C000302352

HOMES OF BRITISH
ICE HOCKEY

HOMES OF BRITISH
ICE HOCKEY

MARTIN C. HARRIS

This book is dedicated to the memory of my father, Donald C. Harris (1907–96), who first kindled my passion for ice hockey over half a century ago and to my wife Barbara and children Judith and Aidan who, over the years, have endured with remarkable patience and forbearance.

First published 2005
Reprinted 2007

STADIA is an imprint of
Tempus Publishing Ltd
The Mill, Brimscombe Port
Stroud, Gloucestershire GL5 2QG
www.tempus-publishing.com

© Martin C. Harris, 2005

The right of Martin C. Harris to be identified as the Author of this work has been asserted by him in accordance with the Copyrights, Designs and Patents Act 1988.

All rights reserved. No part of this book may be reprinted or reproduced or utilised in any form or by any electronic, mechanical or other means, now known or hereafter invented, including photocopying and recording, or in any information storage or retrieval system, without the permission in writing from the Publishers.

British Library Cataloguing in Publication Data.
A catalogue record for this book is available from the British Library.

ISBN 10: 0 7524 2581 1
ISBN 13: 978 0 7524 2581 8

Typesetting and origination by Tempus Publishing.
Printed and bound in Great Britain.

CONTENTS

ACKNOWLEDGEMENTS

The author wishes to acknowledge the assistance that has been received from many quarters in the process of researching and compiling this book. The catalyst was Cardiff-based hockey fan and author Andy Weltch, to whom I will always be grateful. It was Andy who suggested that the notes on rinks and ice hockey that I had compiled over the years would be worthy of a wider audience and introduced me to Tempus Publishing. Regrettably Andy had to drop out of this project due to terminal illness in his immediate family.

Many people gave unstintingly of their time without thought of reward, therefore I particularly wish to thank: Michael Chambers, John Denyer, Wilf Gibbons, David S. Gordon, David Harris, Mark Lewishon and Chris Woodward.

Others who have provided information and to whom I am indebted are: John Baster, Russ Chamberlain, the late Nancy Chisholm, Alison Crockett, Stewart Davidson, Tom Forrest, David Graham, Ian McGregor, Adam Goldstone, Steve Hallum, Catherine Healey, Norman de Mesquita, Ronnie Nichol, James Phillis, Stewart Roberts, Nicola Walker and Stan Wiltshire.

The help and patience of the staff of the Westminster Archives Centre and the Guildhall Library is also greatly appreciated, as is that of Chris Munroe for his assistance with the computer techniques of word processing.

Photographs: where the photographer is known they have been credited. David Huxley, whose company, Midlands Publishing Holdings Ltd, is owner of the title of *Ice Hockey News/Review*, has kindly granted permission for the reproduction of photographs from that magazine.

INTRODUCTION

The intention of the author, in compiling this volume, is to provide the reader with both a combination of facts and figures and an overview as to the history and salient points of this unique type of facility in the United Kingdom and the sport of ice hockey played within these 'homes'.

The building of ice rinks then the invention of mechanically frozen ice surfaces and the progressive development of an outdoor pastime without rules into ice hockey are inextricably interwoven. The sport we recognise today as ice hockey was shaped, formed, and given substance by constraints imposed by the dimensions made necessary by the construction of an enclosing roofed envelope to an ice surface.

A brief history of the early development of artificially frozen enclosed ice rinks and the sport of ice hockey are included.

'Homes' should prove a useful guide to ice hockey fans in learning more of the venues in which they watch their favourite sport, or to those who wonder when their local rink closed or had been relocated. Where known, details of the architect and builder and significant design or construction features are noted. The inclusion of this information is intended to stimulate and widen interest beyond those who follow ice hockey. It is hoped that this publication will also serve as a work of reference to architectural and sports historians, researchers and others with an interest in specialist-building types in Britain and their heritage.

Depending on the source consulted, dimensions of ice surfaces (pads), together with total spectator and seating capacities, differ, particularly in relation to the older buildings. Those given are considered to be the most accurate. For venerable venues spectator capacities have sometimes been reduced from those originally permitted, as more stringent safety regulations have been applied. Where known the reduced figures are also included.

Virtually all sports and recreational pastimes do not require a specialised mechanically produced and maintained surface. In Britain general ice skating and ice hockey in particular are the exception. With a temperate climate, winters in the United Kingdom are rarely cold for long enough to enable natural ice to be sustained safely for more than a few days. Following many unsuccessful attempts to create a workable substitute, the first indoor mechanically frozen ice rinks appeared in Britain in the last quarter of the nineteenth century. From almost their first opening they have provided a home to enthusiasts who wished to practise and play ice hockey. Since that time, over a hundred such venues have supported ice hockey in some form.

To demonstrate the extent to which rinks have provided a 'home', all teams that have played in an organised league, the league in which they competed and the years of participation are listed. The senior team (in bold) is listed first and then earliest-formed next. A 'senior' team is defined as that playing at the highest standard, from all the adult teams based at a particular rink. This will enable readers to observe the number of years a particular team functioned in relation to a rink's total life span. Ice hockey's fluctuating strength down the years and its development and growth pattern can also be tracked.

Observant readers may notice a few gaps in the continuity of Scottish youth league teams (and to a lesser extent the English equivalent). Published records of this area of the sport are incomplete and verification from governing bodies has not proved fruitful.

Regrettably limitations of space dictate the exclusion of those teams comprising players below the age of ten, 'recreational', women's and old-timers ice hockey.

Rinks are listed alphabetically, to accord with the city or town in which they are located e.g. Kirkcaldy rather than Fife.

Any errors of fact are entirely the author's. Corrections and additional information is welcomed and should be addressed, in the first instance, to the Publishers.

Martin C. Harris
Ealing, London W5
June 2005

INDOOR RINKS – THE BEGINNINGS

From as early as 1837 Canadian curling clubs had utilised indoor ice, although they were probably rinks laid down within existing barns and sheds. Purpose-built covered rinks appeared in Canada around 1860 when the vogue for skating was at its height. Continual frosts allowed prolonged periods of skating but heavy downfalls of snow often spoilt the ice. So sheds, called 'ice rinks', were constructed, usually of wood, over sheets of naturally frozen ice. These provided the same day-to-day conditions, free from snow in all weathers, except for periods of thaw. At night gas lamps illuminated them.

The earliest may have been in Quebec. A long narrow structure, with few amenities, was re-erected each winter from the early 1850s at Queen's Wharf. Others venues were the Club House (1856), also at the harbour in Quebec City and the Montreal Skating Club on St-Urbain Street in 1859.

By 1870 purpose-built skating and curling rinks, often with gaps low down in the walls to facilitate the formation of a natural ice surface, were comparatively common in eastern Canada and the north-east of the United States. The most famous and best remembered, for its influence in turning an outdoor pastime into the game we know today as ice hockey, was the Victoria rink, opened in 1862 in Montreal. Designed by local architects Lawford and Nelson, the 250ft-long by 100ft-wide building enclosed a 202ft x 80ft naturally frozen ice surface. From contemporary illustrations it appears that the semi-circular arches, springing from ground level to support the roof 50ft above, were made of steel. Spacious dressing and cloakrooms were attached, all lit by mains gas lamps.

Initially it was a fashionable resort for the leisured and wealthy, with periodic fancy dress masquerades taking place on the ice, to the strains of an orchestra positioned on a high level balcony along one side. This all changed in March 1875. Members of the local skating club, some of whom were students at McGill University, contested the first indoor version of a long-established outdoor pastime known variously as shinny, rickets or hurley on the ice.

As the game of ice hockey developed and progressed the lack of provision for tiered seating forced the increasing numbers of spectators to pack the timber broadwalk surround, only inches above the ice. Players often crashed into the packed ranks of fur-coated, mainly male cigar-smoking fans, to be pushed vigorously back into the action.

When the Westmount Arena in Montreal opened in 1898, it was the world's first venue built specifically to stage ice hockey. Beyond the 4ft-high boards that surrounded the ice rose 6,000 tiered seats. Reserved tickets could be ordered in a heated lobby and blankets to rent were offered to those who considered the rink draughty. It was the home to Montreal AAA, Shamrocks, Wanderers and Canadiens but it burnt down in 1918.

It was not until 1911 that equipment for making an artificially produced sheet of ice was introduced into Canada. The hockey-pioneering Patrick brothers Frank and Lester constructed arenas in the West Coast cities of Vancouver and Victoria to facilitate the formation of the Pacific Coast Hockey Association. Vancouver's Denham Street Arena could accommodate 10,500 spectators. A year later the first mechanically frozen ice pad in the east opened in Toronto.

Circular buildings, up to 160ft in diameter, were popular in eastern Canada during the nineteenth century, housing cattle and agricultural fairs in the summer and an ice sheet in winter. They died out as hockey took hold, but they probably influenced the shape of the early European artificially frozen rinks.

With ice skating fashionable among the leisured classes in early Victorian England, would-be entrepreneur inventors came up with many varied alternatives to ice, as produced by nature. The first recorded commercial attempt produced a surface with the consistency of hard cheese. It was quickly cut up by skates and spoilt by moist or hot conditions. Falls were odious, as the inventor, William Bradwell (chief machinist at London's Covent

GardenTheatre), in conjunction with Henry Kirk, had produced a surface by heating crystallised alum, mixed with hogs' grease, which was guaranteed to last two years. Skate gouges were eliminated by the application of a little heat and a daily application of French chalk. This remarkable substance was installed in 1841 as a trial at the Baker Street Bazaar at Portman Square, but closed the following March.

Four months later a surface of a similar substance, based on soda, was laid in a rotunda known as The Coliseum, which faced onto London's Regents Park. Initially only 23ft x 16ft, the area was soon considerably increased, but closed to the public later that year. The operation was transferred back to Baker Street, opening there in December 1842, with a 70ft x 50ft rink known as the Glaciarum, which lasted until February 1844.

It had been known for a long time that evaporation is an agent for producing intense cold; a scientific paper describing such experiments was read to the Royal Society in London in December 1812. Between 1840 and 1876 seven patents for 'artificial ice' and thirteen for 'real ice manufacture' were received by the Patent Office in London. In New York in 1870 William E. Newton, a civil engineer, produced a design for skating, by adopting an invention by which ice could be formed by the circulation of ammoniacal gas, ether or carbonic acid, through tubes located below the surface of water.

The man who first solved the problem of creating a workable mechanically frozen ice rink, patented in 1870, was Dr John Gamgee (1831–94), a veterinary professor. He was looking for a method of freezing meat to be imported by sea from Australia and New Zealand. Adopting a vacuum and condensing pump, and using a mixture of ether and peroxide of nitrogen, water and glycerine, he built an ice-making machine in a building off London's King's Road in Chelsea.

He utilised part of the plant to form an artificially frozen skating surface, of 24ft x 16ft, under a canvas tent and opened it as an experiment on 7 January 1876. This was followed by a larger version, the Glaciarium, which opened two months later in a more substantial building nearby at 379 Kings Road. This housed a rink of 40ft x 24ft and had a gallery for an orchestra and spectators. The walls were decorated with views of the Swiss Alps with membership by subscription only.

According to an article in *The London Illustrated News* of 13 May 1876 the skating floor was formed with a series of oval copper pipes, immersed in water, laid on a half-inch layer of tarred cow hair, which in turn sat on 2in timber planks. Below these

The world's first mechanically frozen ice rink – Kings Road, London. (*The Illustrated London News*)

The Victoria Skating Rink, Montreal in 1868. (*The Illustrated London News*)

were further layers of cow hair, 4in of earth and a 6in concrete base. The pipes, connected at the ends, allowed the refrigerating liquid to flow through them. This produced ice that was 2in thick. The nearby machinery house contained a steam engine driving a refrigerating machine operating on the vapour-compression system, using ether as the refrigerant. The evaporator consisted of a copper casing about 5ft square with a number of vertical tubes passing through it. This was submerged in a solution of glycerine in water contained in a timber tank about 10ft above the floor. The glycerine solution flowed by gravity through the pipes in the rink floor to be pumped back into the evaporator. A much later source refers to 'freezing by means of Raoul Picet's process and W.E. Ludlow's rotary engine and pump'.

Two more Gamgee rinks opened the same year. At Rusholme near Manchester a rink operated for about twelve months, whereas at Charing Cross the 'Floating Glaciarium', a 115ft x 25ft surface opened on 20 October but closed after five months. A more successful venture at Stockport in Lancashire remained in business for ten years as the world's first successful large ice surface. Although the ice produced by mechanical means was acceptable to skaters, these early rinks gave rise to environmental conditions prone to excessive dampness and thick mists. It would be a while before balanced heating and ventilation systems caught up.

By the mid-1890s three rinks operated simultaneously in London, with one each in Brighton and Glasgow. The latter two were circular, as was London's Niagara, with the capital's Hengler's ice being curved at one end and wedge shaped at the other. Rinks also opened during the roaring '90s in Berlin, Brussels, Munich, Nice, Paris (two) and in America at Baltimore and Philadelphia, with two in New York. Being constructed for skaters, they all possessed very limited spectator accommodation and, like in Britain, many were circular.

To counter crowding on London ice, the long-established Princes sporting club opened their members-only rink in Knightsbridge in 1896. As the second rink in Britain, after Stockport, with a rectangular ice surface, albeit narrow in relation to its length, this facility proved a major influence on ice sports. Ice hockey in particular benefited; it provided a base for expatriate Canadians to demonstrate their new sport and enabled homegrown enthusiasts to acquire the basic skills.

By 1909 three rinks had opened in Australia. In the same year the world's first open-air artificially frozen rink came into use in Vienna. Created by engineer Edward Engleman, the Austrian capital had three by 1914. By the same year Berlin possessed three full-size rectangular enclosed rinks, with accommodation for numerous spectators. The small circular buildings in Britain closed by, or soon after, the dawn of the twentieth century. But by the outbreak of the First World War in 1914, five rinks with more regular dimensions were doing good business, three being in Scotland. Only two, Edinburgh's Haymarket and the Manchester Ice Palace, survived the social and financial changes wrought by war.

By the late 1920s vast improvements in the efficiency of refrigeration and principally electrically powered plants led to a burst of ice rinks opening to the general public, both in Britain and to a lesser extent in Western Europe. Although most lacked adequate seating accommodation, their spread enabled ice hockey to become a permanent feature of many rinks in Britain and more so on the Continent, where many open-air facilities adopted mechanically frozen ice.

ICE HOCKEY – THE BEGINNINGS

Theories are plentiful, facts are few as to the origins of ice hockey. What is certain is that the sport as we know it today originated in Canada. Most historians on the subject agree that the game has many roots but the plant first flowered in Montreal. The event that gave rise to the shape and form of the sport, recognisable today as ice hockey, is well documented. On 3 March 1875 the *Montreal Gazette* noted that 'a game of Hockey' was to be played that evening at the indoor Victoria Skating Rink by members of the local skating club. The next day the same journal reported the contest, which at that time appeared to be unique. It is the earliest eyewitness account known, in that a specific game of 'ice hockey', between two identified teams (of nine players), at a specific time and place is recorded and with a score. James Creighton's team beat that captained by Fred Torrance 2–1. Creighton (1850–1930) hailed from Halifax, Nova Scotia where an earlier form of a nondescript outdoor, and later indoor, game persisted until the late 1880s, with off sides permitted.

The *Gazette* stated that 'a flat circular piece of wood' would be used rather than a ball. This forever changed the nature of stick handling, and greatly influenced the design of the stick. The 202ft x 80ft ice surface became almost the exact dimensions of standard ice hockey rinks used throughout North America to this day. The first printed reference to a 'puck' occurred a year later, also in Montreal.

Of course, for the initial germination of such a sturdy plant, many strands had to join together to form the roots. The sport was not invented in one day. Ice skating goes back many centuries in Europe. Numerous paintings by Dutch artists, as early as the sixteenth century, depict figures on skates wielding sticks, with a small object lying nearby on the ice. What is not in dispute is that Scottish and Irish immigrants to the New World brought their field-based pastimes of shinty and hurley with them. The English would have contributed bandy. This is a game played on skates with stick and ball on ice the size of a football pitch that prevailed on the shallow fens of East Anglia, which readily froze in the then generally colder winters.

Illustrations and printed references to games played on ice such as wicket or ricket, break-shins and hurley-hockey (with or without skates), occur from New York to Nova Scotia, from the late eighteenth century. The earliest ones linking skates, ice, sticks and ball-like objects date from 1829 and can be classified as pastimes without rules. British soldiers based in Kingston, Ontario are also reported in 1843 as playing 'hockey on ice'.

The controversial assertion that 'ice hockey' originated in Windsor, Nova Scotia around 1800 is based on a remark by a character in a work of fiction, published in London, England in 1844.

As the game moved indoors more formal rules were required and in 1877 the first such appeared in print in the *Montreal Gazette*. Only one word – ice – distinguished them from field hockey rules issued two years previously in England. Hockey then grew and spread, in fits and starts, to other parts of Quebec, Ottawa, Toronto and Kingston. The first organised league was held in 1887/88 as five teams formed the Canadian Amateur Hockey Association.

By 1890 the first formal controlling body – the Ontario Hockey Association – came into being in Toronto with, surprisingly an Englishman, the Honourable Arthur Stanley (1865–1948), son of the Governor General of Canada Lord Stanley, being a driving force in its creation. The exploits of Arthur and his brothers on the ice with the Rideau Rebels influenced their father to donate the Dominion Hockey Challenge Cup, now better known as the Stanley Cup, when he returned home in 1893.

By this time the game in Canada was well enough established to attract the attention of promoters. Surreptitious payments or the promise of a job were starting to be commonplace. By 1904 the International Pro Hockey League appeared with two USA and three Canadian-based teams. In Europe payments to players were not made until the mid-1930s, and then only by a handful of clubs in two or three countries (Britain being one) to imported Canadians. Sinecure jobs or the label of 'independent' generally disguised this practice.

Historians of the sport are all agreed that printed references to 'ice hockey' in Europe in the nineteenth century must be regarded with the utmost caution; it was a game more akin to bandy. As with Canada, there is no exact date for the dawning of a recognisable form of ice hockey, with many myths as to its exact original location in Europe.

What is certain is that the introduction of workable artificially frozen ice rinks, usually circular and of modest diameter, in the larger, more cosmopolitan cities, attracted the privileged classes. They enjoyed the leisure time and money to take winter sports holidays in the new resorts of Switzerland, where they learned to skate. Canadians, in Europe either for business or study, also gravitated to these startling new facilities. Both groups were fundamental to the first attempts at ice hockey.

George A. Meager in his 1900 book *Lessons in Skating,* claims to have introduced Canadian ice hockey five years earlier in Glasgow, London and Paris. In London the National Skating Palace and Niagara Hall were operating. Contemporary illustrations of games at these two venues, described as 'hockey on ice', show a puck in play. A contest, in the mid-1890s at the Skating Palace, is billed as England *v.* Canada.

Victoria Rink, Montreal c. 1894.

The Stanley brothers played in an open-air match on a pond at Buckingham Palace, during a cold snap early in 1895. They continued to turn out for the occasional match at Niagara until the close of the century.

It would appear that the influence of Meager died out, as an indoor version of bandy was reported at Glasgow in 1896 and at a circular rink in Brighton three years later. The transitional mix, at this time, of bandy type games and Canadian hockey is illustrated by the use of a combination of bandy and cut-down ice hockey sticks and a lacrosse ball at the first Varsity match in 1900, held indoors at Princes rink in London. Native British pioneers, such as the career soldier Major B.M. 'Peter' Patton (1876–1939) had to await the formation of London Canadians in 1902 for the sport to further progress into the true Canadian game.

Britain and Europe's first ice hockey league was held in London the following season. Five teams were spread between the Skating Palace and the more acceptable 250ft x 52ft ice surface at the Princes club in Knightsbridge. The Canadians, who were resident in the capital, won by two points from Princes.

In 1905 the Canadian Ruck Anderson, studying in Prague, showed the local bandy players how hockey played in Canada. Three years on the sport had grown sufficiently in Europe for representatives from Belgium, England, France and Switzerland, under the chairmanship of French ice hockey pioneer Louis Magnus (1881–1950), to found a world governing body – the Ligue Internationale de Hockey sur Glace (LIHG). Bohemia joined that November and Germany a year later. The Canadian amateur rulebook was adopted by the LIHG at their 1911 congress.

Differences between the longer-established Canadian game and the version emerging in Europe, apart from an absence of body checking, concerned off sides. Basically the Europeans did not have any, permitting forward passing providing a member of the opposition was between the attacker and the netminder. At this time no forward passing was allowed in Canada; players skated towards the opposition passing the puck laterally. The Canadian Pacific Coast Hockey Association first introduced the two blue lines in 1914, with forward passing only allowed in the neutral zone.

Oxford Canadians, formed in 1906 by postgraduate Rhodes scholars at the university, provided a major influence on the development of ice hockey in Europe prior to the First World War. They demonstrated the teamwork that could be achieved between moderately skilled skaters with deft stick handling and puck control. The students' five successive annual tours, to the mainly open-air rinks of Western and Central Europe where they defeated national and club teams, earned praise from opponents and spectators alike. Crowds of over 2,000 were not uncommon when Berlin SC was the opposition. The German magazine *Deutscher Wintersport* stated in January 1913 that 'European teams playing against Oxford Canadians have learnt much'.

The London-based Princes were another influential and successful club but, by 1914 consisted almost entirely of Canadians. This is a contentious feature of the British game, which has persisted to the present day.

By the outbreak of the First World War a form of ice hockey that we would recognise today was well established in the Old World.

ABERDEEN

Opened:	1 February 1992	Address:
Ice Size:	184ft x 85ft (56m x 26m)	Link Ice Rink
Total Spectator Capacity:	1,200	Beach Leisure Centre
Seating Capacity:	1,118	Beach Esplanade
Ice Hockey – First Match:		Aberdeen
Youth hockey training from Under-12 to sixteen-year-		AB2 1NR
olds commenced in 1992.		Scotland

Teams:

Aberdeen North Stars	1992–2005 (recreational only)
Aberdeen Alligators	1997–98 Scottish Under-21 League; 1998–2000 Scottish League
Aberdeen Flames	2000–03 Scottish Under-18 League & 2004–05 Scottish Under-19 League
Aberdeen Atoms	2003–04 Scottish Under-19 League
Aberdeen Flames	1996–97 Scottish Under-16 League & 1998–99 Scottish Under-17 League
Aberdeen Wasps	1999–2000 & 2000–02 Scottish Under-16 League
Aberdeen Roughnecks	2002–05 Scottish Under-16 League
Aberdeen Red Wings	1995–97 Scottish Under-14 League
Aberdeen Wasps	1997–2000 Scottish Under-14/15 League
Aberdeen Eagles	2000–05 Scottish Under-14 League
Aberdeen Red Barons	1995–98 Scottish Under-12/13 League
Aberdeen Eagles	1998–99 Scottish Under-13 League
Aberdeen Atoms	1999–2004 Scottish Under-12 League

Cold winds blowing off the North Sea are often sufficient to keep the ice pad frozen without need of the refrigeration plant.

Progress in developing ice hockey was initially slow, primarily due to the distances to the nearest rinks of Aviemore (closed 1998), Elgin and Inverness. Canadians based in the oil industry helped, with the first team being the recreational North Stars. Although by definition non-competitive, games attracted several hundred spectators. On 19 August 1996, in an exhibition match, Paisley Pirates defeated the Norwegian side Vikings Stravenger 7–5.

The interior of the Link Centre. (City of Aberdeen Council/*IHNR*)

ALDERSHOT

Opened:	24 July 1987	Address:
Closed:	15 October 1991	Aldershot Ice Rink
Ice Size:	145ft x 73ft (45m x 22.5m)	Pool Road
Total Spectator Capacity:	Approximately 600	Aldershot
Seating Capacity:	Approximately 300 on benches	Hampshire
	on one side only	GU11 3SN
Ice Hockey – First Match:		England

8 November 1987: Aldershot Colts 2 *v.* Havering
(Romford) Hornets 13 (EJL 'B' – South)

Teams:

Aldershot Colts	1987–92 English Junior League
Aldershot Pistols	1987–92 English Pee-Wee League
Aldershot Bullets	1989–90 English League Division 3 – South 1991–92 English Under-21 League (withdrew after one match due to rink closure)
Aldershot Pistols	1991–92 English Under-12 League

Developed by Gaul & Company, an organisation that consistently promoted mini rinks, on the basis that an undersized facility was better for the local community than none at all. Their buildings proved unsuitable to the full development of the majority of ice disciplines, with the company failing in September 1991, prior to completion of their third such venture.

    Aldershot's rink was built on a restricted site with limited car parking, at a cost of £1.6 million, adjacent to a housing estate. The Mayor of Rushmoor Council laid the foundation stone on 28 April 1987. At that time the *Aldershot Courier* claimed it to be 'the biggest ice rink in Britain'.

    As the ice surface was only two-thirds of the minimum required size, the national governing body (British Ice Hockey Association), ruled in the summer of 1987 that only youth ice hockey could be sanctioned.

    A change of ownership, with plans to reopen the rink in December 1991, foundered. Rushmoor Council subsequently leased the building to the Camberley Gymnastics Club.

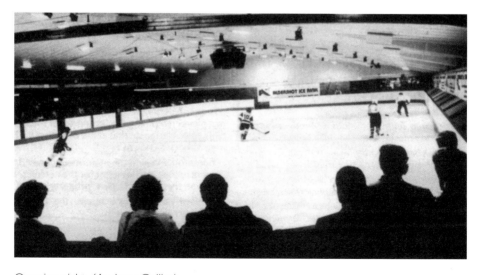

Opening night. (Andrew Collins)

ALTRINCHAM

Opened: 2 December 1960   Address:
Closed: 30 March 2003   Altrincham Ice Rink
Ice Size: 190ft x 85ft (58m x 26m)   Devonshire Road
Total Spectator Capacity: 1,800 (originally 2,100)   Broadheath
Seating Capacity: 1,250   Altrincham WA14 4EZ
Ice Hockey – First Match: Greater Manchester
4 February 1961: Altrincham Aces 5 v. Glasgow Flyers 9   England

Teams:

Altrincham Aces   1961–70 Challenge games and 'Home' tournaments; 1968-69 Northern 'Second' League; 1970–78 Southern 'A' League; 1978–82 Inter-City 'A' League and 1981–82 English National League; 1982–83 British League – Division 1 – Section C; 1983–86 British League – Division 1; 1995–98 English Conference – North; 1998–2000 English League – Division 1; 2000–03 English National League – North

Cheshire Cats   1962–64 Challenge games and Blackpool Tournament.

Trafford Tigers   1974–78 Southern 'B' League; 1978–80 Midland League – Division 2; 1982–84 British League – Division 3; 1984–87 British League – Division 2; 1987–90 English League – Division 2; 1990–94 English Under-21 League; 1994–95 English Under-19 League

Altrincham Tigers   1995–96 English Under-19 League; 1997–2003 English Under-19 League

Trafford Metros   1986–92 and 1993–95 British League – Division 1; 1992–93 English Conference A

Trafford Jets   1987–95 English Junior/Under-16 League
Altrincham Jets   1995–03 English Under-16 League
Altrincham Hurricanes   2000–01 English Under-16 League
Trafford Tomahawks   1992–95 English Under-14 League
Altrincham Tomahawks   1995–2003 English Under-14 League
Trafford Spitfires   1994–95 English Under-12 League
Altrincham Spitfires   1995–03 English Under-12 League

Honours:

Aces   1972/73 Champions Southern League; 1975/77 Winners Midland Section Southern 'A' League

Tigers   1983/84 Winners British League Division 3 North
Jets   1999/2000 Winners English Northern Under-16 B League
Tomahawks   1999/2000 and 2001–03 Winners English Northern Under-14 'B' League
Spitfires   2002/03 Winners English Northern Under-12 'A' League

Originally developed by the same owner as the Solihull rink, Albert Allen, who first discussed plans for a rink with Didsbury Council in 1948. It took twelve years to resolve planning difficulties.

Although the senior teams – Aces and Metros – never attracted capacity crowds, the Altrincham rink played a significant part as a base for ice hockey in the North West of England for over forty years. The loss of this facility to the Greater Manchester community deprived many promising youngsters of the chance to progress in their chosen sport and created a gap that cannot be filled without a replacement rink. A joint bid in 1997 by the rink owner and Trafford Borough Council for lottery funding failed.

Home fixtures of the original Aces, composed mainly of players based in North-East England, were curtailed in February 1963 due to poor support and a lack of players to form a strong opposition. From then on rink management concentrated on other skating activities, leaving enthusiasts to run ice hockey. Emphasis was therefore then placed on developing local talent. In 1970 Aces became founder members of the Southern League as the sport slowly expanded.

Two of the earlier locally developed players, Tim Owen and Bob Gilbert, were later selected for England in the annual clash with Scotland. Gilbert, a netminder who died in 1996 aged forty-eight, went on to represent Great Britain in the 1975 Pondus Cup held in Denmark.

Among the earlier 'imported' Canadian players forward Jim Francheschini stands out, as do the Sims brothers – Brian and Bruce – a little later, along with American netminder Jeff Johnson.

As costs of players' salaries rocketed, Trafford Borough Council made cash available in 1986 to enable professional hockey to continue, hence the change of name from Aces to Trafford Metros. This era also saw coach Roy Warren sign some smooth-skating Ukrainians. Far and away the best of these was Oleg Sinkov with 267 goals from 122 matches.

A clutch of local talent made an impact during the 1980s and 1990s including Ged Smith, who made his debut for Aces at fifteen, Dave Shepherd and the Broadhurst brothers Pete and Paul. All of them played 300 or more competitive matches in local colours. Several played professionally either for Aces/Metros, and in 1995 for the inaugural season of Manchester Storm, who included Alan Crawley and Alan Hough.

The higher echelons of the professional game proved uneconomic so Aces reverted to semi-pro/amateur status in the regionalised English League, with popular Aro Pekka Mikkola staying on as coach until 1999.

Although the club were late on the scene in entering the youth leagues, by the dawn of the twenty-first century hard work and persistence began to pay off, with success from the Under-12s through to the sixteen-year-olds.

The rink closed permanently on 30 March 2003 as the site had been sold to Barratt Homes for development, having been put on the market two years previously. During that day the final ice hockey matches were staged, involving many past and present players from Aces and Metros, in a four-team exhibition tournament.

AVIEMORE

Opened:	14 December 1966	Address:
Closed:	Demolished Spring 1998	Aviemore Centre Ice
Ice Size:	200ft x 100ft (60m x 30m)	Rink (Mountain
Total Spectator Capacity:	Approximately 1,000	Resort)
Seating Capacity:	Approximately 250	Aviemore
Ice Hockey – First Match:		Highland PH22 1PF

12 April 1969: Highland All-Stars 4 *v.* Murrayfield Racers 13   Scotland

Teams:

Badenoch Wolves	1969–70 challenge games
Badenoch Cubs	1969–70 Midget challenge games
Aviemore Blues	1970–71 challenge games; 1992–95 Scottish League – Division 1
Aviemore Cubs	1970–71 Junior challenge games
Aviemore Blackhawks	1976–79 & 1981–82 Northern Reserve League; 1979–81 Northern League; 1984–87 British League Division 2 (Scottish); 1987–88 British League – Division 1 – North; 1988–90 Scottish League – Division 1
Perth Panthers	1995–96 Scottish League – Division 1

Interior view.

Honours:

Blackhawks   1978/79 Winners of Northern Reserve League – Scottish
                          Section; 1984/85 and 1986/87 Champions British League
                          Division 2 – Scottish

Blackhawks, when competing in leagues that contained teams from outside Scotland, frequently travelled understaffed to away matches, as many players were employed in the hotels or ski facilities, whose busiest time was at weekends when most league matches were scheduled. With its small population Aviemore was never able to produce sufficient players either to sustain a senior team consistently or, for the same reason, attract a large enough spectator base to cover the cost of overseas 'imports'. In April 1988 a Scottish Select side defeated the Danish club Esbjerg 2–1 at the Centre.

Having been originally conceived as an open rink, climate conditions dictated that the ice sheet, the largest in Britain since the late 1930s, be housed indoors. A rectangular steel-framed shed-like structure, with a clerestorey along the entire length of the roof provided natural light. The rink was designed by the later-disgraced corrupt architect John Poulson, as part of a multi-sports entertainment complex, in the concrete 'New Brutalist' style of the 1960s.

The Starkis Hotel chain operated the resort and rink in the late 1980s. The newly revived Blues were sponsored for the 1992/93 campaign by the Sheffield-based development company Barclay de Vere who took over the hotel group. The Scottish Under-21 Cup finals were held here in June 1997. The site of the rink is now a car park.

AYR – BERESFORD TERRACE

Opened: 13 March 1939   Address:
Closed: 16 April 1972   Ayr Ice Rink Ltd
Ice Size: 200ft x 100ft   21 Beresford Terrace
Total Spectator Capacity: 4,616   Ayr
Seating Capacity: 3,800 (originally 4,616) Ayrshire
Ice Hockey – First Match: Scotland
22 March 1939: Scottish Select 2 *v.* Trail Smoke Eaters 4
Last Match:
16 April 1972: Ayr Bruins 5 *v.* Dundee Rockets 6
(Northern League)

Teams:

Ayr Raiders   1939–40, 1946–54 Scottish National League; 1954–55 British
                          National League; 1955–56 Scottish Amateur League
Ayr Spitfires   1946–53 Scottish 'Junior' League(s)
Ayr Hurricanes   1958–61 English 'Home' Tournaments
Ayr Balmorals   1961–62 Blackpool Tournament
Ayr Rangers   1962–66 Scottish League English 'Home' Tournaments
Ayr Bruins   1963–72 'Home' Tournaments;1966–67 and 1969–72 Northern
                          League; 1967–69 Northern Second League
Ayr Bearcats   1971–72 Northern Second League

Honours:

Raiders   1951–53 Champions Scottish National League; 1952/53
                          Winners of Anderson Trophy (Play-offs); 1950–52 Winners
                          Scottish Autumn Cup
Rangers   1962/63 Winners of Scottish League – Section A
Spitfires   1947/48 Winners West of Scotland League; 1949/50 Winners
                          Frame League Cup – West; 1949/50 Champions Banner Trophy

Publications:

Raiders Review compiled and edited by A.H. Stanley, 1948. Hockey Publications.
Raiders of the Lost Rink by David Gordon, 2004. Tempus Publishing Ltd.

The idea for the rink was first proposed in 1937 by a group of wealthy local sportsmen, headed by Colonel T.C. Dunlop, who had played ice hockey at Glasgow in the early part of the century.

Designed in 1938 by architect James Carrick and built by Robert Loudon Ltd of Glasgow at a total cost of £90,000, with an ice-making plant by L. Sterne & Co. It was claimed at the time to have the largest single-span roof in Britain at 206ft. It was certainly the largest and best equipped in Scotland, with a heating system running below the seats for the comfort of spectators. The Lord Lieutenant of Ayrshire performed the opening ceremony, with the opponents at the first match nine days later being Canada – the newly crowned World Champions.

By August 1939 a large number of boys between twelve and seventeen years of age were receiving hockey coaching every Saturday morning. Dressed in black, with a white aeroplane logo on their chests, the all-Canadian inaugural Raiders tied their first home game against Dunfermline 2–2, on 3 November in front of over 3,000 spectators. They also drew the largest attendance of all the Scottish League teams that winter.

Also, unlike most rinks, Ayr remained open during the Second World War but only a few matches were played after 1940. These mainly featured Canadian servicemen. With the coming of peace a near all-Canadian Raiders, on £7 a week each, returned to the SNL. Thanks to the rink's early and almost continuous effort at youth level, Raiders soon recruited the most promising local lads. The first two were Hugo Hamilton and seventeen-year-old Lawson Neil, the latter a defenceman, who went on to serve eight consecutive seasons in 319 games for Raiders. These included the back-to-back league championships between 1951–53. It was during this period that player-coach Keith Kewley from Toronto, with fellow countrymen Al Holliday in goal and the attack trio of Orville Martini, Andre Girard and Ernie Domenico, served up the greatest hockey seen by Ayr fans. All played over 200 games for the club, except Martini, who appeared 137 times, with Domenico the top scorer on 261 goals. Over the years Raiders also entertained several visiting national sides, including the USA and Czechoslovakia in the late 1940s.

The 'Junior' Spitfires continued to collect trophies and produce Ayr-born material for the senior team including Dave McCrae and Stan Christie, both of whom, along with Neil, represented Great Britain at the World Championships in the early 1950s. Ken McMurtrie, a forward, although not picked for GB, turned out 253 times for Raiders.

The architect's 1938 proposal
for neon lighting.

Professional hockey came to an end at Beresford Terrace in the spring of 1955, as Raiders' one-year spell in the newly instigated British National League was their last. The Scottish rinks lost money on the experiment and, apart from Paisley, all pulled out. The attempted substitute of a five-member Amateur Scottish League also failed as Raiders, with Holliday as coach, withdrew the following January.

For a few years interest in the sport was sustained by a handful of local enthusiasts travelling to other rinks for the occasional game. During 1961/62 they were granted ice time at home and took the name Balmorals, soon to become Rangers, for the subsequent two winters in the Scottish League. At this time the Bruins came into being to cater for lads from nine to nineteen years, making their first appearance before the public in January 1964. International material continued to be produced as Andy McCubbin played in a two-game World Championship eliminator against France that winter. Rangers then lost their home ice a year later to the curling fraternity, leaving a young and inexperienced Bruins to join the newly formed Northern League.

Jackson McBride (1946–2003) of Paisley relocated to Ayr at the end of the 1960s, and this, along with an influx of players resulting from the closure of the Paisley rink in 1970, considerably strengthened the Bruins. Increasing interest generated sufficient players to form a reserve team – the Bearcats – and enter the 'Second' or reserve league in the autumn of 1971.

In early 1972 the majority of shares of Ayr Ice Rink Co. Ltd were sold to Scottish and Metropolitan Developments. Despite a massive local protest the building was demolished by summer 1972, although the front façade was incorporated into the Safeway supermarket built on the site. Even this fragment was pulled down during late winter 2004.

AYR – LIMEKILN ROAD

Opened:	October 1973	Address:
Ice Size:	154ft x 88ft (46m x 25m)	Ayr Ice Rink
Total Spectator Capacity:	650	Limekiln Road
Seating Capacity:	250	Tam's Brig
Ice Hockey – First Match:		Ayr
5 October 1975: Ayr Bruins 10 v. Durham Wasps 6		South Ayrshire
(Northern League)		KA8 8DG Scotland

Teams:

Ayr Bruins	1975–82 Northern League; 1981/82 Scottish National League; 1982–89 British League – Premier Division
Ayr Bruins	1989–91 Scottish League, 1991/92 Scottish Under-18 League; 1992/93 Scottish Under-19 League; 1996/97 Scottish Under-21 League; 2000–02 Scottish National League
Ayr Rangers	1975/76 Northern Second League; 1977–81 Northern Reserve League
Ayr Aces	1975–81 Northern Junior League
Ayr Beavers	1987–89 Scottish League
Ayr Raiders	1989–92★ British League – Premier Division; ★1991/92 'home' games played at Glasgow, 1992/93 Autumn Cup only 'home' games played at Paisley
Ayr Bears	1986–91, 1992/93, 1994–96 Scottish Under-16 League
Ayr Buzzers	1987–91 Scottish Under-13/14 League; 1992/93 Scottish Under-14 League; 1994–96 Scottish Under-14 League
Ayr Braves	1994–96 Scottish Under-12 League
South Ayr Tornadoes	1999–2002 Scottish Under-18 League; 2004/05 Scottish Under-19 League
South Ayr Storm	1999–2005 Scottish Under-16 League
South Ayr Flames	1998–2005 Scottish Under-13/14 League
South Ayr Sparks	1999–2005 Scottish Under-12 League

Honours:

Bruins	Winners 1975/76 'Icy' Smith Cup
Aces	1976/77 Champions Northern Junior League

Built on the site of a former greyhound racing stadium primarily for, and by, curling enthusiasts, originally without a vertical barrier at the perimeter of the ice. A barrier was installed in the summer of 1975 with financial assistance from David Sinclair, a hockey-playing Glasgow businessman, and with the aid of a local authority grant. A very small separate ice sheet is also housed within the same building.

The all-amateur Bruins' greatest achievement in the 1970s was in their first year at Limekiln Road in winning the 'Icy' Smith Cup. The two-leg play-off with the winners from the Southern League was recognised as the British Championship.

Two further Ayr-born players made the GB side that year as Jimmy Young and John Gibson travelled to Poland for the World Championships. Gibson was also selected in 1977 and again two years later.

The period 1982–83 saw the dawn of a new era with the introduction of a British League and better quality paid imports, mainly Canadians direct from college hockey. Although attendances had plummeted, for the next autumn Bruins, with an injection of cash from a new chairman, moved from the initial regionalised Division One to the Premier Division. The reign of import player-coach Paul Bedard boosted the crowds as a competitive Bruins contested for honours with successive fourth-place finishes and a place at the Wembley finals weekends, followed by a bronze medal in 1986. Three years later-under charismatic coach Rocky Saganiuk, only a 0–3 third period let-down at Wembley prevented a British Championship.

Although the foundations of the club were well represented in the ever-expanding Scottish youth leagues, with entries from Bears, Beavers and Buzzers, the Premier Bruins were struggling. Escalating wage costs, expectations of the increasing quality of imports and opposing clubs all found the limited ice dimensions and off-ice facilities of the building lacking. In autumn 1989 the principal backer, local businessman Glen Henderson and developer of the nearby Centrum Centre, revived the Raiders tag.

And still the production line for the national squad continued. Netminder John McCrone, Alastair Reid and John Kidd joined Great Britain, back in the World Championships in 1989 after an absence of thirteen years.

Failure to complete and open the long-delayed Centrum and poor results on the ice, and then the collapse of Henderson's business empire in November 1990, resulted in the bank taking over the derelict Centrum. Raiders, under pressure from their opponents, had been forced to call Glasgow 'home' having returned from their brief sojourn at the Summit Centre. Autumn 1992 found Raiders playing out of Paisley in front of a near full house. When the latest potential backer's promise to provide cash remained unfilled Raiders, on the recommendation of the Scottish IH Association; withdrew from all competitions.

In spite of the loss of professional hockey the sport at the younger level continued to flourish as the Braves joined the Under-12 league. When the long-delayed Centrum finally opened in time for the 1996/97 campaign three of the junior squads moved up the road, to be followed by the Under-21 Bruins a year later.

As a consequence a new vigorous set-up – South Ayr youth hockey – came into existence in July 1997. Six age groups from Under-10 upwards continue to make the most of this small but invaluable ice surface.

AYR – CENTRUM

Opened:	25 August 1996	Address:
Closed:	August 2002 – see below.	Centrum Centre
Ice Size:	203ft x 104ft (61m x 31.5m)	123 Ayr Road
Total Spectator Capacity:	2,733	Prestwick
Seating Capacity:	2,733 (four VIP boxes)	Toll
Ice Hockey – First Match:		KA9 1TR

1 September 1996: Ayr Scottish Eagles 8 v. Telford Tigers 2 (Autumn Cup)

South Ayrshire
Scotland

Teams:

Ayr Scottish Eagles	1996–2002 Ice Hockey Superleague
Ayr Centrum Bears	1996–99 Scottish Under-16/17 League
Ayr Centrum Buzzers	1999/2000 Scottish Under-16 League
Ayr Centrum Eagles	2000–02 Scottish Under-16 League
Ayr Centrum Buzzers	1996–99 Scottish Under-14/15 League
Ayr Centrum Rapiers	1999/2000 Scottish Under-14 League
Ayr Centrum Eagles	2000–02 Scottish Under-14 League
Ayr Centrum Braves	1996–99 Scottish Under-12/13 League
Ayr Centrum Raiders	1999/00 Scottish Under-12 League
Ayr Centrum Eagles	2000–02 Scottish Under-12 League
Ayr Centrum Bruins	1997/98 Scottish Under-21 League
Ayr Centrum Bears	1999/00 Scottish Under-18 League
Ayr Centrum Eagles	2000–02 Scottish Under-18 League

Honours:

Eagles	1997/98 Champions Superleague and Play-offs and Winners Autumn Cup and Challenge Cup (Grand Slam); Winners Challenge Cup 2001/02.
Centrum Bears	1998/99 Winners Scottish Under-17 League – Division 2
Centrum Eagles	2001/02 Champions Scottish Under-14 League

The interior. (Mike Smith/*IHNR*)

The official opening of the Centrum took place ten years after work had commenced. Planning permission had been granted in 1984. The original developer, local businessman Glen Henderson, spent £7 million with an intended opening in 1988. At a reputed £4 million over budget work ceased in November 1990, as his motor dealership business went into receivership. Five years later the derelict structure was purchased for £100,000 by Barr Construction Group and completed with the aid of a £500,000 grant from the lottery fund (sportScotland) and a further £1.25 million from the new owners.

Professional ice hockey returned to Ayr in the autumn of 1996. Coached by Jim Lynch and the late Milan Figla, Scottish Eagles were the only newcomers to the inaugural eight-team Superleague.

The combination of Czechs such as Jiri Lala and Italian-Canadian Angelo Canternaro soon had the crowds flocking in for a season's average attendance of 2,383, as Eagles made it to the final of the Benson & Hedges-sponsored Autumn Cup and the end-of-season play-off quarter-finals. Only two Scots, Colin McHaffie, who learned his hockey at Ayr, and Steven Lynch, had been signed. It smacked of poor public relations when neither was retained in the next year's all-foreign roster.

Spring 1998 saw unqualified success as Eagles carried off all the trophies – Superleague, British Championship Play-offs, Autumn and Challenge Cups.

Early 1998/99 season successes in the European League, including two defeats of Ak Bars Kazan – the reigning Russian champions, were not sustained. Injuries during 1998/99 to key players such as Jamie Steer took their toll. Ayr could only finish fifth in the league, although they did contest the Autumn Cup final.

Tony Hand, about the best player Scotland has ever produced, joined Ayr for the start of the next campaign, along with ten new signings. Again injuries to key players almost downed Eagles, with another fifth-place Superleague finish, although they did get to the finals weekend. For the first time the average attendances slipped below the 2,000 figure.

Paul Heavy, the only Scottish and British coach in the Superleague, took over in mid-autumn but even with the league's two top scorers from the previous year – Ed Courtney and Teeder Wynne – in the line-up, silverware continued to elude Eagles. By conceding a goal, fourteen seconds from time, they missed out on the play-off final.

Backstopped by Joaquin Gage – the ex-Edmonton Oiler from the NHL – Eagles flew high, in what, unbeknown to the players or fans, turned out to be the team's last season at Prestwick. A runners-up spot in the league was surpassed by an amazing 5–0 blanking, in Belfast, of the Giants in the Challenge Cup final in early March.

During Eagles' tenure at the Centrum several players stand out either for longevity or their skills, usually both. Face-off specialist Shawn Bryam amassed the most points at 268 in 279 appearances, while defenceman Scott Young clocked up the most games at 301 for 192 points and 744 minutes in the penalty box. Dino Bauba from Lithuania ranked third in number of appearances at 260.

Ayr recruited a string of outstanding netminders, although most moved on after one season. The best was Rob Dobson from Smith Falls, Ontario, who, during the 1997/98 grand slam campaign, achieved a saves percentage of .922.

With Bill Barr's construction business making a loss of £3.1 million in 2002, he stated that pro hockey at the Centrum did not make commercial sense. Average attendance had stubbornly stayed a couple of hundred or so below the 2,000 figure since Eagles' second campaign. Barr remained a director, but a new operating company – Eagles Hockey Ltd – was formed and Scottish Eagles moved to Braehead (Glasgow) for the start of season 2002/03.

The Centrum-based youth hockey development programme had to cease, as the rink closed to the public following the holding of a hockey school in August. The ice was removed on 6 February 2003. At the time of writing, discussions with various interested parties as to the long-term future use of the Centrum remain stalled.

BASINGSTOKE

Opened:	30 April 1988	Address:
Ice Size:	197ft x 98ft (60m x 30m)	Silver Dome Arena
Total Spectator Capacity:	1,600 (2,000 when opened,	Basingstoke Leisure Park
	reduced in 1998)	Worting Road
Seating Capacity:	1,300	Basingstoke
Ice Hockey – First Match:		Hampshire

17 July 1988: Basingstoke Beavers 27 v. Bournemouth
Sharks 2

RG22 6PG
England

Teams:

Basingstoke Beavers	1988–90 English League-Division 1; 1990–93 British League – Division 1; 1993–95 British League – Premier Division
Basingstoke Bison	1995/96 British League Premier Division; 1996–98 Superleague; 1998–2003 British National League; 2003–05 Elite League
Basingstoke Bears	1989–91 English League Division 3; 1991–94 English Conference
Basingstoke Junior Beavers	1988–96 English Junior/Under-16 League
Basingstoke Junior Bison	1996–2005 English Under-16 League
Basingstoke Muscrats	1989/90 & 1991–96 English Under-14 League
Basingstoke Bison	1996–05 English Under-14 League
Basingstoke Bruins	1989–91 English League Division 2; 1991–94 English Under-21 League
Basingstoke Muscrats	1990–96 English Under-12 League
Basingstoke Bison	1996–98 and 2001–05 English Under-12 League
Basingstoke Panthers	1998–2001 English Under-12 League
Basingstoke Bulldogs	1992/93 English League; 1994–99 English Under-19 League
Basingstoke Bison	1999–2005 English Under-19 League
Basingstoke Buffalo	1996–2005 English Conference/National League

Honours:

Beavers	Winners 1989/90 English League Division 1 promotion Play-offs; Champions 1992/93 British League Division 1; Winners 1992/93 Group A British League Division 1 promotion Play-offs
Bison	1999/00 and 2000/01 Winners Benson & Hedges Plate
Buffalo	2000–03 Winners English National League – Division 1 – South; 2002/03 Champions ENL
Bruins	1991/92 Winners English Under-21 'A' League – South

| Bison | 1996/97 Winners English Under-14 'A' League – South; 1998/99 Winners Under-14 'B' League – South |
| Bison | 1996/97 Winners Play-offs English Under-12 'B' League – South |

Opening a year later than scheduled, it was originally known as the Playground, and is adjacent to a swimming pool under a shared roof. The rink is enclosed in a basic steel frame, clad with insulated aluminium panels. The majority of seating is tiered along one side. Some of the seats and to a greater extent those in the balcony opposites, suffer from poor sight-lines due to steel railings and protruding platforms.

Refurbishment, mainly to the exterior, was carried out during 2002. Since the local authority, as the buildings' owner, relinquished control several companies, including Crossland Leisure, Basingstoke Sports Trust and Civic Leisure, managed the rink and the senior team, prior to Planet Ice taking over in the summer of 2000. The new operators remodelled the entrance foyer during 2003/04, with a dedicated rink entrance. The first-floor bar was also revamped.

Basingstoke has been a continual home to ice hockey, aided initially by an influx of Southampton players, whose own rink closed shortly after the opening of the Playground. Beavers won promotion into the semi-professional British League at the end of their second campaign, guided by player-coach Don Yewchin. Average attendance increased to 1,469.

Four seasons on and they were in the top flight following another play-off series triumph. This time they were masterminded by sophomore coach Peter Woods and led by the high-scoring trio of Canadian marksmen Rick Fera, Kevin Conway and Mario Belanger, to top Division 1 by 9 points.

Never finishing higher than seventh, the three years in the Premier Division of the Heineken-sponsored British League has to be viewed as a disappointment. The return of Peter Woods in spring 1995 followed three coaching changes in less than two seasons. Woods soon changed the nickname to the more aggressive Bison, with the team referred to as 'the Herd'.

One of the founder members of the Superleague, in 1996, Bison struggled on the ice and with the relatively small spectator capacity suffered unsustainable financial losses over the next two seasons. This was despite averaging over 1,600 spectators. From the all-North American line-up of the Superleague, the decision by team operator Vardon to drop a level to the British National League, founded a year earlier, enabled Bison to compete on equal terms. New coach Don Dopoe added the retained Rich Stachan to a fresh mix of imports and Brits as Bison ended as BNL runners-up. Although a league title eluded the Herd they won the Benson & Hedges Plate the next year and twelve months on became the only team to retain the trophy.

Season 2001/02 produced a mediocre campaign from Bison, despite the line-up looking impressive on paper. A fourth place finish was the best that could be achieved as average attendance levels fell to 1,130. However Neil Liddard was awarded the Best British Defenceman Trophy.

The next winter even new player-coach Steve Moria could only equal the previous fourth place in a league reduced to eight members. On the plus side eight Brits each iced in over 40 games apiece.

From the 2003/04 campaign the Planet Ice-owned Bison threw in their lot with the new Elite League, created as a successor to the Superleague. It was not until the final weekend of the regular season that Bison conceded the sixth and final play-off place. Ottawa-born netminder Curtis Cruickshank (25) was voted onto the All-Star 'A' team. The move to an out-and-out professional league did not lift the crowds back to a four-figure average, as the next campaign's new coach-manager Mark Bernard failed to lift Bison out of the cellar.

Among the teams from overseas seen over the years on Basingstoke ice are Team Canada, Ukraine Select, SKA Leningrad and on several occasions Manitoba University. BBC Grandstand TV cameras were present for the Benson & Hedges Cup Final in 1989 between Murrayfield Racers and Durham Wasps.

BELFAST – KINGS HALL

Opened:	Mid-October 1939 as an ice rink: the Kings Hall opened 29 May 1934	Address: Belfast Ice Rink
Closed:	October 1969 as an ice rink: the Kings Hall remained open for other activities	Kings Hall Lisburn Road Balmoral
Ice Size:	198ft x 98ft	Belfast
Total Spectator Capacity:	7,000	Northern Ireland
Seating Capacity:	3,000 in 1939, reduced to 1,473 by 1949	

Ice Hockey – First Match:

2 December 1939: Wembley Colts 8 v. Wembley Terriers 6. First house league match held on 17 February 1940 for the Gaston Cup – won by Harlandic Wolves 4–3 over Wasps.

Teams:

Belfast Eagles 1946/47 challenge games; 1950/51 Liverpool Tournament
Ulster Monarchs 1951/52 Liverpool Tournament; 1953–54 challenge games; 1968/69 Blackpool Tournament

A house league operated between 1940–42 (Balmoral Tigers, Harlandic Wolves, Short Brothers Raiders, Thornton Wasps); 1951–54 (Harlandic Wolves, Balmoral Wasps, Racers, Shorts Redwings) and 1965–69

The Kings Hall was constructed over a ten-month period to serve as the headquarters for the Royal Ulster Agricultural Society. Officially opened on 29 May 1934 by the Duke of Gloucester, the building is probably better known as a venue for boxing.

With the shipyards enjoying a wartime boom Belfast took to hockey, with large crowds watching four locally sponsored teams. They were all manned by native-trained lads, except for Archie Greer and Ernest Johnston who had both lived in Canada, although were Belfast born.

As an ice rink it closed in 1942; the hall was used for aircraft reconstruction. Re-opened as a rink in 1946, it closed again during April 1949. In that brief period hockey had resumed with many of the previous players. The best formed the Eagles and occasionally travelled to Glasgow to take on the Mohawks.

Reopened under new management on 20 October 1949, Canadian coach ex-Durham Wasps' Pat McMurray soon revived hockey. Crowds of 2,000 regularly watched the local league matches, with teams sometimes bolstered by Canadian students at Queens University. Attendances of 3,000 were common for visiting clubs from over the water such as Liverpool, Glasgow and Richmond. Then rink operations ceased in 1954.

The hall reopened as a rink again on 26 December 1964 under promoter Peter Kane. After the ten-year gap it took some time for ice hockey to return, with a house league first. By 1968 a revived representative Ulster Monarchs came into being to take on Blackpool. The building finally ceased operating in October 1969 when the army requisitioned the hall as a temporary barracks due to the worsening civil unrest and sectarian strife, known locally as 'The Troubles'.

BELFAST – ODYSSEY

Opened:	2 December 2000	Address:
Ice Size:	197ft x 98ft (60m x 30m)	Odyssey Arena
Total Spectator Capacity:	7,300 for ice hockey.	Queens Quay
Seating Capacity:	7,300 (maximum for ice hockey but variable downwards)	Belfast BT3 Northern Ireland

Ice Hockey – First Match:
2 December 2000: Belfast Giants 1 *v.* Ayr Scottish Eagles 2 (Superleague)

Teams:
Belfast Giants   2000–03 Superleague; 2003–05 Elite League

Honours:
Giants   2001/02 Champions Superleague; 2002/03 Champions
                             Superleague Play-offs

Publications:
Champions in the Land of the Giants by Nigel Ringland and Peter Collins, 2002, Belfast
Giants Ltd

The waterfront arena, on a site of regenerated docklands, is housed within an overall building which includes a twelve-screen Warner Cinema, the Sheridan I-MAX Theatre, W5 – an interactive science centre – and a Pavilion containing restaurants, night clubs and bars. This creates the largest entertainment complex on the island of Ireland. The £91 million construction cost was made possible by the Millennium Fund with the largest injection of money at £45 million. The venue operators SMG-Sheridan Group put in £16.9 million, Northern Ireland's Department of Education added the same amount and the Sports Council of Northern Ireland provided £2.5 million. The arena absorbed £35 million and is managed by SMG, who negotiated a ten-year contract with the owners – the Odyssey Trust.

An expensive advertising campaign, with the slogan 'Torvill and Dean it ain't' ensured full houses for Belfast's first professional ice hockey team. Canadian-Dutch merchant banker Albert Maasland is the majority owner. Montreal-born Bob Zeller, the first GM, held a minority holding. The tag 'In the Land of the Giants Everyone is Equal' firmly established a non-sectarian stance, encouraging support from both side of the religious divide. The Northern Irish took to their exclusively North American side, aided by pre-game presentational razzamatazz, to average 6,448 fans for the 19 contests at the Odyessy. The visit of Bill Clinton thirteen days after the Arena opened boosted the Giants image. The American president was presented with a Giants sweater. Retaining ten members from the Giants' inaugural campaign, coach Dave Whistle's masterstroke was in signing ex-NHL goalminder

The opening
night –
2 December
2000.

The complex from the waterside.

Mike Bales. The addition of American Sean Berens, to link with Kevin Richl and Jason Ruff, provided a high-scoring attack. On 19 January Giants clinched the league title with six weeks remaining, for a final 21-point margin over Ayr. Although Belfast lost their league title by a single point, the 2002/03 campaign ended with a triumphant Giants heading their group of the play-offs. They went on to defeat London in the championship final at Nottingham. However, with debts reputed to be near £1 million Giants' creditors had to accept a twenty per cent return in the summer of 2003, or see Giants founder.

The Elite League, with its much lower wage cap, took the place of the Superleague in the autumn of 2003. Giants signed several locally trained players. Mark Morrison contributed seven points from his 55 games. Whistle left for Germany with his assistant Rob Stewart taking over. Belfast finished fourth. Ruff made the All-Star First Team, while average attendances dropped to 3,345 as marketing was drastically reduced. Edinburgh-born Tony Hand (37) came in as player-coach in autumn 2004 to lead Giants to a runners-up place. He was named 'ELPlayer of the Year' and led in play-making with 49 assists.

Other highlights seen at the Odyssey have been the staging of the Challenge Cup finals in 2001 and 2002. In the semi-final round of the Continental Cup in November 2002, Belfast won all three of their encounters. Swedish, German and Norwegian clubs have also met the Giants on Odyssey ice.

BILLINGHAM

Opened:	17 July 1967. Officially opened by the Queen on 19 October 1967	Address: Billingham Forum
Ice Size:	180ft x 80ft (55m x 24m)	Leisure Centre
Total Spectator Capacity:	1,200	Town Centre
Seating Capacity:	800	Billingham
Ice Hockey – First Match:		Stockton-on-Tees
3 February 1973: England 5 v. Scotland 5		TS23 2LJ England

Teams:

Billingham Bombers   1974–77 Northern Second League; 1977–82 Northern League; 1981/82 English National League; 1982/83 British League Division 1 Section B; 1991–93 British League Premier Division; 1995/96 British League Division 1; 2002–05 English National League – North

Cleveland Bombers	1983–87 and 1990/91 British League Premier Division; 1987–90 British League Division 1
Teeside Bombers	1993/94 British League Premier Division; 1994/95 Autumn Cup only
Billingham Eagles	1996–98 English League North Con and 1997/98 English National League; 1998–2000 English League Division 1; 2000–02 English National League – North
Billingham Buccaneers	1977–81 Northern Reserve League; 1983–87 British League Division 2; 1987–91 English League; 1991/92 English Under-21 League; 1995/96 English Under-19 League
Billingham Wolves	1997–2002 English Under-19 League
Billingham Bombers	2002–05 English Under-19 League
Billingham Bullets	1976–81 Northern Junior League; 1983–96 English Junior Under-16 League
Billingham Bears	1996–2002 English Under-16 League
Billingham Bombers	2002–05 English Under-16 League
Billingham Bayonets	1984–90 English Pee-Wee League; 1991–95 English Under-14 League
Billingham Falcons	1996–2002 English Under-14 League
Billingham Bombers	2002–05 English Under-14 League
Billingham Bombardiers	1991–96 English Under-12 League
Bullingham Pumas	1996–2002 English Under-12 League
Billingham Bombers	2002–05 English Under-12 League

Honours:

Cleveland Bombers	1987/88 Winners British League Division 1 – North
Eagles	1998–2000 Winners English League – North and 1998/99 ELN Play-offs and 2000/01 English National League Conference – North
Buccaneers	1989/90 Winners English League Division 2 – North and ELN Play-offs
Bullets	1990/91 Winners English Junior League – North
Wolves	1999/2000 and 2002/03 Winners English Under-19 'A' League – North
Bayonets	1994/95 Winners English Under-14 League – North
Pumas	1996–98 Winners English Under-14 'A' League – North
Bears	1997/98 and 1999/2000 Winners English Under-16 'A' League – North

Part of a sports and leisure complex that includes a swimming pool and 675-seat theatre, designed by architects Elder Lester & Partners. The convex roof is suspended from externally expressed angled columns at each corner. The rink portion of the complex cost around £400,000. Leased from Stockton-on-Tees Borough Council by Durham Ice and Sports Stadiums Ltd, the Forum was run for more than twenty years by the Smith brothers Bill and Sid.

Youth coaching schemes did not get under way for more than four years. By then plastic had replaced most of the original glass windows. A mix of teenage rink rats, a Swedish student, a couple of lads with hockey experience at Durham and a Canadian called Jim Black combined to enter the Northern Reserve League in 1974. It was Black, a forty-something ex-RCAF flyer, who had been based at nearby Thornaby airfield during the Second World War, who suggested the tag 'Bombers'. It stuck. Three years later came promotion to the senior, but still mainly amateur Northern League. The first two imports, recruited from Sweden, did not last the season. Terry Matthews, a Whitley Bay veteran, joined a bit later. Under his guidance, with first Canadian Paul Mitchell at £20 a week, and next year

A view of the
unique roof design.

fellow countryman Ted Phillips, Bombers blossomed. Both led the club in scoring as
Billingham ended as NL and Autumn Cup runners-up for 1979/80, repeating this the following winter. Local lad Brian Cadman, earlier named 'Rookie of the Year', developed into
a high scorer. Crowds built up to around 900.

Behind the scenes the Billingham club, under the chairmanship of Jack Wharry, were
active in facilitating the formation of an English National League in 1981, then the transition to an all-British three-division version two seasons later. Bombers developed a fierce
rivalry with nearby Durham Wasps and Whitley Warriors, all in the top-ranked Premier
Division. The prefix Cleveland was later adopted to appeal to a wider audience beyond the
confines of Billingham Town.

With the increasing emphasis on bringing in paid Canadian imports, the club moved
away from rink ownership, becoming a limited company by 1989. The restricted spectator
accommodation, mainly seating on a balcony along one side of the rink, constrained
income. During this period forward Jim Earle thrilled the Forum crowds with his scoring,
accumulating 240 points between 1983 and 1985. Bombers gradually lost ground to finish
bottom by spring 1987, with relegation to Division 1.

Winning the divisional title the next winter, Cleveland were defeated by Telford in the
promotion play-off. It would be two years before Bombers climbed back into the Premier
Division, aided by the talents of imports Tim Cranston, Kevin Conway and Andre Malo.
The latter coached the Eagles and represented GB in the 1993 World Championships.

Attendances during this decade rose to between 900 and the 1,200 capacity. Three years
back in the top echelon was the high point for ice hockey at the Forum. For 1992/93 a
local entrepreneur, Ian Rennison, took control and in January Bombers defeated Durham
at the forty-sixth attempt, ending with their best-ever league placing. Unfortunately crowd
averages of barely 900 could not sustain the increasing cost of players' wages.

The name change to Teeside coincided with a struggle to maintain a place in pro hockey. By January 1995 money troubles led to the demise of the club. Resurrected late the next
summer, thanks to the efforts of John Rogers and Alan Moutrey, a return to senior hockey
ended with a thirteenth-place finish in Division 1 of the BL. More changes came the following autumn as Bombers became Eagles, with a drop to the English League on financial
grounds. Fewer imports did little to tempt back the fans. Throughout this period the youth
development programmes' teams picked up titles.

A low point came in 1997/98 when a late start due to problems with the barriers and ice
plant led to further erosion of home support. From the following winter the predominate-
ly locally trained Eagles soared to land three consecutive Conference titles and contest the
play-off finals, winning these in the spring of 1999. The club was reconstituted in 2002

under the guidance of Terry Ward, a former Billingham goalminder for many years, as all teams down to the Under-12s reverted to the Bombers tag.

The Forum played host in March 1982 to three matches in Pool C of the European Under-18 Championships. Billingham ice had previously seen the staging of two games in an international tournament involving England, Holland and Spain during October 1978.

BIRMINGHAM – SUMMERHILL ROAD

Opened:	1 September 1931	Address:
Closed:	18 April 1964	Birmingham
Ice Size:	190ft x 80ft in 1931. Some post-	Ice Skating Rink
	Second World War sources state	Goodman Street
	187ft x 78ft or 179ft x 87ft	Summerhill Road
Total Spectator Capacity:	Approximately 1,500	Birmingham
Seating Capacity:	750	Warwickshire
Ice Hockey – First Match:		England

6 November 1931: London Lions 7 v. Scotland 0

Teams:
Warwickshire	1931/32 challenge games; 1932/33 English League – Division 2; 1933–35 English League – Division 1
Birmingham Maple Leafs	1935/36 English League North; 1936–38 challenge games (away only)
Birmingham Barons	1961–64 Blackpool Tournament and 1963/64 *Hockey Fan Cup* (away only)

Honours:
Warwickshire	1932/33 Champions English League Division 2
Birmingham Maple Leafs	1935/36 Champions English League – Winners Northern Section & Play-off

Built at a cost of £75,000 without thought for ice hockey, although the sport featured from the beginning. The first matches, which included Ottawa Shamrocks and England, sparked off the formation of a local side – Warwickshire. Built around a core of four experienced players, including Peter Churchill (awarded the DSO as a wartime secret agent for SOE) and P.R. Tingley (a Canadian) the team lost out 3–5 to Oxfordshire on 6 January 1932 in their first home match. Zurich SC and Vienna EV also visited. Crowds of over 1,000 were commonplace that first season.

The next autumn saw Warwickshire join seven other teams in the Second Division of the English League. They won their home opener, backstopped by ex-Manchester 'keeper Stan Bookbinder, defeating Ps and Qs (Princes & Queens) 11–5. By January they headed the division and took the title with a 6-point margin, suffering just 2 losses in 13 games.

The team found promotion to the top level hard, being badly beaten by London sides Grosvenor House and Queens. Both had introduced the practice of importing paid Canadians. A fifth-placed finish with 8 points was the best that could be achieved. Next winter the dark-blue-and-red-clad Warwickshire team missed the cellar of the eight-member league by two points. This was despite signing Canadians Dean Gee (a goalie), Bert Shaw and Chuck Littlewood.

For 1935/36 the leagues were reorganised. Rink management took full control of hockey, with Sid Blissett appointed player-coach. The club became the Maple Leafs and moved to the Northern Section of the English League where they won all ten of their matches, scoring 106 for the 17 goals conceded. The most successful of Birmingham's four seasons of league hockey was crowned on home ice when Leafs defeated Streatham Royals 4–3 in the

An unusual team picture.

play-off for the EL championship. The losing London squad included GB Olympic gold medal winners Erhardt, Davey and Stinchcombe.

Several professional teams that formed the new English National League met the Maple Leafs at Summerhill Road. Brighton Tigers, Wembley Canadians, Kensington Corinthians and Streatham all suffered defeats. The season's 24 games had the fans flocking in. Attendances of nearly 3,000 were reported, with the doors closed before the opening face-off.

By autumn 1936 the rink management, for reasons that were probably commercial, due to the limited number of seats, turned away from backing a team. Maple Leafs were denied ice time. Wembley's two teams twice provided exhibitions that October, to bring to a close ice hockey in front of the citizens of Birmingham.

Maple Leafs played a handful of challenge games in Bristol and Scotland, with an initial following of over 200 fans, but the better players soon drifted away. An R.C.A.F. team played some hockey at the rink during the Second World War.

Bought in the early 1960s by Silver Blades, a subsidiary company of Mecca, the new owners granted a group of local lads a small amount of ice time. From December 1964 Barons were able to stge a few home matche before Mecca finally closed the doors.

BIRMINGHAM – PERSHORE STREET

Opened:	21 April 1964	Address:
Closed:	9 February 2003	Planet Ice
Ice Size:	180ft x 80ft (54m x 24m)	Birmingham Arena
Total Spectator Capacity:	300 (600 in 1964)	73–75 Pershore Street
Seating Capacity:	Minimal	Birmingham
Ice Hockey – First Match:		B5 4RW

19 September 1987: Birmingham Eagles 10 v. Bristol Phantoms 19 (EL Division 2)

West Midlands
England

Teams:

Birmingham Panthers 1980/81 Midland League Division 2; (1982/83 British League Division 3 – North; games 1983/84 British League Division 2 all away games only)

Birmingham Eagles 1987/88 British League Division 1; 1988/89 English League Division 1; 1989/90 English League Division 2 & English League Division 3 (all games away); 1990/91 English League Division 3 ('home' games at Telford)

Birmingham Hawks	1988–90 English Junior League (1989/90 all games away)
Birmingham Rockets	2000–02 English National League – Conference
Birmingham Barons	2002/03 English National League – Conference
Birmingham Rockets	2001/02 English Under-19 League
Birmingham Rockets	2000–02 English Under-16 League
Birmingham Rockets	2000–03 English Under-14 League
Birmingham Rockets	2000–03 English Under-12 League

Honours:

Eagles	1989/90 Play-off Champions English League Division 3; 1990/91 Play-off Champions English League Division 3 and Winners Central section
Hawks	1989/90 Winners English Junior 'B' League – North (all games for 4 points)

Built by Mecca as a pleasure-skating-only venue, similar in design to Bradford. The ice pad was at first floor level above a ten-pin bowling centre. For years Mecca maintained their anti-ice hockey stance, although they did permit training facilities in 1981 to a group of local lads, to practice at night behind closed doors. The Panthers, originally an offshoot of the Solihull-based Barons, played all their league games on opponents' ice.

Finally dropping their opposition, Mecca Leisure decided to sponsor a team. They invited Bob Bradberry, previously involved with the sport at Solihull, to form the Eagles in the summer of 1987. Canadian Mark Budz joined as player-coach, along with Bob Koral as the second import. Eagles finished fourth in the fourteen-member Second Division of the British League. Budz contributed 205 points.

Next winter Birmingham met tougher opposition, as BL2 became Division 1 of a revived English League. Eagles pulled off a coup in signing Larry Sacharuk, who had played 151 games in the NHL for New York and St Louis. He left after 6 matches and 14 goals as Mecca failed to pay his wages. Koral also soon departed. Eagles ended seventh from eight. That summer Mecca closed the rink at two day's notice. Eagles struggled on for a further two seasons, in the Under-21 EL Division 3, before folding under the strain of playing all their fixtures on the road.

The building operated as a roller skating venue, closing in summer 1990. Planet Ice reopened it as an ice rink in the mid-1990s; the first of several subsequent rink purchases.

David Graham, an ex-GB goalie, formed a club for youth hockey, with around forty players, in 2000. The same label – Rockets – was applied to all teams. Dressing rooms were refurbished and a team joined the Southern Conference of the English National League.

The 'senior' Rockets finished seventh in their inaugural season, moving to the Northern group next winter for a similar placing. For the final season of senior hockey in Birmingham, there was a change to the nickname – to Barons – and a move back to the Southern Conference. With 4 victories from 20 matches the renamed side ended sixth and last.

A severe fire on the evening of 9 February 2003 closed the rink. As a consequence both Rocket's Under-19 and Under-16 teams, with outstanding fixtures, withdrew from their respective leagues. The rink, now a shell, remains closed.

Two games have been held at the National Exhibition Centre (NEC). A £250,000 temporary 60m x 30m ice floor installed in the 7,200-seat Hall 7 during 1986, supported the final of the Norwich Union Autumn Cup. On 15 November, in front of 5,263 spectators Nottingham Panthers defeated Fife Flyers 5–4. Two years later on 3 December, this time in the 5,700 capacity Hall 5, Durham Wasps beat Tayside (Dundee) Tigers 7–5 in the final of the same competition, watched by a 3,580 strong crowd. On both occasions the later stages of these afternoon games were shown the same day on BBC TV's *Grandstand* programme.

BLACKBURN

Opened:	25 January 1991	Address:
Ice Size:	197ft x 98ft (60m x 30m)	Blackburn Arena
Total Spectator Capacity:	3,500	Lower Audley
Seating Capacity:	3,200	Waterside
Ice Hockey – First Match:		Blackburn
26 January 1991: Blackburn Blackhawks 6 v. Oxford City		Lancashire BB1 1BB
Stars 3 (EL)		England

Teams:

Blackburn Blackhawks	1990/91 English League Division 1; 1991/92 British League Division 1
Blackburn Hawks	1992–96 English League Division 1; 1996/97 Northern Premier League; 1998/99 English Premier League; 1999/2000 English League Division 1 – North; 2000–05 English National League – North
Lancashire Hawks	1997/98 British National League
Blackburn Seagulls	1993–97 English League/Conference
Blackburn Phoenix	1997/98 English Conference
Blackburn Seahawks	1993/94 English Under-16 League
Blackburn Eagles	1994–2005 English Under-16 League
Blackburn Kestrels	1994–2005 English Under-14 League
Blackburn Thunderhawks	1995–2005 English Under-19 League
Blackburn Sparrowhawks	1996–2005 English Under-12 League
Blackburn Ice Hawks	1998–2000 English Under-16 League
Blackburn Fire Hawks	2002–05 English Under-16 League
Blackburn Harriers	2001–04 English Under-14 League
Blackburn Ice Hawks	2000–05 English Under-19 League

Honours:

Kestrals	1997/98 Winners English Under-14 'B' League – North
Eagles	1997/98 and 2000/01 Winners English Under-16 'B' League – North

The site owners and developers – Peel Investments (North) – had the good sense to involve C.M. and C.D. Bennett Builders Ltd and their sister company Arena Associates Ltd in the ice design and fitting-out stages. Colin Bennett had direct knowledge of the needs of ice hockey, having previously played for Southampton and Bournemouth.

The rink opened with excellent sight lines from all but the lowest banks of seating along both sides, and was fully fitted out with plexi-glass. A capacious bar runs along almost the entire balcony at one end.

'Senior' ice hockey has had a chequered history with several changes of ownership, name, coach and varying playing standards in a selection of leagues. Its reputation among spectators as the coldest rink in Britain does not help. It was three years after the building opened before a basic heating system was installed.

Blackhawks' first season commenced later than had been intended, as the rink had been scheduled to open on 1 November. The team was formed mainly from players acquired from nearby clubs. Canadian import Fred Perlini, who had played 8 games for Toronto in the NHL, became a one-man scoring machine with 83+49 in his 21 matches. By season's end crowds had built to nearly 2,000. A one-campaign appearance in the British League followed, which started well with the appointment of coach Doug

Early 1991. (Walter Bayliss/*IHNR*)

McKay. However his aspirations were not met by the budget, which upset his paymasters – the rink owners.

For 1992/93 an amended name (the Black had been dropped), plus the acquisition of Steve Moria as player-manager proved inspirational. Crowds reached 2,600 for the season's end clash with local rivals Trafford. Fourth in Conference 'A' of the English League was a fair reward. The next winter, with a shift to the British League, Milton Keynes Kings proved too strong in the battle for promotion to the Premier.

The rink and club owners initially appeared reluctant to provide the necessary finances. Moria was not retained and attendances did not rise much above 1,000. Imports came and went. Then came a change of heart; money became available as Rocky Saganiuk, who had played 265 games in the NHL, was engaged as coach. A six-game winning streak in the spring of 1995 and extensive marketing produced a crowd of 3,127. Ryan Kumma, who replaced Saganiuk, recruited virtually a new side. A winning run took Hawks to the head of the EL. The highlight of 1995/96 came on Manchester ice where the rookie Storm suffered a 12–9 beating in front of Sky TV cameras. The fan base remained stubbornly weak at around 800.

With a stint in the Northern Premier League came a change of import, to two less-expensive Scandinavians. Canadian Todd Bidner, with 12 NHL games to his credit, joined them later and for the first time the club ran at a profit. Player-coach Jim Pennycook encouraged the youth development, which blossomed as Billy Price and Tom Burridge helped GB win promotion at the Under-18 European Championships. A brief flirtation as Lancashire proved futile. Better-funded teams with up to ten imports outplayed them. Six young lads gained experience by icing for Hawks and the Under-14s and Under-16s won their leagues. For 1998/99 Hawks reverted to the Blackburn suffix to compete in the English Premier League. With club stalwart Bobby Haig appointed player-coach Hawks rose to head the standings by four points. Then management stepped in to axe six players as attendances remained too low to sustain the outlay on wages. A bronze medal finish resulted.

From the following winter onwards Hawks, with a near-all-amateur side, have been members of the English League – North, the fourth level of hockey in Britain. Other than eighth in Millennium year Hawks have ended fourth twice and fifth in 2002/03. Compensation came in the Premier Cup with second place in Group A, competing against sides from the league above. Attendances were initially around 1,000 but nearly halved by 2005 with a third-place finish and a play-off spot.

Great Britain Select defeated Romania 6–4 on 18 February 1992 in a warm up for the World Championships. The next October a round of the European Cup was held at Blackburn, featuring Durham Wasps, Valerengen IF (Norway), Txuri Urdin (Spain) and Steaua Bucharest (Romania).

BLACKPOOL

Opened:	July 1937	Address:
Ice Size:	130ft x 95ft (40m x 27m)	Blackpool Leisure
Total Spectator Capacity:	2,400 (reduced to 2,000 by 1980)	Beach Arena
Seating Capacity:	2,000 (reduced to 750 in 1980s)	(originally Ice Drome)
Ice Hockey – First Match:		Ocean Boulevard
4 December 1937: London Canadians 6 v. Queens (London) 4		South Shore
		Blackpool Lancashire
		FY4 1EZ England

Teams:

Blackpool — 1939 challenge games

Blackpool Seagulls — 1951 in Blackpool Tournament and 1951–55 Midland Intermediate League; 1970–78 Southern League; 1978–81 Midland 'A' League; 1981/82 English League North and English National League; 1982/83 British League Division 1 – Section C; 1983–88 British League Division 1; 1988/89 English League Division 2 – North; 1989–91 English League Division 3; 1991/92 English Conference National Division; 1992/93 English Conference Wharry Division

Blackpool Beavers — 1974–78 Southern 'B' League; 1978–81 Midland League Division 2; 1983–86 British League Division 2; 1987/88 English League

Blackpool Otters — 1976/77 Southern Junior League

Blackpool Seahawks — 1988–93 English Junior/Under-16 League

Honours:

Seagulls — 1953/54 Champions Midland Intermediate League; 1977/78 Winners Midlands Section of Southern 'A' League; 1980/81 Champions Midland League; 1981/82 Champions English League – North

Beavers — 1976–78 Winners Midlands Section of Southern 'B' League; 1978/79 Champions Division 2 Midlands League

Built as an 'ice theatre' for ice shows. With a horseshoe-shaped ice pad plus a squared-off stage at one end not conducive to ice hockey, the sport had a slow start. Apart from a handful of exhibition games it took a couple of years for Roy Smith to form a local club, with Bert Halliday and Jack Culverwell prominent among the pioneer players. Then the Second World War intervened.

By 1950 the Seagulls were well established and ready to take on other teams, rather than scrimmage among themselves. The Blackpool Ice Drome Trophy (IDT) consisted of Seagulls meeting, on their own ice, the opposition. The visiting team with the best goal average returned to contest the Trophy final. For nearly thirty years Blackpool became a haven for amateur teams with little or no ice time to host games at their own rinks. A trip to the Ice Drome, with a Lancashire hotpot supper provided after the game, was often a season highlight in the 1950s and '60s.

Blackpool, with the advantage of knowing the peculiarities of the irregular shape of their ice, were usually triumphant in the final, although Liverpool were the first winners in 1952. It was eight years before Seagulls lost again, as Perth Blackhawks skated off with the silverware. In between Blackpool competed in the four-year reign of the Midlands Intermediate League. Coached by Bud Reginier, a Canadian, they won the title in 1953/54 with Ken Atkinson topping the scorers' list with 16 goals and 15 assists.

The interior in 1937. (*Skating Times*)

During the lean years for ice hockey in the 1960s 'Gulls beat the opposition to hold the IDT in 1963 and the next year and again between 1967 and 1969. Prominent were Stuart Lester on defence with Brian Singer and Tommy Patterson up front.

Blackpool were founding members, in 1970, of the five-team Southern League, whose band of clubs spearheaded the resurgence of ice hockey in the south of Britain. With an all-home bred squad Seagulls found it increasingly difficult to compete with the newer teams from the larger urban conurbations. The latter were often able to attract foreign players who were studying or working nearby. 'Gulls also commenced the season about six weeks after other teams, due to the long-running summer ice show.

When the Southern League split in the summer of 1978 Seagulls were again successful, winning two titles. With the formation in 1981 of the English National League, Blackpool engaged three paid imports. The twenty-seven-year-old Sims twins Brian and Bruce, together with Steve Currie (twenty-two) all came from the Toronto area. Seagulls were fifth in the ENL but the Sims ended first and second in the points scoring table. They repeated the trick next year in a regionalised all-British League (BL). When released, attendance figures showed increases from 300 to 700, sometimes rising to over 1,050.

In 1983/84 the BL separated into three sections, headed by the newly formed Premier Division. Blackpool was in Division One as the Sims moved to Southampton. For the next five years Seagulls entertained their fans at this level, often with only two imports to their rivals' three. Just one defeat in the second half of the campaign edged 'Gulls past Glasgow and Sunderland for third spot in the spring of 1985. Dave Anthony, in his first of four winters in Blackpool, led the way with 102 points. Their secret weapon – the horseshoe rink – assisted as standards continued to rise, with better imports on higher wages.

Local lads had not been forgotten. They were a necessity, hence the mainly Under-21 Beavers, who enjoyed some success in the late 1970s. Being a holiday resort put pressure on ice availability, although the club did enter a team into the Under-16 league for five years.

Problems with the ice plant and the continuing absence of a major sponsor forced Seagulls to give up the struggle and drop down to the near all-amateur BL Division 2 for 1988/89. In their five years of BL Division 1 they won 46 of their 120 games, tying a further four.

In the first, and only, campaign at the lower level Seagulls achieved third and provided the English League's Division 2 top scorer in Mark Clegg with 32+21. The two following years Blackpool's 'senior' squad toiled in the non-import Third Division. Another reshuffle by the authorities placed Seagulls in the English Conference – National Division. They ended third from nine and skated to a Knockout Trophy final. Ice hockey came to an end at the Ice Drome, not with a bang but a whimper, as Seagulls slipped down to seventh with only eight home fixtures. No announcement appeared as to the reasons for ice hockey's demise after fifty years at Blackpool. The sport had moved on, away from a horseshoe ice configuration. Seagulls and the Under-16 Seahawks moved east to the two-year-old Blackburn Arena.

A quartet of annual Oxford *v.* Cambridge Varsity matches were held at the Ice Drome – 1967 and 1968 then again in 1971 and the following year. The Dark Blues won all four.

BOURNEMOUTH

Opened: 19 December 1930   Address:
Closed: 6 January 1991   Westover Ice Rink
Ice Size: 120ft x 80ft (37m x 24m)   Westover Road
Spectator Capacity: 1,000   Bournemouth
Seating Capacity: 400   Dorset BH12 2BW
Ice Hockey – First Match: England
22 January 1931: Westover Ice Club 6 *v.* Hammersmith 10
(challenge)
Modern Era:
24 October 1982: Bournemouth Stags 20 *v.* Brighton Royals 8 (challenge)

Teams:
Westover Ice Club   1930/31 challenge games; 1931–33 English League Division 2
Bournemouth   1933/34 English League Division 2; 1934/35 challenge games;
                          1935/36 English League – South
Bournemouth Stags   1938/39 London & Provincial League 1982/83 British League
                          Division 2; 1983–87 British League Division 1; 1987/88
                          British League Division 2
Bournemouth Bucks   1984–87 British League Division 2; 1987/88 English League
Bournemouth Sharks 1988–91 English League Division 2
Bournemouth Hounds   1983–88 English Junior League
Bournemouth Barracudas 1988–91 English Junior League
Bournemouth Terriers   1983–88 English Pee-Wee League
Bournemouth Piranhas   1988–91 English Pee-Wee/Under-12 League
Bournemouth Sharks   1991/92 English Under-21 League (all games played away)

Honours:
Bournemouth   1933/34 Champions English League Division 2
Terriers   1985/86 Winners English Pee-Wee League – South

The rink was at first-floor level above a garage. It was closed during the Second World War,
to be used initially as an emergency hospital for French servicemen from the Dunkirk evac-
uation; then as an RAF store. It reopened as an ice rink on 9 November 1946 with long-
running ice shows and boxing tournaments interspersed with public skating.

The interior,
1933. (*Skating
Times*)

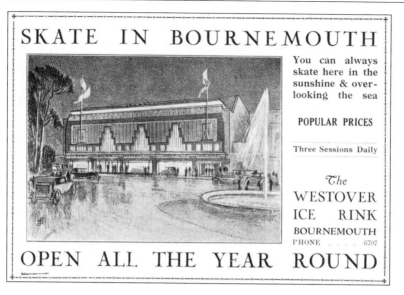

SKATE IN BOURNEMOUTH

You can always skate here in the sunshine & over-looking the sea

POPULAR PRICES

Three Sessions Daily

The
WESTOVER
ICE RINK
BOURNEMOUTH
PHONE 6707

OPEN ALL THE YEAR ROUND

An artist's early 1930s exterior view.

Peterborough-based C.L. Gaul & Co., the then-operators, claimed in January 1991, that the rink was making a substantial loss every week and promptly closed it down. Later that year Gaul & Co. went into liquidation. As of August 2003 the first floor, which had housed the rink, was empty and derelict.

Ice hockey at Bournemouth falls into two periods, separated by over four decades. A club was formed almost as soon as the rink opened with Leslie Cliffe and his two brothers at the core. The first game attracted 'between 500 to 600 residents who were stunned by the daring displays of the players'. Several other London-based teams, plus Sussex and Oxfordshire, visited the seaside rink that winter.

Next season Westover entered the six-member Division 2 of the English League (EL) to finish third. Sussex were defeated in the first game with L. Cliffe netting a hat-trick. Southampton went down 11–7 in the first meeting between the near neighbours. On 30 January a London Select visited with the founder of British ice hockey B.N. 'Peter' Patton in goal. He first played in London in the late 1890s. Carl Erhardt, was on defence and scored as the Select won by 8–4.

With an additional two teams in the league for 1932/33 Bournemouth held onto third spot. Face-off time shifted from Saturday afternoon to 7.30pm. Ivor Nesbitt, who learnt the game in Canada, became a prominent player. Two matches were held on New Year's Eve as Grosvenor House Canadians were defeated 9–3 in the afternoon, but recovered in time to win 7–4 five hours later. At the third attempt Bournemouth won Division 2, going undefeated at home. They needed overtime to see off Streatham by the odd goal in thirteen on the first Saturday of 1934 with Harry Cooke, originally from Montreal, netting the winner.

Season 1934/35 opened on 6 October with a visit of the newly formed professional Wembley Canadians, resulting in a 3–3 tie. A week later, Wembley Lions won 7–4. For these matches, and others against opponents of a similar calibre, Bournemouth normally borrowed a couple of visiting players. What newcomers to England made of the truncated ice pad can only be imagined. Usually each side dropped a skater to compensate for the short length of the ice. The full Streatham, Warwickshire and Richmond Hawks English League clubs also came to Dorset that winter. Bournemouth suffered their first league defeat on home ice in two years, in late February. Queens won 3–2 despite a late goal from F.W. Taylor. The biggest crowd of the season turned up on 27 March to watch a women's international, as England, with a goal from Jean Bayes, blanked the French ladies 1–0. The second tier EL divided into two regions for 1935/36 with Bournemouth in the southern. Despite sparkling displays in the nets from C.K. Harper, a Canadian who had been with the club for four years, it was a poor season. They lost most of their home games until 14 December when they forced a 3–3 deadlock with Streatham.

Bournemouth Stags were formed in the autumn of 1938 to compete in the eleven-team London Provincial League. Newcomers J. March and H. Dohn joined Nesbitt and Cooke and returnee 'Tiger' Leigh. In goal R. Blakeney replaced Harper. Stags came away from Wembley having taken a point from both Colts and Terriers to finish fourth, two points adrift of Princes.

Ice hockey returned to Westover in 1982 when a disaffected group from the Southampton club entered a reformed Stags into the Second Division of the British League (BL). Led by player-manager Colin Bennett they drew crowds of around 650. The docking of 10 points for use of ineligible players did not help a move to the BL Division 1. Glasgow-born netminder Bill Morrison achieved the fourth-best average; his team ended six places lower in the division. A youth coaching programme was set-up, almost from the return of hockey. A further three years in BL 1, with two successive seventh places, ended in the spring of 1987 with more deducted points and relegation. Two outstanding imports skated for Bournemouth. Daryl Lipsey, who remains in this country, topped Stags' scorers in 1985/86 with 119 points. He was joined by Don Yewchin, who stayed on for the start of the next campaign to contribute a total of 89 goals. Seventeen victories provided Stags, now mainly a locally based amateur squad, with a fifth place, one point behind Birmingham.

For the final three years of ice at Bournemouth, the club management adopted marine-based team names. The 'senior' Sharks competed in Division 2 of the English League with varying success.

BRACKNELL

Opened:	1 November 1987	Address:
Ice Size:	197ft x 98ft (60m x 30m)	Bracknell Ice Rink
Total Spectator Capacity:	3,100	John Nike Leisure
Seating Capacity:	2,870	Complex
Ice Hockey – First Match:		John Nike Way
1 November 1987: Bracknell Bees 13 *v.* Medway		Bracknell
Marauders 3 (British League Division 2)		Berkshire RG12 4TN
		England

Teams:

Bracknell Bees	1987/88 British League Division 2; 1988–90 English League Division 1; 1990/91 British League Division 1; 1991–95 British League Premier Division; 1995/96 British League Division 1; 1996–2003 Superleague; 2003–05 British National League
Bracknell Drones	1988–91 English League Division 2; 1991–94 English Under-21 League; 1994–2005 English Under-19 League
Bracknell Hornets	1994–2005 English Conference/National League
Bracknell Bumble Bees	1988–2005 English Under-12 League
Bracknell Hummers	1989–2005 English Pee-Wee/Under-14 League
Bracknell Stingers	1988–2005 English Under-16 League
Bracknell Workers/Swarm	2003–05 English Under-14 League
Bracknell Wings	2003/04 English Under-12 League
Bracknell 'B'	2004/05 English Under-16 League

Honours:

Bees	1989/90 Champions English League; 1991/92 won British League Division Group 'A' Play-offs; 1999/00 Champions

	Superleague; 2004/05 Champions British National League and Winners Winter Cup
Bumble Bees	1990–92 Winners English Under-12 'A' League – South; 1992–96 Winners English Under-12 South-West Conference; 1993/94 English Under-12 Champions
Hummers	1990/91 Winners English Pee-Wee 'B' League – South; 1992/93 & 1995/96 Winners English Under-14 South-West Conference & English Champions; 1997/98 Winners English Under-14 'A' League – South
Stingers	1991/92 Winners English Under-16 'B' League – South
Drones	2001/02 Winners English Under-19 'B' League – South

John Nike OBE, the millionaire rink and club owner, first applied for Town Planning permission for a dry ski run, ice rink and associated facilities at Amen Corner in 1979. Building work on the rink commenced in February 1985, a year after the ski slope opened. He had been advised by the Sports Council to go for a smaller rink, but held out for a 3,000 seater and the first Olympic-sized ice in England. Like several rinks of a similar date, sight lines from the side balconies are restricted.

Bracknell were an ambitious club from the beginning with Nike being quoted as saying: 'breaking even is the target rather than making a profit'. The ambition was achieved by the end of year four, but Bees lost their way since winning Superleague in 2000, until season 2004/05.

In the absence of local players, the inaugural Bees were based around the core of iceless Brighton Royals. Canadian-born Jamie Crapper was engaged in the dual roles of player-coach and youth development. He signed Grant Clark, as the second import. From a thousand spectators for the first game, attendances rose steadily to 2,600. High-scoring league encounters enabled Crapper to pile up 150+100 in 25 games as Bees finished their first season in sixth place. Moving to Division 1 of the English League (EL1) Bees finished one point off the top. The excellent leadership of new recruit Darin Fridgen pulled Bracknell out of an early slump, backstopped by the formidable Mike Kellond. Both were retained for 1989/90, along with Crapper, as Bees took the EL championship and third place in the

Rink entrance to the right. (Mike Smith/*IHNR*)

play-offs. They were again runners-up in two other competitions – the Southern Cup and Autumn Trophy. Crapper represented GB in the World Championships, and Bees replaced Streatham Redskins in Division 1 of the British League. With Clark coaching, a defence strengthened by Ottawa-born Matt Cote, soon a crowd favourite, and prolific British scorers Bob Breskal and Nigel Rhodes, with Gary Brine in goal, the Bees gained promotion to the Premier Division.

The years in the Premier were not the best of times. Player unrest, as Fridgen departed during 1991/92, contributed to the need to win the relegation play-offs to avoid the drop. Next winter's fifth position was the highest from the four Premier campaigns. With Cote back, and Chris Brant retained, to be joined by Dave Whistle and Ron Stewart, Bees narrowly missed a place in the Premier Division in 1996.

Disquiet with the national governing body for the sport – the British Ice Hockey Association (BIHA) – among newer club owners resulted in the formation of the Superleague in the summer of 1996. Bracknell were founder members with the inaugural game staged at the Beehive on 21 September. In a pre-game ceremony John Nike, BIHA President Frederick Meredith and Superleague chairman David Temme, owner of the opposing club Cardiff, who won 5–4, unveiled the Monteith Bowl, to be contested by the eight teams. From an initial sixth, Bees climbed a place for the next two seasons. With Whistle's appointment as coach in 1998 ex-NHLers P.C. Droin, Denis Chasse and Paxton Shulte joined Bracknell. With the superb Bruno Campese in goal Bees only dropped two points in the play-offs to reach the British semi-finals for the first time. Whistle said: 'We can build on this'.

Playing stylish, open ice hockey to an average audience of over 2,000 Bees won the Monteith Bowl in Millennium year. They were also finalists in the Benson & Hedges and Challenge Cup. A motorway bus crash the following winter injured several players but Bees made it as far the finals weekend at Nottingham. Between 2001 and 2003 Bracknell underachieved as attendances dwindled. In 2003 Bees elected not to join the replacement for the defunct Superleague. With a reduced budget they competed the British National League, ending as runners-up in the cup and play-offs. Next winter, under second-year coach Mike Ellis, Bees won the cup and league. Goalie Stevie Lyle and defender Danny Meyers, both Brits, were named to the All-Star squad along with Canadian forward Peter Campbell and Lukas Smital – a thirty-year-old Czech. He also collected the BNL 'Player of the Year' award as Ellis was named 'Coach of the Year'.

On 11 April 2005 ALP, the company running Bees, announced they would no longer be running pro ice hockey and were closing down the next month.

Throughout the 1990s the vibrant Bracknell youth programme produced numerous winners at all levels, although until 2003 few lads gained a permanent place on the Bees' roster. In March 1989 four matches in the World Junior Pool 'C' championships took place on Bracknell ice.

BRADFORD

Opened:	2 December 1965. Official opening 4 January 1966	Address: Bradford Ice Rink
Ice Size:	180ft x 80ft (55m x 24m)	Great Cause
Total Spectator Capacity:	Approximately 300	19 Little Horton Lane
Seating Capacity:	Approximately 150 on benches	Bradford
Ice Hockey – First Match:		West Yorkshire
Unknown		BD5 0AE England

Teams:

Bradford Bulldogs

1979/80 Midland League Division 2; 1980–82 Midland League Division 1; 1982–87 British League Division 2; 1987/88 English League – North; 1988–90 English League Division 2; 1991/92 English Conference – National Division; 1992/93 English Conference – Wharry Division; 1993/94 English League Division 1; 1994–98 English League Conference – North; 1998–2000 English League Division 1 – North; 2000–05 English National League – North/Conference

West Yorkshire Raiders
1980/81 Midland League Division 2 all games forfeit

Bradford Renegades
1981/82 Midland League Division 2; 1982/83 British League Division 3

Bradford Pirates
1982–84, 1985–91 and 1992–2005 English Junior League

Bradford Oilers
1989–91 English League – Division 3

Bradford Buccaneers
1993–96, 1997–2002 and 2003–05 English Under-14 League

Bradford Blades
1995/96 English Under-19 League

Bradford Vipers
1997/99 and 2001–05 English Under-19 League

Bradford Ice Knights
1997–2001 and 2003–05 English Under-12 League

Honours:

Bulldogs
1991/92 Winners English Conference – National Division; 1992/93 Winners English Conference – Wharry Division

Oilers
1989/90 Winners Northern Section of English League Division 3

Vipers
2003–05 Winners English Under-19 'B' League – North

Originally constructed for Mecca as part of a purpose-built entertainments complex, with the rink located on the first floor of a multi-storey block. Closed in 1990 and sold to two local businessmen, whose company Greatcause Ltd came to the rescue financially. Rink reopened in July 1991 with new roof, light and sound system plus café.

Bradford is the only one of the three similar Mecca rinks where there has never been any attempt to launch a professional or semi-professional senior team. The very limited spectator accommodation rules out that form of the sport.

Karl Stanek, who had played for the Czech Army before settling in Bradford, began coaching a group of raw local lads in the spring of 1976. Three years later Stanek considered they had sufficient grasp of the fundamentals to launch Bulldogs into Division 2 of the Midlands League. The rookies finished fourth in front of the longer-established Deeside, Solihull, Trafford and Sheffield. Stanek was second in the league points scoring table with 16 goals and 8 assists from the fourteen-match schedule.

The leading scorer in the league (44+2), and for many years with Bulldogs, was Paul Holdsworth. He learnt the game in Canada and came to England as a young teenager. He returned to Canada in the mid-1990s. Although promoted next winter to the 'senior' Midlands League, to end one spot above the cellar, Holdsworth contrived to finish second in the scoring race, amassing 30 points from 11 outings. In those early days the Villancourt brothers, Luc and Marc, played regularly.

The youth development programme spawned the Pirates, as the Under-17s in 1982 entered the inaugural English Junior League, a continuity that continues today. The Under-14 Buccaneers commenced in their age group a decade later. By the mid-1990s the youth teams each had an hour of ice time a week on alternate days.

The club's greatest successes came in the late 1980s and the early years of the following decade. Bulldogs finished in 1989/90 as runners-up in Division 2 of the English League, three points behind Billingham. Holdsworth (57+40) and Paul Mahon (56+39) ended first-second in points scoring. The same season Oilers won their section of Division 3 of the same league. For the next two winters Bulldogs lost only one match in each campaign,

The exterior at the time of opening in 1966. (C.H. Wood [Bradford] Ltd)

spearheaded by the scoring exploits of Mahon with 50 and 55 goals respectively, in winning their division of the English Conference.

Once, in 1993/94, the club paid an import – John Standing. A true amateur set-up, at that time it cost each of the Bulldogs at least £500 each season, but as a close-knit group of friends, they enjoyed each other's company travelling the country. Small local businesses over the years have provided a limited amount of cash.

An alumni member of Bulldogs is Andy Carson. He went on to become a referee with international experience and several years of officiating at the top level in Britain's Super and Elite leagues.

Charlie Dacres, a prolific scorer as a player, who took over from Stanek as club coach in 1997, told *Ice Hockey News Review* that year: '… I think [hockey's] great for the kids. It gets them about the country, keeps them out of trouble and I think it's valuable to stress that it's about learning, living and having a bit of fun.'

In spite of the lack of recognition in multi-cultural Bradford, little press coverage and shortage of funding Bradford Bulldogs and their youth programme are still a valued member of the ice hockey community. Ice Knights returned to the Under-12 league in autumn 2003 after a two-year absence.

BRIGHTON – MIDDLE STREET

Opened:	16 October 1897	Address:
Closed:	circa March 1900	Real Ice Skating Rink
Ice Size:	Circular – 90ft diameter	52–58 Middle Street
Total Spectator Capacity:	Unknown	Brighton
Seating Capacity:	Loose tables and chairs on	East Sussex
	a wide promenade that	England
	encircled the ice.	

Ice Hockey – First Match:
4 January 1899: Brighton 4 *v.* Princes 2

Team:
Brighton   1899–1900 challenge games

The building, specifically designed as an ice rink by Louis Karslake, is based on, and is very similar to, Niagara Hall in London, which opened two years earlier. It only operated from October to March each season, no doubt partly because early ice-making plants could not cope with summer temperatures. The architect's drawings indicate a rink diameter of 98ft, but these are likely to be 'as designed' drawings and not 'as built'.

Beyond the wide carpeted promenade surrounding the ice were a series of green-draped arches, embellished with mirrors. Above the ice within the dome were drapes hanging in folds, illuminated by incandescent gas lamps.

After three years the owners – brothers Ellis and Humphrey Brammall – engaged the theatre architect Frank Matcham to convert the rink into a venue for circuses; opening in August 1901 as the Hipperdrome. Further alterations and a change of ownership saw the building reopen in December 1902 as a variety theatre. The building is now operated as a bingo hall by Mecca.

Major B.M. 'Peter' Patton, in his book, *Ice Hockey*, states that during 1899/1900 his club Princes (London) and Brighton met several times. The 'hockey' played was more an indoor version of bandy, with field hockey sticks and a ball, rather than the sport we know today.

The Real Ice Skating Rink – the architect's drawing. (Reproduced with the permission of the Brighton & Hove City Council Record Office)

BRIGHTON – SPORTS STADIUM

Opened:	16 October 1935 (as an ice rink – see Remarks)	Address: Sports Stadium
Closed:	10 October 1965	West Street
Ice Size:	175ft x 75ft (180ft x 80ft or 185ft x 85ft according to varied sources)	Brighton 1 East Sussex England
Total Spectator Capacity:	3,000	
Seating Capacity:	1,700	

Ice Hockey – First Match:
24 October 1935: Brighton Tigers 6 *v.* Richmond Hawks 1 (Sussex Cup)

Teams:

Brighton Tigers	1935–39 English National League; 1946–54 English National League; 1954–60 British National League; 1960–65 'Home' Tournaments
Sussex	1935–37 challenge games; 1937–39 London Provincial League and 1949–52 Southern Intermediate League
Sussex Vikings	1938/39 challenge games
Sussex Tigers	1939–41 challenge games
Brighton Monarchs	1956/57 'Home' Tournaments (away games only)
Brighton Ambassadors	1963–70 'Home' Tournaments (away games from 1965-70)
Brighton Tiger Cubs	c. 1956–65 Junior challenge games

Honours:

Tigers	1946/47 and 1947/48 Champions English National League; 1957/58 Champions British National League; 1946/47 Winners National Tournament; 1946/47 and 1950/51 Winners English Autumn Cup and 1957/58 British Autumn Cup; 1959/60 British Play-off Champions; 1961–63 Winners BIHA Cup and Brighton Tournament 1960–65

Designed by architects Jackson & Greenen, the famous 'SS' initials on the front of the quasi 'Art Deco' facade stood for 'Swimming Stadium'. The building was built by W. Hayward & Sons (Bournemouth) Ltd, and was billed as 'the world's first indoor sea water swimming pool', when opening for business on 29 June 1934. It failed, closing next year on 29 September. Within sixteen days the empty pool had been scaffolded out to support an ice pad.

Brighton became a hotbed of hockey interest with rabid fans almost from the opening fixture. Percy Nicklin recruited the first Tigers. Although only gaining nine points from their twenty-four scheduled English National League (ENL) matches, attendances were encouraging. Next autumn new coach Don Peniston engaged French-Canadian Gordie Poirer and twenty-two-year-old Bobby Lee. Both had a few games in the NHL in the early 1940s and starred post-war with Tigers. Trips to Europe interrupted the league campaign as Tigers finished mid-table. Lee ended as the club's best points getter with 22 goals and 21 assists. With Billy Boucher as coach Brighton finished fifth in 1938 in an ENL reduced to seven.

The interior, prior to conversion to an ice rink.

In May of that year two exhibition games between Montreal Canadiens and Detroit Red Wings, during the National Hockey League's (NHL) first tour outside North America, took place on Brighton ice. The following winter ex-NHL player Gillie Farrand joined the regulars. He became the first Tiger to gain All-Star recognition.

Talented British lads and a few resident Canadians founded the Sussex club and by 1937 competed in the London Provincial League, designed to provide a place for indigenous players. Vikings came into being the next winter for the less experienced.

With the outbreak of hostilities the Sports Stadium formed the Sussex, then Brighton, house league. The four teams – Spitfires, Hurricanes, Demons and Furies – were named after fighter aircraft. Matches at noon on Sunday regularly drew a large crowd. By March the best combined into Sussex Tigers to meet opposition as diverse as Oxford University, Wembley, Earls Court and the RAF. Games between Canadian armed forces' teams commenced the same month and continued throughout the war with many NHL stars involved. The Sussex league resumed in 1941 with attendances building to near capacity. Sussex won 12 and drew 3 of their 28 games.

Pro hockey came back to the SS in the autumn of 1946 with the return of Lee and Gib Hutchinson in goal. Tigers swept all three major trophies, much to the surprise of the pundits. Lee, now player-coach, set a new ENL record with 111 points, as did 60-point man Poirer on defence, with 28 goals. Left-winger Lorne Trottier joined the following year as Brighton retained the league crown by a six-point margin. Bobby Lee again led the scorers on 86 points. 1949/50 was poor year although Tommy Jamieson won 'Rookie of the Year', as did Doug Verity the next winter as Tigers gathered in the Autumn Cup.

During the post-war years the national teams of Sweden, Switzerland, the USA, Canada, Czechoslovakia and Russia visited Brighton. In 1957 the all-powerful USSR national squad suffered a rare defeat at the hands of a club side, when Tigers came from behind to win 6–3 at an emotional and packed stadium. The team also travelled extensively across Europe most winters, taking on national and club sides.

An innovative manager – Benny Lee (no relation to Bobby) – joined that summer. He introduced wrestling, boxing, snooker, table tennis and later pop concerts and political con-

The on-ice ceremony after the final match on 23 May 1965. Not a dry eye in the house.

The exterior, 1935.
(*Skating Times*)

ferences as the SS became multi-purpose. Extended runs of the Christmas season ice pantomime shifted hockey nights to Sunday.

Bobby Lee retired in 1954 as the first player in England to score 400 goals. Silverware eluded Tigers until after the amalgamation of the English and Scottish circuits in 1954. They won their only British League title in 1958 by a ten-point margin. Tom Rendall at right-wing collected the scoring crown with 46 goals, and an All-Star 'A' selection, along with long-serving defender 'Red' Kurz. The momentum carried over with the Autumn Cup added to the trophy cupboard, by a two-point margin from Edinburgh. Goalie Tony Parisi and Kurz were named to the season-end All-Star 'A' sextet. Third in the league, Tigers went all the way in the newly introduced play-offs in spring 1960, defeating Nottingham Panthers 6–5 over two legs for the British Championship. A few weeks later the BNL folded.

The previous September the stadium had acquired a new owner in Nicholas van Slocham. He renamed the building Brighton Palladium. This lasted for three years until a new company was formed, with the flamboyant cigar-smoking Benny Lee as managing director. Both Bobby and Benny Lee are now honoured in the British ice hockey Hall of Fame.

The only one of the previous BNL clubs to continue with the sport post-autumn 1960, the gamble paid off. Admission prices reflected the reduced operating costs as fans flocked back in increased numbers to prove the pessimists wrong. They watched a Tigers with more native players than Canadians. 'Home' tournaments, similar to the long-standing affairs at Blackpool and Southampton, took the place of league-based competitions. The Brighton Cup was won, but Edinburgh took home the BIHA Cup. An all-British Tigers were victorious next winter in the Cobley and BIHA Cups. Scotsmen 'Red' Imrie, Johnny Carlyle and Jack Dryburgh stood out along with Mike O'Brien and netminder Ray Partridge. A mere handful of Canadians, who included Gordon Merritt and Bob McNeil, were recruited for the next three campaigns as Brighton achieved a hat-trick of Cobley and Brighton Tournament Cups.

Top Rank purchased the rink in 1964 and by the following 23 May it was all over in a tearful farewell to thirty years of continuous ice hockey, in the pressure-cooker atmosphere SS. In a belated post-war attempt to foster local talent the Tiger Cubs came into being in the mid-1950s, coached by the Canadian Tigers. Older amateur players formed the Ambassadors in 1963, with ice time provided by the sympathetic Benny Lee, with their own 'home' tournaments, usually directly after Tigers on Sunday evenings. All lost out with the closure of the Sports Stadium. The rink was soon demolished with the site providing car parking until the construction, in the early 1990s, of the Oak Hotel, which is now called the Comfort Hotel.

BRIGHTON – TOP RANK

Opened:	10 December 1966	Address:
Closed:	19 September 1971 (see below)	Top Rank Ice Rink
Ice Size:	180ft x 80ft (55m x 24m)	Kings Road
Total Spectator Capacity:	1,000. (Skaters, as not designed for spectators.)	Brighton East Sussex
Seating Capacity:	Loose seating only – surrounding the ice surface.	England

Ice Hockey – First Match:
No public matches staged although occasional training games held with Southampton Redwings. (See below)

Teams:
Sussex Senators   1970–72 Southern League

Honours:
Senators   1970–72 Champions Southern League (all games away)

Promoted by Top Rank, as a replacement for the Sports Stadium (SS), in the face of massive public opposition to the closure of their town's previous rink. The new venue was designed by architects Russell Diplock Associates and formed part of an entertainment complex, with the ice at first-floor level. Minus surrounding barriers and with minimal seating accommodation it could never replicate the SS.

The management only latterly gave grudging permission for practice time to the local amateur ice hockey players, with the inadequate facilities unable to support matches in front of paying spectators. The building officially closed on 18 October 1971, following the holding of a party political conference the previous month.

It was converted into a three-screen cinema complex, which opened on 13 April 1973, adjacent the contemporary Brighton Centre. The structure, now named King's West, still exists facing the Brighton seafront.

BRIGHTON – QUEEN SQUARE

Opened:	25 May 1978	Address:
Closed:	May 2003	Sussex Ice Club
Ice Size:	60ft x 40ft (18m x 12m)	11b Queen Square
Ice Hockey – First Match:		Brighton

Ice hockey club formed in 1980. Ice surface too small to stage matches. Practice facilities only with all games played at opponents' rinks.

East Sussex BN1 3FD
England

Teams:
Brighton Royals	1981/82 Inter-City Intermediate League; 1982–84 British League Division 3; 1984–87 British League Division 2; 1987–92 English League/Conference
Brighton Tiger Cubs	1981/82 Inter-City Junior League; 1982–89 English Junior League
Brighton	1984/85 English Pee-Wee League
Brighton Bobcats	1985–89 English Pee-Wee League

The rink was based in a sports centre that catered for minor activities such as table tennis. Royals made the best use of the small ice patch, ending runners up in 1982/83 in the southern section of Division 3 of the British League. Three years later, in Division 2 – South, they were second. Local boy Bob Breskal progressed to spend a year at Dundee with Rockets in the Premier Division of the BL. The ice hockey club ceased operations some years ago.

The rink closed as the building required extensive repairs and no offers had been received for the lease. As at February 2004 Brighton Council were considering plans for residential accommodation on the site.

BRISTOL – COLISEUM

Opened:	22 November 1934	Address:
Closed:	24 November 1940	The Coliseum
Ice Size:	155ft x 65ft (length 150–160ft	Park Row
	according to one source consulted)	Bristol
Total Spectator Capacity:	900	England
Seating Capacity:	200	

Ice Hockey – First Match:
15 January 1937: Bristol Bears 3 *v.* Bristol Cubs 2 (exhibition)

Teams:
Bristol Bears   1936–38 challenge games
Bristol Bombers   1938/39 challenge games

Tentative enquires by young enthusiastic skaters, and Canadians resident in the area, regarding ice hockey were discouraged. The Coliseum management would not risk the financial outlay, citing the small ice surface and insufficient seating to make the game pay.

Then, nearly halfway into the 1936/37 season rink manager Angus Baxter approached Ronald May, a speed skater, saying he wished to try the experiment of a Friday evening exhibition game. Buying their own equipment the local lads were coached by the more experienced Canadians Les Keel (a lanky defender), Norm Plummer, Jack Tweedie and Roy Button. Three inter-club exhibitions between Bears and Cubs in late January and February were well received by press and public, although the standard was low. Cubs then merged with the Bears.

With a badge depicting an aggressive bear on their blue and white uniforms Bears were defeated 5–3 on 26 February 1937 by their first visitors, Earls Court Marlboroughs. Three more encounters were lost, before the team gelled in a 4–4 tie with Richmond. This was followed by Bears' first victory, as Earls Court lost 3–1 in the return on 9 April, the last game of the season.

Next winter the rink took over the management of Bears. Seating capacity was increased and stronger opposition found for sixteen challenge games at Bristol. Goaltender Bruce Thompson arrived from Canada to be joined by fellow countrymen Murray Munro, Danny Muir and Johnny Hunter and a little later George Acott and Gus McLeod. Attendances increased with wins over Cambridge and London Provincial League sides Earls Court, Sussex and United Hospitals. Birmingham Maple Leafs proved too good, beating Bears on all three trips to the Coliseum. Two minutes of the final period of the 4–4 deadlock with the sponsored Philco Radio team, were broadcast on the West Region of the BBC Home Service. Attendances were reported as capacity at around 1,200. In February, Tommy Grace, an Englishman, joined for 3 matches and scored 3 goals.

With the rink unsure as to whether to continue promoting hockey, the final peacetime campaign did not commence until 9 December. Bears became Bombers – the squad was now composed of Canadians serving in the RAF. Bill Chowen took over in goal, with other changes being Don Ross and Ron McPherson at centre and Don Hamilton and Jack Tennian on the right wing. Richmond, Earls Court and United Hospitals were all well beaten. Bournemouth Stags went down 15–1 on 6 January. In the New Year Wembley United and London Select visited the Coliseum. Next month Bombers travelled north to take on Glasgow Mohawks and Perth Panthers of the pro Scottish National League. They lost 13–5 and 6–1 respectively. Upon their return home Bombers were downed on 10 March by the odd goal in nine by Wembley Colts.

The Coliseum was destroyed on 24 November 1940 by enemy action during an air raid.

BRISTOL – FROGMORE STREET

Opened:	21 April 1966	Address:
Ice Size:	180ft x 80ft (55m x 24m)	John Nike Leisuresport
Total Spectator Capacity:	650 (1,000 in 1966)	Bristol Ice Rink
Seating Capacity:	150	Frogmore Street
Ice Hockey – First Match:		Bristol BS1 5NA

15 January 1972: Bristol Redwings 4 v. Blackpool Seagulls 2 (SL), 6 December 1971 (behind closed doors): Bristol Redwings 6 v. Oxford University 5)

Address:
John Nike Leisuresport
Bristol Ice Rink
Frogmore Street
Bristol BS1 5NA
England

Teams:

Bristol Redwings	1971–74 Southern League; 1974–76 Southern 'A' League
Avon Arrows	1974/75 Southern 'B' League; 1975–78 Southern 'A' League; 1978–82 Inter-City 'A' League
Avon Darts	1975–78 Southern 'B' League; 1978–81 Inter-City 'B' League
Bristol Blackhawks	1982/83 British League – Division 1 – withdrew
Bristol Phantoms	1984–86 British League Division 2 – South; 1986–88 British League Division 2 – Midlands; 1988/89 English League Division 2 – South-East; 1989–91 English League Division 3 – Central
Bristol Bulldogs	1992/93 English League-Conference 'A'
Bristol Demons	1983–87 & 1989–91English Junior League
Bristol Terriers	1992–2005 English Junior/Under-16 League
Bristol Devils	1984–87 English Pee-Wee League
Bristol Demons	1987/88 English Pee-Wee League
Bristol	1991/92 English Pee-Wee League
Bristol Beagles	1993–2005 English Under-14 Conference/League
Bristol Devils	1988–91 English Under-12 League
Bristol Puppies	1992–94 and 1995–2001 English Under-12 Conference/League
Bristol Huskies	2001–04 English Under-12 League
Bristol Boxers	1995/96 and 1998–2005 English Under-19 League

Honours:

Avon Arrows	1974/75 Champions Southern 'B' League
Beagles	1999/2000 Winners English Under-14 'B' League – South
Boxers	2003–04 Winners English Under-19 'B' League – South

The rink is located on the first floor, originally as part of a multi-purpose entertainment complex, developed by Mecca within a concrete-clad building. The fabric did not lend itself to ice hockey as the barriers presented a plastic sloping face to the ice and the first floor bar overhung one end.

The Redwings practising,
April 1973.

Mecca's apathy to the sport was overcome after the amateur Southampton Redwings were shown the door at their Rank-owned rink. In November 1971 a phone call, then a quick dash to Bristol by Colin Bennett and Tony Highmore, resulted in ice time for practice. Courageous rink manager Barrie Wilson braved head office to permit the staging of matches in front of the public from the January. The first such attracted a crowd of around 600. Most came back for more.

'Wings achieved respectable positions in the league over the next four years, including a runners-up slot in the second winter. Experienced players living nearby, and sometimes not so near, joined, including Devon-based ex-Glasgow Dynamos Tom Taylor. Swedish-born Hans Kedelv and Canadian Walter Dirks, both aged twenty-four, signed for 1973/74. Veteran ex-pros Roy Shepherd and Mike O'Brien, both in their early forties, iced a few times the next winter. The biggest attendance, recorded before Redwings decamped back to Southampton, occurred in their final campaign when 700 turned up on 7 February to watch them take on Avon Arrows.

From autumn 1971 local skaters were encouraged to take up hockey. Several joined Redwings prior to the founding of the local Avon club in January 1974. The Wiltshire family provided massive support behind the scenes as Stan sr had watched the sport at the pre-war Coliseum. Arrows first entered the 'B' League for a season before taking Redwings' place at the higher level. The Under-23 Darts replaced Arrows.

John Lively had picked up the basics of hockey in Canada. Goalie Chris Lowden, Paul Farmer on defence and seventeen-year-old Steve Couzens had previously iced with the Redwings. Arrows won the 'B' League at their first attempt in 1975. During their eight years in existence Arrows hovered mid-table, slipping a little by the early 1980s. Canadian students in the city helped out. One of the most talented – Paul White, a twenty-three-year-old drama student, at left-wing, topped the inaugural Inter-City League in points with 33 (25+8) for 1978/79. He also gained an All-Star 'A' team placing. Canadian teenage defenceman Richard Tucker, a pupil at a nearby public school, amassed most goals and assists for Arrows during 1981/82 with 34 points.

Following the success of ice hockey at their refurbished Streatham rink, Mecca installed Britain's second set of plexi-glass at Bristol in 1981.

Two attempts at launching semi-pro hockey have not been successful, no doubt due to the limited seating, some with restricted views of the ice, and the generally basic off-ice facilities. At the beginning of 1982/83 Nick Harris, a Canadian-born member of the now-defunct Arrows, entered Blackhawks into the Heineken-sponsored British League – Division 1. The enterprise, backed by Ian Wright Sponsorship to the tune of £6,000, failed after three months. Casual management was probably a factor.

The rink closed on 31 August 1991. Purchased by John Nike Leisuresport (owners of Bracknell) it reopened in April 1992 with ex-Bee Jamie Crapper (Craiper) as manager.

By early autumn Bristol Bulldogs were ready. Good imports in Derek Higdon and Darren Mattias, with Lee Odelein as coach and hockey programme co-ordinator, were leavened with former Avon Arrows. These included Robbie Morris, the best of the locals, Paul Farmer, Justin Young and Tim Steadman. Winning 19 of their 32 games, to finish runners-up to longer-established Solihull, in Conference 'A' of the English League, was no mean accomplishment. With home game attendances running at 200–400 spectators and lacking major sponsorship, expenditure outstripped income. Bulldogs withdrew from further competition.

Youth hockey continued, with occasional gaps in continuity at some age levels. Beagles were particularly successful in millennium year, winning 15 of their 16 league games. However, lacking a 'senior' team, Bristol's over-19-year-olds need to travel further afield to continue their chosen sport.

CARDIFF

Opened:	18 November 1986	Address:
Closed:	12 June 2006	Wales National Ice
Ice Size:	180 x 79 feet (56 x 26 metres)	Rink
Total Spectator Capacity:	2,700 (increased from 2,334 in 1996)	Hayes Bridge Road Cardiff CF1 2GH
Seating Capacity:	2,400 (increased from 2,051 in 1996)	Wales

Ice Hockey – First Match:
30 November 1986: Cardiff Devils 32 v. Ashfield Islanders 0 (BL Division 2)

Teams:

Cardiff Devils
1986/87 British League Division 2 – Midlands; 1987–89 British League Division 1; 1989–96 British League Premier Division; 1996–2001 Superleague; 2001–03 British National League; 2003–05 Elite League

Cardiff Satans
1989–91 English League Division 2; 1991–94 English Under-21 League; 1994–2004 English Under-19 Conference/League

Cardiff Bears
1987/88 English League; 1989–91 English League Division 3; 1991–94 English Conference

Cardiff Capitals
1994–97 English League

Cardiff Rage
1998/99 English League Division 1

Cardiff Junior Devils
1988–2005 English Junior/Under-16 League

Cardiff Devils B/2
2003–05 English Under-16 League

Cardiff Pee-Wee Devils
1988–2000 English Pee-Wee/Under-14 League

Cardiff Devils
2000–05 English Under-14 League

Cardiff Devils 2
2004/05 English Under-14 League

Cardiff Mini-Devils
1988/89 English Under-12 League

Cardiff Little Devils
1989–2005 English Under-12 League

Cardiff Devils
2004–05 English Under-19 League

Cardiff Devils 2
2004–05 English Under-19 League

Cardiff Devils
2004–05 English National League – South

Honours:

Devils
1986/87 Winners British League Division 2 – Midlands; 1987–89 Winners Autumn Trophy; 1988/89 Winners British

	League Division 1 and Promotion Play-Offs; 1989/90 and 1992–94 Champions British League Premier Division and British Championship Play-Offs; 1992/93 Champions Benson & Hedges Autumn Cup; 1996/97 Champions Superleague; 1998/99 Champions British Play-offs
Satans	1992–94 Winners English Under-21 League – South; 1992/93 English Under-21 League Champions; 2001/02 and 2003/04 Winners English Under-19 'A' League – South
Capitals	1998/99 Winners English League Division 1 – South and play-off South
Junior Devils	1989/90 Winners English Junior 'B' League – South; 1992/93 Winners English Junior League – South-West; 1997/98 Winners English Under-16 'A' League – South & English Under-16 Champions; 1999/00 Winners English Under-16 'B' League – South
Devils	2001/02 Winners English Under-14 'B' League – South; 2002/03 Winners English Under-14 'B' League – West
Little Devils	2000/01 Winners English Under-12 'B' and 2002/03 'A' League – South

Publications:
The Official Cardiff Devils Year Book 1988-89, Beer, A., King, H. and Weltch, A.
It's Funny When you Win Everything, Beer, Anthony, 1994, Rover Publications
Images of Sport – Cardiff Devils, Weltch, Andy, 2001, Tempus Publishing

Arena construction cost £2.5 million. It was designed by Cardiff architects Alex Robertson, Peter Francis & Partners for the developers – Sports Nationwide Ltd. The Duchess of York performed the formal opening on 29 April 1987. Two years on the Brent Walker Group bought the building. The original heat reflective aluminium ceiling was removed during the general refurbishment of summer 1996, with plexi-glass surrounds replacing the nylon netting.

The sensational entry into British ice hockey and the rise and rise of Cardiff Devils is fairly well documented The appointment of Canadian player John Lawless (25) to form an ice hockey team proved an outstanding success. A season in the Second Division of the British League (BL) pulled in over 50,000 paying spectators and promotion to Division 1. By the end of 1988/89 Devils won the promotion play-offs to the Premier Division.

The ice after the 1996 refit with the addition of plexiglass surrounds and centre ice four-face timer. (Mike Smith/*IHNR*)

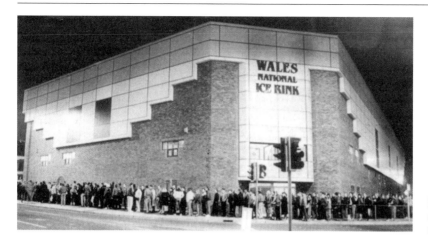

Fans queuing for entry during season 1986/87.

Nicky Chinn and Jason Stone, both local lads, made regular appearances, both scoring their first league goal as Devils became BL champions at the first attempt. All home matches were played to a full house.

The first appearance at the Wembley season-ending weekend saw the Heineken British Championship trophy in Cardiff hands. Having won the inaugural Benson & Hedges Cup and then the 1992/93 BL title Devils swept the play-offs and British Finals without a loss. The league title was retained in 1994 with Chinn scoring four times in the British Championship-winning final. Pool D of the World Senior Championships, won by Britain, took place at Cardiff in March 1990. Devils met foreign opposition in Denmark in the 1990/91 European Cup. Next year SKA Leningrad visited the city.

In 1994 a £250,000 sponsorship with BT commenced. Devils, with fourteen-year-old Cardiff-born goaltender Stevie Lyle, defeated two ex-Soviet Union clubs to qualify for the semi-finals of the European Cup. In April 1996 the rink and club were purchased by Celtic Leisure (Cymru) Ltd from the Brent Walker Group. Money was made available to engage netminder Frank Caprice and Ken Hodge, both ex-NHL. Devils lifted the first Superleague title following spring. Attendances increased by around 400 a game. During the subsequent season the rink was sold to Compco Holdings for £2 million with the club taking a three-year lease back. In October 1998 Devils hosted a Continental Cup Group in the rink now known as the BT Ice House. Cardiff defeated Nottingham 2–1 at Manchester for the British Play-off Championship.

In March of the next year David Temme – the club's chairman – resigned to be replaced by Bob Phillips, as Devils plummeted to seventh. Prior to 2000/01 commencing Celtic Leisure failed with significant losses. At season's end Phillips put the club into liquidation leaving Devils players unpaid, while still holding the building's lease. The rink, now owned by Cardiff Council, reverted to its original name. The lease ends in Spring 2006 with the site earmarked for retail development. Devils, nominally run by Teamplan Ltd, dropped down to the British National League for 2001/02 to finish last with a mainly Welsh-born squad as attendances averaged 500. Turmoil followed as the Swiss-based Chris McSorely sought to rescue the club, then handed over to Paul McMilan. Devils finished fifth and made the play-off finals; crowds crept up to the 900 level.

Cardiff, now back in Phillips' control, joined forces with the rookie Elite League for 2003/04 .With crowds back to a healthier 2,000 wounds healed. With Dave Whistle behind the bench Devils secured third place in spring 2005 proceeding to a 2–1 semi-final play-off defeat to Nottingham. Vezio Sacratini topped the points scorers in all competitions with 28+48 to gain an All-Star rating.

The structured youth development programme continues to turn out winning teams at all age levels with a stream of skilled youngsters. To cater for the over-nineteens Devils placed a squad in the ENL – South for autumn 2004 that made the play-offs.

CHELMSFORD

Opened:	31 March 1987	Address:
Ice Size:	184ft x 85ft (56m x 26m)	Chelmsford Riverside
Total Spectator Capacity:	1,200 (reduced from 1,500 by 1995)	Ice and Leisure Centre
Seating Capacity:	750	Victoria Road
Ice Hockey – First Match:		Chelmsford
5 September 1987: Chelmsford Chieftains 11 *v.* Peterborough		Essex CM18 6YQ
Titans 4 (challenge)		England

Teams:

Chelmsford Chieftains	1987/88 British League Division 2; 1988–92 English League – Division 1; 1992/93 English 'B' Conference; 1993–96 British League – Division 1; 1996–98 English League – Southern Conference; 1998–2001 & 2002–05 English National League – Premier Division; 2001–02 English National League – South
Chelmsford Renegades	1987–89 English League; 1991–94 English Under-21 League; 1994/95 English Under-19 League
Chelmsford Mohawks	1996–2005 English Under-19 League
Chelmsford Tomahawks	1988–91, 1992/93 and 1994–2005 English Junior/Under-16 League
Chelmsford Tomahawks B	2004–05 English Under-16 League
Chelmsford Mini Chieftains	1989–2005 English Under-12 Conference/League
Chelmsford Mini Chieftains B	2003–05 English Under-12 League
Chelmsford Braves	1990–93 & 1994–2005 English Under-14 Conference/League

Honours:

Chieftains	1992/93 Winners English League 'B' Conference Promotion Play-Offs; 1999/2000 Champions English National League Premier Division & Play-Offs
Mohawks	1989/99 & 2000/01 Winners English Under-19 'B' League – South
Tomahawks	1997/98 & 2001–03 Winners English Under-16 'B' League – South Mini Chieftains 1998/99 & 2001–03 Winners English Under-12 'B' League – South
Chelmsford Braves	2000/01 Winners English Under-14 'B' League – South

Virtually identical in design to Slough – as both venues were designed by the same architects, Building Design Partnership (BDP) – except the rink is located at first-floor level above a swimming pool, with external pedestrian approach via a curved ramp. Riverside is a local authority-owned complex, initially run by Sports Nationwide Co.

The various owners and sponsors of the senior team at Chelmsford have recognised the limitations of spectator capacity and catchment area. Chieftains have competed at a level that could be sustained financially. Mike Urquart, previously with Nottingham Panthers, was engaged as assistant rink manager and hockey co-ordinator. He assembled a team of mainly British boys, paying only travelling expenses and suppling equipment, plus himself and Dave Tweedy as the two permitted imports. A runners-up placing in Division 2 of the British League drew around 700. Foreign opposition was also met as a Swedish and a Swiss club visited Riverside.

In the following four years Chieftains competed in the 1st Division of the English League (EL). Rick Smith (24) joined from Oxford City in the autumn of 1989, to assist Chelmsford to the semi-finals of the Autumn Trophy (AT). The next winter a decisive home 13–7 victory over Richmond on 27 October clinched the AT. Urquart's wife Laura managed the team. By the following autumn the pair had left. Smith took over as player-coach to be joined by Karl Goebel (24) who hailed from Enderby BC.

The EL was relabelled 'Conference' with Chieftains in Group B. The team gained promotion to Division 1 of the Heineken-sponsored British League without losing a game in the play-offs. Chieftains found the going tough, never finishing better than eighth in the three years at the higher level. Goebel became player-coach for 1993/94 with Smith once again leading the club on total points at 71+54. Smith took a year out as Jim Fyarchuk took over as bench coach. In spite of signing Ukrainian Alexei Kuznetsov (27), the squad was inconsistent and ill disciplined. For the final BL campaign Chieftains gained new management and sponsorship. When Smith retired in New Year 1997 he had accumulated 1,106 points, which included 689 goals from 298 games. Rick's penalty minutes totalled 58.

In the summer of 1996 the English League was reorganised to suit low-budget clubs. Chieftains' new owner Roger 'Ollie' Oliver appointed Goebel to a second spell as coach, to achieve runners-up spot in the league and their play-off group. Near-neighbours Romford Raiders were defeated, then Billingham, to reach the final. Along with coaching and goalie changes the next winter the success was repeated in the Southern Conference.

Losing only one out of ten of the play-off group games, they were overcome in the final by Solihull Blaze of the English Premier League. Chelmsford joined this higher-level competition in 1998/99, for clubs unable to meet the cost of the British National League. Ending fourth, Chieftains tied with Solihull in Group A of the play-offs, losing out on goal difference. After eight seasons and over 400 games Karl Goebel retired.

The Premier provided a winning environment. Chieftains, in tying 1 and losing 4 of the 24-match schedule, won the league championship. Imports Duane Ward (23) and Andy Hannah (30) were second and third in the league points chart, both on 48. In front of a home crowd of 750, with a 5–2 lead from the first-leg of the play-off final they drew 2–2 with Swindon Chill. They had previously beaten the same team to win the Millennium Cup and £1,000 in prize money. Shaun McFadyen replaced Douglas Erskine as coach, signing Adam Collins (21) and Ryan Mair (25) next autumn. Enforced team changes contributed to the loss of the league title, by three points, to Swindon. The 'Tribe' did make it to the cup semi-final and the league play-off final.

Spending 2001/02 out of the Premier, Chelmsford regained their place next winter for a creditable fifth position in the twelve-team circuit as Erskine Douglas returned. Imports Kyle Amyotte (23) and Andrew Power (26) on 113 and 105 points respectively ended sixth and eighth in the league points scoring.

With crowds at around 500 and no more than three or four non-British players, the Premier Division of the ENL should provide Chieftains a comfortable home for the foreseeable future. Steve Lipinski took over club ownership for autumn 2004 as Roger Oliver transferred to rivals Romford. The Chelmsford youth development programme is paying off in the new millennium. It is providing many skilled recruits to Chieftains.

CLACTON

Opened: December 1981
Closed: c. 1984
Ice Size: 60ft x 40ft (18m x 12m)
Ice Hockey – First Match:
None known.

Address:
Clacton Pier
Clacton-on-Sea
Essex
England

Teams:
Essex Eagles 1982

An ice pad within an existing building located on the pier. Team reported to be formed in spring 1982 but there are no records of any games, at home or away.

COATBRIDGE

Opened: 10 August 1991
Ice Size: 155ft x 52ft (50m x 16m) with
 irregular shaped corners
Total Spectator Capacity: Approximately 250
Seating Capacity: Minimal (bench seating)

Address:
Time Capsule
100 Buchanan Street
Coatbridge
Lanarkshire ML5 1DL
Scotland

Ice Hockey – First Match:
No home games possible – rink unsuitable

Teams:
Coatbridge 1997/98 Scottish Under-17 League – 'A' Conference
Coatbridge Sabres★ 1997/98 Scottish Under-13 League – 'A' Conference
★ Some sources state Rapiers

Part of a local authority-owned sports centre that includes a swimming pool, adventure playground and health suite. The leisure rink, themed to represent the Ice Age with models of woolly mammoths etc., is not suited to the playing of ice hockey. For season 1997/98 all ice hockey matches wer played away.

A new club was formed in season 2002/03 but restricted to two practice sessions each per week for Juniors and over-sixteens.

COLERAINE

Opened: August 1990
Closed: February 2000
Ice Size: 134ft x 81ft (41m x 25m)
Total Spectator Capacity: Approximately 500
Seating Capacity: Approximately 400 (benches on
 one side only)
Ice Hockey – First Match:
Unknown

Address:
Coleraine Jet Centre
Leisure Complex
Riverside Park
Coleraine
Co. Londonderry
Northern Ireland

Teams:
Coleraine Jets *c.* 1990–93 (Carlsberg recreational 'League') and 1996–2000.

Closed *c.* 1993, to reopen during summer 1996. As at summer 2002 the rink stood empty and disused. It formed part of a large leisure complex consisting of a bowling alley and cinema that remain open.

In the early 1990s Jets met an All-Ireland Select team at Coleraine in a match that was filmed by BBC Northern Ireland.

COVENTRY

Opened:	15 April 2000	Address:
Ice Size:	184ft x 92ft (56m x 28m)	Planet Ice at Skydome
Total Spectator Capacity:	2,616 (originally set at 3,000)	Arena
Seating Capacity:	2,200 (4 VIP boxes)	Skydome Arena
Ice Hockey – First Match:		Croft Road

27 August 2000: Coventry Blaze 4 *v.* Milton Keynes Kings
1 (challenge)

Coventry CV1 3AZ
West Midlands
England

Teams:

Coventry Blaze	2000–03 British National League; 2003–05 Elite League
Coventry Blaze	2002–05 English Under-16 League
Mercian Menace	2003–05 English Under-16 League
Coventry Blaze	2002–05 English Under-14 League
Mercian Menace	2004/05 English Under-14 League
Coventry Blaze	2002–05 English Under-12 League
Mercian Menace	2004/05 English Under-12 League
Coventry Blaze	2003–05 English Under-19 League
Mercian Menace	2004/05 English Under-19 League

Honours:

Blaze	2002/03 Champions British National League and Play-offs; 2004/05 Champions Elite League, Play-offs and Winners Challenge Cup
Blaze	2004/05 Winners English Under-16 League – North 2

The game record sheet of the inaugural match on 27 August 2000.

Developed by Rank Entertainment, at a cost of £6 million, to sit alongside their adjacent cinema and nightclub complex. Tiers of seating on three sides, commencing from about the height of the plexi-glass, provide a clear view for the spectator. Ice hockey was not in Rank's plans; they stated it would 'take four or five days to cover and uncover the ice'. Fortunately for the sport Planet Ice gained the contract to operate the Skydome.

Blaze, who had joined the British National League (BNL) the year before, and were previously based at Solihull, moved the fifteen or so miles east, as did many of their followers. A crowd of 1,177 watched the opening game at the Skydome. By spring 2001 attendances hit around 2,000. Coached by Paul Thompson, a Brit, the Blaze roster contained four imports – Anthony (AJ) Kelham, Mats Samuelsson, Mathias

The entrance.

The ice before the
opening match on
27 August 2000.

Soderstrom and Henrik Sjodin, a goalie. Veteran all-star GB defenceman Stephen Cooper joined mid-season. Fourth from twelve in the league and semi-finalist in the Christmas Cup created strong foundations in a city new to ice hockey. Steve Carpenter (30) and Steve Roberts arrived to some effect for the next campaign. The team were BNL runners-up and finalists in the play-offs and Challenge Cup. Brit Shaun Johnson ended third-highest scorer with 84 points. Cooper announced his retirement at season's end. His number 55 sweater was retired to hang above centre ice. With the additional signings of goalie Jody Lehman and Andreas Moborg on defence, Blaze entered the Superleague's season-opening Challenge Cup. They collected two creditable ties on home ice from their six games.

A long winning streak took Coventry to the league championship, followed by clinching the play-offs over Cardiff Devils. They met Devils on a regular basis in 2003/04 as Coventry left the BNL to join seven other clubs in the new Elite League with its higher wage cap. By spring 2005 this well organised and ambitious club completed the EL 'Grand Slam' by winning all three trophies. Britisher Paul Thompson collected 'Coach of the Year', with four of the six first All-Star Team slots going to Blaze. Their captain Ashley Tait was inspirational, scoring the overtime winner to clinch the British Championship final.

A youth development programme had been initiated early on. Two years later, in an action to be applauded, teams were courageously entered into the English Youth Leagues at Under-12, Under-14 and Under–16 levels. For 2003/04 the Under-19s entered league competition with an additional Under-16 team, Mercian Menace, joining the Junior Blaze. Next autumn three further Mercian youth teams were added.

CUMBERNAULD

Opened:	September 1990	Address:
Closed:	c. 1996	The Ice House
Ice Size:	184ft x 85ft (56m x 26m)	St Mango's Road
Total Spectator Capacity:	approximately 1,500	Cumbernauld
Seating Capacity:	Nil	North Lanarkshire
Ice Hockey – First Match★:		G67 1RQ Scotland

4 October 1992: Tayside Tigers 13 v. Irvine Jetstream Flyers 4 (Scottish League Division 1)
★ Other than recreational

Teams:
Tayside Tigers — 1992/93 Scottish League Division 1
Cumbernauld Kings — 1991–95 (recreational only)

Construction commenced in 1988 by Pimley Estates (who were also developers for rinks in Bangor, Northern Ireland and Glenrothes), but was then suspended for two years. Opened without any permanent seating although at the time the operator said it was intended to install some when demand became apparent.

Tayside, a Dundee-based club whose rink had been demolished the previous summer, also used the Livingston rink during 1992/93 to stage fixtures.

DEESIDE – ORIGINAL

Opened:	29 December 1973	Address:
Closed:	Early August 1998	Deeside Leisure Centre
Ice Size:	185ft x 85ft (56m x 26m)	Chester Road West
Total Spectator Capacity:	2,000 (reduced to 1,500 by 1996)	Queensferry
Seating Capacity:	1,700 (1,000 permanent plus 700 temporary – reduced to 800 by 1996)	Deeside Flintshire Wales

Ice Hockey – First Match:
26 March 1974: London Lions 11 v. Altrincham Aces Select 3

Teams:
Deeside Dragons — 1974/75 Southern 'B' League; 1975/76 Southern 'A' League – South; 1976–78 Southern 'A' League – Midlands; 1978–81 Midland League; 1981/82 English League North; 1982/83 British League Division 2 – North; 1983–85 British League Division 1; 1985–87 British League Division 2 – Midlands; 1987–89 British League Division 1 – North; 1994–96 English League – North

Deeside Dragons 92 — 1991/92 English Conference – National; 1992/93 English Conference – Wharry; 1993/94 English Conference

Deeside Flames — 1974/75 challenge games; 1975/76 Southern 'B' League

Deeside Flames — 1976/77 Southern Junior League; 1990–98 English Junior/Under-16 League

Deeside Cubs — 1984/85 English Junior League

Deeside Warriors — 1979/80 Midland League Division 2

Clwyd Flames	1983/84 British League Division 3 (expelled for use of ineligible players); British League Division 2
Deeside Demons	1987–90 British League Division 2; 1994/95 and 1997/98 English Under-19 Conference
Deeside Dynamos	1990/91 English League Division 2 'B'
Deeside Sparks	1990–95 and 1996–98 English Under-12 League/Conference
Deeside Dragons	1991/92 English Under-21 League
Deeside Steelers	1993–98 English Under-14 Conference/League

Honours:

| **Deeside Dragons 92** | 1993/94 Champions English Conference |
| Deeside Flames | 1996/97 Winners English Under-16 'B' League – North |

The first local authority-owned and operated ice rink in the UK. Due to deterioration of the refrigeration plant and the breaking up of the ice pad a new rink was constructed virtually next door. This opened in 1998 without interruption to the schedules of the numerous youth teams playing out of Deeside – see next entry. The original building was retained and converted into a multi-purpose sports hall and inline roller hockey centre.

Queensferry is too small to support seriously any form of senior team not composed of mainly amateurs. More than one attempt at semi-pro hockey has failed. Also at times the rink management has been ambivalent towards the sport.

The opening exhibition match, involving the Detroit-owned professional London Lions from Wembley and the amateur Altrincham Aces inspired the formation of Deeside ice hockey club. Six months later a group of enthusiastic youngsters with the active backing of the rink management entered league competition. Coached by Scotsman Bill Wilson Dragons drew a session-high audience of 405 in the match with Liverpool.

During the 1970s and early 1980s Steve Parry, Chris Dean and Bryan Tudor were the best of the locally based lads forming the core of the Dragons. In spring 1978 they achieved second place in the 'A' section of the Midlands League. A season-ending highlight was the annual Horace Roberts Memorial Junior Tournament, one of the first such to be held in Britain. At the end of the 1970s pop concerts were disrupting hockey, proving more profitable than ice-based activities. By now Dean Walch and Graham J. Jones were regular first-team players.

In autumn 1983 Dragons joined Division 1 of the Heineken-sponsored British League, where rivals regularly iced two and sometimes three paid Canadians. Deeside had one – Dan Walker. He ended as Dragons' leading scorer with 25+9, and also donned the pads to spend 100 minutes guarding the nets. His team finished eleventh and last, winning one match. Even then the points were forfeit for use of unregistered players. Walker left soon after the next campaign opened. Dragons enjoyed two wins and a draw to end in the cellar again.

The return to Division 2 for 1985/86 produced six victories, for ninth place. The following year only the rookie Cardiff side kept Dragons from gold. Deeside's only loss came

As a tennis court in the mid-1970s.

in the Welsh capital. Back at Queensferry they held Devils at 3–3. The ex-Southampton imports Don Wright and Mitch Prpitch finished fifth and six in league scoring on 80 and 78 points respectively, followed by Steve Parry and Barry Evans. A third import – Doug Rigby-kept goal.

Next winter Deeside were back in Division 1 of the British League. With the return of all three imports the going was tougher. Dragons won 10 of their 28 fixtures, for sixth place in the eight-team northern section. The club almost folded before their final season at the higher level began. Promoter Kerry Wycherly stepped in to secure the services of the vastly experienced Fred Perlini as player-coach, to be joined by a second import Mike Oliverio. Lack of depth, combined with netminder John Wolfe breaking a leg, led to a string of defeats and the team finishing eighth out of thirteen. Perlini ended the third-best scorer in the division with 103 goals and 69 assists.

Senior hockey came back to Queensferry with a new three-year set-up dubbed 'Dragons 92' in the non-import English Conference. Improving from fifth to third, the final year ended in triumph. Dragons did not lose a game on the way to the 1992/93 Conference championship. Jason Titmus led the attack with 62 points (38+24) for third best. Alan Steele, Steve Parry, Pete Founds, Lawrence Paul and Gary Shaw all made the top eleven Conference points table. Dropping the '92' tag Dragons struggled for a further two years before calling it a day, ending just one place out of the basement, and firmly in it by spring of 1996.

The youth programme continued. Twelve months on Flames won 15 of their 16 games to top the Northern group of the Under-16 League.

DEESIDE – REPLACEMENT

Opened:	19 September 1998	Address:
Ice Size:	197ft x 98ft (60m x 30m)	Jackson Ice Rink
Total Spectator Capacity:	1,200	Deeside Leisure Centre
Seating Capacity:	1,000	Chester Road West
Ice Hockey – First Match:		Queensferry
26 September 1998: Flintshire Freeze 3 v. Great Britain		Flintshire CH5 1SA
Under-18 13		Wales

Teams:

Flintshire Freeze	1998–2000 English League Division 1 – North; 2000–02 English National League – South; 2002–05 English National League – North
Deeside Demons	1998/99 English Under-19 League
Flintshire Avalanche	1999–2005 English Under-19 League
Deeside Flames	1998/99 English Under-16 League
Flintshire Flames	1999–2005 English Under-16 League
Deeside Steelers	1998/99 English Under-14 League
Flintshire Hurricanes	1999–2005 English Under-14 League
Deeside Sparks	1998/99 English Under-12 League
Flintshire Flyers	1999–2005 English Under-12 League

Honours:

Freeze	2003/04 Winners English National League – North
Hurricanes	2004/05 Winners English Under-14 League – North 2

Constructed with the aid of £2 million of matching funding by Flintshire County Council and SPORTLOT (Lottery Sports Fund for Wales). The replacement rink has a larger ice surface and smaller spectator capacity than its predecessor. The Secretary of State for Wales officially opened it on 6 October 1998.

The local authority appointed Mark Stokes (32), originally from Canada, to the dual roles of ice hockey co-ordinator and player-coach. This involved overseeing the existing youth teams and forming the new senior Flintshire Freeze, as well as obtaining funding in the form of sponsorship. In Flintshire's first home game, held on 11 October 1998, Freeze defeated Blackburn Phoenix 18–1 in an English League Division 1 – North contest. The average attendance was around 400 by the New Year. The side proceeded to win twelve more contests in their eighteen-game schedule for a fourth placed finish in the ten-team group. Davey Clancy topped the goalminders' averages. He progressed to become a full-time professional with Manchester during 2003/04.

Next winter Freeze slipped two places in the standings. For 2000/01 Flintshire moved to the South, to even up the numbers in both regions. Freeze overcame all opposition, other than Basingstoke, to finish runners-up. Clancy came second among goalies, while Stokes led all scorers with 55 points. They won their group in the English Cup. Twelve months on Freeze narrowed the gap on Basingstoke to one point. Stokes proved to be the best sniper again, raising his points take to 64. Third-placed Peter Founds totalled 22+34. In the play-off semi-finals Freeze finished second best to the ultimate winner, Whitley Warriors. Autumn 2003 found Flintshire back in the stronger ENL – North, seventh from 6 wins and 12 losses. Their sixth campaign marked a major improvement. Freeze competed on equal terms to win the Northern section and progressed to the play-offs. Manchester staged a handful of their 'home' games at Deeside when the Manchester Arena was unavailable during 2003/04.

DUMFRIES

Opened:	August 1992	Address:
Ice Size:	184ft x 95ft (56m x 29m)	The Ice Bowl
Total Spectator Capacity:	1,200 (originally 1,000)	King Street
Seating Capacity:	600 (originally 200)	Dumfries DG2 9AN
Ice Hockey – First Match:		Dumfries & Galloway
7 September 1992: Ayr Bruins 13 *v.* Kirkcaldy Falcons 4		Scotland
(Under-19)		

Teams:

Dumfries Vikings	1992/93 challenge games; 1993–95 British League Division 1
Dumfries Border Vikings	1995/96 British League Division 1; 1996/97 Northern Premier and Scottish League
Solway Sharks	1998/99 Scottish and Border Leagues; 1999–2005 Scottish National League
Dumfries Kings	1994–96 Scottish Under-16/17 League
Dumfries Raiders	1999–2005 Scottish Under-16 League
Dumfries Raiders	1994–2000 Scottish Under-14/15 League/Conference
Dumfries Warriors	2000–05 Scottish Under-14 League
Dumfries Ice Warriors	1994–2000 Scottish Under-12/13 League/Conference
Dumfries Invaders	2000–02 and 2003–05 Scottish Under-12 League
Dumfries Sharks	1995–98 Scottish Under-19/20 League
Dumfries	1999–2000 Scottish Under-18 League
Dumfries Kings	2000–05 Scottish Under-18/19 League

Honours:

Sharks	1998–2000 Champions Scottish National League

Warriors	1994/95 Winners Scottish Under-12 League and 1996/67 Scottish Under-12 Conference 'B'
Raiders	2000/01 Winners Scottish Under-16 'B' League

The rink forms the second phase of an 'L'-shaped sports complex, which includes an indoor bowling hall, designed and constructed by Condor Engineering at a cost of £4 million. Seating within the rink is located along one side. Additional seats were installed some time after opening.

Like many similar rinks in a small town, the formation of any form of professional or semi-pro team is a gamble. Sensibly for their opening season in hockey the local authority-managed team met sides of recreational players or those from the all-amateur Scottish League.

In their first match on 10 October 1992 Dumfries defeated Glenrothes Cougars 11–6. Most visiting clubs were easily beaten and this, plus the novelty value, soon attracted capacity crowds. Early on emphasis was placed on youth development. Fourteen months after opening there were around 100 registered youngsters with four organised teams at various age levels – Invaders, Raiders, Warriors and Pee-Wee.

Next winter much tougher opposition was met in the inaugural assault on the First Division of the British League. Vikings, in the northern group, lost more than they won, which reduced the spectator level to a hard core of around 500.

Early signings Greg Ware, twenty-year-old John Haig, Vasily Vasilenko – a Ukrainian – and Dino Bauba struggled as early changes failed to settle the squad, which finished seventh.

With Division 1 teams now back into one countrywide group for 1994/95 there were no easy games. New coach Rab Petrie was not helped by the use of an ineligible player, resulting in the deduction of two points. Vikings slipped to eleventh. At season's end the club released the coach and players.

A new board of directors inserted 'Border' within the team title to attract a wider audience. They recruited Jim Lynch to coach, along with his assistant, the late Milan Figala, to great effect. The Autumn Trophy was won and Craig Lyons joined. Post-Christmas injuries took their toll, but even so Vikings secured fifth spot and a place in the play-offs. The high point was a 6–5 defeat of Manchester Storm in front of the best home crowd of the season.

With the advent of the fully professional Superleague for 1996/97 came the semi-pro Northern Premier League. Faced with crippling debts from the previous winter, reduced travel costs and the efforts of team owner Stevie Marshall plus a hard working band of volunteers ensured that the fixtures were completed. New Canadian coach Rob Barnes and his two Swedish imports, plus goalie Moray Hanson, left before Christmas. Youngsters from the

The entrance – the rink is to the right.

recently defunct Durham Wasps became the unsung heroes on King Street, especially Michael Tasker. He led Vikings in scoring, finishing on 39+34 and adding 15 points in the play-offs.

Senior hockey and the crowds returned to Dumfries in 1998 with the birth of Solway Sharks, in the near all-amateur Scottish League. Player-coach Martin Grubb led the way with 116 points, third overall in the league, as Sharks swallowed their rivals, winning the SL championships with a 12-point margin over Glasgow. Solway were also runners-up in the five-member Anglo-Scottish Border League. A younger version of the Sharks won the Scottish Under-21 Cup.

Dumfries repeated the success next term to head the ten-team league, with a clear margin over Ayr Centrum Bruins. Although those triumphs have not been repeated, the Scottish League provides an affordable home. With a mainly locally produced roster, which includes some near veterans such as John Churchill, Roberts Chalmers and Gary Curruth, Sharks usually finish around mid-table. In spring 2005 they ended three points away from the title and were runners-up in the Spring Cup.

With Scottish League attendances hovering around the 300 mark, and five teams competing from Under-10 to Under-18-year-olds, ice hockey has a secure hold in Dumfries.

DUNDEE – DUNDEE-ANGUS

Opened:	1 October 1938 (for skating)	Address:
Closed:	April 1989	Dundee Angus Ice Rink
Ice Size:	195ft x 97ft (59m x 30m)	Kingsway West
Total Spectator Capacity:	3,665	Dundee
Seating Capacity:	3,045	Tayside
Ice Hockey – First Match:		Scotland

30 September 1938: Dundee Tigers 5 *v.* Fife Flyers 2 (challenge)

Teams:

Dundee Tigers	1938–40 Scottish National League; 1946–54 Scottish National League; 1954/55 British National League; 1987/88 British League Premier Division
Tayside Tigers	1977–79 Northern Reserve League (all games away); 1988/89 British League Premier Division
Dundee Rockets	1947–50 Scottish 'Junior' League(s)
Dundee Rockets	1968/69 and 1980/81 Northern Reserve League; 1969/70 & 1971–77 Northern League; 1981/82 Northern and Scottish Leagues; 1982/83 British League Division – Section 'A'; 1983–88 British League Premier Division
Dundee Tiger Cubs	1946/47 Scottish 'Midget' League; 1988/89 Scottish Pee-Wee League
Dundee Meteors	1971–75 Northern Second League
Dundee Earl Greys	1987/88 Scottish Junior League
Dundee Bengals	1988/89 Scottish Junior League
Dundee Unicorns	1988/89 Scottish League Division 1
Dundee Discoveries	1987–89 Scottish Under-13/12 League

Honours:

Tigers	1938/39 & 1947/48 Champions Scottish National League and Canada Cup; 1949/50 Champions Scottish Autumn Cup
Rockets	1972/73 Champions Northern League; 1973/74 Champions

	Spring Cup Play-offs; 1968/69 Champions Northern Second League; 1980/81 Champions Northern Reserve League – Scottish Section and Play-offs; 1981/82 Champions Northern & Scottish Leagues, British Play-offs, 'Icy' Smith & Spring Cup; 1982/83 Winners British League Division 1 – Section A and Champions British Play-offs; 1983/84 Champions British League Premier Division, Play-offs and Autumn Cup; 1985/86 Champions Scottish Cup
Bengals	1988/89 Champions Scottish Junior League and British Junior finalists
Discoveries	1988/89 Champions Scottish Under-12 League

Designed by architect William Wilson in a careful 'art deco' style. Internally very similar to several rinks built in Scotland immediately pre-Second World War, with banked seating along both sides.

Tigers, an all-Canadian team, entered the virtually professional Scottish National League. That first season of 1938/39 brought instant success as Dundee won the League Tournament for the Canada Cup, with a five-point margin over Perth. In the 20-game Scottish Points Tournament Tigers came second. Leading the attack were Merrick Cranstoun from Merrickville, Ontario and Winnipeg-born Al Rogers. Defender George McNeil became an outstanding coach in post-war Scottish hockey, being elected to the British Hall of Fame in 1956. All three remained for the next winter. During the war years a few games took place at Kingsway West, mainly involving Canadian armed forces teams.

McNeil returned in 1946, this time behind the bench. The following year he steered Tigers into the play-offs by topping the Eastern Section of the SNL. Tigers then beat Ayr and Dunfermline for the league championship to lift the Anderson Trophy. The Canada Cup joined the two other trophies. In 1949/50 a one-point margin over Fife brought the Autumn Cup to Kingsway. In 1951/52 Dundee finished as runners-up to Ayr Raiders and occupied the same position the year after in the Scottish Cup.

Bobby Burns served from 1946 to 1950, accumulating 105 goals and 159 assists. Johnny Rozzini, born in Montreal in 1925, also joined Tigers in 1946, spending six years on Tayside. During nearly 350 games he contributed 284 points, including 130 goals. In the summer of 1954 the Scottish and English leagues combined. For Dundee and six other Scottish clubs the experiment failed. Tigers won 20 of their 62 scheduled matches, but crowds remained static. By spring 1955 professional hockey died in Dundee. Dundee-born Marsh Key started playing hockey at Kingway West as a schoolboy. As an eighteen-year-old

Dundee Tigers v. Glasgow Mohawks on 19 October 1938. The Tigers won 8-2. (Perth Star)

The interior in 1938.
(*Skating Times*)

he played five times for Tigers during 1947/48. By the following winter he had progressed to appear in 60 matches, scored 18 goals and continued in every campaign until spring 1955, for a total of 316 points.

In summer 1968 a group of local enthusiasts pressed the new manager at the Dundee-Angus rink for a return of the sport. Approval was granted for Rockets to hire the rink and stage Sunday evening, Northern Second League fixtures. The first against Murrayfield Raiders on 18 January 1969 was a day of foul weather but 2,200 spectators turned up. By the third game the full-house signs were out with over 1,200 turned away. Rockets won the league title on goal difference over Paisley Wildcats. Among these pioneers were coach Ally Turnbull, top scorer George Reid, Bill Murray and Tam Stewart. Next season Rockets joined the expanded Northern League. Key took over as coach, with veteran Canadian Mike Mazur and experienced Scots Pete Reilly and Sammy McDonald signing, to clinch fifth place among the faster opposition.

Following completion of the Autumn Cup schedule personality clashes forced Rockets to drop out of hockey. Back a year later with new coach Ian Forbes' masterly tactics and seventeen-year-old Mike Ward in the nets Rockets ended NL runners-up, assisted by the sharp shooting of Jim Spence. Twelve months later the Northern League crown was theirs, followed by a runners-up medal in 1974, plus the Spring Cup.

Closed in summer 1975 for installation of a new ice pad, the boards surrounding the ice were removed with ice hockey no longer permitted. Tam Stewart and friends regained home ice for the start of 1981/82. British ice hockey, amateur for some years past, was revolutionised by the signing of three paid Canadians – Chris Brinster, Kevin O'Neil and Roy Halpin. Rockets won all the trophies, including the newly instigated British Championships held in London. They became champions, in 1984, of the inaugural Premier Division of the Heineken-sponsored British League (BL). The three paid import quota was firmly established as Halpin and Mike Walker occupied first and third placings for BL points scorers. Attendances were 2,000 for most games.

Hockey at the Premier level became increasingly costly. Seventh place the following season spurred team boss Tam Stewart to sign, in the autumn of 1985, Gary Unger, a previous NHL 'iron-man' with 914 consecutive appearances. Dundee finished as finalists in the British Championship, with the Scottish Cup as consolation. Crowd levels built from a low 800 of the previous year to 1,400.

Imports Craig Homala, Glen Sharpley and Czech international Jaroslav Lycka gave impressive performances as they took the team to a league silver medal and were finalists in the British Championships. Stewart resigned as the club piled up reported debts of £89,000 and Lycka claimed he was owed money. The following winter the rink took over the running of hockey, reverting to the Tigers tag. An eighth place and retention in the Premier

Division of the BL was quite an achievement. Crowd levels slipped back to around 700. Rebadged as Tayside, Tigers reached the Autumn Cup final with six straight victories.

Successful efforts by new coach Lawrie Lovell to escape relegation in the spring of 1989 proved bittersweet. The rink closed as the youth development programme blossomed, with the Under-12s and Juniors winning their leagues the same year.

The building was sold in August 1989 to Surrey-based businessman Richard Williams, to end up with supermarket chain William Low. The rink did not reopen and was demolished in June 1990.

DUNDEE – 'BACK-RINK'

Opened:	December 1984 (for ice hockey October 1989)	Address: Curling Rink
Closed:	17 May 1992	Kingsway West
Ice Size:	147ft x 85ft (45m x 26m), extended to 180ft (55m) by January 1991	Dundee Tayside Scotland
Total Spectator Capacity:	250, increased to 600 by January 1991	
Seating Capacity:	Minimal	

Ice Hockey – First Match:
29 October 1989: Dundee Bengal Tigers 4 *v.* Glasgow Tigers 3 (Under-16) & Tayside Tigers 11 *v.* Livingston Rams 1 (Scottish League – Division 1)

Teams:
Tayside Tigers	1989–92 Scottish League – Division 1
Dundee Tiger Cubs	1989–92 Scottish Under-14 League
Dundee Discoveries	1989/90 & 1991/92 Scottish Under-12 League
Dundee Bengal Tigers	1990–92 Scottish Under-16 League
Dundee Cougars	1991/92 Scottish Under-18 League

Honours:
Tigers	1989–91 Champions Scottish League – Division 1

The existing curling rink, backing onto the older Dundee-Angus rink, was used in October 1989 to stage a hockey match in front of the public. An entertainment licence had not been granted so entry then became all-ticket with capacity restricted to 250.

The building was closed for ten months and extended, with private finance by the lease-holder Malcolm Reid, to the minimal standard for staging ice hockey at the non-professional level. The first such match took place on 6 January 1991 as Tayside defeated Murrayfield 13–3. Two imports were engaged for 1990/91 – American Paul Mollard, then Canadians John Nobb and Dave Wilson. A third import was permitted the next winter. Tigers' trio were returnee American Chris Brinster as player-coach, Czech Robert Koutny and Canadian Dan Threfall, later replaced by Bobby Brown. The Scottish Association deducted 4 points for infringement on player registration, Tigers therefore lost a third con-secutive SL title to Livingston, and were ruled out of the play-offs for promotion back to the British League.

The free-holder demolished the rink in June 1992, in accordance with original terms of sale for the site. A Tesco supermarket, Burger King, filling station and car parking now occupy the site of both rinks.

DUNDEE – CAMPERDOWN

Opened:	22 September 2000	Address:
Ice Size:	197ft x 98ft (60m x 30m)	Dundee Ice Arena
Total Spectator Capacity:	2,400	Camperdown Leisure
Seating Capacity:	2,300	Park
Ice Hockey – First Match:		Kingsway West
1 October 2000: Dundee Tigers 3 *v.* Kirkcaldy Kestrals 3		Dundee City
(Scottish League)		DD3 2SQ
		Scotland

Teams:

Dundee Tigers	2000/01 Scottish National League
Dundee Tigers	2001–05 Scottish National League
Perth Panthers	2000–02 Scottish National League
Camperdown Stars	2002–04 Scottish National League
Dundee Stars	2004/05 Scottish National League
Dundee Stars	2001–05 British National League
Dundee Bengals	2000–02 Scottish Under-18 League
Dundee Tigers	2004/05 Scottish Under-19 League
Camperdown Cobras	2002–04 Scottish Under-18/19 League
Dundee Stars	2004/05 Scottish Under-19 League
Dundee Bengals	2000/01 Scottish Under-16 League – Division 1
Dundee Tigers	2001–05 Scottish Under-16 League
Camperdown Destroyers	2002–04 Scottish Under-16 League
Dundee Stars	2004/05 Scottish Under-16 League
Dundee Tigers	2000–05 Scottish Under-14 League
Camperdown Demolition	2002–04 Scottish Under-14 League
Dundee Stars	2004/05 Scottish Under-14 League
Dundee Tiger Cubs	2000–04 Scottish Under-12 League
Dundee Tigers	2004/05 Scottish Under-12 League
Camperdown Coyotes	2002–04 Scottish Under-12 League
Dundee Stars	2004/05 Scottish Under-12 League

Honours:

Tigers	2000/01 Champions Scottish League
Stars	2001/02 Champions British National League; 2001/02 & 2004/05 Champions Play-offs
Camperdown Stars	2003/04 Champions Scottish National League & Winners Autumn & Scottish Cups
Dundee Stars	2004/05 Champions Scottish National League

Constructed on the site of a previous NCR factory, not far from the location of Dundee's original rink. Sportscotland Lottery fund contributed £2 million to the total cost of £6.7 million. The building is owned and operated by Dundee City Council.

In the first winter the local Tigers and Perth Panthers were devoid of imports in the amateur Scottish National League. Panthers' own rink was only suitable for youth teams. Dundee drew a crowd of around 1,000 for the opening match, with 1,500 turning up for their second game. Among Tigers' regulars back at Kingsway West, Craig Phillips, John Dolan, Craig Smith and Niall Stott, who also played field hockey for Scotland, stood out. Paul Guicher, son of coach Joe, also featured. Tigers beat Ayr 5–2 to clinch the SNL crown by a six-point margin from Edinburgh. By mid-season crowds averaged 1,500. Panthers were less successful – they finished seventh on 10 points. Fourteen-year-old Charlie Ward kept goal on occasions for Perth. Alain Baxter and brother Noel turned out when skiing commitments allowed. To provide variety Fife Flyers, from the British National League (BNL), visited twice in March. Whitley Warriors also travelled north for an Anglo-Scottish Cup fixture. Tigers and Panthers entertained the Scottish Under-19 squad.

The Ward brothers, Charlie, Mike (formally a goaltender with Dundee Rockets and Tigers) and Steve, directors of the family-owned construction company, formed Dundee Stars in the spring of 2001. Both Stars and Tigers applied to join the semi-pro BNL. Only Stars were accepted. The Wards engaged Edinburgh-born Tony Hand (34) as player-coach. He signed an expensive sparkling roster, including defenceman Jan Mikel (26) a former Czech international and Teeder Wynne, previously with Sheffield Steelers. Seven others who had learned their hockey abroad were also on the books. Nearly 2,000 spectators watched Stars for the first time at Dundee on 26 August, as they drew 5–5 with Superleague Ayr Scottish Eagles. Winning 40 of their 44 games Stars took the BNL title at a canter. They proceeded to lift the inaugural John Brady Bowl as play-off Champions. Only the Challenge Cup escaped, with Dundee as finalists. Attendance averaged a fraction above 1,600. The club's top scorer Hand, with 39+106 from all competitions, led the league with 104 points.

Tigers, now drawing around 300 fans, lost their SNL title, by 3 points to Edinburgh. The capital also beat Dundee to the Spring and Scottish Cups. Perth struggled, collecting a mere 6 points for a second successive penultimate place. By autumn 2002 Perth Panthers had metamorphosed into Camperdown Stars. The change spurred the players to SNL runners-up, while Tigers dropped to seventh.

Ken Priestly (35), with two Stanley Cup rings to his credit, came out of retirement to join Stars. With seven other imports, Dundee finished top of their group in the qualifying round of the Findus Cup. A few weeks later they could not get beyond the semi-final at Newcastle. Five home losses relegated Stars to second. Even so Hand, Wynne and Priestly occupied the top three slots in the scoring race. The sudden departure of coach Hand, not long before the play-offs, unsettled the team. A controversial semi-final at the Ice Arena on 23 March 2003 knocked Stars out of contention. Spectator support fell by 8.6 per cent.

For winter 2003/04 Roger Hunt, promoted to head coach, made eleven new signings. Priestly and Murphy had left, to be replaced by Dave Trofimenkoff. Dino Bauba, Johan Johansson and Magnus Sjostrom from Sweden were among the newcomers. Two home wins from six forced Dundee to sixth in the Findus Cup. A disappointing BNL mid-table position dulled the sparkle on Kingsway West. The 'other' Stars shone brightly as Camperdown topped the SNL table, while the longer-established Tigers slid towards the cellar. Stars retained the SNL crown the next winter.

Fifth-place finishes for 2004/05, in the BNL and play-off standings gave way to a surprise three-game sweep of Guildford in the play-off finals. Not one Stars player made either the First or Second All-Star sextet although Calgary born right-winger Corey Morgan (26) headed the PO scorers with 10+9. Scott Barnes and Patrick Lochi were third and fourth on 18 points apiece.

DUNDONALD

Opened:	22 September 1986	Address:
Ice Size:	197ft x 98ft (60m x 30m)	Dundonald
Total Spectator Capacity:	1,500	International Ice Bowl
Seating Capacity:	1,500	111 Old Dundonald Rd
Ice Hockey – First Match:		Dundonald
22 September 1986: Castlereigh Cougars★ 14 v. Lee Valley		Castlereigh BT6 0XT
Lions 2 (challenge).		Co. Down
★Streatham Redskins represented 'Castlereigh Cougars'.		Northern Ireland

Teams:

Dundonald Redwings	1988/89 Scottish League Division 1
Dundonald Kings	1989/90 Scottish League Division 1
Castlereigh Flames	1989–93 Scottish League Division 1
Castlereigh Knights	1995/96 Scottish League Division 1; 1996/97 Northern Premier League
Castlereigh Goldwings	1996–98 Scottish Under-21 League; 1998–2000 Scottish League Division 1
Northern Ireland	2002/03 expelled from Scottish National League for use of ineligible players
Castlereigh Hawks	1995–2000 Scottish Under-16/17 League/Conference
Castlereigh Kestrels	1995–2000 Scottish Under-14/15 League/Conference
Castlereigh Falcons	1997–1999 Scottish Under-13 Conference/League

Honours:

Castlereigh Flames	1990/91 Champions SNL Spring Cup
Castlereigh Knights	1995/96 Champions Scottish Cup

This complex includes ten-pin bowling, sports hall and a function room. At a total cost of £8.5 million, the rink, at £4.3 million, was made possible by a £4 million grant from the European Regional Fund. The bulk of the seating is upstairs along one side, similar to Billingham. Two London-based clubs flew over to provide a taste of ice hockey, at the opening performed by Peter Robinson, the Member of Parliament for East Belfast.

The following winter a hundred local players were undergoing ice hockey training. The best players combined as Northern Ireland All-Stars to take on the visiting English recreational Billingham Comets, winning the series 7–3 and 18–7 in early June. A four-team house league consisting of Lions, Racers, Redwings and Wolves commenced operations in September 1987.

A year on the pick of the best entered the Scottish League. A second entry – the Flames – followed twelve months later. P&O Ferries underwrote travel costs to the mainland. Double headers were played in Scotland, with the Scottish teams playing both their fixtures in Northern Ireland over the same weekend. The visiting teams attracted crowds of around 400.

The initial coaching by John Harkness – originally from Montreal – administration by Jack Cash and the support of the Brannigan family paid off. Castlereigh Council decided to back the sport with funds and staffing, appointing Jim Graves early in 1993 as hockey

The entrance to the ice bowl.

The Project

It was back in 1980 that the interim report from John W. Whittaker (Consultant Architect) was presented to Castlereagh Borough Council regarding the:

" Provision of ice skating in the Borough ... at Ballyhanwood, Dundonald ..."

Having considered many, varied proposals, all providing a wide range of leisure facilities on the site, a design brief was formulated in 1984 which incorporated:

1. A 60 x 30 metre Ice Rink with all ancillary accommodation
2. A Ten-Pin bowling installation of 20 lanes.
3. A 400 sq. metre multi-purpose hall.
4. A function suite complete with independant catering facilities.

EXTERNAL VIEW

It is the Council's intention to encourage the full range of activities and provide fun and enjoyment for participants and spectators alike. To enhance the family atmosphere and increase the attractiveness of the centre, a modern, bright cafeteria is provided.

The second phase of the complex introduces another first in the form of ten-pin bowling, an experience not to be missed and sure to be another hit with the public. This is scheduled for completion in the New Year and in common with the rest of the centre is completely up to date, incorporating electronic scoring systems.

The inclusion of a 400 sq. metre sports hall makes the complex a true family centre catering for all preferences and age groups. The ultimate leisure experience. A modern approach to management and the desire to please will make it an experience you will want to repeat many times.

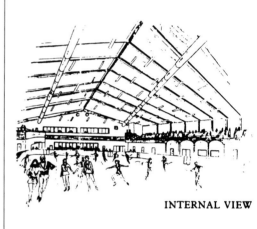

INTERNAL VIEW

The external and internal views from the opening day programme.

co-ordinator and head coach of the Flames. Jim had the brief of expanding and developing a programme that included youth, recreational and women's hockey. Among Flames' roster, now resident in NI, were Zhenting Fo (37) who had served with the Chinese national team, Romanian Roberto Cosmo and Canadians Brian Servetnyk and Pete Campion, a church minister. Helped by complimentary tickets, attendances rose to around 900. During their tenure of the Scottish League Flames enjoyed modest success as runners-up and Spring Cup champions in 1990/91 and a mid-table position in other years.

Knights spent season 1995/96 in the Scottish League culminating in a penalty shoot-out at Aviemore to win the Scottish Cup. Servetnyk the captain, local boy Stevie Hamill, Will Mansour and netminder Mike Johnston formed the backbone. Dundonald also hosted, on 6 January, the first North *v.* South club clash, as Flames beat Dublin Flyers 20–2. That autumn Knights, now a semi-pro outfit, joined the new Northern Premier League. Work permit-holding Ukrainians Vas Vasilenko and Igor Urchenko had vast experience. Kevin Doherty, a Canadian and two Scots – Dean Smith and Mark Slater – joined the hard core of Dundonald regulars, including Hamill and Jamie Brannigan. Their netminder, American-born Chris McGimpsey, joined the fully pro Belfast Giants in 2003.

In Castlereigh's first home game, on 14 September 1996, they achieved a stunning 3–2 victory over long-established Whitley Warriors, in front of a capacity crowd. Inevitably the travelling took its toll; locally based players, with jobs outside hockey, could not always get away. Money problems hit as the local authority cut back the funding. Doherty and several other players from the mainland departed during December. The dedication of the two imports and the Northern Irish contingent ensured the league programme was fulfilled. Without a win at home in the New Year the spectator level dwindled. Knights finished last. Sixty goals and 34 assists pushed Vasilenko to seventh in the scoring race. A final and long-awaited home 6–5 win over Dumfries came in the play-offs.

A form of 'senior' hockey returned to Dundonald in 1998. Goldwings' experience, gained from two winters in the Scottish Under-21 League, was now tested in Division 1 of the Scottish League. Tough competition pushed 'Wings towards the lower end of the standings. In 1995 the maturing youth programme entered Kestrels and Hawks into the Scottish Under-14 and Under-16 Leagues. Two years on the Under-13s Falcons followed their older brethren into league competition. Several prospects emerged, under the tutelage of Doherty, in charge of development since 1997. Graeme Walton and David Gibson represented Scotland at Under-17 and Under-19 levels. Gareth Martin made the Scots Under-14 team, with Mark Morrison selected for the Scottish Under-16s and a Great Britain Under-20 trial. By autumn 2003 Walton, Morrison and Martin were full-time professionals with Belfast Giants.

From summer 2000 Scottish league participation ceased across all age ranges. Five older players joined Solway Sharks and one moved to Ayr. A simmering dispute between factions within the ice hockey community at the Ice Bowl came to a head. At the time of writing it appears that problems still exist between these factions and the Northern Irish Association. The NIIHA is recognised by Ice Hockey UK as being responsible for control of the sport within the province. Northern Ireland joined the Scottish League in the autumn of 2002. They were soon expelled for use of unregistered players.

Some hockey activity is being maintained at Dundonald in the hope that the current impasse will soon be broken.

DUNFERMLINE

Opened:	20 October 1939	Address:
Closed:	April 1955	Dunfermline Ice Rink
Ice Size:	200ft x 100ft	Halbeath Road
Total Spectator Capacity:	3,400	Dunfermline
Seating Capacity:	2,600	Fife
Ice Hockey – First Match:		Scotland

27 October 1939: Dunfermline Vikings 5 *v.* Perth Panthers 9 (challenge)

Teams:
Dunfermline Vikings   1939/40 Scottish National League; 1946–53 Scottish National League; 1954/55 British Autumn Cup

Dunfermline Royals   1946–50 Scottish 'Junior' League(s); 1948–53 Northern Tournament

Honours:
Vikings   Champions 1946/47 Play-offs – Anderson Trophy, Winners Canada Cup & League Flag; 1939/40, 1948/49 & 1952/53 Winners Scottish Cup; 1949/50 Winners Association Cup; 1950/51 Winners Canada Cup

Royals   1945/46 Winners Banner Trophy; 1948/49 Champions (Durham) Northern Tournament Play-off

Dunfermline Ice Rink Limited came into being in autumn 1938. Work commenced on the £40,000 project early the next year under the control of Company Secretary J.C. Rolland.

The exterior in 1988. (David Gordon)

Yorkshire-born forward Jimmy Chappell (24), of GB's 1936 gold medal-winning team, was the inaugural Vikings' best-known member. Tommy Durling (23), Scotty Cameron, defence-man Ernie Batson and Chick Kerr, in goal, had all previously been seen with other clubs in Britain. Although last in the professional Scottish National League (SNL), with only 4 victories in 20 matches, Dunfermline won the Scottish Cup. Contested on a knockout format they tied Falkirk Lions 3–3 in the final's first leg. They triumphed at Falkirk by the odd goal in seven.

The rink remained open during the Second World War. This enabled some of the local lads, who formed the Royals in 1940, to compete on near-equal terms with the Canadian imports when hostilities ceased. Royals, coached by Cameron, won the Banner Trophy in 1946, scoring 46 goals to the 6 conceded. The trophy was put up by the father of Frankie Banner, a pre-war Royal, who was killed while flying with the RAF.

For 1946/47, and the following years, Vikings consisted mainly of Canadians. Several of the Royals increasingly gained ice time, principally the Syme brothers and Johnny Roland, son of director J.C. All three went on to represent Great Britain at the 1950 World Championships held in London. Vikings stamped their authority on Scottish hockey, as runners-up in the league, three points behind Perth. Fife Flyers were defeated 5–2 and 2–0 in the play-off finals to lift the Anderson Trophy. Vikings also won the league format-based Canada Cup and the League Flag Tournaments. All in front of capacity crowds at Halbeath Road. Goalminder Ivan Walmsley and Joe Lay on defence gained All-Star 'A' status with Johnny Myke topping the SNL scoring on 39+18. Although the next winter did not provide silverware Randy Ellis's 57-point total was the league's highest. 'Tuck' Syme played for GB at the 1948 Olympics in Switzerland.

Dunfermline never won the SNL but consistently triumphed in other competitions during the next three seasons, as well as finishing runners-up in the 1948/49 play-offs and the Canada Cup a year later. Vikings won the Canada in 1950/51 and missed out on a tie for second place in the league by one point. Tom 'Tuck' Syme (23), a coalminer from nearby Blairhall, became the first Scottish and British-trained player to be named to a season ending All-Star 'A' sextet. In 58 matches he scored 10 goals and contributed 13 assists.

Attendances started falling as Vikings had a poor season with hockey-minded rink manager Bill Creasey moving to Paisley in 1952. Performances picked up the following season, but spectator levels did not, as Vikings won the league-based Scottish Cup. An All-Star 'B' rating came 'Tuck's' way. Among the Canadians, Jerry Hudson spent four years with Dunfermline, as did Nebby Thrasher, born in 1928 at Timmins, Ontario, who totalled 246 points and led the club in scoring between 1949 and 1951. Hudson, from Gananoque, Quebec, amassed 319 points between 1950 and 1953.

The rink was put up for sale in November 1953, with Vikings absent from the Scottish League that winter. A new board of directors came into being the next year, chaired by J.C. Rolland, and Vikings returned with the amalgamation of the Scottish and English National Leagues. The roster was virtually unknown to Dunfermline fans, other than Rolland and Jim Thompson – a local boy – as the team failed to gel. With only two wins the Autumn Cup closed with Vikings seven points adrift in the cellar. Crippled by the cost of travel, falling gates and with one victory in eleven British League outings the board met in January 1955 to withdraw Vikings from competition. Their British League statistics were expunged from the records. Johnny Rolland, in nearly 300 games, scored 88 goals plus 76 assists.

Closed three months later, the building served as a naval barracks, before conversion to a showroom and offices for the electricity board until 1987, then briefly as a furniture warehouse. It was demolished in the late 1980s. A mosaic depicting a Viking's head, from the floor of the rink entrance foyer, is preserved in the wall of the Carnegie Centre – a local leisure facility.

DURHAM

Opened:	6 March 1940 as an open air rink, 21 December 1946 with permanent roof.	Address: Durham Ice Rink Walkergate
Closed:	8 July 1996	Durham City
Ice Size:	180ft x 80ft (55m x 24m)	Co. Duham
Total Spectator Capacity:	2,860 (as at 1988; 4,000 during 1940s and 1950s)	DH1 1SQ England
Seating Capacity:	2,247 (as at 1988)	

Ice Hockey – First Match:
From late 1941 the Canadian YMCA organised a league of twelve RCAF teams. First game featuring local team – 18 October 1947: Durham Wasps 4 v. Kirkcaldy Flyers 5

Teams:

Durham Wasps
1948–55 & 1956–61 Northern Tournament; 1957/58 North British League; 1966/67 'Home' tournaments; 1966–82 Northern League; 1981/82 English National League; 1982/83 British League Division 1 Section 'B'; 1983–95 British League Premier Division

Durham University
1951–55 challenge games

Durham Hornets
1953–55 'Home' tournaments; 1973–77 Northern Second League; 1977–81 Northern Reserve League; 1983–87 and 1988–91 British League Division 2; 1987/88 English League; 1991–94 English Under-21 League; 1994–96 English Under-19 League

Durham Mosquitoes
1948–51 challenge games; 1975–81 Northern Junior League; 1983–96 English Junior/Under-16 League

Durham Midges
1983–96 English Pee-Wee League

Durham Stingers
1990–96 English Under-12 League

Durham City Wasps
1995/96 English League Division 1

Honours:

Wasps
1949/50, 1951–53 & 1963/64 Winners Northern Tournament Play-offs; 1982/83 Winners British League – Section 'B';

	1984–86, 1988/89 & 1990–92 Champions British League; 1984/85, 1987–89 & 1990/91 Winners Autumn Cup; 1986–88 and 1990–92 Champions British Play-offs
Hornets	1987/88 Winners English League; 1991/92 Champions English Under-21 League Play-offs; 1994/95 Champions English Under-19 League Play-offs; 1995/96 Winners English Under-19 League – North
Mosquitoes	1983–87, 1988/89 & 1991–93 Winners English Junior League – North & Champions English Junior League Play-off; 1986/87, 1988/89 & 1992/93 British Junior/Under-16 Champions; 1993–95 Winners English Junior League – North & Champions English League Play-offs
Midges	1983–87 & 1990/91 Winners English Pee-Wee League – North & Champions English Pee-Wee League Play-off; 1990–93 Winners English Under-14 League
Stingers	1990/91 Winners English Under-12 League – North & Champions English Under-12 League; 1992/93 Winners English Under-12 League – North

John 'Icy' Smith (1889–1965) manufactured ice for use in chiller cabinets. At his riverside premises, in Bishop's Mill alongside the river Wear, he installed a water-driven turbine generator to provide electricity. By the late 1930s 'Icy' realised that the days of selling ice were numbered. He utilised his knowledge and machinery to build an ice rink. Work commenced in June 1939. With the ice surface in place the outbreak of war prevented completion of a permanent enclosure. Although open-air skating proved popular, the sun and rain frequently curtailed activities. So seven posts driven into the ice, three down the middle and two at the ends, supported a 19,000sq ft tarpaulin roof.

Canadian airmen based at the nearby RCAF Bomber Group airfields of Croft, Leeming, Middleton St George and Topcliffe soon organised a ten-team league. In the first match, in

1944 wartime ice hockey. Note the post in the ice on the right supporting the roof. (Durham Ice Rink)

Early morning practice, 1989. (Alex Wilson/*IHNR*)

late 1941, Bombers defeated Spitfires 5–1. In the next three years many stars of North American professional hockey were seen on Durham ice. These included, from the NHL, Roy Conacher, Lloyd Gronsdel (Boston), Alf Pike (New York), Paul Platz (Chicago), Jimmy Haggerty (Montreal), Johnny Whitelaw, Sid Abel (Detroit) and Howard Meeker (Toronto). Rival player-coaches and former Boston Bruins linemates Milt Schmidt and Woody Dumart agreed that the timbers embedded in the ice revolutionised the mechanics of their sport; woe betide the man skating with his head down. The most outstanding series occurred in 1944, in play-off contests between Leeming and Middleton, for the Group title. Leeming, with Pike, won the first game 3–2. Middleton took the second 7–1. In the final game they iced Schmidt, Haggerty and Conacher who could not shake off the close checking of Leeming – the winners by 3–0. Gronsdal netted the final goal.

In November 1944 a gale ripped away the roof and a few weeks later fire destroyed the remaining structure. Open air skating resumed for a while but closed on 31 March 1946. In spite of post-war shortages 'Icy' managed to have a concrete and steel-framed asbestos-cement-clad permanent rink built in nine months by Cargo Fleet Iron Co., at a cost of £64,000. Seating was reputed to have been formed from firewood and coffin lids

Early on lads with improvised sticks had played a form of hockey, more like shinny. After the war Mike Davey, from Ottawa, an airman player who married a local girl, became Wasps' first coach. Fellow countrymen Earl Carlson, Gordie Belmore and netminder George Gibson, who had all stayed on, assisted. Equipment was improvised and twice weekly training sessions held, for those living or working in Co. Durham; a homegrown policy that continued until the early 1980s. The first season consisted of 32 challenge games, mainly with Scottish amateur teams. 2,500 spectators turned up for Wasps' first appearance. For the visit of Nottingham Wolves, who included Zamick and Westerman from the professional Panthers, 4,000 packed the building on 27 December 1947, with hundreds turned away. Davey resigned mid-season to be replaced by Pat McCurry, another ex-RCAF man. After ensuring the future, by setting up Hornets (Under-20) and Mosquitoes (Under-15), McCurray moved on. Bill Booth, a professional defenceman with Brighton, replaced him. Next winter the Northern Tournament (NT) was introduced. Visiting teams travelled to Durham twice, in later seasons three or four times. Those with the best goal average returned to contest the play-offs. From 1948 to 1954 Wasps topped the standings. In that inaugural campaign Dunfermline Royals knocked Wasps out 6–5 in a semi-final and defeated Kirkcaldy 3–2 for the cup. Wasps won next year, beating Paisley Wildcats 3–1 with goals from Belmore (2) and Carlson. Wembley Terriers and Earls Court Marlboroughs triumphed before Wasps again won a final.

By now talented younger players were regulars, including Derek Adamson, Mike Jordan, Derek Elliott and Dave Lammin. Apart from NT clashes Wasps bravely took on Harringay

Racers, Lou Bates' Select of pros and blanked the full Great Britain squad 5–0. In 1954 Terriers captured their second NT Cup. Next year Wasps slipped to second in the standings behind Falkirk Cubs, and lost by the odd goal in nine to Glasgow in the semi. With less than half the number of teams available, compared with the first year and falling attendances, the rink disbanded Wasps. Following the success of hockey at the recently opened Smith family-owned Whitley Bay rink, Wasps and the Northern Tournament returned to Walkergate on 5 October 1957.

The first encounter with Whitley Bees took place a month later with Dicky Herkes shutting out the interlopers. A new generation of Smiths – Tom (Durham) and Bill skated on opposite sides. For the next four years Wasps and Whitley simultaneously hosted the NT. Durham contested the final unsuccessfully in 1958 and 1961. Carlson's goal total reached over 600. England v. Scotland clashes were held in 1960 and 1961. The team lost home ice in 1961 following a dispute with the rink over the level of out-of-pocket expenses. The players banded together as The Wasps and provided strong contenders at opposition rinks around the country.

For two years, from 1962, Durham-based teams – Dynamos and Leopards – competed in the North East League. This introduced many players to the sport including Ronnie Stark and Peter Johnson. With the formation of the Northern League in autumn 1966 Wasps regained ice at Durham. As Booth had retired Hep Tindale became player-coach with Tom Smith as captain. During the sixteen years of the Northern League and associated competitions Wasps' best efforts were runners-up in the 1975/76 Autumn Cup and a third NL place. Around the rock-like presence of Tindale, Johnson, Kenny Matthews and Derek Metcalfe in goal, many newcomers blossomed. John Hudson, Denny Brown, Ivor Bennett and Paul Smith were among the forwards plus Rolly Barrass. England took on Scotland in 1970, 1971, 1974 and then bi-annually until 1980. Wasps contributed up to five players on several occasions. Season 1981/82 saw the English National League revived, leading to a regionalised British League next winter. Helped by their first import – goalminder Ron Katernyuk – Wasps topped Section B of Division 1. With the stream of lads emerging from the Hornets, via the Mosquitoes, Durham were well placed at the birth of the Heineken, British-wide, multi-divisional league.

The approach of team and rink owner Tom Smith, with his revolving door policy – 'any import who doesn't produce the goods will go' – engendered a winning ethos. The high-quality, high-scoring imports that stuck include many who gained All-Star recognition. Paul Tilley and Jamie Crapper are early examples. Now dubbed 'The Big Blue Machine' as Mike O'Connor joined in 1984, Wasps won the Autumn Cup – their first major title for thirty-four years. A settled roster saw the emergence of the homebred Cooper brothers, Stephen and Ian, as Durham remained unbeaten at home for fourteen months, winning the Premier Division in 1985. The title was retained as Pete 'Jonker' Johnson took over behind the bench. His sons Anthony and Shaun formed the 'Kid Line' with Ian Cooper.

The British Championship at Wembley followed, imports Kevin Conway and Mario Belanger forming the CBS line with Paul Smith, son of Tom. Attendances at the Riverside rose by around 1,200 in 1982, from a couple of hundred in the Northern League days, to average 3,203. During the next five winters trophies came thick and fast. The fallow season was 1989/90, when Wasps were Autumn Cup finalists. The Cooper brothers had left for Cardiff the previous year. The dawning of the 1990s saw Wasps achieve the HBL Grand Slam with the Autumn Cup, League and British Championship titles. The return of the Coopers and the acquisition of ex-NHLer Mike Blaisdell helped. As an encore Durham retained both league title, for a record fifth time, with an unbeaten run of 27 games, plus the British Championship at Wembley in April 1992. From that high point Wasps plunged downhill. The Cooper brothers moved back to Cardiff, Blaisdell left and Tim Cranston was replaced. Wasps dropped to the foot of the BL with a virtually new squad, the sixth place in spring 1994 was not good enough for coach P. Smith. The rink's founders and owners, the Smith family, sold the building on 24 September 1994 to Rex Brown, a local business-man. Three weeks later their company Incredo Ltd went into voluntary liquidation with reported debts of around £400,000. Brown replaced the charismatic coach Rocky Saganiuk with returning player Richard Little.

Next May Tom and Paul Smith sold the Durham Wasps title to Sir John Hall – the chairman of Newcastle FC. They bought up the players' contracts and, amid much acrimony moved the club to Sunderland for 1995/96. A new team, Durham City Wasps, with one import and an influx from the successful conveyor belt of league-winning youth teams, ended fourth in the English League – North, drawing crowds of around 1,000. On 12 May, City won the first leg of the play-offs. This proved to be the last game at Walkergate. Brown claimed the venue needed renovations costing £250,000.

Following closure as an ice rink the building became, by 1997, the Kascada Bowl, a twenty-lane ten-pin bowling alley and a Meridan Health and Fitness Centre.

EDINBURGH

Opened:	7 August 1952	Address:
Ice Size:	200ft x 97ft (61m x 29.5m)	Murrayfield Ice Rink
Total Spectator Capacity:	3,800 (4,500 in 1952)	Riverside Crescent
Seating Capacity:	3,300	Murrayfield
Ice Hockey – First Match:		Edinburgh EH12 5XN

19 September 1952: Edinburgh Royals 4 *v.* Falkirk Lions 4
(challenge)

Scotland

Teams:

Edinburgh Royals 1952–54 Scottish National League; 1954/55 British National League; 1955/56 Scottish Amateur League; 1958/59 British Autumn Cup; 1959–61 'Home' tournaments

Murrayfield Royals 1957/58 North British League; 1962–66 'Home' tournaments; 1962/63 & 1964/65 Scottish League; 1995/96 British League – Division 1; 1996/97 Northern Premier League; 1997/98 British National League

Murrayfield Racers 1966–82 Northern League; 1981/82 Scottish National League; 1982/83 British League Division 1 Section 'A'; 1983–94 British League Premier Division

Edinburgh Racers 1994 /95 British League Premier Division

Edinburgh Capitals 1998–2005 British National League

Murrayfield Raiders 1968/69 & 1971–76 Northern Second League; 1977–82 Northern Reserve League; 1987–91 & 1998–2000 Scottish League Division 1; 1991–93 Scottish Under-18 League; 1997/98 Scottish Under-21 League

Edinburgh Capitals 2000–05 Scottish National League

Edinburgh Capitals 2004/05 Scottish Under-19 League

Murrayfield Ravens 1976–81 Northern Junior League; 1986–93 Scottish Junior/Under-16/17 League; 1994–99 Scottish Under-16/17 League/Conference; 1999–2004 Scottish Under-18/19 League

Murrayfield Racoons 1999–2003 Scottish Under-16 League

Murrayfield Raptors 2003–05 Scottish Under-16 League

Murrayfield Racoons 1986–93 and 1994–98 Scottish Pee-Wee/Under-14/15 League/Conference

Murrayfield Rapiers 1998–2005 Scottish Under-15/14 League

Murrayfield Racers 1988/89 Scottish Under-12 League

Murrayfield Rapiers 1990–93 & 1997–99 Scottish Under-12/13 League/Conference

Murrayfield Rascals 1999–2004 Scottish Under-12 League

Honours:

Royals	1957/58 Champions North British League
Racers	1969–72, 1975/76 & 1979–81 Champions Northern League; 1968/69, 1971–73 & 1977–79 Winners Northern League Play-offs (Spring Cup); 1965/66, 1968–72, 1974/75 & 1978–81 Winners 'Icy' Smith Cup; 1970/71, 1974/75, 1977/78, 1979–81, 1989/90 & 1993/94 Winners Autumn Cup; 1986–88 Champions British League – Premier Divison; 1985/86 Champions British Play-offs
Raiders	1971–73 & 1976/77 Champions Northern Second League; 1977/78 & 1979/80 Champions Northern Reserve League; 1987–89 Champions Scottish League & Play-offs; 1992/93 Winners Scottish Under-18 Cup
Capitals	2001/02 Champions Scottish National League and Scottish Autumn and Spring Cups; 2002/03 Champions Scottish National League
Ravens	1977/78, 1979/80 & 1986/87 Champions Northern Junior League; 2000/01 Champions Scottish Under-18 League
Raptors	2003/04 Champions Scottish Under-16 League
Racoons	1986/87 Winners Scottish Pee-Wee League Play-offs; 1996/97 Champions Scottish Under-14 Conference 'A'; 1997/98 Champions Scottish Under-15 Conference 'A'
Rapiers	2000–02 Winners Scottish Under-14 'B' League
Rascals	2000–02 Winners Scottish Under-12 'B' League

Publications:
Murrayfield Racers Supporters Club Handbook 1984-85, Mizen, Ian, 1985

Conceived by James Walker and designed in 1938 by architects Dunn and Martin, the rink is adjacent to the famous Murrayfield rugby stadium. The building, completed in 1939 at a cost of £60,000, was due to open on 15 September. Instead the government requisitioned it for use by the army. In January 1952 a licence was issued to repair the building. It changed hands in the summer of 1957 for £48,000 and is now owned by the Kerr and Neil families. The front façade is Grade B listed. In 1976 the boxing and closing ceremonies of the Commonwealth Games were held here.

With the rink not opening until 1952 the Scottish Association waived their rule of a minimum of two home-bred players, as Royals signed twelve Canadians. Sixth in the Scottish National League was disappointing to coach Alex Archer. They did win the Bairns Trophy, a tournament for finishing below mid-point. Moe Fife from Hastings, Ontario, was the best of the forwards with 38+12. Only Cece Cowie, Vern Greger and Henri Lemonie were retained. Twenty-one-year-olds Dorry Boyle and Jimmy Dunlop came in as the mandatory Scots. Royals moved two places up the standings under player-coach Bobby Burns, a defenceman who gained an All-Star 'B' accolade.

The Scottish and English National Leagues combined for 1954/55. Royals were probably the most balanced team, so fourth in the Autumn Cup and sixth in the league were an underachievement. George Townsend, from Edmonton, proved the best sniper with 59+48. In spite of the queue round the rink at the opening three years earlier, attendances slumped.

Murrayfield tried pro hockey again in September 1958. Dundee-born Marshall Key led the club in scoring, potting 51 points in the 25-match Autumn Cup schedule, six ahead of Ted McCaskill, who later served briefly in the NHL. 'Red' Imrie, Jim Mitchell, Johnny Carlyle and Jack Dryburgh were Royals' other Scots. Insufficient spectators turned out, forcing Murrayfield to fold by Christmas. Next autumn Royals joined the Scottish Amateur League, which faded out before spring. Murrayfield won the short-lived North British

League in 1958. Royals dropped 1 point in their 12 fixtures scoring 114 times, and were an amalgam of talent generated from several Scottish rinks. Among those who had recently learned their skills on Murrayfield ice were goalminder Willie Clark and Glen Reilly on defence.

For several years the team regularly appeared at Southampton and Brighton. They also contested the Scottish League, although dropping out for 1963/64 as facilities at Murrayfield were withdrawn. This was the winter that first saw Racers on the ice.

Scottish League hockey returned to Murrayfield in autumn 1964 with fortnightly matches. They won 11 of 18 encounters to finish second in Section A. With no league the next winter and few games the players drifted away. By February 1966 Royals were no more.

Racers, formed as a reserve team, were established with plenty of talent. Freddie Wood, Derek Reilly and Lawrie Lovell were examples benefiting from the coaching of Johnny Carlyle. By the close of the decade the crowds were coming back as Racers won their first major trophy – the knock-out 'Icy' Smith Cup in 1969. They held onto it for the next three seasons. The Northern League title followed, to be retained for a further two campaigns. Goal-getting ace Lawrie Lovell gained a trio of scoring titles. Reilly was never out of the top ten, named an All-Star four years running. 'Player of the Year' accolade went to defender Gordon Inglis in 1970.

League Champions again in 1975/76, Racers proceeded to another hat-trick of titles in the early 1970s, plus 'Icy' Smith Cup triumphs, emblematic of the British Championship. Ronnie Wood, Jim Pennycook (who was 'Rookie of the Year' for 1973/74) and John Hay and Stevie Hunter joined Reilly and Lovell in the top ten scoring lists.

Murrayfield produced a string of leading goalminders from Willie Clark, with a five-year consecutive run of All-Star ratings from 1968, to John Pullar (1978 & 1980) and Mike Ward (1981). Moray Hanson was awarded the Pete Smith Memorial Bowl as 1981/82 'Netminder of the Year'. The first 'imports' joined Racers for 1978/79 – Oke Alm (Sweden) and Alex Dampier (Canada) – immediately to gain All-Star status. Fellow countryman and defenceman Chris Kelland arrived for 1980/81 to also gain All-Star 'A' recognition. The pinnacle of two consecutive British League titles (1986–88) had been preceded by Racers as runners-up, followed by two further silver medals. Finalists at Wembley two years running culminated in the British Championship in 1986. Success continued with Autumn Cup victories in 1989 and 1993. From an average attendance of around 550 in 1982 through to 1,235 during 1986/87 the crowd levels at Riverside Cresent rose to 2,141 by 1992/93.

In 1986 Edinburgh native Tony Hand won a trip to Calgary Flames' training camp as 'Young British Player of the Year'. He first skated for Racers in the final campaign of the Northern League in 1981/82. Other prospects included Tony's brother Paul, cousin Scot Neil, Lindsay Lovell and Paul Pentland. All were products of a development programme consisting of the Under-14 Racoons, Under-16 Ravens and the older Raiders, league title-winners during this period. A lot of the credit goes to the far-sighted Willie Kerr (1911–83), rink manager from 1959 until his death. At a time when the British-based game had been in decline he encouraged and provided ice for local lads and homeless teams from other rinks. From 21–27 April 1984 Murrayfield hosted Pool C of the European Under-20 Championships.

Following a mass exodus of players a consortium headed by Derek Reilly and Robert Adams took control in 1992. The import attack of Chris Palmer and John Newberry provided effective Murrayfield came second in the Premier Division. During the next campaign, in spite of winning the Autumn Cup: a dispute over finances between the club owners and the rink broke out. This resulted in Racers finishing the season at Livingston. Attendance average fell to 1,147.

Local businessman Alan Maxwell and enthusiast Stewart Robertson formed a new club – Edinburgh Racers. With the addition of Ivan Matulik they made it through the play-offs to the Wembley final. In June 1995 ownership of Racers reverted to the rink and they changed the name to Murrayfield Royals. Hand moved to Sheffield. Royals joined thirteen other teams in Division One. They sank to the bottom. The year 1996 saw Royals in the new Northern Premier League. With Roger Hunt as player-coach they escaped the cellar, with crowd levels well below those of 1980. Heroics by Scots-American netminder John Finnie failed to save Royals from last in the revived British National League.

Another transformation came in summer 1998 as Scott Neil and Raymond Lumsden joined forces to raise finance with a further change of name to Edinburgh Capitals. Further money troubles in 1999 caused Lumsden to depart. Coach Jock Hay made the most of Steven Lynch, a Scot, and passing imports, notably Angelo Catenaro and Jason Lafreniere. Financial prudence and the signing in 2002 of Czech imports Jan Krajicek and goalie Ladislav Kudrna, plus Paddy Ward and the return of native son Tony Hand, for winter 2003/04, turned the rebuilding Capitals into serious title contenders. A third-placed finish by spring 2004 was the best yet as spectators started to return in increasing numbers. A team of the same name provided competition for younger players in the Scottish National League and for 2004/05 an Under-19 side was added.

ELGIN

Opened:	30 July 1993	Address:
Ice Size:	148ft x 82ft (45m x 25m)	Elgin Ice Rink
Total Spectator Capacity:	200	Borough Briggs Road
Seating Capacity:	Minimal	Elgin
		Morayshire IV30 1AP
Ice Hockey – First Match:		Scotland
Not known		

Teams:

Moray Tornadoes	2002–05 Scottish National League
Moray Firth Tornadoes	1996/97 Scottish Under-21 League
Elgin Tornadoes	1997/98 Scottish Under-21 League
Elgin	1999/2000 & 2001/02 Scottish Under-18 League
Elgin Buccaneers	1995–98 Scottish Under-16/17 League/Conference
Elgin Moray Lightning	1998–2000 Scottish Under-17/16 League
Elgin Buccaneers	2000/01 and 2002–05 Scottish Under-16 League
Elgin Moray Buccaneers	1995–2000 Scottish Under-14/15 League/Conference
Elgin Sky Pirates	2000–05 Scottish Under-14 League
Elgin Sky Pirates	1995–99 Scottish Under-12/13 League/Conference
Elgin Ospreys	1999–2005 Scottish Under-12 League

The rink is an integral part of the Moray Leisure Centre, which also contains a swimming pool. When first opened minimal facilities existed for ice hockey. The most northerly of British hockey rinks, its comparative isolation would have been a factor as to why it took a while for the sport to become established on the Moray Firth. Inverness, along the A96 to the west, and Aberdeen to the south east ,were the nearest rinks.

FALKIRK

Opened:	30 November 1938	Address:
Closed:	28 September 1977	Falkirk Ice Rink
Ice Size:	195ft x 97ft	138 Grangemouth Road
Total Spectator Capacity:	4,500	Falkirk
Seating Capacity:	4,000	Lothian
Ice Hockey – First Match:		Scotland

30 November 1938: Falkirk Lions *v.* Perth Panthers.

Teams:

Falkirk Lions 1938–40 Scottish National League; 1946–54 Scottish National League; 1954/55 British National League; 1955/56 Scottish Amateur League; 1961/62 'Home' tournaments; 1964/65 'Home' tournaments

Falkirk Cubs 1946–55 Scottish 'Junior' League(s) and 'Home' tournaments

Falkirk Cougars 1961/62 'Home' tournaments

Honours:

Lions 1938/39 Champions Scottish Points Tournament; 1948/49 & 1951/52 Winners Scottish Cup; 1948/49, 1951/52 & 1953/54 Winners Play-offs (Anderson Trophy); 1948–50,1951/52 & 1953/54 Winners Canada Cup; 1955/56 Winners Scottish Amateur League Play-offs

Cubs 1950–52 Champions Frame League; 1950/51 Winners Frame Cup and Banner Trophy; 1954/55 Winners Northern Tournament

Designed by architects Wilson and Wilson. The main elevation is a coherent two-storey rectangle with a glazed semi-circular bay in the middle, with the main entrance set to one side. Duncan Stewart (Bonnybridge) Ltd built the largest rink in Scotland in ice size and spectator capacity, until Ayr opened four months later. York Shipley of Glasgow installed the ice-making machinery.

British-born Gerry Davey (24), of 1936 GB Olympic fame, was appointed the first player-coach by rink manager R.J. Buck. Both had previously been employed at Streatham. Canadian recruits, with experience of this side of the Atlantic, included goalie 'Buster' Amantea, Bob Beaton, George McWilliams, Nels McCuaig and 'Red' Thompson, who took up refereeing in Scotland post-Second World War. The rookie squad won the 20-game Scottish Points Tournament, and were finalists in the Bairns Trophy. Glasgow-born Tommy Forgie took over the coaching spot for the second and last pre-war season. Although Davey stayed on, only three others were retained. With Maurice Gerth in the net Lions took second spot in the league, were Scottish Cup finalists and won the Airlie Trophy. Forgie and Davey finished fourth and fifth in the Points Trophy scoring list.

When peace and hockey resumed McCuaig took over as manager/coach. Johnny Savicky, Rennie Platt and Frank Davis were the only holdovers for 1947/48. Lions won the Bairns Trophy, were finalists in the Scottish Cup and runners-up in both the newly instigated Scottish Autumn Cup and the Canada Cup. All-Star 'A' recognition went to centre-ice Savicky with a 'B' rating to Bob Palmer at right-wing, both twenty-year-olds. Home-bred boys Johnny Carlyle and Bill Sneddon played a few times. With the signing of George McNeil, originally from Nova Scotia, as manager and coach a new era dawned at Grangemouth Road.

He had pre-war playing experience in London and Dundee, and more recently coached Dundee. Although Lions were never league champions – the nearest they came were

Summer 1938.

The exterior in 1988. (David Gordon)

runners-up in 1948/49 and 1953/54 – under McNeil's guidance silverware was won in every year except 1950/51. They almost made the Anderson Trophy their own, clinching the end-of-season play-offs in 1949 and 1950 and again in 1952 and 1954. Outstanding were goalminder Hap Finch, who was voted an All-Star 'A' 1949–51, and Rennie Platt on defence with an All-Star 'A' rating for 1948/49. In that and the following season Pat Casey, at right-wing, collected a 'B' sextet rating. In spring 1952 Nebby Thrasher (24) from Timmins, Ontario, sixth overall in league scoring with 66 points, gained an 'A' vote.

In the inaugural twelve-member British Autumn Cup Lions placed second, four points behind Harringay Racers. Con Switzer (25) and Gerry Hudson (26) were fifth and tenth in scoring with 42 and 39 points respectively. Lions finished the league as the second best of the Scottish entries, at fourth, three points behind Paisley.

During these years the coaching achievements of McNeil were continually recognised by All-Star accolades. An 'A' in 1949 was followed by five 'Bs' including 1955. His consecutive run was broken, at the request of the Scottish IH Association, by a year as senior referee. He was far sighted, with a belief in nurturing home-bred talent. Among his outstanding discoveries are many who gained regular places with Lions and continued in the sport. They include, with games played in brackets, Sneddon (258) from nearby Grangemouth, Falkirk-born Carlyle (328), Tom 'Red' Imrie (98), Joe McIntosh (26), Tommy Paton (221) and Alex Ormond (93). Many others graduated via Cubs to play lesser parts. The most prominent were Gus Adams (19), Art Williams (24), Jake Morrison (49) and Mike Smith (71). The Cubs' greatest achievement has to be topping the 1955 Northern Tournament standings. To win four out of four at Durham, putting 25 goals past Wasps, demonstrated a high level of hockey. Cubs reached the semi-finals in 1949, 1951 and 1954.

Next spring professional hockey ended as Falkirk, like the other Scottish teams except Paisley, pulled out of the BNL and joined the new, but short-lived, Scottish Amateur

League. In the play-offs Edinburgh Royals lost in the final as Lions roared to a 13–1 triumph. In the second leg goals came from Carlyle (3), McGeever (2), Smith and Imrie. In summer 1956 the rink directors stated that hockey would no longer be staged as there were insufficient teams for worthwhile competition.

During April 1964 the rink presented two exhibitions, featuring a 'Falkirk Lions' consisting mainly of players with Fife and Murrayfield, against Scottish clubs including Paisley. Two more took place in November. Some of the old stalwarts turned out including Roy Reid in goal, McIntosh, Williams, Carlyle and Sneddon. On 16 December 1964 The Rest defeated Great Britain 3–2. Joe McIntosh (Fife) and Carlyle (Murrayfield) represented GB. For the victors Sneddon served on defence. Despite fairly large attendances rink management did not repeat the exercise. Ice had been obtained a couple of years earlier and again in 1964 for some late-night practices, with Lions playing a few away games at the handful of rinks staging 'home' tournaments.

The rink remained open mainly for curling, with limited public skating. The last session was held on 28 September 1977. Festus Moffat, the rink's MD and one time secretary of the Scottish Ice Hockey Association, announced there were serious defects in the ice plant, making repairs impracticable. In December a Leeds businessman spent £70,000 converting the rink into a skateboarding venue. When that venture failed the rink lay empty for some time before becoming a car auction centre. The building was adapted and opened as Coasters rollerskating rink on 12 November 1982, has served as a basketball arena, housed Scotland's biggest indoor climbing wall and is now an indoor market with a bingo hall.

GILLINGHAM

Opened:	22 September 1984	Address:
Ice Size:	185ft x 85ft (56m x 26m)	The Ice Bowl
Total Spectator Capacity:	1,500	Ambley Road
Seating Capacity:	980	Gillingham Business Park
Ice Hockey – First Match:		Gillingham
3 March 1985: Islington All-Stars 8 v. Southampton		Kent ME8 0PP
Knights 4 (BL Division 2)		England

Teams:

Medway Bears	1985/86 British League Division 2 – South; 1986–91 & 1992–96 British League Division 1; 1991/92 English League; 1996/97 Premier League
Invicta Dynamos	1997/98 English National League & EL Conference – South; 1998–2003 English Premier League; 2003–05 English National League – South
Medway Marauders	1986–91 British League Division 2; 1991–94 English Under-21 League; 1994–96 English Conference; 1996/97 English Under-19 League
Invicta Devils	1998/99 English League Division 1; 1997/98 and 1999–2002 English Under-19 League
Invicta Mustangs	2001/02 English National League; 2003–05 English Under-19 League
Medway Rangers	1993/94 English Conference
Invicta Dynamos	1997/98 English Conference – South
Medway Bear Cubs	1986/87 English Junior League
Medway Junior Bears	1987–97 English Junior/Under-16 League
Invicta Junior Dynamos	1997–2005 English Junior/Under-16 League
Medway Pee-Wee Bears	1987/88 English Pee-Wee League

Medway Kodiaks	1988–97 English Pee-Wee/Under-14 League/Conference
Invicta Dynamites	1997–2005 English Under-14 League
Invicta B	2003/04 English Under-14 League
Medway Kodiak Kubs	1988–97 English Under-12 League/Conference
Invicta Dynamites	1997–2003 English Under-12 League
Invicta Dynamites B	2000–02 & 2003/04 English Under-12 League
Invicta Devils	2004/05 English Under-12 League

Honours:

Bears	1985/86 Champions British League Division 2 & Winners South; 1991/92 Champions English League and Winners Play-off promotion Group 'A'
Dynamos	1997/98 Winners English League Conference – South; 2001/02 Champions English Premier League and Play-offs; 2003–05 Winners English National League – South
Mauraders	1988/89 Winners English League Division 2 – South East; 1989/90 Winners English League Division 2 – South
Dynamos	1997/98 Winners English Conference – South
Junior Bears	1994/95 Winners English Junior League – South East
Dynamos	2000/01 Winners English Under-16 'B' League – South
Kodiaks	1991/92 Winners English Under-14 'B' League – South
Dynamites	1999/00 Champions English Under-14 League and Winners 'A' South
Kodiak Kubs	1990/91 Winners English Under-12 'B' League – South; 1993/94 Winners English Under-12 Conference – South East; 1996/97 Winners Southern Under-14 'A' League
Invicta Dynamites	1998/99 & 2004/05 Winners English Under-12 'A' League – South

Publications:
The Bears – Season 1987/88, ed. Stamp, Phil, 1988, Medway Bears Ice Hockey Ltd
The Bears – Season 1988/89, ed. Stamp, Phil, 1989, Medway Bears Ice Hockey Ltd

A privately financed, owned and operated ice rink, designed in 'warehouse/shed' form, located in a trading estate on the edge of the Medway Towns; it was officially opened by The Queen. For ten months from its opening a Canadian – Ron Barr – was employed to provide power-skating and hockey lessons. Islington All-Stars staged a few of their 'home' games at the Ice Bowl during spring.

For the first season of the Medway Bears two Canadians from Saskatoon – Kevin McNaught as coach and Dale Lambert – were engaged. They recruited a mix of youth including goalie Russell Jackson and Peter Roden, leavened by veterans John Holtham and Tony Whitehead. In the first of their 14 league matches on 6 October 1985, Bears defeated Islington 18–4. Unbeaten, Medway hosted the promotion play-offs in early May. In front of a packed rink they swept past Nottingham Trojans to a 26–4 victory over Grimsby Buffaloes and onto the following winter's British League.

The club surprised the experts by taking Division 1's runners-up slot. The permitted third import Gord Jeffrey was joined by key signings Rob Breskal (Brighton), Andy Steel (Telford), Geoff Williams (Lee Valley) and Jason Wood, a netminder from Streatham. With crowd levels averaging around 1,400, sometimes rising to over 1,600, packed into the tiered seating running down both lengths of the building and standing two or three deep, the noise generated created a spine-tingling atmosphere. Two years later, Bears missed promotion to the Premier by a whisker. One point separated them from Cardiff. Luc Chabot had replaced Lambert, with goalie Gary Brine and Tony Goldstone joining from Streatham. Medway never came this close again. Next term was a disappointment. Robin Bartel could not

The interior, c. 1987.
(*Ice Hockey World*)

settle and returned to Canada as several other imports came and went. The season closed with a dispute between club and rink over finances, which continued into early autumn. The cash-strapped team failed to win the end of season relegation play-off.

Dropping to the English League provided a chance to rebuild. The success of the second-tier Mauraders, fed by the Under-14 Kodiaks, was paying off. Darren Masters, Andy Thorncroft, Paul Slaughter and Scott Hughes with netminder Sam Russell-Samways were major contributors under the tutelage of McNaught, inspired by a 225-points total from Chabot. A capacity crowd thrilled to the 8–4 victory over Streatham in the promotion decider. The one-point margin over new boys Sheffield Steelers ensured British League hockey from autumn 1992. New directors Brian Smith and Jack Middleton exercised fiscal prudence, but the next four years were a struggle for Bears. Third in the southern group was the best that could be gained. In 1996/97 Medway joined richer clubs in the new Premier League. With a mix of nationalities and homebred talent such as Greg and Jamie Randall and seventeen-year-old Simon Smith in goal the small squad ended seventh.

Kent hockey had a new owner from 1997 onwards as David Hodge and colleagues out-bid Medway Bears for use of the Ice Bowl. Player-coach Mark Mackie recruited shrewdly, including the Cotton brothers from Peterborough, as the new Invicta Dynamos lost once on the way to the EL Conference South title. Dynamos did the double in 2001/02 by winning the English Premier League and play-offs under the leadership of Sean Clement and Phil Chard. Significant contributions to victory came from popular Finn Mikko Skinnari, goalie Matt van der Valden, a Brit, and imports Carl Greenhous and Duane Ward. Exciting prospects continued to join from Invicta's youth system including Mike Wales and, in 2003, Daniel Fudger and Adam Smith. For 2003/04 Dynamos dropped a level, to win ENL – South by late winter, repeating the feat the following season.

In the early years visiting clubs included Laki from Findland, Kagedaleus AIF and AC Camel (Sweden).

GLASGOW – REAL ICE SKATING PALACE

Opened:	May 1896	Address:
Closed:	1897	Glasgow Real Ice
Ice Size:	Probably circular	Skating Palace
Total Spectator Capacity:	Unknown	Sauchiehall Street
Seating Capacity:	Unknown but likely to be minimal	Glasgow
Ice Hockey – First Match:		Scotland
June 1896		

Originally built in 1892 as the Hippodrome to house a diorama. In 1896 showman Arthur Hibner turned it into an ice skating palace. In the following year it became Glasgow's first cinema. In 1902 the building reopened as the Hipperdrome to stage circus and spectacular water-based shows. The Hipperdrome was rebuilt in 1924 as the Regal cinema, which later on became the ABC.

A team from the National Skating Palace in London travelled to Glasgow to defeat the local side in a bandy match in June 1896 (this game on skates is played with a ball, and sticks more akin to field hockey).

GLASGOW – CROSSMYLOOF (ORIGINAL)

Opened:	1 October 1907	Address:
Closed:	February 1918, when acquired by	Crossmyloof Ice Rink
	the authorities for war purposes.	Titwood Road
Ice Size:	149ft x 89ft (42m x 29m – Les	Glasgow G1
	Sports D'Hiver c. 1912)	Scotland
Total Spectator Capacity:	Minimal	
Ice Hockey – First Match:	1908	

A line of steel columns, set in the ice down the length of the building towards one side, supported a gallery and the roof above. As this was the only rink in Scotland permitting ice hockey pre-First World War, the sport at Crossmyloof would have been mainly inter-squad games, similar to a 'house' league.

The short sticks initially used, more like those for bandy, were soon abandoned for more conventional long-handled ones. Among the players were H.R. Orr, J. Ritchie, D. McGill and J.B. Warrie. With the latter in goal, along with MacGuffie, Dunlop, Strathern, Taylor and Pittigrew, the visiting London-based Princes club were defeated by 8 goals to 3, on 15 December 1910. Strathern scored five times for the Scots. Later accounts classify this encounter as a Scotland *v.* England match, the second such to be held.

Purchased in 1917 by engineering firm Beardmores for aero engine manufacture, it later became derelict and mainly used as a store.

See next entry.

GLASGOW – CROSSMYLOOF (REBUILD)

Opened:	14 January 1929	Address:
Closed:	End of December 1985	Crossmyloof Ice Rink
Ice Size:	225ft x 97ft (67m x 30m)	Titwood Road
Total Spectator Capacity:	2,000 (3,000 pre-Second World War)	Glasgow G1
Seating Capacity:	950 (2,600 pre-Second World War)	Scotland
Ice Hockey – First Match:		

2 March 1929: Glasgow Canadians 4 *v.* Bearsden 0 (challenge)

Teams:

Kelvingrove	1929–39 Scottish League
Queens University	1929–36 Scottish League
Glasgow Lions	1936–38 Scottish League
Glasgow Mohawks	1929–39 Scottish League; 1946–59 Scottish 'Junior' League(s) & 'Home' tournaments

Glasgow Mustangs	1935–38 Scottish League; 1947–51 Scottish 'Junior' League(s)
Glasgow Flyers	1958–65 'Home' tournaments
Glasgow Dynamos	1966–82 Northern League and Scottish National League 1981/82; 1982/83 British League Division 1 – Section 'A'; 1983–86 British League Division 1
Paisley Mohawks	1971–77 Northern League
Glasgow Redwings	1968/69, 1971–73 & 1974–82 Northern Second/Reserve League
Glasgow Mustangs	1975–81 Northern Junior League

Honours:

Mohawks	1936/37 Champions Scottish League
Dynamos	1966/67 Winners 'Icy' Smith Cup; 1969/70 Champions Northern League Play-offs (Spring Cup)
Mustangs	1975/76 & 1978/79 Champions Scottish Junior League

In 1928 the Scottish Ice Rink Co was formed and the site bought back from Beardmores. A cantilevered roof replaced the pillared one and the ice pad was reconstructed and extended with the ice plant installed by L. Sterne & Co. The rink closed during Second World War to be used as refrigeration store and reopened in October 1946. There was also a 144ft x 100ft annex devoted exclusively to curling. Following the final closure in 1986 the building was damaged by fire the next year, vandalised and subsequently demolished.

During a frosty November and December 1928 Canadians and Glaswegians met at some improvised outdoor hockey games. Four of them – Canadians Stewie Lindsay and Hugh

The annual international. Scotland 1 England 1 at Crossmyloof, Glasgow, 14 March 1936. From left to right, standing: J.R. Gilmour (Hon. Sec. SIHA), W.L. MacDonald (Referee), P. McPhail, W.S. Montford, J.C. Kelly, J. Kenny (Scotland), J. Coward (England), J. Fullerton, W. Fullerton (Scotland), E.J. Ramus, J. Shannon (England), R. McAlpine (Scotland), A. Dick (Referee), G. Graser (Coach, SIHA). Seated: S. Cameron, R.O. McDonald (Scotland), C.A. Erhardt (England), J. Foster (Scotland), A. Child, J. Groome, J. Brenchley, A. Archer, J. Kilpatrick (England). (Weir, Glasgow & Greenock)

Reid together with J. Gilmour and G. Scott – held meetings in early 1929 with rink directors Frank Stuart and Andrew Mitchell. An association was formed and a few games took place on Crossmyloof ice. Next winter ten clubs inaugurated the first Scottish League. After a preliminary round of matches teams were seeded into two divisions, with Mohawks winning the first and Kelvingrove the second. Doonside dropped out and for the next two years nine teams contested the league. For 1932/33 Actungs and Glasgow S.C. folded to be replaced by Juniors. By next winter Queens had gone leaving seven teams. The Bears were the next to go, enabling the six survivors to play each other three times.

From the first year additional knockout competitions took place for the Mitchell Trophy, with from time to time the President's Silver Pucks and the Scottish Cup. From 1935/36 a separate Junior League was formed with each of the remaining clubs providing an entry, except Queens University, back for a last time. Bridge of Weir and Dennistoun Eagles were replaced by Glasgow Mustangs and Glasgow Lions. Games were played in front of a near-capacity house. Prominent in this period were Art Bradly, Gordon Rowley, Jack Easton, Andy Dick, Keith Thompson, Don Porter – all Canadians – Dave Cross, Hugh Reid and Scots Sid Montford and Johnny Fullerton.

In October 1936, with Perth Panthers joining the four Glagow teams, the sport underwent change. Blackhawks joined Panthers for 1937/38 and both rosters were nearly all professional. For the next campaign only Kelvingrove and Mohawks remained at Crossmyloof. A demand by the Canadian players for additional money saw them shown the door. From now on it was amateur hockey only in Glasgow. The home-bred lad benefited, especially in the immediate post-war years under the coaching of Jim Kenny. Sadly he collapsed and died in the engine room at the rink in March 1965. Winning the Banner and Mitchell Trophies during 1946/47 and being finalists in the McPherson Trophy was not a bad start. The Banner was retained the following season, in the 3–2 final victory over Ayr. Mohawks were also finalists in 1950/51 and in the Young Cup.

Prominent at this time were Bill Crawford, Paul Logan, Gus Munro, Frank Jardine and Charlie Huddlestone, a netminder. Jardine was good enough to play for Great Britain at the 1948 Olympics in St Moritz. Crawford served for many years in the pro ranks, principally with Paisley Pirates. Huddlestone's enthusiasm and organisational skills maintained a Mohawks team in competitive hockey well into the 1960s. Up to the late 1940s Mohawks and Mustangs played to large crowds. But this second level of hockey lacked support from the authorities, schedules were not completed, standings not published and teams faded away by early in the next decade, including Glasgow Mustangs.

Mohawks continued, taking part in the one-year Scottish Amateur League of 1955/56 and the similarly short-lived North British League two winters later. By now their home ice was at nearby Paisley. Twice they reached the semi-finals of the Durham-based Northern Tournament and were finalists in 1955. Glasgow Flyers came into being in 1958 to compete in most of the 'home' tournaments around the country, and Section 'B' of the 1963–65 Scottish League. Home-bred players such as John 'Jumbo' Milne, Robert Stevenson and Fred Soulis were regular members of the roster. Practice ice had been regained at Crossmyloof. With the introduction of the Northern League, in the autumn of 1996, Dynamos came into being with new talent emerging such as Tommy Taylor, Rab Ormond, Barrie Stevenson with Jim McDougall in the nets. Reserve side Redwings was formed in 1967. Glasgow won the 'Icy' Smith Cup the same year and the play-offs for the Spring Cup three years on. They were also 'Icy' Smith finalists in 1969 and 1970 and Autumn Cup runners-up. The next campaign Dynamos finished one point behind league champions Murrayfield Racers. By 1971 crowd levels were increasing. R. Stevenson either led the league in scoring or placed second from 1967, for four consecutive years, with an All-Star run to match. He then emigrated to Australia. The advent of the junior Mustangs, coached by Sam Stevenson, unearthed and nurtured Paul Heavey on defence, among others. As the 1980s dawned Martin Shields and John Hester had moved onto the top-ten points scorers list. For three seasons from 1978 Steve Tubb, a Canadian, gained All-Star 'B' accolades for his netminding prowess.

By now the rink had suffered ice plant breakdowns of several weeks duration and a fire or two. With the advent of the British League from 1982/83 Glasgow were naturally grouped with the other four Scottish clubs from the defunct Northern League. For the next campaign a Premier Division emerged with Glasgow, the only Scottish team, pushed down into Division One. With Swedish coach Oke Alm and three imports, the travelling, plus early season injuries, left Dynamos in fifth spot. Under eighty-three-year-old coach Sam Stevenson they moved up to fourth by spring 1985. For Dynamos' final season at Crossmyloof, with crowds of around 350, the team made a sensational start in inflicting Solihull's only league defeat. In early December, at Lee Valley in London, the team disputed a refereeing decision and refused to continue. A player and the coach were suspended. Later that month the rink closed for roof repairs, never to reopen. The Summit Centre had just been completed, which enabled all Glasgow-based hockey activities to continue.

The first radio broadcast commentary on an ice hockey match in Scotland came from Crossmyloof in early January 1937. Local journalist and hockey player, W.S. Montford, described the final play-off contest, won 9–1 by Glasgow Mohawks from Perth Panthers for the President's Silver Puck. Pre-Second World War several annual Scotland *v.* England matches took place, as well as visits by Berlin SC, the University of Manitoba and the national teams of Canada and the USA. English clubs such as Manchester and Grosvenor House Canadians met Scotland on the broad expanse of Crossmyloof ice.

GLASGOW – SUMMIT CENTRE

Opened: 13 February 1986   Address:
Closed: Early 1998   The Summit Centre
Ice Size: 184ft x 85ft (56m x 26m)   Minerva Way
Total Spectator Capacity: Approximately 1,000   Finnieston
Seating Capacity: 600   Glasgow G3 8AU
Ice Hockey – First Match: Scotland
8 March 1986: Glasgow Dynamos 6 *v.* Lee Valley Lions 7
(BL – Division 1)

Teams:

Glasgow Dynamos 1986 British League Division 1; 1992/93 & 1994–96 Scottish
Under-19 League; 1996–98 Scottish Under-21 League

Glasgow Summit Eagles 1986–89 British League Division 1

Glasgow Saints 1990/91 British League Division 1 and Scottish League

Glasgow Redwings 1987–90 & 1995/96 Scottish League Division 1; 1992–93
Scottish Under-18 League

Glasgow Tigers 1987–93 & 1994–98 Scottish Junior/Under-16/17
League/Conference

Glasgow Blackhawks 1990/91 & 1992–98 Scottish Under-14/15
League/Conference

Glasgow Comets 1992/93 & 1994–98 Scottish Under-12/13 League/Conference

Honours:

Tigers 1996/97 Winners Scottish Under-16 Conference 'A'; 1997/98
Winners Scottish Under-17 Conference 'A'; 1997/98
Champions Play-offs

Blackhawks 1993/94 Champions Scottish Under-14 League

Comets 1996/97 Winners Scottish Under-12 Conference 'A' &
Champions Play-offs

The view across the ice. (Russel T. Hutcheson)

Developed and operated by Scotia Arenas Limited, a company owned by ex-Glasgow player David Sinclair, this £1 million-plus shed-like structure was financed by Municipal Insurance Ltd. Located opposite the Scottish Exhibition and Conference Centre, its opening enabled Glasgow Dynamos to switch from the Crossmyloof rink, along with the youth teams, to complete their 1985/86 schedule. Summit's first match was delayed due to the Building Control Officers requiring adjustments to the surrounding plexi-glass and handrails for public safety. With their first training session for nearly three months Dynamos completed their home games in the season's remaining five weeks, drawing an average attendance of around 300. Considering the winter's dramas a fourth-place finish was a reasonable achievement.

For the next season contractual arrangements between the rink's financial backers and the management of the building required Dynamos to be relabelled Glasgow Summit Eagles. Three fresh imports were engaged to blend with the Scots-bred players, with Kenny Redmond (18) proving an effective attacker on 113 points. Spectator attendances averaged 258 with the best at 532. The trio of imports absconded in spring 1988 before the completion of the schedule, leaving a trail of damaged accommodation and debts. Eagles finished fifth. The Under-17 Tigers, in their first year of competition, were runners-up in the Junior Play-offs.

With the abandonment of the one-year regional groups experiment, Glasgow, as the only Scottish club in Division 1, again faced expensive travel costs. Constant personnel changes and financial problems saw Eagles, with only four wins, face relegation.

After a year away from semi-pro hockey John Hester formed the Glasgow Saints. With imports Todd Annand, Terry McCutchoen and Doug Marsden plus Tony and Kenny Redmond and backstopped by Gerry Anderson, they won over twice as many games as Eagles. Fourteen successive losses, followed by five straight victories were insufficient to avoid the relegation play-offs. The losing steak returned and Saints were no more, in spite of the efforts of coach Martin Shields, who returned to the ice on a diet of painkillers. Crowds averaging less than 300 did not help.

The youth programme continued, with some success, until the rink finally shut down in early 1998. It is now used as a gymnasium which includes a swimming pool.

GLASGOW – BRAEHEAD

Opened:	21 September 1999	Address:
Ice Size:	197ft x 98ft (60m x 30m)	Braehead Arena
Total Spectator Capacity:	4,000	Kings Inch Road
Seating Capacity:	4,000	Glasgow G51 48N
Ice Hockey – First Match:		Scotland

29 September 2002: Scottish Eagles 3 *v.* Manchester Storm 2 (Challenge Cup)

Teams:
Scottish Eagles   2002 Superleague and Challenge Cup

Braehead is part of a £285 million ice and retail complex developed by Braehead Park Ltd and Capital Shopping Centres. There is also a 50m x 35m curling rink at first-floor level and a circular leisure rink located on the ground floor at one end of the retail mall. The complex, sited adjacent to the Clyde waterfront on the western edge of Glasgow, opened for the 1999 World Curling Championships. Since April 2000 it has been operated by SMG (Spectacor).

With crowd levels dropping at the Bill Barr-owned Ayr Centrum, he decided a move nearer to the Glasgow conurbation, for his Scottish Eagles, would prove a better draw. A subsidiary company, Eagles Hockey Ltd, was set-up with Belfast Giants' owner Albert Massland as a director, holding twenty-five per cent of the shares, with Bob Zeller, Giants' previous MD. A crowd of 2,466 watched Braehead's first ice hockey match, 700 up on the previous season's average at the Centrum. Manchester's Geoff Peters scored the first ever goal on Braehead ice within the first minute. In the succeeding four matches, split between the Challenge Cup and the Superleague, attendances varied between 984 and 2,429. With franchise transfer arrangements completed seven weeks before the opening fixture, it was a wildly over-optimistic timescale in which to recruit a team and carry out marketing in an area new to the sport. The roster, under their Glaswegian manager-coach Paul Heavy, was remarkably successful. Their finest performance was at Rouen in the Continental Cup in mid-October. With four regulars missing, and Paddy Ward the sole Scot, Eagles overcame Storhamer of Norway 2–1. The following evening Rouen went down 6–2, with Jeff Johnstone netting four goals. Nottingham on 3 November witnessed the last appearance of Scottish Eagles. The company operating the Eagles went into liquidation, after running up debts of £153,839 in less than six months. All players were released on 8 November 2002 after just 14 games, their statistics being expunged from the records. The Friends of Eagles Hockey's fundraising produced £21,000 to pay off the wages owed to the players and coaching staff. Ice hockey has not been held since at what is a superb viewing facility.

GLENROTHES

Opened:	14 September 1984	Address:
Closed:	October 1993	Crystals Arena
Ice Size:	146ft x 73ft (44.5m x 28.5m)	Viewfield Estate
Total Spectator Capacity:	150	Glenrothes
Seating Capacity:	Minimal	Fife
Ice Hockey – First Match:		Scotland

Glenrothes Jets playing challenge games during 1985/86

Teams:

Glenrothes Jets	1986/87 British League Division 2 – Scotland (Scottish League Division 1); 1987/88 & 1989–93 Scottish League Division 1
Glenrothes Harriers	1986–88 & 1989–92 Scottish Junior League
Glenrothes Spitfires	1986–88 & 1989–91 Scottish Pee-Wee League; 1992/93 Scottish Under-14 League
Glenrothes Hawks	1989/90 & 1991–93 Scottish Under-12 League
Glenrothes Tornadoes	1991/92 Scottish Under-18 League; 1992/93 Scottish Under-19 League
Tayside Tigers	1989/90 and 1992/93 Scottish League Division 1

Developed by Pimley Estates, with the shed-like structure resembling a similar Pimley venture at Bangor, Northern Ireland. The rink covered half of the overall building, with a mix of carpet bowls, a disco venue and bar occupying the remainder. The small ice, with minimal spectator facilities, suffered commercially from the presence of the full-sized Kirkcaldy rink about five miles to the south.

Jets v. Paisley Pirates in 1993. (Simon Walton/*IHNR*)

The senior team's best performance was Jets' fourth place at the end of 1987/88, in the eight-member Scottish League Division 1. They also made it to the play-off semi-finals. Fourth was again achieved in spring of 1992, with six teams participating. Jets were coached by the late Milan Figala, who hailed from Czechoslovakia. At the end of the previous campaign Milan, recently with Fife Flyers, coached Jets to the Spring Cup final. Ake Alm, originally from Sweden, also stood behind the bench in 1992/93. During most of these years Richard Latto spent many hours each week on club management.

Jets continued for two seasons, based at Livingston, following the closure of Crystals. Homeless Tayside Tigers also used Glenrothes as their base for a couple of seasons.

A youth development programme was established at the same time as the senior Jets. Both were interrupted by the temporary closure, resulting in the loss of the 1988/89 season. Harriers made it to the semi-finals of the Junior League Play-offs in their second campaign. Andrew Samuel of Tornadoes was near the top of the Under-19 scoring list in spring 1994. By early April his stats stood at 28 goals and 14 assists from 9 matches.

Prior to the rink's final closure, when the management company went into liquidation owing £50,000 in rates, the facility had ceased operations in the summer of 1988, to reopen on 1 September of the following year. The mortgage holder – Glenrothes Development Corporation – informed the ice hockey clubs using the rink at the time of closure that the ice facility would be retained. In the spring of 1995 the authorities announced that the rink would never reopen.

GOSPORT

Opened:	6 October 1989	Address:
Ice Size:	145ft x 73ft (40m x 20m)	Gosport Ice Rink
Total Spectator Capacity:	800	Forest Way
Seating Capacity:	Approximately 300 on benches	Fareham Road
Ice Hockey – First Match:		Gosport
7 October 1989: Southampton Knights v. Slough Harrier		Hampshire PO13 0ZX
Hawks (English League Division 2)		England

Teams:

Southampton Knights   1989–91 English League Division 2 – South; 1991/92 English Under-21 'A' League – South; 1994/95 English Conference – South

Gosport Dreadnoughts   1989/90 English League Division 3 – South; 1990/91 English League Division 3 – Central; 1991/92 English Conference National Division; 1992/93 English Conference – Wharry Division

Gosport Knights	1992–94 English Conference – South
Bournemouth Whalers	1992/93 English Conference – South
Gosport Seakings	1993/94 English League; 1994–99 English Conference – South
Solent Lightning	1999/2000 Millennium Cup – Group A
Solent & Gosport Sharks	2003/04 English National League – South
Gosport Lightning	1996–99 English Under-19 League
Solent Storm	1999/2000 English Under-19 League 'A'
Gosport/Solent Devils	2001–05 English Under-19 League
Gosport Cruisers	1989–92, 1993–99 & 2000–04 English Junior/Under-16 League/Conference
Solent & Gosport Cruisers	2004/05 English Under-16 League
Gosport Hunters	1990/91,1992–95,1996/97,1998–2002 English Under-14 League/Conference
Solent & Gosport Hunters	2002–05 English Under-14 League
Gosport Hunters	1989/90 & 1997/98 English Under-12 League
Gosport/Solent Destroyers	1990–92 & 1998–05 English Under-12 League

Honours:

Knights	1990/91 Winners English League (Under-21) Division 2 – South 'A'; 1992/93 Winners English Conference – South Division
Devils	2004/05 Winners English Under-19 League – South Division 2
Cruisers	2004/05 Winners English Under-16 League – South Division 2

Almost a carbon copy of the Aldershot rink and developed by the same business, Gaul & Co., which, not long after Gosport opened, went into receivership. At two-thirds the minimum required ice size for hockey the British Ice Hockey Association (BIHA), prohibited 'import' hockey. As the Southampton rink closed in the summer prior to Gosport opening, large numbers of their younger player pool formed the Gosport club. A further influx occurred when Bournemouth shut early in 1991. A Bournemouth-based league team operated out of Gosport for two years, until the strain of the continual travelling took its toll.

Sensibly, those controlling the various ice hockey programmes have never attempted to run any form of semi-pro senior team and continue to abide by the ruling of the now defunct BIHA. As a consequence a seeming myriad of youth teams from Under-12 up to Under-19 are able to utilise the ice. The club changed their name to Solent & Gosport in spring 2002. With the closure of Southampton and then Bournemouth, where the sport had been played on and off since the early 1930s, Gosport is the only remaining ice surface along the South Coast with any form of league-based ice hockey.

In 1999 Planet Ice took over the management of the rink. It is now run by Parkwood Leisure.

GRIMSBY – LADYSMITH ROAD

Opened:	9 August 1930	Address:
Closed:	1956	Grimsby Ice Rink
Ice Size:	165ft x 58ft (156ft x 55ft prior to 1936)	Ladysmith Road Grimsby
Total Spectator Capacity:	1,000	Lincolnshire
Seating Capacity:	Nil	England
Ice Hockey – First Match:		

First intercity – November 1937: Grimsby 4 *v.* Manchester 6 (challenge)

Teams:

Grimsby Redwings   Founded 1937, reformed 1947; 1950–59 'Home' tournaments;
                        1951–55 Midland League.
A local City League (house league) operated on Monday nights for many years, consisting
of four teams – Red Hawks, Wolves, Columbia and Lions.

Honours:

Redwings   1952/53 & 1954/55 Champions Midlands Intermediate League;
                        1950–55 Winners Grimsby Tournament

Built as an experiment by F.A. Wood Ltd and C.W. Edwards Ltd, there were columns down
the centre of the ice. These were removed in the summer of 1936 with the ice surface
increased in size during general upgrading, for a reopening on 19 September of that year.
A form of ice hockey was first played in 1932 at Ladysmith Road. As the nearest teams were
at Manchester and Birmingham, 120 miles distant, the Grimsby and District Ice Hockey
League came into being. A year later the best players formed the Redwings. Reg Mason,
one of these pioneers, coached and captained Redwings post-Second World War when they
reformed in 1947. The team's first match was held on 8 January 1949 as Grimsby defeated
Liverpool Leopards 7–6. Redwings won every final of their own Grimsby Tournament,
before a packed house.

   The years of the four-club Midland League were 'Wings finest, twice becoming champions. The pick of the scorers, all home bred, were Dave Baxter, Doug Smith and Steve
Gibbs. Their star, Pat Mudd, learnt to play while an evacuee to Canada. He represented
Britain at the 1953 World Championships. Netminder Don Oslear made a name for himself as a Test match cricket umpire. John Letton bought the loss making facility in 1950 and
overhauled the freezing plant. After the rink closed in 1956 Redwings managed to continue
for a further three seasons. The building was then used for some years by Birdseye Foods as
a potato crisp factory. It was demolished in the late 1960s.

GRIMSBY – CROMWELL ROAD

Opened: 14 February 1975   Address:
Ice Size: 120ft x 60ft (36.5m x 18m)   Grimsby Leisure
Total Spectator Capacity: 1,000 (1,300 when first opened)   Centre
Seating Capacity: Nil   Cromwell Road
Ice Hockey – First Match: Grimsby
6 September 1975: Grimsby Buffaloes 3 v. Solihull Barons 12   Lincolnshire
                                                               DN31 2BH England

Teams:

Grimsby Buffaloes   1975–78 Southern 'A' League; 1978–82 Midland League;
                         1982/83 British League Division 2 – North; 1983–85 British
                         League Division 1; 1985–87 British League Division 2 –
                         North; 1987/88 English League North; 1989–91 English
                         League Division 2; 1991–93 English Under-21 League;
                         1997/98 English Under-19 League; 1998/99 English League
                         Division 1 – North; 2000–04 English Conference – North
Grimsby Redwings   1990/91 English League Division 3 – North; 1991/92 English
                         Conference National Division; 1992/93 English Conference
                         – Wharry Division; 1993/94 English Conference; 1994–96
                         English Conference – North
Grimsby Tornadoes   1977/78 Southern 'B' League; 1978–82 Midland League
                         Division 2

Grimsby Dynamos	1976–78 Southern Junior League; 1979–82 Inter-City Junior League; 1982–86, 1987–97 and 1998–2005 English Junior/Under-16 League/Conference
Grimsby Ghosts	1980/81 Inter-City Pee-Wee (Under-13) League; 1996–2005 English Under-12 League
Grimsby Jets	1989/90, 1993–98 English Pee-Wee/Under-14 League
Grimsby Vikings	1998–2005 English Under-14 League
Grimsby Blackhawks	2001–05 English Under-19 League

Honours:

Buffaloes	1982/83, 1985/86 and 1986/87 Winners British League Division 2 – North; 1990/91 Winners English League Division 2 North 'B' (Under-21)
Tornadoes	1980/81 Champions Midland League Division 2
Dynamos	1976/77 Winners Southern Junior League Midland Section; 1979/80 & 1981/82 Champions Inter-City Junior League; 1982/83 Champions English Junior League; 1991/92 Winners English Junior 'B' League – North
Redwings	1990/91 Winners English League Division 3 – North
Vikings	2000–01 Winners English Under-14 'B' League – North
Ghosts	1998/99 Winners English Under-12 'B' League – North

Part of a Grimsby Borough Council developed and owned sports complex, which includes a sports hall, indoor bowling, squash and a 'fun swimming pool'. Virtually as soon as the ice was laid players from Grimsby's previous rink reformed the club. Prominent were secretary Alan Woodhead, who first held that post in 1951, chairman Ron Burnett and treasurer Bob Baxter. The latter, along with Harry Finning, Art Smith and Roy Southwell was among others from the previous Redwings to don skates to become the core of the new Buffaloes. To finish fourth in the Southern 'A' League was a commendable beginning for coach Reg Mason.

A capacity attendance of 1,300 was achieved on 21 February in a 5–10 loss to Sheffield Lancers. The four-team local league was soon re-established. Promising youngsters such as Martin Hall, who later played for Cambridge University, Mike Tutty, a GB Under-18 by 1979, Dave Welch and netminder John Wolfe were emerging. Defenceman Martin Weddell has been the CEO at Bracknell for some years. Dynamos won the Southern Junior League in their first year of competition, a feat repeated three campaigns later.

With the coming of the British League for 1982/83 Buffaloes were allocated to Division 2. They won their regional 20-game schedule, losing out to Solihull, and their two imports, 8–5 in the play-off. Sean Blisset on 49 points and Mike Sleath with 32 were first-second in North section scoring. Crowds were around the 750 mark. Next winter the two regions were amalgamated to form BL Division 1. Without imports, against most other teams' three, Buffaloes slipped to fifth. Blisset made the British Under-18 squad in the European Championships. Grimsby moved back to the second division table as the richer clubs, based on full-sized ice surface, attracted better and costly imports.

Winning the Northern group took Buffaloes to the play-offs at first year Cardiff. Losing their semi-final to the rookie Devils, the Lincolnshire lads poached the third place in a 9–6 win over Streatham Bruins. With the advent of Hull's full-sized arena, and their local authority-funded Seahawks in September 1988, Grimsby players migrated over the Humber. Among them were Lee Barley, Blissett, Sleeth, Jon Patterson and netminder Steve Yorston. From twenty-five registered players nine remained. Buffaloes were forced to withdraw from senior hockey.

Ice hockey at Hull has remained a continual draw for players and their followers from south of the Humber. Buffaloes returned to the ice and the lower ranks of the English League in autumn 1989. From the following season they competed at the Under-21 level, then the Under-19s as the English I.H. Association reduced the qualifying age. This enabled a switch, from 1990/91, to a revived Redwings label. Both squads won their respective league group in the first season of this new arrangement. Mike Sleeth and Sean Blisset, back at Cromwell Road, topped the Division 3 scoring chart at 94 and 79 points respectively. Next winter the junior Dynamos followed the example set by their older club mates, winning their region of the English Under-16 'B' League.

By the mid-1990s the club needed to raise £10,000 per annum at senior level. Although all the players were simon-pure amateur, travel costs to away fixtures and match officials' expenses for home games had to be met. Some assistance was obtained in the form of an annual £1,000 grant from the Humberside County Council. Redwings folded at the commencement of the 1996/97 campaign as players defected to the new Kingston Hawks. A period of consolidation followed as Jets, then Vikings and Ghosts maintained a continuing presence in the Under-14 and Under-12 leagues. From 1998 until spring 2004 Buffaloes competed in senior hockey, helped by Nick Chambers' scoring prowess. In 2001 the Under-19 Blackhawks completed the final stepping-stone in the Grimsby youth programme.

The one constant is Alan Woodhead, club secretary in 2005, over half a century from first undertaking the role.

GUILDFORD

Opened:	January 1993	Address:
Ice Size:	197ft x 98ft (60m x 30m)	Guildford Spectrum
Total Spectator Capacity:	2,200 (including 5 executive	Parkway
	boxes)	Guildford GU1 1UP
Seating Capacity:	1,800	Surrey
Ice Hockey – First Match:		England

23 January 1993: Guildford Flames 13 v. Stevenage Sharks 3 (EL).

Teams:

Guildford Flames   1992/93 English League Division 1 – Conference 'B'; 1993/94 British League Division – South; 1994–96 British League Division 1; 1996/97 Premier League; 1997–2005 British National League; 1997/98 Southern Premier League

Guildford Firestars   1993–2005 English Under-16 Conference/League
Guildford Firestorm   1993–2005 English Under-14 Conference/League
Guildford Fireflies   1993–2005 English Under-12 Conference/League
Guildford Phoenix   1994–2005 English Under-19 League

Honours:

Flames   1992/93 Winners English League Division 1 South; 1997/98 Champions Southern Premier League; 1998/99 Winners Benson & Hedges Plate; 1997/98 & 2000/01 Champions British National League and Play-offs; 2000/01 Winners Christmas Cup; 2003/04 BNL Play-off Champions

Phoenix   2002/03 and 2004/05 Champions English Under-19 League
Firestars   1995/96 Champions British and English Junior (Under-16) Conference; 1996/97 Winners English Under-16 'A' League – South; 2003/04 Champions English Under-16 League
Firestorm   1994/95 Winners English Under-14 Conference – South West; 1998/99 & 2001–04 Winners English Under-14 'A' League – South; 2003/04 Champions English Under-14 League
Fireflies   2001/02 & 2004/05 Winners English Under-12 'A' League – South

Publications:
Guildford Flames 1992/93–2001/02 10th Anniversary Annual (2001), Sportfact Ltd

The rink is part of a £30 million local authority-owned and managed sports complex, which also includes swimming pools, squash courts, a bowling alley, conference facilities and a health suite. As with several other rinks of this period, the smart and crisp design is marred by poor sightlines from the balcony seating along both lengths of the rink. This time the shallow rake of the seating and steel front handrail are to blame.

Flames' first owner Barry Dow, an American international banker who had worked in London for the previous eleven years, engaged the husband-and-wife team of Mike as player-coach and Laura Urquart as team manager. Flames were forced to spend the first four-and-a-half months of their existence in the English League 'on the road'.

The rink's original opening date of 4 October 1992 failed to be met. Mike recruited the Canadian attack duo of Sean Murphy and Dave McGahan, previously with the Isle of Wight, defender Darrin Zinger as the third import with Mike Kellond in goal, supported by a myriad of British bred talent. The delayed opening game attracted a capacity crowd. Packing the remaining 15 home fixtures into eleven weeks drew an average attendance of 2,122 as Flames won Conference 'B' by four points. Restructuring of the British League saw Flames in Division 1 – South for the next campaign. Three new college-educated imports – Paul Thompson (born in Grimsby), Rob Friesen and Ryan Campbell – joined. Nineteen-year-old Danny Thompson took over as first choice netminder. Results took a dive after Christmas. By March the suspected cash crisis surfaced over unpaid player wages. A deal was patched up and Flames survived for a fifth-placed finish in the eight member Southern Section. The plus side to the season was the entry of Firestars, Firestorm and Fireflies into the Under-16, Under-14 and Under-12 leagues. Mike Urquhart is renowned for his work at youth level.

This second season at the Spectrum saw Canadian John Hepburn, an investment banker and vice-chairman of Morgan Stanley International's London operations, volunteer his services to assist the cash-strapped club. From helping with the youth training Hepburn, who has four sons, joined with Ryan and a local councillor to put together a business plan acceptable to Guildford Council. A consortium was formed with the necessary commercial acumen to secure extensive and continuing sponsorship. A regime still in place in 2005 with Hepburn at the helm as chairman.

Ex-referee and netminder Ron Charbonneau became general manager. The much-travelled imports Terry Kurtenbach and Fred Perlini joined the five retained players. Their experience benefited Brits Andrew Sparks, Nicky Iandoli and Elliot Andrews – a GB Under-20 team member. Flames finished seventh. Bob Zeller came in for a one-year stint as MD. A one-place improvement to mid-table in an expanded Division 1, the last for the two-division BL, was reasonable progress. Sparks retired, along with his playing number, to become the first Flame to be so honoured. At Wembley Arena Firestars defeated Fife 3–2 in the British Junior Championship.

With the formation of the Superleague for 1996/97 Guildford resisted blandishments to throw in their lot with the 'Arena' based group. They joined the new eight-member Premier League with Valerie Vassie in charge day-to-day. The Bosman ruling significantly increased the number of non-British-trained players, including deadline signing Petri Engman, a Finnish goalie. A drop-off in form ensured fourth in the league and the play-offs. Crowds levelled out to average 1,515, a figure that has since stayed fairly constant. The advent of the British National League (BNL) from autumn 1997 coincided with the arrival of ex-Swindon coach Stan Marple. Triumph followed as Flames garnished a trio of titles. Pearce Barclay, Mike Harding and Pete Karowski, all from Alberta, put the puck in the opponents' goal. Jamie Organ and Englishman Simon Smith kept them out at the other end. Next winter the offensively talented and hard-working Flames' third place was an anti-climax. Cohesion was lost when a controversial incident at the Spectrum in January 1999 caused a season ending injury to outstanding netminder Organ. The 4–3 victory over

Opening night. (T. Benbrook/*IHNR*)

Telford in the B & H Plate final in December was the only silverware as the campaign closed with a play-off semi-final.

Two years on and Marple and his team repeated the triple collection of trophies. Scotsmen David Smith and John Haig from Fife were signed, with veteran Wayne Crawford added. Fourth at the turn of the year, Marple snapped up Welshman Nicky Chinn. Flames went on a 24-match winning streak. They nicked the BNL title by three points from local rivals Basingstoke, and pipped Bison to the play-off crown. By Flames' standards the next two years were fallow, although most clubs would consider being semi-finalists in the play-offs (twice) and Challenge Cup satisfactory. During 2002/03 Marple signed up five players with NHL credentials. Next autumn they had been replaced by five East Europeans including Ratislav Palov, Marian Smerciak and Milos Melicherik. Flames topped the Challenge Cup standings, contested the final and won the play-offs. Flames were 2004/05 BNL losing play-off finalists in the three-match series with Dundee with NHL refugees David Oliver and Jamie McLennan as late additions. Veteran British defender Paul Dixon gained an All-Star 'A' place.

The efforts put into youth development also paid off, especially for the Under-14 Firestorm, with three successive titles from 2001. The future of ice hockey burns bright at the Spectrum.

HAMILTON

Opened:	1968	Address:
Ice Size:	145ft x 95ft (45m x 27m)	Lanarkshire Ice Rink
Total Spectator Capacity:	Nil (a lounge bar overlooks the ice)	Low Parks off Muir Street
Seating Capacity:	Nil	Hamilton ML3 6BS
Ice Hockey – First Match:		South Lanarkshire
c. 1985 – details unknown		Scotland

Teams:
Hamilton Hawks   *c.* 1985–2004 (recreational only)

Built primarily for curling. Public skating is usually limited to one day a week. Hawks founded as a recreational ice hockey club in mid-1980s.

HASTINGS

Opened:	December 1980	Address:
Closed:	*c.* 1987	White Rock Ice Rink
Ice Size:	80ft x 40ft (24m x 12m)	White Rock
Total Spectator Capacity:	Minimal	Hastings
Seating Capacity:	Nil	East Sussex
Ice Hockey – First Match:		TN34 1JY
Club formed in spring 1984. All games away.		England

Teams:
Hastings Arrows   1984/85 British League Division 2 – South
Hastings Monarchs   1986/87 British League Division 2 – South; 1987/88 English
                   League – South

Formally the White Rock swimming baths, then a skateboard arena, prior to the area below the seafront promenade being utilised for an ice rink. By summer 2002 this had reverted to a skateboard centre and is now (March 2004) derelict. Not surprisingly, with such a small piece of ice, both teams fared badly in league play. They won only 2 of their 44 games, plus a draw in 1987/88 and tied one during 1986/87.

HOVE – DENMARK VILLAS

Opened:	23 December 1929	Address:
Closed:	27 February 1932	Hove and Brighton Ice Rink
Ice Size:	180ft x 85ft	84–86 Denmark Villas
Total Spectator Capacity:	2,000	Hove
Seating Capacity:	Unknown	East Sussex
Ice Hockey – First Match:		England
11 February 1930: England 1 *v.* Canada 11(challenge)		

Teams:
Sussex   1930 challenge games; 1931/32 English League Division 1
Sussex County   1931/32 challenge games

The rink was located adjacent to Hove railway station and was constructed in four months at a cost of £70,000, on open land that had been a nursery garden. The mayor of Hove, Arthur Bartlett, laid the foundation stone on 14 September 1929. There was limited seating at ice level and on the first-floor balcony, which contained a spacious gallery at the eastern end.

In late February 1930 London Lions came to Hove, to win 17–3 in the first game featuring a locally based team. Sussex then entered the knockout 'Junior' Cup. Given a bye into the semi-final J. Langmead and R. Hill scored at home in the 4–3 loss to Princes II on 9 April. The Sussex line-up was A. Langmead, H. West, W.P. Tretheway, C. James, P. Hill

The frontage to Denmark Villas
(Brighton & Hove Libraries)

Interior view. (Brighton &
Hove Libraries)

and R.P. Morgan. Almost as many internationals were held as domestic games. The BIHA beat Berlin SC, billed as 'Germany', 5–2 on 12 March. Seven days later England defeated Switzerland 4–2. Sussex were represented by W.P. Tretheway. France went down 4–1 on 2 April, with the veteran B.M. 'Peter' Patton in goal for England. Carl Erhardt of Princes, later of 1936 Olympic GB gold medal fame, was also in the line-up. Princes played two of their British League matches at Hove in early spring. Next autumn Hove again witnessed internationals. England met Berlin SC in November, and on 3 March lost 7–0 to the University of Manitoba. They beat Davos eleven days on, lost to France on the 25th and drew 2–2 with Austria on the last day of that month. Sussex also met Davos, when the Swiss won.

For the third and final season of the sport at Denmark Villas Sussex competed in Division 1 of the English League without much success. Tretheway netted the only goal in Sussex's first EL match at home on 21 November, a 5–1 victory by Princes. Two weeks later Hill was the only scorer in the 3–1 loss to Grosvenor House Canadians. They did manage a draw with Manchester before Oxford University, ultimately the league champions, came to Hove to administer a 9–1 walloping on 1 February. The only international that winter was a 1–1 cracker, in front of a packed rink on 2 January as Sussex met the Scottish League. West, for Sussex, scored in the first period with H. Tingley, a Canadian, replying in the second frame. It may have been the comparative lack of on-ice success by Sussex that caused the rink owner to publish, in the local press, a notice stating that the rink would close on Saturday 27 February. This was also the day of the last ice hockey match at Hove as Sussex hosted Princes. Four fixtures went unfulfilled.

As the 'talkies' had arrived the ice rink was converted into the Lido Cinema. Around 1960 it became a Top Rank bowling alley, followed by use as a builders' merchants. The building was demolished in 1969.

HOVE – SEAFRONT

Opened:	June 1976	Address:
Closed:	June 1977	King Alfred Centre
Ice Size:	60ft x 20ft (18m x 6m)	Seafront
Total Spectator Capacity:	Minimal	Hove
Seating Capacity:	Nil	East Sussex
Ice Hockey – First Match:		England

Youngsters practised on Sunday mornings.

Teams:

Brighton Royals   1976/77 challenge games (away games only – mainly at Streatham)

Brighton Tigers Cubs   1976/77 challenge games (Under-16 away games only – mainly at Streatham)

Part of a complex that included a swimming pool originally constructed in 1938 and extended in 1982. The ice pad, which cost £10,000, was laid in the basement that previously housed a car wash. It was operated as a private club with a membership of 500. The people behind this venture were Bill Burn and Valerie Moon.

Brighton and Hove City Council have selected architect Frank Gehry for the proposed £290 million redevelopment of the site as a landmark sports and housing complex.

HULL

Opened:	14 September 1988	Address:
Ice Size:	197ft x 98ft (60m x 30m)	The Hull Arena
Total Spectator Capacity:	2,000	Kingston Street
Seating Capacity:	1,400 (originally 2,000 on pull-	Kingston upon Hull
	out benching)	HU1 2DZ East Riding
Ice Hockey – First Match:		of Yorkshire

18 September 1988: Humberside Seahawks 13 *v.* Solihull Knights 4 (English League Division 1)

Address:
The Hull Arena
Kingston Street
Kingston upon Hull
HU1 2DZ East Riding
of Yorkshire
England

Teams:

Humberside Seahawks   1988/89 English League Division 1; 1989–91 British League Division 1; 1991–93 British League Premier Division

Humberside Hawks   1993–96 British League Premier Division

Kingston Hawks   1996/97 Premier League; 1997–99 British National League

Hull Thunder   1999–2003 British National League

Hull Stingrays   2003–05 British National League

Humberside Hurricanes   1989–91 English League Division 2; 1991–93 English Under-21 League; 1994–96 English Under-19 League

Kingston Hurricanes   1996/97 English Under-19 League

Humberside Cobras   1989–91 English League Division 3; 1991/92 English League National Division; 1992–94 English Conference

Humberside Jets   1994–96 English Conference

Kingston Jets   1996–98 English League Conference; 1998–2001 English League Division 1; 2001–05 English National League

Kingston Predators   1997–2005 English Under-19 League

Humberside Blades	1990–98 English Under-16 League/Conference
Kingston Crunch	1998–2005 English Under-16 League
Humberside Spitfires	1991–96 English Under-14 League/Conference
Kingston Spitfires	1996–98 English Under-14 League
Kingston Aeros	1998–2005 English Under-14 League
Humberside Humdingers	1990–95 English Under-12 League/Conference
Humberside Flyers	1995/96 English Under-12 Conference
Kingston Flyers	1996/97 English Under-12 League
Kingston Rivermen	1997–2005 English Under-12 League

Honours:

Seahawks	1988/89 Champions English League and Winners Autumn Trophy; 1990/91 Winners British League Division 1
Jets	1995/96 Winners English Conference – North
Hurricanes	1993/94 & 1996/97 Champions English Under-21 League
Predators	1997/98 Champions English Under-19 League; 1998/99 & 2000/01 Winners English Under-19 'A' League – North
Blades	1995/96 Winners English Under-16 Conference – North
Crunch	2001/02 Champions English Under-16 League
Spitfires	1993/94 Champions English Under-14 Conference
Aeros	1998/99 Winners English Under-14 'B' League – North; 1999/00 Winners English 'A' League – North
Humdingers	1994/95 Winners English Under-12 Conference – North
Rivermen	1998/99 Winners English Under-12 'A' League – North; 2000/01 Champions English Under-12 League

Publications:
End Of An Ice Age – History Of The Humberside Seahawks: 1988-93, Mowforth, Ian, 2005

Originally known as Humberside Ice Arena, set in what had been derelict docklands. A local authority (now Hull City Council) developed and financed the rink, costing £3.2 million – whose foundation stone was laid by The Queen on 17 June 1987. Plexi-glass surrounds were installed prior to staging the World Senior Pool C Championships on 18–24 March 1991– won by Great Britain. Individual plastic tip-up seats were fitted in lieu of the original benches in the late 1990s.

The outstanding youth development programme is partly due to initial finances from the public purse and to the continuing teaching and motivational skills of Peter Johnson. Seahawks achieved a rapid rise, helped by generous local authority funding. Rink manager Adrian Florence engaged Dale Lambert as player-manager and coach. Dale signed Mark Mackie, a fellow Canadian, as the second import, to add to the almost ready-made roster from Grimsby. Seahawks secured the English League title, and promotion, with a game in hand in spring 1989. Spectators averaged out at 1,724. Scott Morrison replaced Mackie, with Ross Lambert joining his brother. A fourth place at the first attempt in Division 1 of the Heineken-sponsored British League was satisfactory. Earlier 'Hawks won the Autumn Trophy. A third-year triumph followed with a division title, and promotion to the Premier with a play-off group six wins from six.

Peter Johnson, a home-bred product from Durham, came in as bench coach. He brought with him his three sons Stephen, Anthony and Shaun. The first two led the scoring at 80 and 73 points. Shaun bagged 41. Scots-Canadian Andy Donald stopped pucks at the other end. By the following campaign, after reaching the Autumn Cup final, injuries took their toll. With import Mike Bishop and Kevin McNaught, several player changes and the addition of Dan Dorian, inconsistency resulted in seventh place in spring of 1993. A 6–4 Group A play-off away victory at Bracknell sent Humberside to the Wembley finals. With the scores locked at 4–4 in the second semi-final, MacNaught broke the deadlock with

Hull interior c. 1989

Nottingham at 6.36 into the sudden-death overtime. Next afternoon Cardiff overcame a tired Seahawks 7–4. Lambert departed Humberside after five years and 171 games, during which he scored 271 goals and 424 points.

Sponsorship from British Aerospace shortened the name to Hawks. Three years later, with newly appointed Keith Milhench behind the bench, Hawks reached the British Championship weekend for the second time. In the last ever Wembley Arena finals Sheffield overcame Hawks 6–3 in the semi-final, to win the championship next day. Scott Morrison, in four seasons on Humberside, piled up 589 points from 297 goals in league matches. With local government reorganisation and the withdrawal of the county council's subsidy Hawks were no more. In came Milhench as owner of the new Kingston Hawks. By mid-November 1996 a season-ending £50,000 deficit loomed. Players came and went, but Hawks survived to spend the next two years in the newly founded British National League.

In the first year a third place and being play-off finalists were a minor triumph on a limited budget. A year on, with Dale Lambert back as coach, a cash-strapped Milhench failed to save the club from sinking in a welter of unpaid bills. In stepped former rink manager Adrian Florence, as the now Hull City Hawks completed 1998/99. A new season brought a new name and owners. For the next four campaigns, under three different ownership regimes Hull Thunder, with numerous roster changes, tried the patience of their long-suffering fans. Crowd levels had fallen to around 1,000. The team dropped from fourth at the end of year one to ninth by the end of the fourth season.

For 2003 Mike and Sue Pack came in, with Rick Strachan as coach, as Stingrays became the sixth semi-pro Hull-based team. They brought financial stability, although a better-than-cellar finish had been hoped for by the core base of nearly 600 fans. Next year they were rewarded with fourth, although 'Rays failed to progress to the semi-finals of the play-offs.

Throughout all the turbulence Hull's youth teams, from the Under-19s down to the eleven-year-olds, had been consistently bringing league titles to Kingston.

INVERNESS

Opened:	22 July 1968	Address:
Ice Size:	168ft x 73ft (51m x 22m)	Inverness Ice Centre
Total Spectator Capacity:	300	Bught Park
Seating Capacity:	Nil	Inverness
Ice Hockey – First Match:		IV3 5SR
4 December 1988: Kirkcaldy Kestrals 7 v. Dundee Cougars		Scotland
6 (challenge) part of an ice sports cavalcade		

Teams:

Inverness Jaguars	2001–03 Scottish National League
Inverness Senators	1994–99 Scottish Under-16/17 League/Conference
Inverness Trojans	1999–2003 Scottish Under-16 League
Inverness Trojans	1994–99 Scottish Under-14/15 League/Conference
Inverness Spartans	1999–2002 and 2004/05 Scottish Under-14 League
Inverness Spartans	1996–99 Scottish Under-12/13 League/Conference
Inverness Titans	1999–2001 Scottish Under-12 League
Inverness Senators	1999–2001 Scottish Under-18 League

Minimal spectator seating is behind the glass-fronted first-floor café. Rink ownership changed hands during 2002 as Aviemore-based businessman David Cameron acquired the rink, as an unwanted portion of a package of properties he purchased. He promptly offered to sell the building for £250,000 to a group of local skaters. They obtained £131,000 in funding from the Lottery and formed a board of directors who now run the rink. An ice hockey club was born in late 1988. It took a further six years until enough players, in the Under-14 and Under-16 age groups, had developed skills for exposure to league-based competitions.

The Inverness club withdrew all their league teams in August 2003 due to insufficient numbers, although the Under-14 Spartans reappeared for 2004/05. As for Elgin, the town's northerly location and relatively modest population act against team-based ice sports.

IRVINE

Opened:	18 September 1976	Address:
Ice Size:	145ft x 95ft (44m x 27m)	Magnum Leisure Park
Total Spectator Capacity:	750	Harbour Street
Seating Capacity:	Minimal	Irvine
Ice Hockey – First Match:		North Ayrshire

11 October 1980: Irvine Challengers 3 v. Glasgow Redwings 2 (Northern Reserve League)

KA2 8PP Scotland

Teams:

Irvine Challengers	1979–82 Northern Reserve League – Scottish Section
Irvine Magnum Wings	1983–85 British League Division 2 – Scotland; 1986/87 British League Division 1; 1987/88 Scottish League Division 1
Irvine Jetstream Flyers	1992/93 Scottish League Division 1
Irvine Flyers	1993–96 Scottish League Division 1
Irvine Magnum Flyers	1998/99 Scottish League Division 1
North Ayr Bruins	2004/05 Scottish National League
Irvine Eagles	1979–81 Northern Junior League
Irvine Flyers	1996–98 Scottish Under-21 League
Irvine Bulldogs	1997/98 Scottish Under-17 Conference
North Ayrshire★ Devils	2002–04 Scottish Under-18 League; 2004/05 Scottish Under-19 League
North Ayrshire★ Predators	2002–05 Scottish Under-16 League
North Ayrshire★ Stars	2001–05 Scottish Under-14 League
North Ayrshire★ Penguins	2001–05 Scottish Under-12 League

★-shire dropped from title for 2004-05.

Honours:

Penguins	2004/05 Champions Scottish Under-12 League

The rink is part of a local authority sports complex including a theatre, swimming pool and general-purpose sports hall, designed by Irvine Burgh Council architects' department. The rink originally opened with square corners and plenty of glass close to the ice. A club was admitted to the Northern Ice Hockey Association in January 1978, with a Junior League entry for season 1978/79. That side failed to materialise. However, teams did compete in the Northern Reserve and Junior Leagues the following winter, playing fixtures away from home. A one-year experiment, during 1986/87, in running a team in the British League proved a financial disaster, not helped by the very limited spectator accommodation at Harbour Street. Never climbing out of the cellar, Wings won only 5 of their 30 matches. The two imports of Blair Hiddleston (89+75) and Kent Davis with 110 points carried a heavy burden, as did the core of local players, who mostly lacked experience. They ended up out of pocket as the team on occasions had to rely on bucket collections at away games.

Five years later a group of players from nearby Kilmarnock formed the Jetstream Flyers to compete in the amateur Scottish League. Until the dawning of the twenty-first century ice hockey progressed in fits and starts at Irvine, with gaps of several years, particularly in the youth development programmes. With the formation of a new set-up, under the label of North Ayrshire, teams participate in stepped age bands up to and including Under-19s. A Scots National League entry was added for 2004/05 with North Ayr Bruins.

KILMARNOCK

Opened:	15 May 1987
Ice Size:	146ft x 75ft (44m x 20m)
Total Spectator Capacity:	400
Seating Capacity:	400 (extendable form)
Ice Hockey – First Match:	

4 November 1989: Kilmarnock Galleons v. Castlereigh Flames (Scottish League Division 1)

Address:
The Galleon Centre
99 Titchfield Street
Kilmarnock
East Ayrshire
KA1 1QY
Scotland

Teams:

Kilmarnoch Galleons	1989/90 Scottish League Division 1
Kilmarnock Jetstream	1990/91 Scottish League Division 1
Kilmarnock Flyers	1991/92 Scottish League Division 1
Kilmarnock Avalanche	1996–98 Scottish Under-21 League; 1998–2000 Scottish League Division 1; 2000–04 Scottish National League
Kilmarnock Jets	1991–96 Scottish Under-16 League
Kilmarnock Storm	1996–2000 Scottish Under-16/17 Conference/League
Kilmarnock Devils	2000–04 Scottish Under-16 League
Kilmarnock	1994–96 Scottish Under-14 League
Kilmarnock Lightning	1996/97 & 1999–2005 Scottish Under-14 Conference/League
Kilmarnock Devils	1997–99 Scottish Under-15 Conference/League
Kilmarnock Lightning	1996–99 Scottish Under-12/13 Conference/League
Kilmarnock Tornadoes	1999–2004 Scottish Under-12 League
Kilmarnock	1999–2000 Scottish Under-18 League
Kilmarnock Storm	2000–04 Scottish Under-18/19 League

Honours:

Jetstream	1990/91 Winners Scottish League Cup
Lightning	1999/2000 Winners Scottish Under-14 League Division 2
Kilmarnock	1999/2000 Winners Scottish Under-18 League Division 2

The site, within walking distance of the town centre, was leased by the district council to a charitable trust set-up in consultation with local government. This trust borrowed £4.5 million to finance construction of the complex, which includes a swimming pool, sports halls, squash courts, sauna suite and fitness centre. Work commenced in February 1986. The name of the centre relates to the Gallion Burn, which formally ran through the site.

The late Jackson McBride, a well-known Ayr-based player and coach, set-up Kilmarnock's first club – Galleons. Although they were stripped of all their Scottish League points for icing unregistered players, John Hester led the league in points with 58 goals and 27 assists. The one-season Jetstream placed third in the eight-team Scottish League, and went on to win the knockout Scottish League Cup. Stevie Andrews was best scorer, ending fourth in the SL on 41 points and netting a hat-trick in the cup final.

For 1992/93 season the core of Jetstream moved to Irvine, to be replaced by Flyers, a new senior team. In their one campaign they occupied the penultimate spot in the standings. Four years elapsed before Avalanche emerged to spend two seasons in the Scottish Under-21 set-up. Senior hockey returned to Kilmarnock in 1998 as Avalanche joined the Scottish League. They won 11 of their 22 fixtures, with Tommy Boll the leading scorer on 116 points including 54 goals. Colin Gooding guarded the nets. Avalanche's best performance was fourth in 2000 and runners-up two years later.

Since 1991 a junior team at either Under-16 or Under-17 years of age has been in league action every winter until 2004. An Under-14 programme commenced three years later, to be joined two seasons on by the Under-12s. The Under-18s won Division 2 of their league at the first attempt. With this integrated youth system the future of ice hockey at Titchfield Street is assured.

KIRKCALDY

Opened:	1 October 1938	Address:
Ice Size:	198ft x 98ft (59m x 30m)	Kirkcaldy Ice Rink
Total Spectator Capacity:	3,280 (4,000 in 1938)	Rosslyn Street
Seating Capacity:	2,500 (2,800 in 1939)	Kirkcaldy
Ice Hockey – First Match:		Fife FY1 3HS
1 October 1938: Fife Flyers 1 v. Dundee Tigers 4 (challenge)		Scotland

Teams:

Fife Flyers — 1938–40 & 1946-54 Scottish National League; 1954/55 British National League; 1961–66 'Home' tournaments; 1962–65 Scottish League Section 'A'; 1966–82 Northern League; 1981/82 Scottish National League; 1982/83 British League Division 1 Section A; 1983–91 British League Premier Division; 1991/92 British League Division 1; 1992–96 British League Premier Division; 1996/97 Northern Premier League; 1997–2005 British National League

Kirkcaldy Juniors — 1946/47 McPherson and Frame Trophy

Kirkcaldy Flyers — 1947–55 Scottish 'Junior' League(s) and 'Home' tournaments; 1968/69 Northern Second League

Kirkcaldy Kestrels — 1947–51 Scottish 'Junior' League(s); 1972–77 Northern Second League; 1977–81 Northern Reserve League; 1984/85 British League Division 2 – Scotland; 1986–88 British League Division 1; 1988–96 & 1998–2000 Scottish League Division 1; 1996–98 Scottish Under-21 League; 2000–05 Scottish National League

Kirkcaldy Sabres — 1975–81 Northern Junior League

Fife Flames	1986–2005 Scottish Junior/Under-16/17 League/Conference
Fife Falcons	1986/87 British League Division 2 – Scotland; 1987/88 Scottish League Division 1; 1992–96 and 2000–05 Scottish Under-19/18 League
Kirkcaldy Chiefs	1986–91 Scottish Pee-Wee League; 1992/93 & 1994–2005 Scottish Under-14/15 League/Conference
Kirkcaldy Cherokees	1988–96 Scottish Under-12 League
Kirkcaldy Redskins	1996–2005 Scottish Under-12/13 Conference/League

Honours:

Flyers	1939/40 Champions Scottish National League and Play-offs; 1948–50 Champions Scottish National League; 1962–64 Champions Scottish League; 1972/73, 1975–77 & 1978/79 Winners Autumn Cup; 1976–78 Champions Northern League and Play-offs for Spring Cup; 1975/76, 1977/78 & 1984/85 British Champions; 1991/92 Winners British League Division 1; 1996/97 Champions Northern Premier League; 1999/2000 Champions British National League and Play-offs; 2003/04 Champions British National League
Kestrels	1973–76 Champions Northern Second League; 1989/90 Winners Scottish Division 1 Cup; 1993/94 Champions Scottish League; 1996/97 Champions Scottish Under-21 League
Flames	1987/88 & 1989/90 Champions Scottish Junior League and Play-offs; 1990–96 Champions Scottish Junior League; 1991/92 & 1994/95 British Junior Champions; 1996/97 Winners Scottish Under-16 Conference B; 1997/98 Winners Scottish Under-17 Conference B; 1999/2000 Winners Scottish Under-16 League Division 1; 2001/02 Champions Scottish Under-16 League and Cup
Chiefs	1986–90 Champions Scottish Pee-Wee League; 1987/88 Champions Play-offs; 1992/93 & 1994/95 Champions Scottish Under-14 League; 1996/97 Winners Scottish Under-14 Conference B; 1998/99 Winners Scottish Under-15 League Division 1; 1999/2000 Winners Scottish Under-14 League Division 1; 2001/02 Winners Scottish Under-14 Cup.
Cherokees	1991–94 & 2001/02 Champions Scottish Under-12 League
Falcons	1992–94 Champions Scottish Under-19 League; 2001/02 & 2002/03 Champions Scottish Under-18 League

Publications:

Champions – The Story of Fife Flyers' Greatest Ever Season, Crow, Allan, 2000

Kirkcaldy is the last of the Scottish pre-Second World War rinks still in operation. Ice hockey has been staged there almost without a break, with the home-bred player encouraged. Designed in 1937 by architects Williamson and Hubbar, with the front entrance in the fashionable 'moderne' streamlining style. Built at a cost of £40,000 by Fraser (Kirkcaldy), with ice plant installed by J&E Hall, the building was opened by Lord Elgin on the same day as the first ice hockey contest. The rink and its hockey club have always been run by a private company, usually as an integral business operation. In March 1995 the rink received a £100,000 grant from the Foundation for Sports and the Arts. This assisted £500,000 of refurbishment carried out that summer.

The original Kirkcaldy Fife Flyers included three home-bred Sots in Alec and Billy Fullerton from Glasgow and Perth's Tommy McInroy. Yorkshire-born Jimmy Chappell, of

1936 Olympic gold medal fame and Norm McQuade, originally from Manchester, were recruited along with Les Lovell Sr, Tommy Durling, Len McCartney and McQuade as Flyers secured third place in the League Tournament. Next year Flyers won the Scottish National League (SNL), and clinched the play-off finals, winning two and tying one. Only McInroy had been retained from the rookie campaign. Other signings included Alloa-born George Horne (29), Arnie Pratt (25) on the right-wing and Paul Rheault from Wembley Lions. The latter two were high in the points table with 50 and 40 respectively by the end of March. The building remained open during the Second World War with a limited amount of Canadian Army and RCAF hockey.

In eight seasons of the post-war SNL the most successful were those of 1948–50. Defenceman Floyd Snider had been with the club since 1946, earning All-Star 'B' ratings in the lean years, as had Bud Scrutton, Flyers' leading scorer for three years, totalling 415 points. He shared in the glory of the first Autumn Cup and league championship in 1948/49, collecting an All Star 'A' vote along with Snider and Chick Mann. Goalie Pete Balanger, Vern Greger on defence and coach Al Rogers all made the 'B' squad. Next winter Fife retained the League title. They also won the Canada Cup and were runners-up in the Autumn and Scottish Cups. Mann was accorded an All-Star 'A' for his defensive work. 'A's also went to Balanger, Snider and Rogers. The remaining years were barren except for the capture of the consolation Bairns Trophy in 1951 and 1952.

The amalgamation of the Scottish and English leagues in late 1954 proved a disaster. Fife managed tenth in the Autumn Cup, moving up one place in the British league with 13 wins. Flyers were no more and hockey was virtually absent from Gallatown for six years. Flyers remerged in 1961, as a home-grown outfit, competing in their own Kirkcaldy 'home' tournament against Scottish amateur sides. Next winter they met Ayr and Murrayfield in Section 'A' of the Scottish League, to win their group and contest the play-off final, defeating Paisley in 1964. Many of the best Scottish players wore Fife colours including Jimmy Spence, Sammmy McDonald, Ian Forbes, Graeme Farrell, Kirkcaldy-born and bred Bert Smith and Lawrie Lovell, son of Les Sr. Flyers appeared on the small screen winning the BBC Grandstand Trophy in 1964 and 1967. They were founding members of the Northern League in autumn 1966. Fife collected silverware throughout the mid- and late 1970s.

Led by the established Lovell brothers Les and Lawrie, Fife were joined by youngsters such as Gordon and later Dougie Latto, Jimmy Jack and Charlie Kinmond. The defence relied on Ken Horne with goalies Willie Cottrell and Roy Reid. Flyers secured the first of four Autumn Cups in 1973, continuing to contest the 'Icy' Smith Cup final successfully, between the champions of the Northern and Southern Leagues. Southampton were vanquished by a double figure aggregate in 1977 and the following winter. By 1980 the first imports of the 'modern era', Jim Lynch and Neil McKay, joined Flyers.

The club's leading import scorer for 1982–84 – Gordon McDougall – piled up 183 points. Next autumn the first player for twenty-five years with NHL experience came to Britain, as Fife signed player-coach Ron Plumb (34) from Kingston, Ontario. Class acts Dave Stoyanovich and Danny Brown also joined. All gained All-Star 'A' honours. Their

A drawing of the rink on the opening day.

The interior in 1939.
(*Skating Times*)

firepower projected Flyers to second place in the Premier Division. Crowd levels at Rosslyn Street doubled to 2,200. Four wins out of four in the quarter-final Play-offs took Flyers to the May weekend Wembley Championships. Fife swept past Streatham 12–3. The following afternoon Flyers defeated Murrayfield 9–4, for their first major trophy in six years. Plumb won the Coach of the Year award, Stoyanovich took the same accolade as Player. Andy Donald contributed as the stand out goalie for the previous four seasons. During April 1984 three matches in the European Under-18 Championships were held at Kirkcaldy.

There were two more visits to Wembley. In 1988 imports Fred Perlini, Steve Moria and Al Sims led Flyers to third in the league as crowds climbed to 2,776. A 13–5 semi-final victory preceded losing the final 5–8 to Durham. Two years on a fifth-placed Flyers failed to get past Cardiff in the semi-final. Numerous player and coaching changes during 1990/91 resulted in Fife in the basement and relegated. But not for long. A mix of seasoned imports and Kirkcaldy youth topped Division 1 and the promotion group play-offs.

Mark Morrison joined in 1993 and has been with Flyers ever since. He was appointed player-coach three years later by Fife Flyers Ltd, a company set up by three local businessmen including Tom Muir, currently chairman. Shunning the Superleague, Mark has since led the team to three BNL championships, the latest being winter 2004. Flyers progressed to the play-offs' final four in spring 2005.

During the past decade Flyers' continuing success is founded on the never-ending stream of home-bred talent that has included Ian Robertson, Derek and Steven King, Les Millie, John Haig, David Smith, Andy Samuel, Colin Grubb, Kyle Horne and many others.

LIVERPOOL

Opened:	2 September 1931	Address:
Closed:	1986	Liverpool Ice Rink Ltd
Ice Size:	Dimensions vary from 159ft x	8 Prescott Road
	78ft to 180ft x 80ft depending	Kensington
	on source consulted.	Liverpool
Total Spectator Capacity:	2,000 (3,000 in 1931)	L7 8LP
Seating Capacity:	600	England

Ice Hockey – First Match:
30 October 1931: North of England 0 *v.* Scotland 9 (challenge)

Teams:
Liverpool Hornets 1936–39 challenge games
Liverpool Leopards 1948–1959 'Home' tournaments; 1950–54 Midland
Intermediate League; 1973–78 Southern 'A' League;
1978–82 Midland League – Division 1

Liverpool Redwings   1972/73 challenge games
Liverpool Trappers   1974–78 Southern 'B' League
Liverpool Cougars   1978–82 Midland League Division 2
Liverpool Cubs   1977/78 Southern Junior League

Honours:
Leopards   1951/52 Champions Midland Intermediate League; 1979/80
    Champions Midland League; 1951/52 & 1954/55 Winners
    Liverpool Tournament
Trappers   1975/76 Champions Southern 'B' League
Cougars   1979/80 & 1981/82 Champions Midland League Division 2

Publications:
See You on the Ice – A History of the Liverpool Ice Rink, Whale, Derek, 1984

Built in 1927 originally as a dance hall, and during 1929/1930 used as a roller rink. In a link between the promoters of the Casino Roller Rink and Ice Rinks Ltd, the company running the Hove and Golders Green rinks in London, architect Sydney Clough was engaged. Work commenced on 19 March 1931. Six months later the building reopened as the 'Casino Ice Rink'.

Following the first ice hockey match a further four internationals took place. In the first, on 14 November, France blanked England 4–0. Among the hosts were Blaine Sexton, who showcased the sport on the continent with his London Lions. Lancashire, who included H. and A. Bridge of Liverpool, lost 1–4 to the Scottish League on 9 January. The following month England, with Peter Churchill, Ernie Ramus and Gerry Davey, went down 1–2 to Boston All-Stars. The last game saw England, who included Dr. Blake Watson, a journeyman Canadian, draw 1–1 with Vienna EV. Inspired by these international matches a local club was in existence by Easter 1932.

Next season Edmonton Superiors travelled to Liverpool twice. On November 28 they overcame England 9–5. Upon their return on 26 January 1933 Great Britain were shut out 7–0. GB included goalie Dave Cross, Gordon Rowley, J.R. Gilmour and Jack Easton from Scottish clubs. The rink closed in the autumn of 1933. Two hundred local skaters formed a limited company and acquired a twenty-one-year lease from the landlord General Theatres Corporation.

It reopened as the 'Liverpool Ice Palace' on 15 November 1935. About a year later Liverpool Hornets emerged. In their first match they travelled to London, where in January 1937 they lost 6–1 to Earls Court Marlboroughs. Further games took place, both at Liverpool and at opposition rinks up to the outbreak of war. Hornets included Canadians Gordon Gibbons, Ken Brown and Jack Ritchie, as well as Charlie Benson and George Brabin. Hit twice by bombs in the space of eleven days in September 1940, the rink reopened for skating the following February. Canadian Armed Services ice hockey finals were held during the hostilities. The players included Milt Schmidt, 'Porky' Dumart and Wilf De Marco, who was later killed in action. Meeting these famous stars sparked local lad Ron Booth's interest in the sport.

Returning home in 1947 from war service, Ron gained permission from Charles Jones, the rink's managing director, to restart ice hockey. Liverpool Leopards' first game, on 18 December 1948, this time on home ice, was with Earls Court Marlboroughs, who again won by the narrow margin of 5–4. Among Leopard's roster were Benson and Gibbons from the pre-war team, Canadians Carl Sturtridge and John Cole, Zazik Zarlikowski, a Polish international, Bob Patterson, who learned to play while in Canada, Harry Barrow, Bob Davies, Jim Parry, Tom Carter, Sid Thorne and John Gallagher. Leopards went on to win 8 of their 16 matches. From 1949 to 1956 Leopards hosted the Liverpool Tournament, modelled on a similar competition held at Durham. A round ten games culminated in a final. In these Leopards beat Streatham 4–2 in 1952 and defeated Southampton 4–3 three years later. Being champions in the inaugural season of the Midland League in 1952, with one loss, was a major triumph. By the early 1950s Canadian Ron Francis, John Smith and young talented Vic O'Hagen were among Leopards' goalscorers. O'Hagen was a product of the junior Merseyside Monarchs.

External and internal views in 1980.

In August 1956 Elstead Investment Trust Ltd bought out the previous shareholders. Hockey ceased at Prescott Road. Leopards soldiered on for three years, with the occasional match at Blackpool, Whitley Bay and Southampton. The rink closed in the summer of 1959 as the lease expired, to be purchased by Star Associated Holdings Ltd who became Silver Blades (later Mecca). Refurbishment included a new ice pad. The building reopened for skating on 18 March 1960.

Twelve years later Ray Walch, the coach of Blackpool's second team, was looking for additional training ice. An approach to Mecca's rink manager proved fruitful. By autumn 1973 Liverpool Leopards were reborn, competing in the Southern League. In their first league match at home, on 6 October, Leopards beat Solihull Vikings 3–2. They won once more to finish sixth. Bob Rowntree (18), Dean Lewis (19) and Mick Lloyd (19) were effective attackers in front of the goaltending duo of Eric Cregan (24) and Roger Thompson (27). By the second campaign the spectators averaged around 300. Trappers were founded for younger players. In 1978 Liverpool moved to the newly formed Midland League. Attendances had increased, sometimes topping 600. Bob Bramah, Bernie Snagg and Carl Riley were starting to make an impression on the sport.

Mecca sold the rink in spring 1978 to Les Williams, a local businessman, who carried out essential works and operated it as a private venture, supported by Sports Council and local authority grants totalling £75,000. Leopards won the Midland League in 1980, undefeated, led by Swedish player coach Ake Alm, and backstopped by Charlie Birch. Next winter deadly rivals Blackpool took three out of four points off Leopards, who dropped to second. Bernie Butler led the club in scoring with 20 goals and 4 assists. In a more competitive revamped Midland League, rebranded as English League – North, Leopards slipped to fifth in a changing roster, which used five netminders. Cougars gained their second title in Division 2. This turned out to be the last season for both teams. Rink owner Williams, who had sponsored the club for the past three years, and was still carrying out major repairs, could not afford both. Hockey lost out. Four years later he gave up the struggle as the rink closed for good.

LIVINGSTON

Opened:	24 April 1987	Address:
Closed:	1996	Summit Ice Rink
Ice Size:	184ft x 85ft (56m x 26m)	Almondvale West
Total Spectator Capacity:	1,000	Livingston
Seating Capacity:	500	West Lothian
Ice Hockey – First Match:		EH54 6QX
11 October 1987: Livingston Rams 9 v. Glenrothes Jets 6 (Scottish League)		Scotland

Teams:

Livingston Rams   1987–89 Scottish League Division 1; 1990/91 Scottish League Division 1

Livingston Kings   1991/92 Scottish League Division 1

Tayside Tigers   1990/91 & 1993–95 Scottish League

Glenrothes Jets   1993–95 Scottish League

Murrayfield Racers   Spring 1994 Play-offs British League

Livingston Stallions   1988–90 Scottish Junior League

Livingston Colts   1988/89 Scottish Under-14 Pee-Wee League

Livingston Chargers   1991/92 Scottish Under-18 League

Honours:

Kings   Champions 1991/92 Scottish League – Division 1

Constructed by the same developer – David Sinclair – as the Glasgow Summit Centre. The life of the rink, originally named The Summit Centre Icelandia, in the New Town with a population of a little over 40,000, spluttered fitfully before dying aged nine. The rink closed in the spring of 1989 to reopen on 23 July 1990. Crossland Leisure, who also managed the Basingstoke rink, took over the running of Livingston in the summer of 1991. The building closed down again on 10 September 1992, due to lack of funding support from Livingston Development Corporation. The building's owners, Municipal Mutual Insurance Company, hoped to sell it, complete with ice plant, as a cold store. The rink did reopen that November, finally ceasing operations in 1996. A shopping and leisure complex, constructed in 1999, is adjacent. The hope at that time that West Lothian Council would bring the facility back into operation was not fulfilled. It is now a retail unit.

Rams, the rink's first senior team spent three-and-a-half seasons in the Scottish League. With only five players with previous hockey experience they won four times in their inaugural campaign, to finish seventh. Next winter six victories and a tie lifted the Rams one position. Officially credited with two wins and a last place Rams withdrew in mid-campaign in 1989/90. Back the next winter, Rams ended in the cellar with two wins. Mike Urquart and his wife Laura ran the rink and hockey in 1991/92, with Mike as player-coach. The new Kings grabbed the SL crown with 16 victories in the 20-match schedule. Eric Bommer and Brian Day were second and third in scoring on 75 and 67 points respectively. Then the Urquarts moved to Guildford. With a late start Kings folded after losing six of their seven games.

Senior hockey returned for a couple of years with the homeless Glenrothes and Tayside utilising the ice. Murrayfield Racers used Livingston for their British League Play-offs schedule in spring 1994. In the late 1980s Scotland's Under-16 and Under-13 squads trained at the rink, as did a British Army team.

LONDON – ALEXANDRA PALACE

Opened:	18 June 1990	Address:
Ice Size:	184ft x 85ft (56m x 26m)	Alexandra Palace Ice Rink
Total Spectator Capacity:	1,250	Alexandra Palace Way
Seating Capacity:	746	Wood Green
Ice Hockey – First Match:		London N22 7AY
26 August 1990: Haringey Racers 4 *v.* Lee Valley Lions 8 (challenge)		England

Teams:

Haringey Racers   1990–92 English League Division 1; 2002/03 English Premier League

Haringey Greyhounds	1990/91 English League Division 3 – Central; 1991/92 English Conference National Division; 1992/93 English Conference – Wharry Division; 1993/94 English Conference; 1994–98 English Conference – South; 1998–2000 English League Division 1 – South; 2000–02 English National League Premier Division; 2004/05 English National League – South
London Racers	Autumn 2003 Elite League
Haringey Phoenix	1990/91 English League Division 3 – South
Haringey Whippets	1991–97 and 1998–2005 English Under-16 League/Conference
Haringey Hounds	1992–2005 English Under-14 Conference/League
Haringey Bulldogs	1991–2005 English Under-12 League/Conference
Haringey Wolves	1997–2001 & 2003–05 English Under-19 League

Honours:

Greyhounds	1999/00 Winners English League Division 1 – South
Hounds	2002/03 Winners English Under-14 'B' League – South East
Bulldogs	1994/95 Winners English Under-12 Conference – South East

The rink, owned and operated by a non-profit making trust, administered by Haringey Borough Council, has been constructed within the Listed brick-walled shell of a late nineteenth century leisure complex, which was severely damaged by a major fire in 1980. Situated in 196 acres of parkland, Alexandra Palace first opened in 1873 to provide a recreation centre; it burnt down. An extended building reopened two years later.

A quarter of a century in financial difficulties caused the enterprise to be administered by the local authority. In 1935 the BBC leased the East Hall. The following year, the world's first regular public high-definition (406-line) TV transmissions commenced. There was a connection between Alexandra Palace and ice hockey, long before the present rink opened. In early January 1940 the professional Harringay Racers and Greyhounds enjoyed a morning practice and scrimmage game on a frozen pond in the grounds of the Palace, having changed into their kit at Harringay Arena. Quite a crowd gathered to watch.

In late summer 1990 John Holtham put together the first Haringey Racers. It was built around import Craig Oster with a core of young English players from the London area – Danny O'Hanlon, Phil Gosbee, Lee Hurley and Perry Tomlinson. Scottish-Canadian Robin Andrew anchored the defence in front of netminders Andy Nunn and Mike Shead. Four imports tried out, with Rich Strachan staying. Holtham said of their English League sixth place: 'We did well considering our lack of strength in depth.' Attendances varied from a low of 150 to 1,000, but usually hovered around 350. Next winter, with a £70,000 budget Barry Blisner and Glen Kehrer from the University of Manitoba were engaged, along with Dave Tweedy. Two wins from six games in the season-opening Autumn Trophy did not augur well. Ten victories came from a 32-match schedule for a seventh place finish. Blisner and Kehrer were Racers' leading scorers with 73 and 58 goals. By spring Holtham left following differences with the rink management. The Trust withdrew all funding.

With a new owner in Greg Vasicek, and little cash, Racers pulled out of the Autumn Trophy on 18 September 1992 after two games. They had been fined £750 for use of unregistered players in both fixtures, with Vasicek suspended. He resigned. For the next ten years Alexandra Palace were represented by the senior amateur Haringay Greyhounds and a continual youth development programme with teams in three stepped age groups. In the first four seasons of the English Conference Greyhounds lingered in the lower half of the table. For 1995/96 'Hounds won ten games, for fifth. Fredrik Sixtensson, in his second campaign with the club, finished as the tenth best scorer in the Conference with 38 goals and 33 assists. Next year two Swedish defencemen were added. Crowds rose to average 500. When Romford Raiders visited on 16 January they played to a capacity house.

With the formation of an English League Haringey stayed with the Conference set-up. New Canadian coach Dave Robb imposed a better disciplinary record. Millenium year

Haringey Racers 1990/91. From left to right, standing: John Holtham (Manager), Franklin John, Lee Horley, Perry Tomlinson, Jonathan Beckett, Darren Peies, Rupert Thompson, Danny O'Hanlon. Seated: Michael Shead, Robin Andrew (Coach), Dave Tweedy, Craig Oster, Andy Nunn.

brought silverware as three years of perseverance paid off. Winning 14 out of their 16 fixtures, in EL Division 1 South, gave 'Hounds the title. Four play-off group wins took Haringey to the two-leg semi-final where they met Whitley. Warriors took both legs with an aggregate of 18–5. The cosmopolitan mix included Zoran Kozic from Belgrade, Dane Rasmus Edmund, Romanians Octavin Sersea and Somfaleanu, combined with Tom Clark from Chelmsford and the established Scotsman Kevin Gray.

The amateurs of Haringey moved to the semi-professional EPL, not a wise move. Kozic and Steve Fullan, a Canadian, took over the team, to be joined by Canadian netminder Tom Wills and ex-Romford Roger Black (three years on this duo, along with Fullan, formed London Racers). Only five games were won on home ice and the rink withdrew its financial support mid-season. Greyhounds finished seventh. Next winter was even worse. One win and a tie meant the basement, below the England youth squad. New team owner Kozic raised funds. In late autumn he picked up a twelve-month suspension. Soon money was unavailable and he left.

For 2002/03 rebranding as Racers, by owner Roger Black, did not assist. Several imports helped out including Cody Mayoh and Brian McLaughlin. The team finished eleventh from twelve. In early November 2003, the first-year professional London Racers, of the inaugural Elite League, transferred their operations to Lee Valley ice. Racers' ninth and last game at Alexandra Palace was a 6–2 loss to Belfast Giants in front of 426 spectators on 31 October. London-funded Haringey Racers were forced to withdraw from the EPL.

With youth hockey continuing unaffected, a new all-amateur Greyhounds was revived in autumn 2004 by Jan Bestic, backed by a long-time hockey enthusiast with realistic ambitions for the team.

LONDON – EARLS COURT

Opened:	1 November 1935	Address:
Closed:	1957	Empress Hall
Ice Size:	200ft x 97ft	Lillie Road
Total Spectator Capacity:	8,116 (7,100 by early 1950s, 10,000 for non-ice events)	Fulham London SW6
Seating Capacity:	7,100 (6,500 by early 1950s)	England

Ice Hockey – First Match:
1 November 1935: Kensington Corinthians 2 *v.* Earls Court Rangers 1 (challenge)

Teams:

Kensington Corinthians	1935/36 English National League
Earls Court Rangers	1935–39 and 1948–53 English National League
Earls Court Royals	1936/37 English National League
Earls Court Marlboroughs	1937–39 London Provincial League; 1948–53 Southern Intermediate League
Oxford University	1935/36 English League
Cambridge University	1938/39 London Provincial League
Earls Court Redwings	1938/39 London Provincial League

Publications:
Earls Court, Langdon, Claude, 1953, Stanley Paul & Co. Ltd

Not a new structure but an adaptation, by architect C. Howard Crane, of a hall erected for the 1886 Indian Exhibition. Known as Empress Stadium from 1935–37. With the lease being taken over by Claude Langdon, it reverted to the original name of Empress Hall. The first of the 'big three' London arenas to drop from running two professional teams, the least successful in attracting sufficient spectators and the first to dispense with ice hockey and close.

The best that Rangers could achieve in the pre-Second World War English National League was third in 1938/39. Sixth among league-leading points scorers with 29, Jerry Brown went onto play pro hockey in the USA. All-Star 'A' ratings went to goalminder Gib Hutchinson and centre-ice Frank Currie, with 'B's to Bobby Lee, another centre, and Jack Forsey at right-wing. Other Rangers acknowledged were Airdrie-born Scotty McAlpine on defence (1935/36), with 'A's, Don Willson at centre and right-wing Johnny Acheson (1936/37). Forsey and Willson later spent time in the NHL. Rangers did win the London Cup at their first attempt.

The short-lived Kensington Corinthians were player-coached by Bobby Giddens. With their ever-changing roster they finished last. That same season Giddens, the first Canadian to captain Harvard University's hockey team, founded the weekly *Ice Hockey World*. For 1936 Corinthians became Royals. Homeless Oxbridge teams used Earls Court as a base, with the 1939 Varsity match, won 2–0 by Cambridge, being televised. A 'house league' – the Sunday League, operated in 1937 consisting of Marlboroughs, St Thomas' Hospital, Kestrals, All Blacks and Barclays Bank, each team playing eight times. Out of this grew the London Provincial League, catering for homegrown players. E.C. Marlboughs were runners-up in the inaugural campaign and finished seventh next winter as the LPL expanded to eleven. Runners-up were Redwings, who had relocated from Richmond. Among the better-known Marlies' British lads were Jock Robin, Maule Colledge, Tommy Grace and Fred Dunkleman. Redwings featured Stan Simon, Ken 'Pip' Perrin and Art Ridley who, along with Grace, represented Great Britain in the 1939 World Championships. In late April and early May 1938 four exhibition games between Detroit Red Wings and Montreal Canadiens, during the National Hockey League's (NHL) first tour outside North America, took place at Empress Hall.

Canadian military teams played before the public in February, March and April 1940. The building closed during Whitsun 1940, to be requisition by the government as a refugee centre. It did not reopen to the public until October 1948. In the first post-war match on 9 October 1948, Rangers narrowly lost by 4–3 to Nottingham Panthers. Although the line-up remained constant, third place in the season-opening Autumn Cup was the only reward. Pint-sized John Bourada kept goal. Willis Mosdell on defence and Alf Harvey at left-wing both had famous brothers in the NHL. Three forwards left their mark in British hockey. Kenny Booth at centre, and wingers Kenny Campbell (left) and Henry Hayes (right), who

The architect's drawing of the exterior, 1935. (*Skating Times*)

An artist's view of the interior, 1935. (*Skating Times*)

pre-war had been with Royals. Campbell picked up a 'B' All-Star award. In 1949/50 goalie Ken Dargeval's (26) performances were recognised with an All-Star 'A' for an otherwise outclassed team. Also signed were two English-bred players – Art Green (27), a defenceman and goalie Stan Simon (28). It was at this time that Marlboroughs lost their ice time, to play their next three seasons' fixtures at their opponents' rinks.

Of the five post-war campaigns Rangers penultimate one proved the most successful under forty-two-year-old player-coach Duke Campbell. Returning after an interval away were Stan Dequoy and Bud McEachern. Rangers' first 'home' fixtures took place at the Richmond rink, due to an extended run of a summer ice show at the hall. As March closed they headed the league table by a point. A sequence of four losses dropped them to third. Four weeks later Rangers were back on top to finish as runners-up to Wembley Lions. Booth led the league in scoring with 22 goals and 46 assists. Les Anning was fourth to make the All-Stars with an 'A' as Booth collected a 'B'. Tommy Jamieson on defence also gained an 'A' with a 'B' for Campbell. Rangers' 1952/53 roster was to be their last. The Autumn Cup ended with Rangers slipping to fifth. League play brought an improvement to fourth. Denny contributed 38 goals and 19 assists, good enough for All-Star 'A' recognition. The last programme said '…ice hockey has been struggling under an increasing load of difficulties… during the past season'. Rangers did not return, although Empress Hall continued to function for a while as an entertainments venue. Alf Harvey had been with Rangers throughout the five seasons, spending 293 games on the blue-line to accumulate 47 goals and 80 assists. Ken Dargavel missed the first winter to spend 239 matches guarding the nets.

Overseas visitors included Canada, USA, Sweden and Davos as well as the Swiss and Scottish League All-Stars. In 1950 Earls Court hosted, along with Harringay and Wembley, the World and European Championships. The opening ceremony, on 13 March, was held at Empress Hall. Great Britain were placed fourth. Harringay Racers played their last seven 'home' games between 21 March and 18 April 1954 at Empress Hall.

The building was demolished soon after closure. A multi-storey office block 'Empress House', originally occupied by government security services as an 'out-station', was built on the site. It has recently been refurbished for occupation by the London Metropolitan Police.

LONDON – GOLDERS GREEN

Opened:	20 December 1929	Address:
Closed:	Spring 1932	Golders Green Ice Rink
Ice Size:	180ft x 85ft	Finchley Road
Total Spectator Capacity:	Unknown, but unlikely to have been large	Golders Green London NW11
Seating Capacity:	Unknown	England

Ice Hockey – First Match:
13 February 1930: Combined Cambridge/Oxford
University 0 *v.* Canada 13

Teams:

London Lions 1929/30 British League – South; 1930/31 challenge games; 1931/32 English League – Division 1

Located near Golders Green tube station, owned by Ice Rinks Ltd and designed as a steel-framed building by ice rink specialist architect Sydney Clough. Following closure the building, which was constructed from new as a rink, was converted into the Regal cinema, later the Odeon, which closed in 1959.

During the first winter England defeated Germany (Berlin SC) 4–2 on 13 March. William Speechly of Oxford University kept goal and captained England, with Oxford University's Larry Bonnycastle scoring. England drew 2–2 with France on 4 April with 'Peter' Patton in the home nets. In March the following year England met the University of Manitoba, Davos, France and Vienna IHC, representing Austria. The home side lost 3–1 to Manitoba and 5–4 to the French and beat the Swiss and Austrians. In a GB trial on 24 January 1931, for the forthcoming World Championships in Poland, The Rest defeated England 3–2.

Golders Green became the base for Blaine Sexton's nomadic London Lions, as the first British League commenced in early January 1930. With the late start many fixtures were cancelled, although play-offs were held. On 1 May at Golders Green, in the southern semi-finals, Lions beat United Services, to meet Princes next day at the same venue in three fifteen-minute periods. Neville Melland with two, the German Henry Ball and John Magwood with one each put Lions through to meet Glasgow in the first British final on 17 May. Gerhard Ball kept goal as Sexton and H.W. Bushell, with a goal apiece, countered the single from Ronald MacDonald for the Scots. With the league not held next winter it was October 1931 before competitive club hockey returned. On 22 October Lions crushed Cambridge University 11–2 with Blaine Sexton scoring four times. Fixtures for November and December were cancelled. January's game was held, as Lions blanked Princes 3–0 and on 11 February sneaked two points from Grosvenor House Canadians 3–2. Eight days later Oxford University came to Town for a 1–0 clean sheet, thanks to Bonnycastle. Lions finished fourth with 12 points from their 9 matches. The gaps in the fixtures were partly filled by internationals. England defeated Germany 3–1 on 15 October. Lions' Vic Gardner was now the home country's regular netminder. New Year's Day saw Lions tie 2–2 with the Scottish League. In March the usual burst of international activity had England win 5–2 over Zurich SC and on the 24th suffer a 1–0 blanking by Boston All-Stars. In the final international on Golders Green ice on 16 April, England tied 4–4 with Vienna EV as Lions' recent signing from Zurich, Frank Morris, netted a hat-trick.

This was the rink where travel agent John Francis 'Bunny' Ahearne (1900–85), a charismatic and shrewd Irish businessman, first saw ice hockey. He worked his way up from assistant secretary for the British Ice Hockey Association to alternate, post-Second World War, as long-serving president and vice-president of the International Ice Hockey Federation (IIHF) – the world governing body for the sport.

LONDON – HAMMERSMITH

Opened:	30 December 1929	Address:
Closed:	28 April 1934	Hammersmith Ice
Ice Size:	175ft x 75ft (or 182ft x 83ft	Drome
	depending on source)	Brook Green Road
Total Spectator Capacity:	Unknown, but unlikely to have	Hammersmith
	been large	London W6
Seating Capacity:	Unknown.	England

Ice Hockey – First Match:
31 January 1930: London 4 *v.* Oxford University 1
(challenge) – 'large audience'

Teams:

Hammersmith	1930/31challenge games
London Lions	1931/32 challenge games; 1932/33 English League Division 1
London Lions 'A'	1932/33 English League Division 2

Built as a tram shed, it became a dance hall – The Hammersmith Palais – prior to serving as an ice rink under the ownership of entrepreneur Claude Langdon (died 1964). It reverted to the Hammersmith Palais after April 1934. The building still exists and continues as a venue for public entertainment and music.

The limited spectator views 'were against any good hockey being seen', although international matches took place at Hammersmith. One of the first involved Japan, comprising a team of medical students from Mukden in Manchuria, taking on Great Britain. The British won 7–1 with Vic Gardner in goal, Neville Melland scoring the first goal. England beat Switzerland 5–4 on 20 March with three goals from Peter Fair and two by Blaine Sexton.

In March 1931 England came close to beating the World Champions Canada, represented by the University of Manitoba. Brian Carr-Harris, followed by Scotsman Jimmy Brown, gave the home side a 2–1 lead and 'sent the crowd wild with delight'. Vic Gardner stopped over 25 shots in the third period before a late Canadian goal gave them a 3–2 victory. Nearly a year later on 16 February 1932 Boston All-Stars overcame England 6–3. Gerry Davey scored a brace for the hosts.

Racing Club de France commenced the 1932/33 campaign on 25 October. With James Robertson Justice (the 1950s film actor) refereeing, Carl Erhart scored the only goal for England in their 2–1 loss. Edmonton Superiors inflicted a 7–1 defeat on 3 December, with England's solo by Harry Mayes. Superiors returned on 17 January. With three Oxford University players in England's line-up, including Herbie Little in goal and 'the rink filled to capacity' it took a third-period goal for Edmonton's 1–0 win. This game was filmed for the cinema. Canada (Toronto Nationals) also shut out England, this time 9–0 on 15 February. On March 20 in the BIHA International Trophy, USA, the 1933 World Champions, represented by Boston Olympics, blanked England 5–0. With 'the rink packed to overflowing' Toronto beat Boston 4–2 in the BIHA IT play-off on 6 April.

Next winter England/Great Britain (the label being interchangeable in the 1930s) met Canada and the USA twice at Hammersmith. England ran Canada (Ottawa Shamrocks) close on 4 December, taking a 2–0 lead from Davey and Frank de Blanc. Lou Bates, later with Wembley Lions, replied with two for a 4–3 Ottawa victory. On 8 January 1934 GB had most of the play in a 1–1 tie with the USA (Boston Rangers). Canada won 7–2 in the return on 8 February, with the Americans also winning on 5 March, by 5–1. George Strubbe netted the home side's goal.

Although Hammersmith gave more prominence to international fixtures, club hockey commenced almost as soon as the rink opened. Two of the founders – T.M. Kellough, a

Hammersmith's interior. (*Skating Times*)

doctor of medicine and Canadian-born Strubbe, who arrived during the First World War, married an English girl and stayed – continued to be involved in the sport for many years, as did Scots-born Don Porter with Wembley Canadians. In one of their handful of games Hammersmith defeated Grosvenor House 5–2, in a challenge game on 16 April 1930.

With the closure of the Golders Green in spring 1932, London Lions played some of their following winter's league fixtures at Hammersmith, for fourth in Division 1 with 9 points. Prominent among Lions that season were John Magwood, Blaine Sexton, William MacKenzie, all from Canada, German-born Frank de Marwicz, Habid Surcock of Egyptian origin and Neville Melland, the only home-bred player.

LONDON – HARRINGAY

Opened:	10 October 1936	Address:
Closed:	28 October 1958	Harringay Arena
Ice Size:	200ft x 90ft	Green Lane
Total Spectator Capacity:	10,000	Harringay
Seating Capacity:	8,220	London N4
Ice Hockey – First Match:		England

10 October 1936: Harringay Greyhounds 4 *v.* Harringay
Racers 2 (challenge)

Teams:

Harringay Greyhounds 1936–40 English National League; 1946–49 English National League

Harringay Racers 1936–40 and 1946–54 English National League; 1954–58 British National League

United Hospitals 1937–39 London Provincial League

Harringay Hornets 1938/39 challenge games; 1949/50 English Junior (Under-17) League; 1951–55 Southern Intermediate League; 1955–58 London Intermediate League

Civil Service Rockets 1948–52 'Home' tournaments (at opposing rinks)

Honours:

Greyhounds 1938–40 Champions English National League; 1938/39 & 1946/47 Winners London Cup; 1939/40 Winners National Tournament

Racers 1937/38 & 1948/49 Champions English National League; 1936/37 Winners London and Coronation Gold Cups;

1947/48, 1949/50 & 1952/53 Winners English Autumn
Cup; 1954/55 Champions British National League and
Winners British Autumn Cup

Publications:
The Story of Harringay Stadium & Arena, Ticher, Mike, 2002, Hornsey Historical Society

Modelled on Maple Leaf Gardens, Toronto, and the brainchild of Calgary-born entrepreneur and promoter Alfred Cecil Critchley DSO (1890–1963). It took an almost-impossible nine months to construct, including the driving of 400 concrete piles to a depth of 45 feet to support a raft of beams to bridge over the twin tunnels of the Piccadilly tube lines running diagonally below the arena. Suspended from the 600 tons of roof steel was an electrically controlled four-faced time clock. The arena was built at a total cost of £200,000, with the ice plant designed and installed by York Shipley Ltd and structural engineering by Dr Oscar Faber CBE.

Greyhounds and Racers were named from the already established dog and speedway racing at the adjacent stadium (1927–87). Strangely Percy Nicklin, Olympic 1936 gold medal-winning GB coach, is listed in the Harringay programmes as coach of both teams. They enjoyed a successful first campaign. Racers ended second with their rink mates third in the league. Racers won the knockout London Cup. Their Toronto-born netminder, Andy Goldie, was awarded an All-Star 'A' as was defender Len Burrage and Bert Peer, a winger. Wally Monson made it to the 'B' squad, along with Greyhounds' Frank Currie. For 1937/38 Racers streaked ahead to take the league crown with a 13-point margin. Burrage and Peer repeated in the All-Star voting, with British born defenceman Bob Whitelaw from Bradford joining them on the 'A' list.

Next winter, back stopped by the Port Glasgow born '36 Olympic hero Jimmy Foster, plus four members who later played in the NHL in Dick Behling, Hazen McAndrew, Joe Shack and Connie Tudin, Greyhounds won the league and London Cup. Shack, with 24 goals and 19 assists, topped the scoring race and won the left-wing All-Star 'A' award, as did Behling on defence. In the only wartime season 'Hounds retained the league crown by one point from Racers. Centre-ice Joe Beaton, in his third year with Greyhounds, headed the league's points scorers with 54, including 32 goals. He gained his second All-Star 'A' accolade. Duke Campbell at left-wing was also an 'A'. The only Racer so honoured that winter was Archie Creighton. This was also the winter that Harringay Arena operated an Under-14 house league consisting of Bantams, Flyers, Midgets and Whippets. It produced Doug Young, Ted Hallum and John Dunkleman.

Canadian armed forces, including 1st, 2nd, 3rd Field Regiments (RCA) and 48th Highlanders played many matches in early 1940. They also met Greyhounds and Racers. The arena closed on 31 March 1940 to be requisitioned and used by the army for stores, reopening in the spring of 1946.

In the first post-war match on 19 October 1946 Racers defeated Greyhounds 3–2 in a challenge, watched by a capacity 10,000 crowd. Nicklin, now general manager of the arena, left coaching to Duke MacDonald. The only pre-war returnee was Duke Campbell for Racers, who were beaten 10–3 in the final of the London Cup by Greyhounds. Next season Racers captured the first of their ultimate haul of four Autumn Cups, helped by defenceman Danny Linton, an All-Star 'A'. After a runners-up placing in the 1948/49 Autumn Cup, Racers streaked to an 11-point winning margin in the league. Shack, who transferred from Greyhounds, was leading scorer with 28+41, followed by teammates Bill Glennie and Pete Payette from Cornwall, Ontario, with All-Star 'A' ratings. After a third place league position in spring 1949 Greyhounds were folded on economic grounds.

Next winter Racers gained their second Autumn Cup, by a 5-point margin. Although third in the league Pat Coburn, Ricky Richard and Glennie, plus coach MacDonald, made the All-Star 'A' team. Season 1954/55 saw major changes. The English and Scottish Leagues combined, with Glennie taking over coaching from Campbell. English home-growns Rupe

The exterior in 1936.

The interior. (*The Builder*)

Fresher and Clive Millard were signed. The inaugural British Autumn Cup and league were won, the former by four points from Falkirk, the league by seven. Racers occupied second to fifth places in the combined scoring tables. Defenders Bill Winemaster and Art Hodgins, plus winger Fred Denny gained All-Star 'A' acclamations with a 'B' to forwards Gene Miller and Roger Maisoneuve. There were no more trophies for Racers; cup and league runners-up in 1956/57 were the nearest, with a trio of All-Star awards, apart from Glennie. He was voted onto the 'B' sextet for three consecutive seasons from 1956. There was no hint of the imminent cessation of ice hockey at the arena in Racers final programme of 26 April 1958, a league 10–4 defeat of Paisley.

The 1937 World and European ice hockey championships were held at Harringay. In a tempestuous contest on 26 February Britain lost their world title in a 3–0 shutout to Canada. With the arena packed to the rafters the crowd went wild when a high stick felled GB's 'Chirp' Brenchley. Debris was flung onto the ice as a spectator joined in. In a reflection on a different time, order was only restored when the band struck up *God Save the King*. The Worlds returned in 1950. Among many other internationals at Harringay, Racers' 5–3 defeat, on 15 March 1955, of newly crowned World Champions Canada, represented by Penticton Vees, stands out.

The Arena had always been a major boxing venue and, in the 1950s, was home to the Horse of the Year Show. Hornets *v.* Richmond Ambassadors, during the Harringay Ice Gala on 3 May 1958, was the last ice hockey.

Following closure it was used as a warehouse by a supermarket chain. The proposed Altrincham rink benefited, gaining the ice plant. The building was demolished in the summer of 1978. A Sainsbury's supermarket and associated car parking and housing now occupy the site.

LONDON – HENGLER'S/NATIONAL SKATING PALACE

Opened:	Mid-January 1896	Address:
Closed:	Spring 1904	Hengler's Ice
Ice Size:	Dimensions unknown; semi-circular	Rink/National Skating
	at one end, tapering at the other	Palace
	– 11,200sq ft in total area	7 Argyll Street
Total Spectator Capacity:	Estimated at approximately 1,000	London W1
Seating Capacity:	Estimated at approximately 700	England

Ice Hockey – First Match:
February 1896: England 4 *v.* 'Canada' 2

Teams:
Argyll 1902/03 challenge games; 1903/04 Ice Hockey League
Amateur Skating Club 1903/04 Ice Hockey League

One of the two venues for Britain and Europe's first ice hockey league, founded at a meeting at Henglers on 6 November 1903. B.M. 'Peter' Patton was elected chairman with Arthur Sullivan as secretary. Matches were held at 6.00 p.m.and 9.30pm. In the first, at the later hour on 26 November, Argyll suffered a 4–2 loss to Princes. In the second on 8 December Argyll edged a 2–1 (0–0; 2–1) win over Amateur Skating Club. In an eight-game schedule the two Hengler clubs finished third and fourth. T.G. Cannon, C.E.G. Vernon, G.L. Ogilvie, N. Montague, M.B. Milne and H.L. Webb were among the Argyll line-up. On 4 February 1904 King Edward VII, Queen Alexandra and the Prince and Princess of Wales watched a specially arranged match with five players a side between the Internationals, who won, and London.

The irregular restricted size and shape of the ice surface, which contained the protruding bases to columns, meant that the sport was very different from the one we know today. The goals were more like low-level chicken coops. Illustrations from 1896 show that a puck was used – this being a clear distinction between ice hockey and bandy which is played with a ball, although at that time the game was often called 'hockey on the ice'. In February 1896 England beat Canada 4–2. The latter were no doubt Canadians resident in London. By June 1896 advertisements appeared in the press informing the public that 'Ice Hockey' could be watched or played with matches twice weekly at 'The Most Magnificent Skating Palace in the World'.

A game in March 1896. What the couple standing on the left are doing is anyone's guess. (*Black & White* magazine)

The refrigeration plant, 1904. (*The Bystander*)

The building, on the site of Argyll House, the home of the Duke of Argyll, and demolished in 1860, was originally built as the Corinthian Bazaar in 1864 and then became the Palais Royal theatre. In September 1871 Charles Hengler staged the opening night of his Grand Cirque of equestrian demonstrations. When the National Skating Association learnt that the circus was to close down they took a lease on the building. This would account for the seemingly interchangeable contemporary references to either Hengler's Ice Rink or National Skating Palace. It took a few months to fit the refrigeration plant, which also produced around 15 tons of ice per day for the commercial market. Electric lighting, then a comparatively new marvel, was also installed.

At the end of the 1903/04 season the rink closed. The main auditorium and back-of-house areas were pulled down in 1908 to be rebuilt as the London Palladium, now a Grade II Listed building. The original Corinthian Bazaar façade fronting Argyll Street was retained. On the rear to Great Marlborough Street is a blue plaque with a brief history of the building.

LONDON – MICHAEL SOBELL CENTRE

Opened:	15 December 1973	Address:
Ice Size:	130ft x 60ft (40m x 20m)	Michael Sobell Sports Centre
Total Spectator Capacity:	200	Hornsea Road
Seating Capacity:	Nil	Islington
Ice Hockey – First Match:		London N7 7NT

14 December 1974: Sobell Colts *v.* Deeside Flames (Under-14 challenge) followed by Sobell Saints 3 *v.* Deeside Dragons 4 (Under-18 challenge)

England

Teams:

Sobell Saints	1974/75 challenge games; 1975–78 Southern 'B' League
Sobell Colts	1974–76 challenge games; 1976/77 Southern Junior League
Sobell Racers	1979/80 Inter-City Junior League
Sobell All-Stars	1979/80 Inter-City Intermediate League (all games away)
London 'All-Stars'	1981/82 Midland League (all games away)
Islington (London) All-Stars	1984/85 British League Division 2 – South (all games away)
London Sobell	1981/82 Midland League Division 2

Honours:

Saints	1975/76 Winners Southern 'B' League Southern Section; 1977/78 Champions Southern 'B' League
Colts	1976/77 Champions Southern Junior League
All-Stars	1984/85 Winners British League Division 2 – South

The first new ice rink to be opened in London for thirty-six years. Part of a larger £2 million sports complex, which includes indoor climbing walls. Financed by industrialist Michael Sobell, it was opened on 21 November 1973 by the Duke of Edinburgh.

Owing to the small size and a handrail, rather than a solid boarded barrier, at the perimeter, the rink is only suitable for beginners and children's ice hockey. Youth coaching commenced in January 1974. The first 'house' league game was held on 31 May that year, as Sobell Saints and Islington Rebels (Under-18) tied 2–2. The prime movers were the first rink manager Tony Mould, soon replaced by Mike Smith, and Dave Richards, who had played junior ice hockey at Harringay. Teams were promptly entered into the Southern Junior and B/Intermediate Leagues. It was soon apparent that as the skating abilities, skills base and age of the players increased the facilities at Sobell were inadequate. However, in the ice-starved London area it enabled many youngsters to gain a taste for ice hockey. Several progressed to other teams as more rinks opened in the 1980s, including goalie Jeff Smith, Freddie Sandford and Ron Austin. The experience of Czechoslovakian netminder Bob Mitura helped the older 'All-Stars.'

In the spring of 1977 Colts defeated Grimsby 17–6 on aggregate, home and away, for the Southern Junior Championship. Denis Philip was the leading points scorer with 18 goals and 11 assists. A year later Saints beat Blackpool by three penalty goals for the Southern 'B' League Championships, after tying 2–2 in regulation time. As the 1980s dawned fixtures were not always fulfilled, Mike Smith moved to Streatham and the youth programme faded away.

LONDON – LEE VALLEY

Opened:	28 January 1984	Address:
Ice Size:	180ft x 85ft (56m x 26m)	Lee Valley Ice Centre
Total Spectator Capacity:	1,000	Lee Bridge Road
Seating Capacity:	850	Leyton
Ice Hockey – First Match:		London
5 February 1984: Lee Valley Lions 11 v. Oxford University 9 (challenge)		E10 7QL
		England

Teams:

Lee Valley Lions	1983/84 challenge games; 1984–95 British League Division 1
London Racers	2003–05 Elite League
Lee Valley Whalers	1988/89 English League Division 2; 1989–91 English League Division 3; 1991–96 English Conference
Lee Valley Cubs	1990/91 English League Division 2 (Under-21); 1991/92 English Under-21 League
Lee Valley Sharks	1986–92 & 1993–95 English Junior/Under-16 League/Conference
Lee Valley Wizards	1985–90 & 1992–95 English Pee-Wee/Under-14 League/Conference
Lee Valley Colts	1999–2003 English Under-14 League
Lee Valley Lions	2003–05 English Under-14 League
Lee Valley Lions	2001–05 English Under-16 League
Lee Valley Colts	1998–2002 English Under-12 League
Lee Valley Lions	2002–05 English Under-12 League
Lee Valley Lions	2002–05 English Under-19 League

Honours:

Lions	1985/86 Winners Division 1 Trophy
Whalers	1989/90 Winners British League Division 3 – South
Sharks	1990/91 Winners English Junior Under-16 'B' League – South
Lions	2004/05 Winners English Under-16 League Division 2 – South

Construction was funded by Lee Valley Recreational Authority and the Sports Council, each contributing £1 million. The architects – Building Design Partnership (BDP) – conceived a new design departure for rinks by specifying nine three-pinned arches, spanning 40m in cold rolled curved steel sections, covered by a profiled metal insulated sandwich roof. A similar design, with adaptations to provide enhanced seating accommodation, was utilised later for the Slough and Chelmsford rinks.

The senior Lions, run for many years by the rink, although not a title contender in later campaigns, gained a loyal, almost fanatical group of followers. They worked very hard behind the scenes to keep the club afloat.

Rink manager Mike Smith recruited several players from Sobell and Geoff Williams from Solihull to combine with a couple of London-based North Americans, including Dave Worthman. With the rink opening late the rookie Lions were restricted to challenge matches. In March the Canadian Old-Timers (over-35) Hockey Association staged a week-long sixteen-team international tournament at Lee Valley.

Competitive hockey commenced in the autumn as Lions, with three imports in Bill Watson, Steve McCormack and Finnish netminder Vesa Pennanen, entered Division 1 of the Heineken-sponsored British League (BL). They set the early pace with four straight victories, tailing off to win only four of their final ten, for sixth from eleven. Pennanen was the division's best goalminder with an 86.4 per cent save record. Next year was Lions' most successful as two more Finns were signed, Janne Lehti and Ari Arvila. Promotion was missed by one point as Solihull Barons piped Lee Valley to the divisional title.

Consolation came with a second leg final 9–1 win over Barons on 20 April at the Lions' den in the Division 1 Trophy. Lehti and Arvila finished fifth and seventh in division scoring, on 133 and 126 points. All three Finns were voted onto the All-Star team. Arvila did not return next winter as Lions failed to build on the success of 1985/86. Imports came and departed, as did a succession of netminders following the sacking of Pennanen after a poor performance in the Autumn Cup. Two Americans, fresh out of Boston College, Neil Shea and Mike Barron, joined to inspire Lions to eight consecutive wins. Shea then assaulted a match official to be suspended for the remainder of the season. Barron also left. Lehti contributed 103 goals and 78 assists for fifth in points, the highest by a defenceman in the division. Average attendances of 583 stood at seventeenth for all British hockey rinks.

Looking towards the bar, 1948.

For the next eight years Lions struggled to stay in contention. For 1987/88 Doug McEwen up front and Jaroslav Lycka on the blue line notched up over 100 points each. The highlight was the defeat of Telford for the first time. With a seventh place finish Lions retained their place in Division 1 due to Richmond electing to drop out. Homegrown Ed Joseph and Tari Suwari became local heroes as import Dave Ducharme, with 124 points from 24 matches, ended as ninth-highest scorer in the division. A year on Deeside saved Lions from relegation in similar circumstances. Midway through the season of 1990/91 Alec Goldstone, previously with Streatham, came in as team manager. He settled the line-up with Greg Cyr and Rod Schluter joining Randy Oswald. Backstopped by Jim Graves, Lions won all four of their relegation play-off matches to retain Division 1 status. Director Terry Mills and player Steve James used some of their own money, assisted by Lions' first major sponsor – British Engine Insurance Ltd.

James, now the team owner, struggled on as all the plexi-glass was stolen. With Graves steady in the nets and veteran Brit Tony Goldstone up front Lions escaped from relegation. The slide continued in 1992/93 with only three wins for a cellar finish. South African coach Lindsey Miles took over in mid-winter from Ed Joseph, import changes continued and discipline improved. This time Lions were saved from demotion as the BIHA decided to decimate the English League by promoting five teams, to enable the BL Division 1 to form two regional sections. Lions, with veteran import Fred Perlini and Darcy Cahill (79+157) helping, gained sixth place with 14 victories. As spring 1995 blossomed, Lions finished bottom for the fourth time in their eleven years. Crowd levels sometimes dropped as low as 111. By June Steve James had had enough and on the 20th Lee Valley withdrew from the British League. After a somewhat disjointed youth programme, a new 'Junior' club came into existence in 2001, using the 'Lions' tag.

London Racers, a first-year professional team in the inaugural Elite League, transferred from Alexandra Palace in early November 2003, bringing senior hockey back to Lee Valley, after an eight-year break. They played their first fixture in their new home on 14 November, losing 6–3 to Coventry. In spite of only winning three games at Lee Valley, Racers reported that they attracted nearly 500 spectators to their Friday night matches. The following winter, with a virtually new team, including Scott Nichol and Eric Cairns from the moribund NHL, they claimed the sixth and final play-off spot.

LONDON – LONDON ARENA

Opened:	29 October 1998 (as an ice arena)	Address:
Closed:	15 June 2003	London Arena
Ice Size:	197ft x 98ft (60m x 30m)	Limeharbour
Total Spectator Capacity:	7,400 (10,000 in 1998; seating at	London
	one end removed in 2000)	E14 9TH
Seating Capacity:	7,400	England

Ice Hockey – First Match:
29 October 1998: London Knights 3 *v.* Nottingham
Panthers 4 (Superleague)

Teams:
London Knights   1998–2003 Superleague

Honours:
Knights   1999–2000 Superleague Play-off Champions

A building conversion in the summer of 1998, costing approximately £5 million, included installation of an ice pad and refrigeration plant, forty-eight luxury high-level ten-seat VIP

Knights being
introduced on
opening night.
(Mike
Smith/*IHNR*)

The entrance.
(Mike
Smith/*IHNR*)

boxes, additional seating and a centre ice video scoreboard. This formed a multi-purpose entertainment arena catering for pop music concerts, conventions, ice shows, boxing and wrestling as well as ice hockey. The previous £23 million non-ice sports arena opened in 1989, being a conversion from tobacco warehouses. It was conceived by a consortium of Mecca, Bovis and GEC and developed further by boxing promoter Frank Warren, whose company Arena Development Europe went into receivership in 1990.

Bought in May 1994 by American stadium operators SMG Management Ltd, they teamed up four years later with the Denver-based Anschutz Corporation. Anschutz initially purchased a 50 per cent share in London Arena and set up London Knights. Initially marketing was directed at the expatriate North American business community and then veered towards the indigenous population of east London. In spite of excellent sightlines from the shallow racked seating, the building lacked atmosphere and seasonal average attendances never rose much above the initial 3,122.

With the arena not opening until late October, the first-year Knights were housed at Milton Keynes, a ninety-minute drive from Docklands, where they also played their opening home fixtures. London's best performance under coach Jim Fuyarchuk was to reach the semi-finals of the Benson & Hedges Autumn Cup. The only home-grown on the roster – Ian Cooper – replaced Bruce Eakin as captain. Highly touted Kelly Glowa missed half the season with injuries.

The best of Knights' five years came during their second campaign. Only goalie Cavallin had been retained. The charismatic and driven Chris McSorley, originally from Hamilton, Ontario was the new coach. Pushing his players hard, the Knights contested for honours all winter. Newcomers to the defence included goalie Trevor Robins from Brandon, Manitoba and ex-NHL blue-liner Claudio Scremin. As B&H Cup finalists London had overcome Ayr by 7–1 in the quarter-finals and Bracknell by identical 5–3 victories in the semis. It took nine penalty shots before Manchester broke the 4–4 tie in the final at Sheffield. Fourth in the league, Knights topped their play-off group. McSorley turned off the rough stuff as Mark Bultje broke the 1–1 deadlock in overtime in the semi-final at Manchester. Next day Knights took Newcastle 7–3 for their only major trophy. All-Star 'A' acknowledgements went to Scremin, Knights' leading scorer, and forward Rob Kenny.

During 2001/02 Knights won over half their home fixtures and contested fiercely in every competition. Newcomer Bryan Richardson ended as top scorer with 47 points. Ex-NHL hard man Dave 'Moose' Morissette averaged nine minutes a game in the penalty box. The eastenders loved it.

With Cooper being sacked prior to the end of the previous campaign, Cardiff-born Nicky Chinn became London's sole Brit. A Benson & Hedges Cup 'home' fixture was played at Milton Keynes due to problems with the ice in Docklands. In the play-off semi-final they faced Ayr at Nottingham. Knights needed to come from behind for the 2–0 victory. Sheffield proved too strong in the final, winning 2–1. Trevor Robins, with the best save percentages, was named to the All-Star 'A' team.

McSorley moved onto to the Anschutz-owned Geneva club, as Manitoba-born Bob Leslie coached for 2001/02. Dave Trofimenkoff from Calgary took over in goal from the injured Robins. London seemed to have a penchant for outstanding defencemen as they signed Montreal-born Maurizio Mansi. He ended as the league's top-scoring defender and an All-Star 'A'. Mike Barrie (20+24) missed many games through suspensions from his 140 penalty minutes. Knights slid to sixth in the seven-member Superleague. In the finals weekend at Nottingham Knights took an early 2–0 semi-final lead over Sheffield but could not hold on, losing 3–2.

Mark Kolesar, in his third year in a Knights sweater, was the best scorer in all competitions with 51 points. A late change of coach, to Swedish-born Jim Brithen, propelled Knights to the 2003 finals weekend. In the last match at London Arena on 26 March Knights blanked Bracknell Bees 6–0 in the play-offs. Dennis Maxwell, a hero to the London fans for his gritty play, exploded for the winning goal with two seconds remaining for a 4–3 semi-final victory over Nottingham. Next day Belfast ran out 5–3 winners.

In the six years many foreign teams met Knights at the Arena, including Hanover and Schwenningen from Germany and the Norwegian clubs Storhamer and Valerengen in the Ahearne Trophy. In August 2002 the Anschutz-owned teams of Berlin Eisbaren, Hamburg Freezers, Geneva Eagles, Sparta Praha and Stockholm Hammarby met in a pre-season tournament. CSKA Moscow also visited.

Following negotiations by a consortium, including Anschutz, for a long-term lease of the nearby Millennium Dome, planning permission was granted, in late 2002, for the redevelopment of the London Arena site by property developer Barrymore. Popular music groups occasionally used the building as a practice facility. The arena was demolished during the summer of 2006.

LONDON – NIAGARA

Opened:	7 January 1895	Address:
Closed:	Late 1902	Niagara Hall
Ice Size:	Circular – approximately 70ft in diameter	20–25 York Street (now Petty France)
Total Spectator Capacity:	Unknown	Westminster
Seating Capacity:	Minimal	London W1
Ice Hockey – First Match:		England

During 1896/97 season: Niagara *v.* Stanley Brothers Sextet

Teams:
Niagara   1896–1902 challenge games

Honours:
Niagara 1897/98 British club Champions

Built as the Westminster Panorama in 1881, to display a panorama of the Battle of Waterloo. The sixteen-sided polygon, 130ft in diameter, designed by R.W. Echs had few architectural pretensions. Called the National Panorama in 1882, next year the building stood empty. It was renamed in 1888 the Niagara Hall with a new façade, to house a spectacular panorama of the Niagara Falls, which is reputed to have attracted over a million visitors.

A new 'Niagara Falls' was painted onto the walls, and remained when the building was converted to an ice rink. For a time it was one of the most popular resorts of fashionable London with skating exhibitions, ice carnivals and in 1902 the World Skating Championships. The rink was small in diameter, with limited spectator accommodation upstairs between the supporting columns.

Although a puck and not a ball was used in the ice hockey matches played at Niagara, it bears little resemblance to the sport we know today. One of the factors was the small and circular playing surface requiring chicken coop type goal cages. There was no off-side rule.

Records of early days are sparse but it is known that in the 1896/97 season the Niagara team were easily beaten by Edward Stanley and five of his brothers. Edward became the 17th Earl of Derby, serving as Secretary of State for War 1916–18. His father Lord Stanley donated the Dominion Hockey Challenge Cup for annual competition in Canada. It is now better known as the Stanley Cup. During 1898/99 Edward, Arthur F. and F.W. Stanley joined R. and J. Gossett, plus B. M. 'Peter' Patton to take on Niagara. Dropping 2–0 behind Niagara came back to win 3–2. Prominent for the victors were J.H.H. Nation, P. Platt and S.R. Beresford. In a sport that only the wealthy had the time to practice, many of these players bore titles or graduated to high ranks in the military. The Stanleys were all Honourables, with A.F. and F.W. becoming colonels and winning the DSO. Nation was also a DSO, brigadier-general and Memmber of Parliament. During February 1902 the Amateur Skating Club from Henglers staged one of the last matches at Niagara. Reds beat Whites 3–1 in a game lasting twenty minutes. Among the players were Bruce Harding, W.A. Webb, Gerald A. Turnout, W. Strange, G. Mayer, H. Uthke, L.H. Turner, Alfred C. von Berg and F. Siegle.

The building became a garage/workshop, first for carriages then motorcars. It was transferred to government control in 1942 and was demolished in 1964 when engineers discovered the ironwork to the dome roof to be in a dangerous condition. Ministry of Defence buildings adjacent to the Home Office complex now occupy the site, which is virtually opposite the current Passport Office.

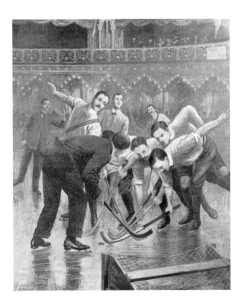

A stylised drawing of a game between members of the amateur skating club in January 1902. (*The Illustrated Sporting & Dramatic News*)

LONDON – PARK LANE

Opened: 1929
Closed: 11 April 1934
Ice Size: 171ft x 71ft (170ft x 77ft according to one source)
Total Spectator Capacity: 1,500
Seating Capacity: 500
Ice Hockey – First Match:
30 April 1930: Princes 3 *v.* Cambridge University 0
(British League play-off)

Address:
Park Lane Ice Club
Grosvenor House
86 Park Lane
London SW1
England

Teams:
Grosvenor House Canadians 1931–34 English League Division 1
Grosvenor House Canadians 'A' 1931–34 English League Division 2

Honours:
Canadians 1933/34 Champions English League
Canadians 'A' 1931/32 Champions English League Division 2

The rink was situated at basement level in the still-functioning Grosvenor House Hotel, built 1926–28. The eminent architect Sir Edwin Lutyens designed the west façade. York Shipley Ltd installed the freezing plant. When the rink ceased to operate it became the ballroom/banqueting suite of the hotel, now known as the Great Room. During the Second World War it served as an American Officers' mess, frequented by Generals Eisenhower and 'Blood and Guts' Patton.

According to Carl Erhardt it was 'too small for the best type of game' and 'it was a terribly hot place to play in', although a team formed soon after the rink opened. On 16 April 1930 Grosvenor House visited Hammersmith, losing 5–2. John T. Moore Brabazon MC kept goal for the visitors with the Hon. J. Mitford on the forward line. Brabazon was the first holder of a pilot's licence in England, and during the war was Minister for Aircraft Production. Fourteen days later Princes shut out Cambridge University in a British League – South semi-final. In April 1931 the seminal Grosvenor House Canadians were formed, pioneering the importation of paid players, along with Queens.

With F.L. Summerhays as president and Canadian George A. Strubbe as secretary and treasurer, the formidable pair recruited a strong side. This included J.E. Elkins in goal, Dr T.M. Kellough, Bernard H. Fawcett, Scottish-born Don A. Porter (21), Bob Rogers, Edward H. Jackson, later manager of Wembley Lions, English-born Harry Mayes (the captain), Eric Hualsoe, Keith Thomson (22) from Ontario and Peter Fair (26) on the left-wing. Fair, born at Kingston, Ontario, was a flying officer in the RAF. They won 7 of their 12 games in the first division of the English League, to finish as runners-up to the unbeaten Oxford University. They lost their first game at Grosvenor House, being shut out 2–0 by London Lions. A victory was achieved on 11 November as Manchester went down 6–2. The most thrilling match of the season occurred at Park Lane on 2 March as the reigning champions Oxford took a two-goal lead in the second period. R. Cossey and W.H. Bostock equalised for Grosvenor House before a long-distance shot by Larry Bonnycastle gave the postgraduates both points. The second team – Grosvenor House 'A' – won 7 out of 9 games for the Division 2 title.

The Scottish League, on tour, was held 1–1 on 6 January, with Jackson scoring for Canadians in the first period. Twelve days later Ottawa Shamrocks shut out Great Britain by 7–0 in the first match to be broadcast over the wireless in Britain. On 30 March Boston Olympics beat England 5–1 with Mayes scoring for the losers in the final period. Rogers, Mayes, Fair and Thomson represented Great Britain in the European Championships held in Berlin in March, where they finished seventh.

Canada attacking the English goal. England 0 Canada 7, 18 January 1932. This was the first match to be broadcast on the wireless in Britain. (*The Illustrated Sporting & Dramatic News*)

Montreal-born Jimmy Carr (20), a regular army officer, the American C. Cunningham and McQuire were added for 1932/33, as Grosvenor House won 8 out of 10 of their league fixtures. The struggle for runners-up position on 8 March saw Canadians blank London Lions 6–0 in, for the standards of the time, a rough encounter. Cunningham and Fair hit a brace apiece. In the Second Division the 'A's managed 3 wins to finish fourth. In the internationals Canadians unexpectedly beat Berlin SC 6–2 on 9 November, taking a 4–1 lead by the first interval. Cunningham and Carr each notched a hat-trick. The South of England went down 4–1 three weeks later to Edmonton Superiors. On 4 January, with four of their best players on international duty, Canadians were beaten 3–2 by Stade Francais. Edmonton blanked Grosvenor House 4–0 on 25 January with Alfred C. Critchley refereeing. Three years later he was responsible for the construction of Harringay Arena. England lost 5–2 on 29 March, in the BIHA International Trophy, to Boston Olympics, the newly crowned World Champions. Gerry Davey and Fair scored for the losers in the first period.

For their third and final English League campaign Grosvenor House engaged several outstanding members. Some stayed to make their mark on the sport in Britain. Defenceman Gordon Dailley from Calgary, Manchester-born Jimmy Borland, both aged twenty-two and homebred Londoner Bob Wyman (20) all collected gold medals at the 1936 Olympics. Albert Duncanson, a centre-ice was a member of Canada's 1932 Olympic gold medal squad. Among others were left-wing George McWilliams (24) from Winnipeg, Glen Morrison (23) on right-wing, H. Yeandle from Western University, Ontario, J.M. Kennedy, a flying officer from the Royal Military College at Kingston, Ontario and goalminder Lyle Holmes. Some, if not all, were paid a form of wage. Canadians lost just 1 of their 12 EL matches in scoring 75 goals and conceding 22. Grosvenor House beat league-leading Streatham 5–4 on 20 December. Although finishing third, on 9 February Oxford University, on their own ice at Botley Road, inflicted a 3–2 defeat on the semi-pros. In the return, five days later, it took overtime before Canadians emerged with a 4–3 win. Gordon Johnson, urged on by a large contingent of students, put the university ahead early on. Playing catch-up Duncanson equalised at 3–3 on a power play. McWilams, with his second of the evening, broke the deadlock with three minutes of overtime remaining. A 7–7 tie was the outcome in the traditional League Champions *v.* The Rest at Park Lane on 28 March. Canadians beat Streatham 3–1 in south London on 6 April for the London Cup in Grosvenor House's last-ever match. The 'A's, with 1 win, finished in the Division 2 cellar.

Austria was the first international visitor that winter, beating Grosvenor House 3–1 on 25 October. Thomson netted for the Canadians in a rough game. Ottawa Shamrocks, billed as 'Canada', opened their European tour by defeating England 7–1 on 29 November. Two weeks later, in a rugged encounter, goals by Duncanson and Kennedy gave Grosvenor House a 2–1 victory over Francais Volants. The USA met England with five members of GH Canadians, in the fifth and last match in this series on 10 January at 9 p.m. A fast game refereed by Blaine Sexton, ended in a 0–0 tie after ten minutes' overtime. The home country came close when they took on the USA on 7 March, losing by the odd goal in three. England's Duncanson opened the scoring in the second period. Outshooting the visitors 20 to 10 England had two goals disallowed in the last period.

In early February Mayes, Fair, Borland and Jackson, with two goals each, helped Great Britain to eighth place in the 1934 World and European Championships at Milan.

Next autumn Grosvenor House transferred almost en bloc, to become Wembley Canadians.

LONDON – PRINCES

Opened:	7 November 1896	Address:
Closed:	Summer 1917	Princes Ice Rink
Ice Size:	210ft x 52ft	Montpelier Square
Total Spectator Capacity:	Not known	Knightsbridge
Seating Capacity:	Not known	London
Ice Hockey – First Match:		England

13 February 1897: Princes 6 v. Fenwick's Team 3 (challenge)

Teams:

Princes	1897–1914 challenge & cup matches; 1903–04 The Ice Hockey League
London Canadians	1902–04 challenge & cup matches; 1903/04 The Ice Hockey League
Oxford Canadians	1906–14 challenge & cup matches

Honours:

Princes	1899–1901, 1905/06,1912 & 1914 English club Champions
London Canadians	1903 English club Champions; 1903/04 Champions The Ice Hockey League
Oxford Canadians	1901, 1910/11 & 1913 English club Champions

The first rink in Britain to house an ice surface with proportions nearer to those best suited for ice hockey. Even these were less than ideal, being more than four times as long as it was wide. Glass adjacent to the ice and the stucco barriers of the grandstand were subject to being holed by flying pucks. The rink had a narrow main entrance at the eastern end of Montpelier Square with the length of the building onto Hill Street (now Trevor Place). It was built as a private club, the preserve of the wealthy and leisured. The owner Admiral Maxe, was favourable towards the sport of ice hockey. In the autumn of 1903 the lease of Princes was purchased in its entirety by Mary Russell – the Duchess of Bedford (1865–1937), – a keen skater who persuaded her husband to invest the money. The three skating events of the 1908 Olympic Games were held here.

According to B.M. Patton in his 1936 book *Ice Hockey*, the Princes ice hockey club was formed a month after the rink opened, with Charlie Napier, English-born Vane Pennell, C. and Robert French-Brewster and Patton among the founders. Their first practice took place on 4 January 1897. During the next few years matches were played at, and with, Niagara, Brighton and the Chatham-based Royal Engineers.

The first Varsity match was held at Princes on 16 March 1900. Oxford insisted that bandy sticks and a lacrosse ball should be used. Jack Cawthra from Toronto captained Cambridge who lost 7–6. Next day a combined Varsity side defeated Princes 7–2. Indicative of the transition of the sport is that in the Varsity match a year later a puck and regulation hockey sticks were used. As with twelve months earlier the Combined Varsities met Princes next evening, this time they lost, by 10–6. In the match for the Admiral Maxe Challenge Cup on 15 March 1902 Cambridge University defeated Princes by 9–5, to become English club champions.

The use of Princes enabled Canadians resident in London as students or on business to join with the locals, who had learned to skate on winter sports holidays in Switzerland. The switch to 'Canadian hockey', as opposed to the European adaptation of bandy to indoor rinks using a ball, was accelerated by the formation of London Canadians in 1902. This team consisted of Donald Hingston, Arthur Sullivan, S.D. McKenzie, G. Furlong and two Royal Engineers based at Chatham – Keith Edgar and F.F. Carr-Harris. The number of games played between Princes, Henglers, Cambridge University and the new Canadian team increased.

On 6 February 1903, in the first match between Canadian teams in Britain, a touring rugby club beat London Canadians 5–3. Princes was one of two venues for Britain and Europe's first ice hockey league, held during 1903/04, with matches at 7 p.m. Canadians defeated Amateur S.C. 8–5 in the league opener at Princes on 17 November. Four days on Princes won their first points as the Cambridge students lost 9–6. In the last game on 24 February Canadians defeated Princes 6–3 to take the title with 14 points from 8 games. Princes, runners-up two points behind, usually iced C.E.G. Vernon in goal, C.H. Hannaford and B.M. Patton as backs, with C. Clayton and Charlie Napier up front. The league was not held again due to the closure of Henglers. In their final match London Canadians beat Princes the next November. On 30 January 1906 SC Lyons paid their second visit to Princes, to lose 9–1, in a game billed as 'England v. France'. 'A large gathering cheered both teams in great style.' England: T.G. Cannon; T.J. Unite, Bethune M. Patton; Harold H. Duden; A. Noel Macklin and Napier. Two months later Paris Palais de Glace came to London to score 1 goal to the 5 for Princes, from C.M. Howell and Napier with two apiece, plus one from Duden.

The same season Rhodes Scholars at Oxford University formed the Oxford Canadians, who had a significant influence on the sport's development at Princes and in mainland Europe. In their first match on 20 March they lost 8–4 to Princes. The following day they won 4–3. The first Oxford Canadians were S. May in goal, Reginald Murray and Ralph Bellamy in defence with Talbot M. Papineau, G. Herbert Bond and Gilbert L. Stairs, the captain, in attack. Papineau was killed in action in October 1917 leading an attack at Passchendaele. Up until the First World War Princes and Oxford met frequently at the Knightsbridge rink, with one or the other winning the Maxe Challenge Cup in the annual encounter for the English championship.

Napier scored four in the 11–1 defeat of SC Lyon at Princes on 9 February 1907. On 16 March C.M. Howell scored 15 goals in the 17–0 thrashing of Brussels Club des Patineurs. Earlier in the evening Princes' first team lost 3–2 to Oxford in the Challenge Cup. A year later Princes regained the Cup in a 7–2 win with five goals from Howell and a pair by C.C. Lewis. CPP Paris visited Princes on 12 December 1908 to go down 8–2 as Macklin scored five. This was the first time the rules of the world governing body (LIHG) were applied in England. The French were back in twelve months to lose 10–6, with Tommy Sopwith, later of aircraft fame, in goal for the victors. USA-born newcomer Dr Robert Le Cron scored four times.

From late December until early February each year, Princes and Oxford Canadians would undertake continental tours. They competed with great success in the increasingly numerous international tournaments. In March 1910 England beat Scotland 11–1 in the first of such encounters. The first visit of a German team to Britain was on 27 December 1910 with Princes winning 8–3 win over Berlin SC. Princes defeated Manchester 5–2 in their visit in March 1911 and 4–1 a year later. In December 1912 Brussels returned to the Princes rink to be beaten 14–1. In a third attempt in London, Manchester were shut out 5–0 on 13 December 1913. Cawthra did all the scoring. The same month the Royal Engineers, a new team, lost 12–3 to Princes, as did Cambridge by 9–2. In March 1914 the REs and Cambridge again lost at Princes by 10–5 and 10–0. In August Europe went mad.

Probably the final match to be staged at Princes was between members of the Canadian armed forces waiting to serve in France. Many had played at the highest level in the National Hockey Association, the precursor of the NHL. The 228th Battalion (Northern Fusiliers), entered a team earlier that winter into the NHA, withdrew on 8 February 1917 and sailed for England later that month. In early April the players divided, five-a-side, into Montreal and Toronto, including four Stanley Cup winners★. The match ended at 6–6 after an hour with Toronto scoring in the first minute of overtime. Toronto: Harry Lockhart; H. or R. Reynolds, George McNamara★ (C); Burns, Gordon Keats. Montreal: Montgomery; Howard McNamara★ (C); Goldie Prodgers★; Amos Arbour★, Myers. A large attendance, included many in khaki, with some of the civilians sitting behind a glass partition drinking tea and eating cakes, greatly appreciated the exhibition, amazed and impressed with the speed and stick handling of the soldiers.

The British Ice Hockey Association, founded in 1914, lost all its files following the rink's closure. In 1931 the Daimler Car Co. was using the building. The site is now occupied by a terrace of five-storey 1970s-style brick-faced flats, with a house facing onto Montpelier Square.

LONDON – PURLEY

Opened:	5 February 1931	Address:
Closed:	Summer 1950	Imperial Ice Rink
Ice Size:	185ft x 85ft	Brighton Road
Total Spectator Capacity:	Approx. 1,500	Purley
Seating Capacity:	700	London
Ice Hockey – First Match:		England

16 March 1932: Grosvenor House Canadians 3 v. Princes 1 (challenge)

Teams:
Purley IHC   1932/33 challenge games
Purley Imperials   1933/34 English League Division 2
Cambridge University   1933/34 English League Division 1

An ice hockey club came into being early in 1932. The first game in March 1932 proved so popular that rink management arranged for Grosvenor House Canadians to meet London Lions on 15 April. Every available seat was sold as Canadians won 1–0. Eight days later the local Purley lads tried their luck against London Lions 'A' (Cubs); the result has not survived.

The entrance to Purley Rink. (*Skating Times*)

Above: The interior of Purley Rink. (*Skating Times*)

Right: London Canadians *v.* All-Canada (a Canadian touring rugby team) at Princes on 7 February 1903.

In the first international at Purley on 7 November 1932 England defeated Berlin SC. Neville Melland and A. Searle Leach scored in the first period, overcoming Rudi Ball's opening goal for the Germans, in front of a 'full house'. Purley shut out London Lions 'A' by 3–0 on 23 October and met Streatham on 16 November for a 1–1 tie. Another draw occurred on 14 December with Grosvenor House 'A' as neither side could score. Boxing Day afternoon London Lions 'A' (Cubs) were defeated. On 18 January Southampton won 3–1. Streatham were also victorious when they returned on 9 February. Purley's outstanding player was goalie George Mason. He progressed to play for England in the 1934 annual clash with Scotland.

Next season, with improved lighting and a PA system installed, greater emphasis was given to hockey. Games were advertised in the press. Purley, with the suffix Imperials, entered Division 2 of the English League with seven local homegrown lads and Canadians Jim Arnott and Potts. Helped by a new forward line of the experienced Arnott, J. Markham and C. Rhodes they won three of their four home games, and two on opponents' ice, to finish second behind Bournemouth. On 29 November Streatham 'A' lost 3–0 to goals from Rhodes, Arnott and Veitch. Queens 'A' were crushed 6–1 on December 13. Bournemouth won by 8–2 on 13 January with Markham getting both of Imperials' markers. After being 5–1 ahead against Grosvenor House 'A', Purley hung on for a 6–5 win. The only international was on 21 November as England, with Lyle Holmes of Grosvenor House in the nets, on a goal from Gordon Dailley, shut out France. Division 1 hockey was seen at Purley as Cambridge University gained 'home' ice at Brighton Road. Two of the students' five games were cancelled, as the university authorities would not grant sufficient leave. They lost the others to Queens 5–0 on 7 December, 4–1 to Streatham on 23 November and on 1 February were shut out 6–0 by Warwickshire. From next autumn Purley featured an 'all-skate' policy; hockey and speed skating were out.

The Canadian YMCA took over the rink during the Second World War and operated armed services hockey. Stewart McPherson broadcast the semi-finals of the Canadian Forces League during a heavy air raid with a 1,500 crowd in attendance. Following closure the ice plant moved to the rebuilt Southampton rink. The building became a Mecca dance hall and still exists as an entertainment venue.

LONDON – QUEENS

Opened:	3 October 1930	Address:
Ice Size:	220ft x 65ft (67m x 20m), since	Queens Ice Rink
	early 1990s shortened to 50	17 Queensway
	metres	Bayswater
Total Spectator Capacity:	1,500 pre-1990	London W2 4QP
Seating Capacity:	1,000 pre-1990 – now minimal	England
Ice Hockey – First Match:		

9 December 1930: Queens Club 0 *v.* Princes 'A' 3 (challenge)

Teams:

Queens   1930–32 challenge games; 1932–35 English League Division 1;
                1935/36★ English League Southern Section; 1936–38 chal-
                lenge games (mainly away)
                ★also played as Earls Court Marlboroughs

Princes   1930/31 challenge games; 1931–32 English League Division 1
Princes II   1931/32 English League Division 2
Ps and Qs 'A'   1932/33 English League Division 2
Queens 'A'   1933/34 English League Division 2

A.O. Edwards, an entrepreneur with a keen interest in skating, had the rink built at the base-ment level of 'Queens Court', a block of flats. The ice plant was by York Shipley Ltd. In 1930 ice hockey practice was at 5.45 p.m. Tuesday and Fridays. According to Carl Erhardt 'the long and narrow character of the ice surface never permitted a game to develop attractively.'

Initially a new team, 'Queens Club', and the existing revived, previously homeless Princes, played at the rink. Occasional challenge matches took place in the spring of 1931. Queens drew 3–3 with Grosvenor House Canadians 'A' on 28 March and met London Lions in May. With the formation of the English League the next season Princes entered both divisions. Their better-known players included seventeen-year-old Gerry Davey, P.M. Davis, Ralph Couldrey, Ernie Ramus, A.J. Grace and Carl Erhardt, with H. Kerr in goal. At home, in their opening Division 1 game on 23 October, Manchester were shut out 6–0. On 6 November Princes defeated Cambridge University 5–1, fourteen days later the Dark Blues won 6–2. Couldrey and Grace scored for Princes. The 4 December 2–1 defeat of London Lions, on goals from Whitakker and Ramus, and an 11–3 win at Streatham took Princes to the head of the table by Christmas Eve. A 3–1 loss, at Queensway on 29 January, to Grosvenor House, combined with away defeats, pushed Princes into a third-place finish. Some Division 2 fixtures were not held, although Princes II won all their home games.

For season 1932/33 the first team remained virtually unchanged. Some fixtures still referred to 'Ps and Qs' but on 12 November 1932 the two teams merged. They beat Cambridge University at Queensway on 12 November and Manchester by 13 goals on 11 February. Coupled with two ties Queens ended fourth. The second team had won four and lost five by late February, to finish well down the table.

Autumn saw the increasing introduction of paid imported Canadians by Queens and Grosvenor House. Goaltender Art Rice-Jones, Frank Le Blanc, a centre-ice from Montreal, Blaine Sexton of the defunct London Lions, Winnipeg-born Archie Creighton (21), Bernard H. Fawcett, Uxbridge-born Ivor Nesbitt and Habbib Sursock, an Egyptian, were among the new recruits. Canadian-born William H. McKenzie of the RAF also joined. In their home opener on 4 November Fawcett with two, Sexton, Kerr, Creighton and Le Blanc were the scorers in the 6–0 shutout of Manchester.

It was Queens' turn when Grosvenor House scored the only goal a fortnight later. By Christmas they lay second to Streatham. At home on 24 January they shut out the current

The interior, 1933.
(*Skating Times*)

champions Oxford University 4–0. A fortnight later Streatham were beaten 4–3 in overtime, for Queens to end runners-up, two points behind Grosvenor House. By March 1934 Le Blanc had contributed 8 goals and 2 assists, in an era of generally low-scoring contests.

With the introduction of Wembley Arena London-based sides were more professional than amateur. Queens added balconies to increase spectator capacity, although attendances were below expectations. Nesbitt, MacKenzie and Sursock moved to Richmond. Replacements were H. Bushell, H.R. Cooke, W.C. Ross, H. Oyler, V. Dick, the veteran Dr T.M. Kellough, Bethman Hollweg, a German, and netminders Dr B.M. Allen and E.A. MacNamara. They lost their first home game 3–1 to Wembley Canadians on 2 November. Two weeks later they went down 5–3 to Richmond. Queens defeated Oxford University by the same score on the last day of that month. On 18 January Wembley Lions won 6–3. Cameron, Ross and Dick scored for the losers. In March Queens entertained Streatham on the 29th to lose 6–1. Neither Manchester nor Warwickshire fulfilled their fixtures at Bayswater, so forfeited the points. Queens finished fifth in the eight-team table.

For 1935/36 Queens opted out of the new near-all-pro English National League, to compete in the Southern Section of the English League. Among a host of players were ex-Purley goalie George Mason, returnees Creighton, Sexton, MacNamara and Fred Towell. Queens won 4 of their 9 matches before the section was disbanded. For the following two years the rink provided practice ice with the team, managed by Dr Kellough, playing the occasional challenge away game.

Before the rink abandoned the sport, internationals featured regularly. On 1 March 1932 England were crushed 8–1 by Zurich SC. The date 13 April saw a third-period goal from Peter Fair to give England a 1–1 tie with Vienna SC. On 21 October Racing Club de France inflicted a 9–4 loss on England, who went down 6–0 on 10 December to Edmonton Superiors. With 'the rink crowded to capacity' on 19 January 1933, Edmonton returned to blank the home country 2–0. Neville Melland opened the scoring, and Fair put England ahead 2–1 in the second period on 22 March, as they lost 5–2 to Toronto Nationals in the BIHA International Trophy. At the seventh attempt England won on Queens' ice, 1–0 over Austria on 23 October. Albert Duncanson netted in the fourth minute. Queens beat Francais Volants 4–2 on 16 December, a match described as 'unnecessarily rough'. Sexton was 'sent off twice'. Great Britain drew 3–3 with USA on 3 January, on first period goals from Davey and Bert Forsyth; Davey equalised in the fiftieth minute. Ottawa Shamrocks, billed as 'Canada', were victorious by 2–0 against the USA on 22 January 1934. Goalie 'Turkey' Harnedy was outstanding for the losers. On 21 December the same year Queens took on England to lose 7–5. England met Winnipeg Monarchs at Queens on 8 March 1935. The newly crowned World Champions won 7–3.

The only 'ice hockey' seen at Queens post-Second World War was on 19 November 1987 when the advertising agency Saatchi & Saatchi hired the entire rink for a pre-Christmas event. Players from the Streatham club represented Saatchi's four main departments, in a mini hockey tournament that included the expected, but staged mock punch-up.

LONDON – RICHMOND

Opened:	18 December 1928.	Address:
Closed:	December 1932 and reopened	Sports Drome
	22 September 1934	Clevedon Road
Closed:	5 January 1992	East Twickenham
Ice Size:	200ft x 81ft (60m x 25m)	Middlesex TW1 2HY
Total Spectator Capacity:	2,500	England
Seating Capacity:	1,250	

Ice Hockey – First Match:

26 December 1928: United Services 4 v. Blaine Sexton's Team 3 (challenge)

Teams:

Richmond Hawks	1934/35 English League; 1935–37 English National League
Oxford University	1934/35 English League; 1948/49 Intermediate Trophy
Richmond Redwings	1937/38 London Provincial League
Richmond Ambassadors	1950/51 & 1952–55 Southern Intermediate League; 1955–58 London Intermediate League; 1958–62 'Home' tournaments
Earls Court Marlboroughs	1948/49 Intermediate Trophy
London Phoenix Flyers	1976–78 Southern 'A' League – South; 1978–80 Inter-City 'A' League
Richmond Flyers	1980–82 Inter-City 'A' League; 1982/83 British League Division 1 Section C; 1983–89 British League Division 1; 1990/91 English League Division 1
London Phoenix Falcons	1976–78 Southern Junior League; 1978–80 Inter-City Junior League
London Phoenix Kestrals	1977/78 Southern Junior League
Richmond Falcons	1980–82 Inter-City Junior League; 1982–91 English Junior League
London Phoenix	1976–78 Southern 'B' League; 1978–80 Inter-City 'B' League
Richmond Royals	1980/81 Inter-City 'B' League; 1983/84 British League Division 3
Richmond Raiders	1980–82 Inter-City 'B' League; 1982/83 British League Division 3; 1983–88 British League Division 2; 1988–90 English League Division 2
Richmond	1979/80 Inter-City Pee-Wee League
Richmond Regals	1982/83 English Pee-Wee League
Richmond Eagles	1983–92 English Pee-Wee League
Richmond Rascals	1989–92 English Under-12 League

Honours:

Flyers	Champions 1979/80 Inter-City League and Play-offs
Falcons	Champions 1978/79 Inter-City Junior League
Richmond	Champions 1979/80 Inter-City Pee-Wee League
Richmond Eagles	Winners 1990/91 English Pee-Wee 'A' League – South
Rascals	Winners 1989/90 English Under-12 'B' League – South

The rink, on the south side of the Thames, was a conversion of the Pelabon munitions factory built in 1916. When first opened the ice was 284ft long by 78ft. The length was reduced for the reopening in 1934, with a temporary bank of seating occupying the area, increasing spectator capacity to 3,000. This seating was removed at the end of the 1936/37 season when professional hockey ceased. A swimming pool briefly occupied this end of the building before a second rink – 'The Arosa', at 85ft x 65ft – opened on 26 October 1938,

The interior
c. 1973. (Ice
& Roller
Skate)

Richmond Hawks 1936/37. From left to right: George Reading (Coach), Joe Beaton, Clarke
Morrison, Foster Dickson, Harry McArthur, Albert Conick, Bob Wyman, John Coward, Biff
Smith, George McNeil, Hamilton Riley, Rudy Pilous, Trainer, George Stubbs (Manager).

was substituted. Richmond remained open throughout the Second World War. Although a
2,000lb bomb penetrated the engine room, it failed to explode.

In the 1970s and 1980s the building went through ownership changes before being
demolished. The site remained fallow for a few years, prior to the building of luxury blocks
of flats. The contentious planning decision that permitted the destruction of a well-loved
amenity, was bitterly contested by the skating community, with allegations of underhand
dealings by the council.

It was the second rink to open in London following the First World War with several
internationals played on the long surface. Sweden defeated England 5–3 (Clarence Campbell,
2) on 27 March 1929 in front of a 2,000 crowd. Blaine Sexton scored twice for England in
the last period in the 2–2 tie with Berlin SC on 20 November 1930. On
21 January 1932 Ottawa Shamrocks defeated England 3–1 with over 3,000 spectators. Larry
Bonnycastle scored for the losers. When the building resumed as an ice rink under the control of Claude Langdon, his Richmond Hawks consisted mainly of imported players.
American goalie Clem Harnedy, replaced late season by Ron 'Scotty' Milne, with William
MacKenzie and W. Leigh formed the defence. In attack were American Tom Robertson, Joe
Beaton (24) from Nova Scotia, Hymie McArthur, Ivor Nesbitt, Habbib Sursock, Harry
Yeandle, W. Leavely and London-born Ernie Leacock – soon to take up refereeing. In the
first of their Tuesday evening home games Oxford University were beaten 4–2 on
23 October. Two further English League games were won at Richmond and one was tied,
giving Hawks fourth place in the EL. The postgraduate students from Oxford finished sixth.
Richmond fared better in the International Club Tournament winning 6 of their 8 matches

in Pool B, winning once in the final four, to end third behind Streatham and Francais Volants.

Next winter only Beaton was retained as a sham-amateur outfit being signed by coach Percy Nicklin, newly arrived in England. Netminder Jimmy Foster, 'Chirp' Brenchley and Johnny Coward were selected for GB and, along with Nicklin, came back from Germany with Olympic gold medals. Winning 14 of their 24 English National League matches Hawks finished on 33 points, as did Wembley Lions, who took the title on goal difference. Foster and Frank Currie were named to the All-Star 'A' team. Beaton, the league's leading scorer with 29 goals and 15 assists collected a 'B'. Most of the team followed Nicklin to the new arena at Harringay. His replacement, George Strubbe, recruited afresh. Neither calibre nor chemistry were right for a league which expanded to eleven. With 8 victories from a 40-game schedule Hawks occupied the cellar, seven points adrift of Manchester. Richmond dropped out of pro hockey. The youth coaching under Leacock continued for a while. Redwings, devoid of home ice, were third in the 1937/38 London Provincial League. Among the internationals held on the shorter ice was a GB trial on 18 December 1934 as England and the resident Canadians tied at five apiece. Hawks' Leacock and Nesbitt scored for England. On 12 March 1935 the World Champions, Canada, represented by Winnipeg Monarchs, suffered a 1–0 blanking by England. R. Dickson scored in the second period, with a 4,000 crowd!

Tuesday evenings in 1948/49 were given over to amateur hockey. The youngsters, under the Greg Ward-inspired 1950/51 Young British movement, became the Ambassadors. The English Under-18s met their Scottish counterparts at Richmond on 29 May 1950 and 26 March 1951, losing 4–1 and 6–1. League games were held behind closed doors on Friday evenings after public skating. Ambassadors achieved third in 1953–55 in the Southern Intermediate League. Ken Harrison led the league in 1954 with 22 goals and 10 assists. Earls Court Rangers opened their 1951/52 campaign at Richmond with six Autumn Cup fixtures before returning to Empress Hall. Apart from those six games the annual Varsity match, held between 1949 and 1966, was the only hockey the public saw during those years.

In October 1975 John Goodson and Len Cole, along with Alan Parker, Bob North and several local lads, gained permission to practice at the Arosa rink. Goodson and Cole founded the London Phoenix club, with about sixty playing members, including Czechs Bob Hrabal and Mirko Cihak plus Tom Hahn, a Canadian. Next autumn Flyers, coached by Dave Iwohn, entered the Southern 'A' League to finish fifth in the eight-team circuit. 'Home' games were held at Streatham, apart from 14 May 1977 when, after the evening public skating session, Flyers beat their south London rivals 4–3 on the larger Richmond ice surface.

Phoenix gained the confidence of rink management and from a monthly late-night match they began to stage a complete schedule in front of the paying public. Fees from a large membership helped finance teams, which usually included several overseas players at each level. In the inaugural winter a second team competed in the 'B' League, with the Falcons joining the Junior League a year later. On 3 February 1979 Flyers broke a 24-game losing run with their first ever win at Richmond, beating Oxford University 4–3. Next month the rink changed hands as Tony Carratu bought a controlling interest for a six-figure sum.

London Phoenix, coached by Dennis Horne, topped the Inter-City League, winning 13 of their 16 games, to set up a final at Southampton. Led by Canadians Bob Bechard and Dave Howden and Billy Walker, a Brit, Flyers won 10–6. Bechard had scored 27 goals in league play. With Chris Scammon, the captain and an All-Star 'A', on defence and Charlie Colon in the nets, both Americans, the Richmond club iced the maximum permitted number of overseas players. Home games were still at 11 p.m. on Saturday evenings, which drew around 150 hardy fans. By contrast an early evening Sunday start in January 1980 pulled in nearly 1,000 spectators. The Pee-Wee (Under-14) side won their league. Next winter Flyers had to give best to Streatham, although Gary Stefan, newly arrived from his native Canada, was the star of Richmond. In the three competitions he scored 60 goals, 18 more than the next highest. Now permitted to carry the prefix 'Richmond' many games were still late-evening affairs. Stefan moved to Streatham. Richmond's lack of sufficient home ice fixtures excluded them from the revived English League.

Despite skilled homegrown players such as Barry Gage, the increasing number of paid imports made it difficult for Richmond to remain competitive, even with financial support from the rink. In 1983/84, they moved to Division 1 for the remainder of the decade. In the following years Canadian law student Cory Gelman, imports Lloyd Clifford – a goalie – Jukka Korhonen, Ron Johnston, John Blais and Davd Sweeny, plus London youngsters Andy Young, Mark Salisbury were prominent in Flyers colours.

Clifford gained All-Star Division 1 ratings in 1987 and 1988. In autumn 1988 Lloyd briefly held the post of hockey co-ordinator. He engaged defenceman Mark Didcott, who took over as coach. Ex-Streatham team manager Alec Goldstone moved in, goalie Jim Graves signed in November. Streatham released Tony Goldstone, Peter Quiney and Kurt Wickenheiser who all joined Flyers. Results improved for a ninth place finish with 10 wins. Runners-up Medway were held 5–5 at Clevedon Road, as crowds improved to not far below 1,000.

In June new rink owners London and Edinburgh Trust plc announced that they were cancelling plans to provide Flyers with a budget and no money would be available. Amateur and youth teams continued, with Rascals winning their section of the Under-12 league. Flyers returned for a final season in the autumn of 1990. The second-team, Raiders, formed the core of an entry into the English League. Imports Mike Cavanaugh, as player-coach, and Darrin Zinger were joined by three homegrown returnees from the 1988/89 Flyers, including netminder Alex Barnes. Five home victories provided seventh place.

Only the Under-14s and Under-12s competed in 1991/92, with the Rascals playing in the last game of ice hockey the weekend before the doors closed forever at the Thames-side rink.

LONDON – ROMFORD

Opened:	11 February 1987	Address:
Ice Size:	184ft x 95ft (56m x 26m)	Romford Ice Rink
Total Spectator Capacity:	1,500	Rom Valley Way
Seating Capacity:	1,250	Romford
Ice Hockey – First Match:		Essex RM7 0AE
31 March 1987: Great Britain Under-19 1 *v.* Medway Bears 6 (challenge)		England

Teams:

Romford Raiders	1987/88 British League Division 2; 1988/89 British League Division 1; 1989/90 English League Division 1; 1990–94 British League Division 1; 1994/95 B&H and Southern Cup only; 1995–98 English League Conference – South; 1998–2005 English Premier League
Romford Buccaneers	1988–92 English League Division 2; 1992–94 English Under-21; 1994–2005 English Under-19 League
Havering Hornets	1987–90 English Under-16 League
Romford Hornets	1990–2005 English Under-16 League/Conference
Havering Hurricanes	1988–90 English Under-14 League
Romford Hurricanes	1990–2005 English Under-14 League/Conference
Romford Mini-Hurricanes	1990–97 English Under-12 League/Conference
Romford Raptors	1997–2005 English Under-12 League

Honours:

Raiders	Winners 1987/88 British League Division 2; Winners 1996/97 English League Conference – South; Champions

	2000/01 Play-offs English Premier League; Winners 2001/02 & 2004/05 Premier Cup
Buccaneers	Winners 1991/92 English Under-21 'B' League – South; Winners 2002/03 English Under-19 'B' League – South
Havering Hornets	Winners 1987/88 English Under-16 'B' League – South
Romford Hornets	Champions 1990/91 English Under-16 League; Winners 1992/93 English Under-16 South-East Conference; Winners 2003/04 English Under-16 'B' League – South
Havering Hurricanes	Winners 1998/99 English Under-14 'B' League – South
Romford Hurricanes	Winners 1992–94 English Under-14 South-East Conference
Romford Mini-Hurricanes	Winners 1992/93 English Under-14 South-East Conference

Publications:
A Decade on Ice, Power, Lee, 1997, Lee Power

Designed by London Borough of Havering's architects department and constructed at a cost of £3.5 million. Alan Weeks – BBC ice sports commentator – officially opened the rink, which has excellent sightlines from the tiered seating along both sides, on 31 March 1987. Rink manager Adrian Florence engaged Gordon Jeffrey, a Canadian, to form Romford Raiders.

Their first competitive match took place on home ice on 13 September 1987, beating Oxford City Stars 9–6 in the British League Division 2. A mix of experience and raw youth with import Marc Chartier from Saskatoon, Erskine Douglas, Gary Bayliss, Delroy Chambers and Lennnox McCatty among others, powered their way to win Divison 2 of the British League. Dropping one point in 26 matches Raiders finished top with a 12-point margin. Chartier and Jeffrey were fifth and eighth-highest scorers in the division with 203 and 171 points respectively. With promotion the first shot at Division 1 hockey proved tough. Bryan Swystun replaced Chartier. Devoid of a major sponsor to cover the cost of the third permitted import, finances were tight. Attendances averaged 1,097. With only three wins and a tie at home Raiders slipped back to Division 2, relabelled English League First Division.

The club was now independent from the rink, with Jeffrey as manager. Chartier returned for autumn 1989. With experienced Brits Steve Condron, Fraser Hopper and Geoff Williams, plus the netminding duo of Jamie Elliot and Andy Nunn, Raiders ended runners-up. Second in the promotion play-off table ensured a return to the British League. Next season proved a triumph. Andy Heinze and Rob Stewart, plus reclassified Mark Budz, were the imports. Several talented home-grown youngsters joined. Fourth by New Year they maintained that pace with 48 points from 40 games. In the promotion play-offs they lost out to Humberside. Funding benefited from a five-figure sponsorship sum from local car dealer Gary Grimstead.

A sketch from a publicity leaflet.

With Budz not returning until late in the campaign, Raiders played most of 1991/92 an import short. Romford-developed sixteen-year-old Richard Tomalin started getting regular shifts. With Dave Whistle as third import the following year Raiders improved to fifth, with success in the promotion play-offs elusive. Slight consolation was the 8–3 defeat of the mighty Durham Wasps at Rom Valley Way on 14 April 1993 in a bad-tempered display. Whistle accumulated 149 points for fifth in the league. Tomalin continued to improve, ending as Raiders' fifth best scorer. Jeffrey left in the summer of 1993 to be replaced by Erskine Douglas as hockey co-ordinator. Three new imports Dave Bankoske, Brad Scott and veteran Terry Kurtenback, as coach, joined holdover Stewart. Financial problems surfaced. Rink MD Phil Jinks, who now ran the club, renegotiated the imports' contracts, underpinned with finances from a local businessman. Player Tari Suwari became team manager. On 5 December 1995 Jinks pulled Raiders out of competition. The need for £30,000 and inadequate administration with imports unsigned, led to one-sided defeats.

The youth hockey programme was unaffected. A team support committee soon formed with Grimstead and Alan Bishop as managers. Troy Walkington returned to coach. Over 700 turned up as a reborn Raiders took to the ice to defeat Slough 10–1 on 10 September 1996, in the Southern Conference of the English League. Apart from Canadian Mike Rows and experienced Brits Jon Beckett and Glen Moorhouse the bulk of the team were Romford homegrowns. Being semi-finalists to Durham in the cup was a disappointment. Next winter three Finnish students, and the return of Nicky Iandoli, played a huge part in a memorable campaign. Also, local lad Danny Marshall was now a prolific scorer. They were Conference champions with only three points dropped, including one loss at home to Essex rivals Chelmsford. Crowds returned with a high of 1,125 in January. The Finns were replaced by Swedish players the following winter, as Raiders slipped to fifth.

For 1998/99 Romford moved up to the semi-pro Premier Division of the English League (EPL), enjoying varying success during the next seven seasons. A new committee came into being in 1999 with John Wright as manager. Apart from clinching the play-offs in spring of 2001 and winning the Premier Cup next winter, third in 2003/04 has been the highest placing in the EPL. A fire in the rink shop on 26 February 2004 closed the rink to the public for a month and delayed the play-offs.

An EPL fourth place, plus winning the Premier Cup and a third place play-off victory over Slough in April 2005 were a relief after the summer's uncertainties.

LONDON – STREATHAM

Opened:	26 February 1931	Address:
Closed:	1940, for use by the army as a warehouse – reopened 5 October 1946	Streatham Ice Rink 386 Streatham High Rd
Ice Size:	195ft x 90ft (59m x 28m) 210ft x 100ft prior to 1951	Streatham London
Total Spectator Capacity:	1,400 (3,000 in 1931; 2,400 in 1946; 3,348 from 1951–62)	SW16 6HT England
Seating Capacity:	120 (1,400 in 1946; 600 in 1962–80; 1,000 in 1980–92, nil 1996–2003)	

Ice Hockey – First Match:
8 March 1931: England 1 v. University of Manitoba 7 (C)

Teams:
Streatham 1931/32 challenge games; 1932–33 English League Division 2; 1933–35 English League Division 1; 1935–40 English National League; 1946–54 English National League; 1959–60 British National League

Streatham 'A'	1933/34 English League Division 2
Streatham Royals	1935/36 English League; 1937–39 London Provincial League; 1949–55 Southern Intermediate League; 1955–58 London Intermediate League; 1996–98 and 2000–05 English Under-19 League
Princes	1938/39 London Provincial League
Streatham Indians	1949–51 English Junior League
Streatham	1973/74 Southern League; 1974–76 Southern 'A' League
Streatham Redskins	1976/78 Southern 'A' League – South; 1978–82 Inter-City League; 1981/82 English National League; 1982/83 British League Division 1 Section B; 1983–89 British League Premier Division; 1989/90 British League Division 1; 1991/92 English League; 1992/93 English Conference B; 1993/94 British League Division 1; 2003–05 English National League – South
Streatham Hawks	1976–78 Southern 'A' League – South; 1978/79 Inter-City League
Streatham Bruins	1975–78 Southern 'B' League; 1978–82 Inter-City Intermediate League; 1982–88 British League Division 2; 1988–90 English League Division 2; 1990/91 English League Division 2 'B'; 1991/92 English Under-21 League
Streatham Scorpions	1976/77 Southern Junior League; 1978–82 Inter-City Junior League; 1982–2005 English Junior/Under-16 League/Conference
Streatham Braves	1979–81 Inter-City Pee-Wee League; 1982–2005 English Pee-Wee/Under-14 League/Conference
Streatham Mini Braves	1988–97 & 1998–2005 English Under-12 League/Conference
Honours:	
Streatham	1934/35 Champions English League and International Club Tournament; 1947/48 & 1949/50 Winners National Tournament; 1951/52 & 1953/54 Winners Autumn Cup; 1949/50 & 1952/53 Champions English National League; 1953/54 Winners London Cup; 1959/60 Champions and play-off Winners British National League and Winners Autumn Cup; 1973–75 Champions Southern League; 1975–77 Champions Southern 'A' League & Play-offs
Redskins	1978/79 & 1980–82 Champions Inter-City League, Play-offs and Winners Southern Cup; 1981/82 Champions English National League
Royals	1935/36 Winners English League – South; 1937/38 Champions London Provincial League
Bruins	1976/77 Champions Southern 'B' League; 1978/79 & 1981/82 Champions Inter-City Intermediate League; 1983/84 & 1986/87 Winners British League Division 2 South
Scorpions	1980/81 Champions Inter-City Junior League; 1982–87 Winners English Junior League – South; 1985/86 Play-off Champions English Junior League and British Junior Champions; 1987–89 Winners English Junior 'A' League – South
Braves	1980/81 Champions Inter-City Pee-Wee League; 1982/83 Champions English Pee-Wee League; 1983–85 & 1986/87 Winners English Pee-Wee League South; 1987–89 Winners English Pee-Wee 'A' League – South; 2004/05 Winners English Under-14 League Division 2 – South
Mini Braves	1988/89 Champions English Under-12 League

Streatham is the oldest operating rink in Britain running a hockey programme. Tesco, who purchased the building in December 2002, intend to build a supermarket on the site. This, along with a swimming pool and 250 flats, will include a replacement 60m x 30m ice pad with 1,000 seats, on the adjacent bus garage site. A condition of the planning permission for the new scheme, known as 'Streatham Hub', allows for the existing rink to remain open until the new one is built.

Robert Cromie, a well-known cinema designer, was architect for the current rink. He specified a front façade faced with a mix of reconstructed Portland stone and black faience. The original interior décor featured a kaleidoscope of motifs. Horace R. Watt of Catford SE6, the builders, took just eight months to complete the rink. The mayor of Wandsworth, Lt-Col A. Bellamy performed the opening ceremony. Carl Erhardt, captain of Britain's 1936 Olympic gold medal winners, considered Streatham 'had a more congenial atmosphere… and in this way is a pleasant contrast to the more severe stadiums'. Some scenes of the 1935 movie *Car Dreams,* with John Mills, were filmed at the rink.

The reduction in ice size during summer 1951 enabled spectator accommodation to be increased by 800 seats. Mecca purchased the building in 1962, closing it on 30 July. After a £100,000 refurbishment programme it reopened on 18 December, with a sloping plastic internally illuminated barrier surrounding the ice. It closed again on 18 May 1979. Mecca obtained a ten-year grant from the Greater London Council, replaced the ice pad and lighting, added a hockey barrier, extra seating, the country's first set of plexi-glass and a four-face electronic time clock.

In April 1990 Mecca sold the rink to Laws Estates, who replaced the roof two years later by means of a £1 million grant from the Foundation for Sports and the Arts, while removing all the seating. With the return of senior ice hockey in autumn 2003 the club restored 120 seats to the south balcony.

A few months after the rink first opened enthusiasts from the Streatham Ice Club, formed a hockey team. Challenge matches were held on opponents' rinks. In spring 1932, during a Sunday morning club session closed to the public, they took on London Lions 'A' losing 4–2. On a Wednesday in early May, with the public admitted, Streatham lost by the odd goal in seven to Grosvenor House Canadians 'A'. Gordon Thomas, D. Young and Chris Westway scored for Streatham. Stan Fitchett kept goal.

Next winter Streatham entered the Second Division of the English League. They gained their first point at home in December, in a 1–1 tie with Princes, to finish mid-table. By autumn 1933, with a core of Princes' first-team players, Streatham entered Division 1. The local pioneers continued at the lower level. With Vic Gardner in goal, Orvald Gratias, a Canadian from Oxford University, and Carl Erhardt on defence and Bert Forsythe, another Canadian, combining with Ernie Ramus and Gerry Davey in attack Streatham presented a formidable challenge. Oxford, champions for the past two seasons, were defeated 2–1 on 3 November, with goals from Gratias and Davey. Shutouts over Cambridge and Manchester helped towards a fourth-place finish in the EL. Undefeated at home next

Interior in 1932.
(Skating Times)

winter, Streatham took the league championship. They also won the International Club Tournament with eight victories and two losses. Maurice Gerth had taken over in goal. Austrian nobleman Von Trauttenberg strengthened the defence with Canadians George Shaw, 'Red' Stapleford and Bob Giddens, as coach, in attack. Next year Streatham were third in the English National League (ENL). Stapleford and Archie Stinchcombe gained 'A' and 'B' All-Star accolades. The team slipped out of contention, twice ending last and were expelled from the ENL early in 1939 for the use of suspended players. The next All-Star awards came in 1939/40 with Gib Hutchinson collecting an 'A' for netminding and Bob McCranor a 'B' for defensive skills.

For the first post-war campaign rink manager Benny Lee signed up many pre-war veterans including Davey and Stinchcombe, Frank and Lorne Trottier from Ottawa, Stapleford as coach, Scots-born George Baille and Londoner Fred Dunkleman. The crowds packed in, with hundreds queuing by 6 p.m. for the face-off nearly two hours later. In October 1948 Art Hodgins joined the defensive corps in front of second-year goalie Monty Reynolds. Both made the All-Star 'A' sextet, along with Stapleford as coach. Keith Woodall took over in the nets as the south Londoners took the league title in 1950, along with winning the mid-season National Tournament. Streatham captured the league crown again in 1952/53 with fine goal-tending from All-Star 'A' Earl Betker. Stu Robertson took the points title with 30+37. Next winter netminder Ron Kilby backstopped Streatham to Autumn and London Cup success. Right-winger Gene Miller was made an All-Star 'B' with Kilby an 'A' along with Stapleford who gained his third coaching citation.

The rink directors pulled out of pro hockey with the birth of the British National League in autumn 1954, citing consistent weekly losses and additional travel costs to Scotland. Streatham returned after five years. The twelve-man squad included two homegrown Scots in 'Red' Imrie and 'Spike' Bremner, with Bill Dobbyn as player-coach. The league title and Autumn Cup fell to the talented dozen who carried off five of the seven 'A' Star awards. Imrie was named Best British Player. Although crowd levels were good and the rink directors admitted to making a profit, they could see no future in the sport and pulled out, precipitating the collapse of the BNL. For the next two years the amateur Royals were permitted training ice and the odd game behind closed doors.

Eleven years elapsed before the homeless Sussex Senators and Wembley Vets gained a modicum of late-night practice ice at Streatham in February 1973. The clubs amalgamated in August to enter the Southern League as Streatham, with a monthly fixture at 8.30 p.m., others being late evening after public skating. In the first, on 29 September the new club lost 6–1 to SL champions Altrincham, who included six Canadians. Streatham had one, Mike Talalay. Among their roster of veterans were goalie Glynne Thomas, 'Butch' Peters, John Cook, 'Red' Devereaux, John Rost, Tony Whitehead, Vic O'Hagen and John Baxter, who scored the goal. Streatham went on to win the league and retained the title next winter undefeated.

The league split into two regions, with Streatham again unbeaten in the south, winning the play-off championship two years running. Expatriate Canadians were signing up, Richard Bacon and Ron D'Amour being prominent. Crowds built to around 600 with youngsters encouraged to take up the sport. To provide them with game experience a second 'senior' team – the Hawks – was formed for autumn 1976. The original side became the Redskins, the first champions of the Inter-City League. For season 1979/80 'home' games were at Southampton as Streatham was refurbished. Redskins returned to the High Road on 28 September with a 5–3 victory over Dunkirk. Unbeaten in the league and play-offs, home crowds averaged 1,204. Streatham repeated the feat next year, additionally carrying off the title of the revived English National League. The first of the commercially sponsored British Championship finals took place at the rink over the weekend of 24/25 April 1982. Redskins, coached by Imrie, lost out 3–2 in the final to Dundee. The first generation of the youth development programme formed the bulk of the team.

From netminder Gary Brine, defenders Trevor Cogan, Erskine Douglas and Gary 'Moose' Cloonan through to the forwards of Tony Goldstone, Dave Rapley, Peter Quiney,

The repainted frontage in 1993. (Andy Collins)

Steve James, Phil Adams, Chris Leggatt and Mark Howell – all were homebred on Streatham ice. Total recorded attendance rose by over 4,000 to 27,071. Streatham provided a showcase for the sport's authorities to demonstrate, to the London-based national print and electronic media, and sponsors, ice hockey's potential. League-wide funding from Heineken and exposure by BBC TV ensued.

The formation of the British League (BL) saw Redskins in the Premier Division, which permitted three paid imports. Streatham's third place in the inaugural season of 1983/84 was their best. Doug Merkosy joined the already-established Robin Andrew and Gary Stefan. Attendances increased by 500 to often above official capacity. Slipping to fifth in the Premier, the team squeezed past Durham for their only Wembley appearance in the British Championships. Imrie stood down as coach to be replaced by former player Bacon, a firm disciplinarian. He could not halt Redskins' slide and resigned next winter. Another ex-player, Danny Wong, took over behind the bench, giving ice time to a new wave of youth, including Neil Brown, Adrian Smith, Jim Johnston and Warren Rost. In front of a crowd of 2,500 at Wembley Arena on 27 April 1986 Scorpions shut out Durham 7–0, in the first British Junior Championship. Streatham 'seniors' struggled, failing to attract financial backing after the one-year sponsorship deal with a hamburger chain ended. Mecca stepped in to fill the breach for a while. J. Rost became coach. Stefan moved to Slough, to be replaced by Brent Hogan for 1986/87. He combined with the fiery Craig Melancon for a total of 296 points. Streatham were relegated in spring 1989 after losing a two-leg play-off to Division 1 winners Cardiff. With the rink changing hands in 1990 the new owner made it clear that there would be no cash for ice hockey.

After a year's absence Redskins returned, entering the English League. The three permitted imports were Brett Kelleher, Fred Perlini and Darrin Zinger. The Redskins' best performance at the High Road was the November defeat of newcomers Sheffield Steelers. With the pyramidal three divisional BL/EL structure destroyed, Redskins found themselves back in the BL D1 – Southern Section for 1993/94. Team spirit could not overcome the combination of changing coaches, imports and a building site for a rink. Eleven wins from 44 starts provided a two-point cushion above the cellar floor. Youth hockey continued, with silverware now elusive.

Ten winters passed before Redskins returned, all-amateur, but with the same intense enthusiasm both on and off the ice. The fans came back in 2003, as did some of the veteran Brits – Peter Quiney, Graeme Collins, Steve Paris and Adam Goldstone as coach. A fifth place in the English National League – South was no mean accomplishment. Next winter third gained the new 'Reds' access to the play-offs, with the Under-14 Braves gaining the first youth-team success of the new millenium.

LONDON – WEMBLEY ARENA

Opened: 25 July 1934

Total Spectator Capacity: 7,900 to 9,018 (10,000 in 1934)

Seating Capacity: 7,900 to 9,018 – dependent on amount of seating at east end.

Ice Size: 200ft x 85ft (60m x 26m)

Ice Hockey – First Match:

25 October 1934: Wembley Canadians 5 *v.* Wembley Lions 4 (challenge)

Address:
Wembley Arena
Empire Way
Wembley
Middlesex
HA9 1DW
England

Teams:

Wembley Lions   1934/35 English League; 1935–40 & 1946–54 English National League; 1945/46 challenge games; 1954–60 British National League; 1963–68 'Home' tournaments/challenge games

Wembley Canadians   1934/35 English League; 1935/36 English National League

Wembley Monarchs   1936–40 & 1946–50 English National League

Wembley Olympics   1935/36 English League

Wembley Terriers   1937–39 London Provincial League; 1949–55 Southern Intermediate League; 1955–58 London Intermediate League

Wembley Colts   1938/39 London Provincial League; 1948–50 Northern Tournament

Wembley Juniors   1949–51 English Junior League

Royal Air Force   1949/50 Southern Intermediate League

London Lions   1973/74 challenge games

Honours:

Lions   1935–37 & 1951/52 Champions English National League; 1935/36 Winners International Club Tournament; 1937–39 Winners National Tournament; 1937/38 & 1939/40 Winners London Cup; 1956/57 Champions British National League; 1957/58 Winners British Autumn Cup

Canadians   1934/35 Winners London Cup

Monarchs   1948/49 Winners International Tournament and Autumn Cup

Colts   1938/39 Champions London Provincial League

Terriers   1950–52 & 1953–55 Champions Southern Intermediate League

Juniors   1949/50 Champions English Junior League

Royal Air Force   1949/50 Champions Southern Intermediate League

Publications:

Wembley Presents – 22 Years Of Sport, Morgan, Tom, 1945

Wonderful Wembley, Low, A.M., 1953, Stanley Paul & Co. Ltd

Wembley Arena was the brainchild of Sir Arthur Elvin MBE (1899–1957), the then managing director of Wembley Stadium. Work commenced in October 1933, to a design in reinforced concrete by pioneering structural engineer Sir Owen Williams, for a combined swimming pool and ice rink. The large external vertical concrete fins, running down the whole length of the building, serve as a counterbalance to the thrust of the pitched roof. The span of 240ft, the largest concrete span in the world at that time provides unobstructed internal viewing. It was built in nine months by Holloway Bros (London) Ltd at a cost of £200,000.

The foundation stone was laid on 15 February 1934 by the 17th Earl of Derby, Edward Stanley, the ice hockey-playing son of Lord Stanley, who donated the famous cup for

An aerial view
c. 1938.

competition in Canada. The stone, with an impression of the Derby coat of arms, could be viewed mounted on a wall at the west end of the entrance foyer. The completed edifice was officially opened on 25 July by the Duke of Gloucester. The 200ft x 60ft x 16ft deep swimming pool housed that summer's Empire Games swimming and diving events as they did during the 1948 Summer Olympics. In 1972 the Department of the Environment protected the future of the building, listing it as being of Architectural and Historic Interest. The arena, now owned by Quintain Estates & Developments Plc, closed in January 2005 for a year-long £29 million refurbishment programme.

In October 1934 a two week shut-down took place to drain the pool, erect decking and lay a wooden floor covered with canvas, placing ten miles of piping laid in sand, through which chilled brine circulated. Water was then sprayed onto the compacted sand, which froze to form the ice pad.

With the Grosvenor House rink closed, their Canadians became ready-made companions to the newly formed Wembley Lions. Canadians added three new recruits in Winnipeg-born netminder 'Buster' Amantea, ex-Kenora Thistles teammates Clarence 'Sonny' Rost (20) on defence and centre-ice Jack Milford. Jimmy Carr, a regular army officer from Kingston, Ontario, Carl Ross and Joe Markham from the Purley club completed the line-up. Rost stayed with Wembley until the league folded in 1960. English-born Ted Jackson (34) and Gordon Dailley (23) from Winnipeg moved across to Lions, whose netminder was the diminutive American Gerry Crosby, who backstopped his country to the 1933 world title. On defence Lou Bates (22) hailed from Ottawa and became the darling of the fans with his solo rushes. Up front the 6ft 2in Edgar Murphy (25) was flanked by Bob Walton (21) and Jimmy Forsythe (21) from Edmonton. Chris Westway and Londoner Tommy Grace (20) joined from Streatham. Both teams of nine-man line-ups entered the eight-strong English League and the two five-team pools of the new European Inter-club Tournament. By the end of the following April over fifty games had been held, generally on Thursday and Saturday evenings. Canadians missed the league crown by two points, with Lions a couple of points lower in third place. The fans also watched Munich, Berlin, Milan, Prague and two teams from Paris. Other visitors included Winnipeg Monarchs, Scotland, Davos and Hamilton Tigers from Ontario. The sensational contest was Lions' 2–0 shutout of Monarchs on 28 February, both goals coming from Murphy. Monarchs, representing Canada, had won the World Championship earlier that month.

The Lemay brothers – Tony and Bert – joined Lions from Winnipeg Monarchs for the 1935/36 season. In a revamped league with 'National' added, the title was not settled until the last match at Wembley on 23 April. Fourth placed Canadians defeated Streatham to leave Lions on top, tied on 33 points with Richmond, but with a better goal difference.

Defender Des Smith and Bobby Walton on the right-wing were named to the All-Star 'A' team, the first such to be voted upon in Britain. The next season Lions retained their title with a three-point margin. The renamed Monarchs finished fifth.

The 1937 World and European Championships took place at Wembley. Britain, who included Alex Archer and Dailley from Lions, plus Monarchs' Norm McQuade, finished second behind Canada. The World event was repeated in 1950.

Lions won the National Tournament next winter. They overcame Harringay Racers 4–2 on 7 April to clinch the two-legged final 9–4 on aggregate and retained the title on 10 November in front of 10,000 fans. Lions snatched the game winner in the fifty-second minute in a 3–2 win over Racers. The ENL crown was lost by one point.

Between 1937 and 1939 a four-team junior (Under-17) house league operated with Cubs, Panthers, Princes (replaced by Bears in 1938) and Wolves, playing two ten-minute periods before the senior matches. Two Panthers and one player from Bears were killed on active service during the Second World War.

Despite wartime restrictions five London-based teams entered the competitions. Monarchs gave English lads Art Green and Johnny Oxley a chance. Lions pipped the season-opening London Cup, tying on seven points with Racers, with a +2 goal difference. The Royal Canadian Horse Artillery became the first of many armed services teams to appear at the Empire Pool as Monarchs beat the Gunners 4–2 on 20 January 1940. Winston Churchill and Anthony Eden met both teams on 24 February, prior to 2nd RCA's 8–2 win over Toronto Scottish.

Some of the troops lifted off the beaches at Dunkirk came straight to the pool, which was turned into a dispersal centre. Afterwards the building gave shelter to hundreds of homeless French, Belgium and Dutch refugees. A few months later several hundred evacuees from Gibraltar were given billets in the arena for the duration of the war.

Ice came back in December 1945 as eight Canadian service teams contested two games every evening for a week, with over 3,000 servicemen being the only permitted spectators. The first official post-war opening match took place on 15 December 1945 as Wembley Lions tied Canadian Military HQ at 4–4. Lions included NHL guests Johnny Mower, John Chad and Sid Abel. Forty-five games later, which had included many featuring stars from the NHL serving in the armed forces, league hockey recommenced. Two Monarchs would not be seen on the ice again – Glasgow-born Jimmy Kelly was killed in Holland and Frank Leblanc, who died on military manoeuvres back home in Canada.

A public skating session c. 1935.

Pre-war stalwarts, Alex Archer the coach and 'Sonny' Rost the captain, guided Monarchs in 1948. They twice came from behind on 25 November to defeat Earls Court 6–3, as Les Anning (21) and Jean-Paul Lafortune (21) netted two apiece, to clinch the Autumn Cup. The line-up included the wacky goalie Stubby Mason, Winnipeg-born 'Red' Kurz (21), a fiery defenceman and the high scoring 'Regina Peach' – George Beach (22). Monarchs also triumphed in the next competition, which included Racing Club of Paris, hence the International Tournament.

Two years on, with Britain involved in the Korean War, the pound devalued and money tight, Monarchs were disbanded. In spring 1952 a run of home fixtures allowed Lions to peak with a seven-game winning streak. The race to the wire was settled on 10 May, in front of a home crowd. Lions beat Nottingham 9–5 to capture the league crown for the first time in fifteen years. Twenty-year-old rookie Bob Cornforth from Montreal backstopped the two solid lines of Ottawa-born Bobby Dennison, Beach, Mal Davidson, Dave Maguire-Ross and Tyrell 'Rip' Riopelle. All-Star placings went to Ottawa-born Frank Boucher as coach. Cornforth topped the netminders' averages.

On 4 December 1952, in a special Royal Command charity event, in front of the Duke of Edinburgh, the *Ice Hockey World* All-Stars met and defeated Lions 2–1 before a crowded house.

In spring 1957 Lions captured the league crown for the second time since the war. Jerry Frizzell was the catalyst, following a switch to defence, paired with Curly Leachman (23), a newcomer from Victoria Cougars. Other new signings included Allan Lee, a defender from Pierson, Manitoba, ex-Nottingham captain Les Strongman, back from coaching in Zurich and Davidson, who returned from two years pounding the beat as a policeman in Winnipeg. Wembley blanked Brighton 7–0 on 23 March to commence an undefeated 12-match home stand. Lions secured the title in the final match at the pool, beating Nottingham 12–6 on 27 April. Ken Booth, from Montreal, lifted the scoring title with 22 goals and 39 assists. Ron Kilby (25) from Kitchener, Ontario, topped the netminder averages for an All-Star 'A' position. Home-grown defenceman Roy Shepherd gained a 'B' rating, with Rost gaining the coaching vote.

Newcomers to the Empire Pool were twenty-four-year-old centre-ice Clare Smith, a Canadian out of Colorado College and Gordie Lomer, last seen in a Wembley sweater during 1954/55. An 8–1 crushing of Paisley got the Autumn Cup campaign underway on 5 October 1958. Rost made his 1,000th league and cup appearance for Wembley on the last day of October. By mid-November Lions had moved to the head of the standings. They remained there, winning the last three games on the road, after the ice show moved into the pool, to clinch the cup with a three-point margin. Booth and Gordie Scott, a London-based sergeant in the RCAF, finished third and fourth in the scoring table, with 43 and 39 points.

For 1959/60 Beach topped the league scorers by a margin of eight points (30+35), to be voted onto the All-Star 'B' team. There were no overseas visitors during the winter, in a not very memorable final season of domestic pro hockey at Wembley.

Over the years one of the highlights of the season had been foreign clubs taking on Lions and Monarchs. These included Canada, represented down the years by RCAF Flyers, Edmonton Mercuries, Lethbridge Maple Leafs, Whitby Dunlops and Belleville McFarlands. Other visitors were the USA, Sweden, Czechoslovakia and the USSR, plus clubs such as AIK Stockholm, HC Davos, LTC Prague, Ottawa All-Stars and Scottish All-Stars.

Three hockey-less years followed, apart from two games between British-based players and Canadian armed forces teams. On 12 October 1963 a virtually amateur Lions returned. They consisted of nine members of Southampton Vikings, whose new rink owners Top Rank had shown the sport the door, plus Canadian defenceman Art Hodgins and twenty-five-year-old Londoner Reg Board. There were six seasons of 'Home' tournaments and challenges games, either side of the long-running Christmas period ice show. The Lions roared for the last time at the pool on 30 November 1968 in a 3–0 blanking of Paisley Mohawks.

In 1973 the owner of the NHL Detroit Red Wings set up the experimental London Lions, without a single Brit, playing a challenge series against European club teams of varying strengths. By then the void of the swimming pool had been filled in with the top-ping of a new solid ice pad. Twenty-two games later, and although well supported, despite fans seeing the same opposition three times in four days, the Lions were no more. The American backers concluded that a European league was not viable.

In April 1959 Boston Bruins and New York Rangers opened their European tour by meeting on successive nights at Wembley. Twenty-three years later Montreal Canadiens and Chicago Blackhawks met twice in September in pre-season exhibitions. Twelve months on, almost to the day, on 11 and 12 September 1993, Toronto Maple Leafs clashed with New York Rangers.

With the advent, from 1983/84, of major sponsorship of the British League by Heineken the sport returned to Wembley for one weekend each spring. Now known simply as Wembley Arena, the sponsors dubbed it 'the spiritual home of the sport in Britain'. Initially, the three-game series of two semis and a final, constituting the British Championships, took place in early May, later on in mid-April, usually with extensive television coverage by the BBC. The crowds quickly built from 2,500 for the first semi-final on 5 May 1984 to peak, with the need for additional seating, nine years later at 9,018 in the Sunday afternoon final as Cardiff beat Humberside 7–4. A fourth game – the British Junior club final – was added in 1986. This soon became a firm favourite with the large number of fans from clubs nationwide, who turned the Wembley weekend into a much loved, and now sadly missed, jamboree with an atmosphere that had to be seen and heard to be believed.

Three years after the cessation of Heineken's sponsorship, the formation of the Superleague, in 1997, ended the last hockey, to date, at wonderful Wembley.

LONDON – WEMBLEY ALPINE

Opened:	8 January 1937	Address:
Closed:	c. Summer 1940	Alpine Open Air Ice Rink
Ice Size:	175ft x 75ft	Empire Way
Total Spectator Capacity:	Estimated at approximately 500	Wembley
Seating Capacity:	Minimal	Middlesex
Ice Hockey – First Match:		England

29 January 1938: Wembley Aces 1 *v.* Wembley Vultures 0
(House 'league')

Teams:

Wembley Aces	1938/39 challenge games
Wembley Comets	1938/39 challenge games
Wembley Panthers	1938/39 challenge games
Wembley Vultures	1938/39 challenge games
Alpine Beavers	1939/40 challenge games

Panthers, Beavers, Dukes and Royals 1939/40 (Alpine House League won by Panthers)

The Alpine was the first artificially frozen public open-air ice rink in Britain. It was made possible, after much experimentation, by D.S. Burleigh of the Wembley Ice & Cold Storage Co. inventing special pipe work.

Under separate ownership and situated a few hundred yards south of the longer-established indoor Empire Pool, caused friction between the two operators. The manager, Al Gordon, had previously been the floor manager at the Empire Pool. A month after opening to the public the pool erected 18ft high hoardings blocking the Alpine frontage, and the local council received complaints about the use of the Alpine public address system on Sundays. The close proximity of the much larger and better-known arena is possibly why the Alpine's hockey teams dropped the prefix of Wembley. There was also a women's team by late 1939 – the Alpine Belles.

A raised timber walkway with café and changing rooms, skate hire etc, with backdrops depicting Alpine scenery surrounded the ice, with floodlighting for evening use. Spectator accommodation would have been limited, mostly standing with few fixed seats. The rink was enclosed from the weather in October 1939 with a partial roll-back roof to preserve the rink's unique character.

Apart from the four-team house league, visits by amateur teams from Earls Court, Sussex, Streatham and Bournemouth Stags are recorded.

A fifteen-storey office block – York House – was built on the site of the Alpine in 1962

LONDON – WESTMINSTER

Opened:	Late 1926	Address:
Closed:	Summer 1940	The Ice Club
Ice Size:	170ft x 90ft	Westminster Ice Rink
Total Spectator Capacity:	Unknown, but not large	20 Millbank
Seating Capacity:	Unknown	Westminster
Ice Hockey – First Match:		London SW1
9 March 1927: England 1 *v.* Montreal Victorias 14		England
(challenge)		

Teams:
Ice Club — 1927–29 challenge games
Princes — 1927–29 challenge games; 1929/30 British League – South
United Services — 1927–29 challenge & Cup games
London Lions — 1932/33 English League Division 1

Honours:
United Services — 1927–29 British club Champions

Westminster, opened by Sir Stephen L. Courtald, was the first rink to be built after the First World War. It enabled ice hockey to develop south of Manchester. According to Carl Erhardt – captain of Britain's 1936 Olympic gold medal-winning team – the Ice Club was 'only just open for hockey players who were merely tolerated, and although they also had to pay a substantial subscription for being permitted to practise from 9 p.m. to 11 p.m. Monday nights, were really looked upon as a nuisance'.

In Westminster's first match England, with only one native-born Brit, 'Peter' Patton, included Clarence Campbell at centre-ice. A postgraduate Rhodes scholar attending Oxford University, Campbell went onto to referee in the NHL and serve as its president for thirty-one years. Blaine Sexton scored the only goal for the home side. Three weeks later GB beat Belgium 3–1. Canada, on their way back from the 1928 Olympics, lent England three players on 8 March. One of them, Frank Fisher, along with Campbell, scored in England's 11–4 defeat. Belgium arrived a month later, Campbell netted twice in the 11–4 win. With George Rogers of Manchester in goal, England got closer to Canada (Toronto Granites) on 17 December 1929, when they lost 6–2. The next February Cambridge University overcame Japan, after overtime, by the odd goal in nine. International ice hockey ceased after 1930, around the time more suitable rinks opened in London. In late April 1927 London Lions beat Manchester 4–0 with three from E. Watts and a Sexton solo. On 14 November Cambridge University held trials, the cut to ten, followed a scratch game next evening with United Services. Two years later fifty players attended on 29 October and 6 November, to be slimmed to ten, including Peter Churchill and Frank de Marwicz.

In 1930, in the British League – South the Light Blues drew 2–2 with London Lions on 5 March, losing 2–1 to United Services five days later. On both occasions Bernard Fawcett

The Ice Club, January 1927. From left to right, back row: -?-, P. Watson, -?-, Basil Johnson, Carl Erhardt. Front row: Alfred Critchley, Victor Tait, B.M. 'Peter' Patton, -?-, W. Tretheway.

The interior, 1934.
(*Skating Times*)

scored for Cambridge. Princes II defeated University Casuals 5–1 on 14 April in the final of Division 2. Ernie Ramus netted the solo.

Club hockey returned briefly in autumn 1932 as London Lions shared their home fixtures between Westminster and Hammersmith. Neville Melland was the only home-grown player. In the final match at Westminster, on 11 March, Lions lost to near-neighbours Grosvenor House, to drop to third in the league.

The building, renamed the Westminster Ice Rink in the mid-1930s, was taken over by the BBC in 1940 to be used as a studio. It has long since been demolished.

MANCHESTER – ICE PALACE

Opened: 25 October 1910
Closed: 11 April 1967
Ice Size: 140ft x 100ft
Total Spectator Capacity: 2,000
Seating Capacity: 1,100
Ice Hockey – First Match:
17 December 1910: Manchester 5 *v.* Princes (London) 3
(challenge)

Address:
Manchester Ice Palace
Derby Street
Cheetham
Manchester 8
England

Teams:

Manchester★ 1910–14 challenge games; 1924–29 & 1930/31 challenge games;
1929/30 British League – North; 1931–34 English League
Division 1; 1934/35 English League; 1935/36 English League
– North; 1937/38 challenge games (away only); 1938–40 chal-
lenge games
★Between 1910–12 also refereed to as Lancashire

Manchester Rapids 1936/37 English National League

Publications:
The Puckchasers of Manchester, Smith, Adrian, 1995, TLH

The Ice Palace was opened by Lord Lytton. The freezer pipework, sitting on a floor of two layers of asphalt on cork, was linked to an ice-producing factory opposite. Closed in 1915, the building was used for the manufacture of observation balloons. It reopened on 21 November 1919 to be requisitioned in 1941 by the Ministry of Aircraft production and reopened as an ice rink 21 March 1947. It was purchased for £130,000 by Silver Blades-Mecca in 1962, who closed the rink for a £100,000 refurbishment on 26 August 1962, reopening it again on 21 November of that year.

A group of local enthusiasts, who had picked up the rudiments of ice hockey during hol-idays in Switzerland, banded together, with Dr Alfred Barclay (1876–1949) as secretary/play-er, to form Lancashire. They were joined by expatriate Canadians, many being medical stu-dents or doctors. The first 'Roses' clash took place on 8 March 1911. The Yorkshire Skating Association, relying for practise on scarce natural ice, had not previously used a puck. Lancashire beat them 14–0 with A. Barnes scoring six. Next year Princes came north to win 4–0, with Manchester's Leslie Hood breaking his nose in a collision with the boards and two opponents. Manchester beat Leeds University and met Oxford Canadians in the winter of 1913/14. Among the pioneers were Edgar Baerlein, Dr W. Bithell, Humphrey Shimwell, C. Clarke, T. Killick, A. Pawson, Norman Fletcher and Percy Rothband.

As the Ice Palace housed the only ice sheet in England for the next eight years, occasional high-profile matches took place. On 27 January 1922 Oxford University's Canadians defeat-ed a group of fellow countrymen serving in the British Army, 4–3. Next March Manchester and London Canadians combined to lose 5–0 to Oxford. In November 1923 The Rest met The Army in a trial for Britain's 1924 Olympic team. Blaine Sexton, with three, Hamilton Jukes, George Clarkson, and Manchester's Joe Cock, originally from Manitoba, scored for The Rest. Two years later Manchester contributed Cock, Millington and Neville Melland to the British roster competing in the European Championships. In November of that year Manchester lost 2–1 to the visiting Cambridge University. With Clarke in goal Cock scored for the seven-man squad.

By 1928 Stan Bookbinder became the regular 'keeper, as Manchester took on a greater variety of opponents. Princes went down 3–1 with a genuine hat-trick from Cock.

The interior c. 1930.

The exterior c. 1932.

Cambridge University Eskimos were shut out 6–0, with a brace from Cock, Dave Davis and Bert Wake. London Lions were also beaten. Next season, in spite of goals from Gerald White and Melland, Lions returned for a 4–2 victory. In March 1929 the Swiss side Kandersteg were defeated 10–3 with Melland scoring four and Cock three. Manchester played United Services on 6 April for the British Championship in front of a capacity 2,000 crowd. Three goals from Cock and two from Melland were not enough. In the third period Services overcame a 4–2 deficit to clinch the title 6–5 with the game winner in the five minutes of overtime.

A five-team house league, the brainchild of Stan Bookbinder, which lasted three winters, commenced in February 1930. Eagles, Medicals and Falcons each won the Spalding Trophy. In early December 1929, in the first game at Manchester with periods increased from fifteen to twenty minutes, the largest Saturday night crowd watched London Lions win 6–2. Later that month Wake, Melland and Revd Geb White scored in each period, in the 3–1 defeat of Scotland. Manchester also drew 1–1 with them later in the season, on a strike from Davies. Early in the New Year, with George Rogers in goal, Cock scored the only goal in the 8–1 defeat by BIHA Internationals. Next season Melland scored the only goal in the win over Scotland. Manchester had a poor season. Only Doctors Boyd and J. Grant on defence and local lad Joe Ferguson in attack shone.

Manchester joined the inaugural English League in autumn 1931. The first and only point gained at Derby Street, was on 21 November. Grant, the captain, netted twice to the single from Cambridge University. Fifth place and financial losses from the travel, mainly to London, ensued. In the next campaign all ten league fixtures went to the opposition. Manchester had difficulty in raising a team and postponed their first two home games. For 1933/34 the increasing use of paid 'imports' could not be matched. Manchester just avoided the cellar. Even with Canadian-trained native son Gordon Johnson, the advent in autumn 1934 of teams packed with Canadian 'imports', ensured another miserable campaign. An opening home 4–3 victory over Warwickshire on 3 November furnished the only points, with goals from P. Tingley (2) and Johnson.

Manchester was relegated to the four-member Northern Section of the English League. Among new signings were Canadians Les Tapp and Bert Shaw, along with Chris Fair, Pete Stevenson from Glasgow and goalie 'Scotty' Palfrey. The opening 7–2 challenge win on 31 October over Wembley Select, drew an enthusiastic record crowd. A switch from Thursday evenings to Saturdays helped crowds build to capacity. Four victories over the two Varsities, plus wins over lesser lights confirmed that 'ice hockey has at last caught on at the Ice Palace'. The 3 January 10–10 shoot out with 'London', followed by the 10–8 defeat of Wembley Lions thrilled the fans. Next month saw a 2–2 tie with Wembley (Johnson and Stevenson) and a loss by the odd goal in eleven to Brighton Tigers with Palfrey outstanding. March closed in a tie with Scots Canadians.

By late autumn the financially troubled French-Canadian Paris Rapides, transferred to Derby Street, although the players would live in London and train at Harringay. Additional tiers were squeezed in, to treble seating and lift total capacity to nearly 2,500 for Wednesday evening fixtures. In the first, on 18 November 1936, virtually all seats were booked prior to Rapids' 4–3 challenge defeat of London 'All-Stars'. Lionel Lafontaine netted Manchester's first goal. The locals' ex-captain, Johnson, drew shouts of 'come on Johnnie' whenever he took the ice. A week later in the ENL, the fans who braved the fog saw Lafontaine force a draw late on with Richmond. From January, weakened by injuries, Rapids hovered near the foot of the table. They ended tenth, seven points above Richmond. Rapids squeezed out Harringay Greyhounds 6–5, on aggregate, to enter the finals of the National Knock-Out Cup. In the first leg at the Ice Palace, with a full house, they drew 2–2 with Earls Court on goals from Ernie Tendreau and Len Godin. In London they lost 3–1. The other members were Johnny Lacelle, Dollar Belhumer, George Pearson, Maurice Gerin, Paul Armand, Larry Laframboise, Frank Cadorette and Dick Prouix. Tendreau ended as highest scorer with 33 goals and 8 assists. Matches late in the evening, combined with a lack of local identity, contributed to the fall in attendances.

With the abandonment of hockey by the Palace management the sport reverted to a handful of locally based members. Ice hockey returned to Derby Street on 12 November 1938, as a sizable crowd watched Grimsby beaten 6–3. Newcomer Jack Culverwell scored three solo efforts, as did Johnson, who netted twice. Next month a packed rink saw the Grimsby-based RCAF Canadians lose 5–4. Culverwell was outstanding with four goals. In early January goals from Johnson, Culverwell and Dyment contributed to the 5–3 win over Liverpool. Two months later slick teamwork from Grimsby proved decisive in their 7–0 shutout.

In the last recorded match at the Ice Palace Liverpool lost 3–2 in front of a large crowd on 3 February 1940. Ice hockey formed no part of the venerable rink's peacetime activities.

The ice was too wide and too short for ice hockey to be played and watched to its best advantage. The limited spectator accommodation was a factor in the lack of continuity of the sport, and its ultimate cessation at the Ice Palace.

For many years the building served as the offices and plant of Lancashire Dairies. The interior had been sub-divided by partitions but the balcony and facades remained. Manchester Council bought it in 2002 for £1 million. Three years later there was a proposal before the council to convert the building to units for warehousing and storage.

MANCHESTER – MEN ARENA

Opened: 15 July 1995
Ice Size: 197ft x 98ft (60m x 30m)
Total Spectator Capacity: 17,250
Seating Capacity: 17,250
Ice Hockey – First Match:
15 September 1995: Manchester Storm 6 *v.* Telford Tigers 5 (B &H Cup)

Address:
Manchester Evening News (MEN) Arena
21 Hunt's Bank
Victoria Station
Manchester M3 1AR
England

Teams:
Manchester Storm   1995/96 British League Division 1; 1996–2002 Superleague
Manchester Phoenix   2003/04 Elite League

Honours:
Storm   1995/96 Winners British League – Division 1; 1998/99 Champions Superleague; 1999/2000 Winners Benson & Hedges Cup

Publications:
The 1998 Manchester Storm Yearbook, Brierley, Chris, 1998

Constructed at a cost of £52 million, with P&O owning a fifty per cent stake. Initiated in part by government support for the Manchester bid to host the 2000 Summer Olympics, it was designed by American architects DLA/Ellerbe Beckett. The arena is built above, with a direct pedestrian link to, the existing Victoria mainline railway station. The complex includes the lightrail Metrolink, 1,075-space multi-storey car park, 100,000sq ft of offices, a multiplex cinema and a food court. It became established as a prototype for European arena design, with thirty hospitality boxes at mid height, separating the seating into two tiers. The upper level can be blanked off with black drapes. A giant video screen, scoreboard and sound system are suspended at high level above centre-ice. Capacious team dressing rooms set a new standard for Britain. The 'Nynex' (Nynex Cable Communications) Arena became the first in Britain to raise revenue via 'naming rights'.

The original operators, the New York-based Ogden Entertainment Services, purchased all the assets of the former Altrincham-based Trafford Metros, from the previous owners, the Cook Group, to form the nucleus of the Storm. They signed a three-year, six-figure deal with sportswear retailers Allsports. John Lawless, who had guided Cardiff to numerous trophies, was engaged as player–manager/coach. Fellow Canadian Daryl Lipsey, from

The aerial view.

The arena was packed with a capacity crowd of 17,245 on 23 February 1997 as Storm tied Sheffield Steelers 4-4. (Andy Yates/*IHNR*)

Swindon, signed as assistant coach. Among newcomers were Hilton Ruggles, Dale Jago, Steve Barnes, Jeff Lindsay and goalie Nathan McKenzie. Admission was set at £4 and £6. A curious 10,034 crowd watched the first game; at the first league match on 1 October 4,886 were present. From that evening's 6–2 win over Dumfries, crowds grew and grew as victory piled on victory. Further strength came with the signing in early November of Manitoba-born Shawn Byram. He was followed by dual national goalie John Finnie (23) who joined from Detroit. The British attendance record was smashed for a third time on 24 March as 16,289 witnessed Storm win their play-off group and with it promotion to the Premier Division. Finnie, Jago and Byram were all elected to the Division 1 All-Star team, with Lawless named Coach of the Year.

The Superleague commenced in autumn 1997 with Storm a natural member. Out went the majority of home-bred players and in came further imports including Brad Rubachuk, German goalie Marc Gonau, Brad Zavisha, Nick Poole and defenceman Jeff Sebastian. Another defender was a rare British signing from Cardiff in Durham-born Stephen Cooper. A succession of injuries intervened as the new league only provided 14 wins from the 42-match schedule, for eighth from nine. Combined with six losses from six starts in the European League, this caused Lawless to admit at season's end '…I underestimated the standard…'. American Kurt Kleinendorst came in as coach, plus twelve new signings. Stefan Ketola, the club's top scorer, Dave Morrison, Kris Miller, Jeff Jablonski and netminder Grant Sjervan stayed the course. In the European League Sparta Prague were beaten home and away. It took Dynamo Moscow an overtime goal to overcome Storm 3–2 at Nynex. Miller and Woodcraft made the All-Star 'A' squad. Attendances averaged 8,379. In Storm's fourth season a Stanley Cup-winning netminder Frank Pietrangelo (34) was engaged. He was joined by ex-NHLer Rob Robinson, Blair Scott, Marco Sten – a Finn – and John Weaver, a British forward from Newcastle. Storm headed the race for the Superleague crown from the beginning, lifting the title with a six-point margin, and won their play-off group. At the finals weekend, Devils shut out Manchester in the first semi-final. Pietrangelo was named Player of the Year and voted onto the All-Star 'A' sextet, as was defender Troy Neumeier. Kleinendorst picked up Coach of the Year. Attendances in the arena, relabelled MEN, were down by eleven-and-a-half per cent on the previous year.

Rick Brebant netted the goal, in the penalty shoot-out with London, to give Storm the autumn 1999 B&H Cup. That summer the arena and Storm changed hands as Philadelphia-based SMG took over. The club's GM David Davies moved on to football. American Terry Christensen came in as coach. By season's end Storm's performance was the worst since their first Superleague campaign. Greg Bullock, as the league's top scorer with 27+33, was the highlight. In April 2001 SMG sold Storm to Gary Cowan, a local commercial TV producer. He terminated Christensen's contract and appointed Daryl Lipsey. In came Joe

Cardarelli, Mark Bultje and Ivan Matulik, all experienced imports. After ending in the league cellar, a strong finish in the play-offs propelled Manchester into the finals at Nottingham. A 2–1 win over Ayr matched Storm in the final with Sheffield, who won on penalty shots. A significant hike in admission charges assisted a massive thirty-one per cent fall in attendance, dropping Storm to third in total crowds. Storm went into receivership on November 2002 allegedly owing around a £1 million, after six games at the MEN.

A new club, Phoenix, with Neil Morris as owner, arose from the ashes in summer of 2003, to join the rookie Elite League. Brebant came in as coach, to be replaced at season's end by Scotsman Paul Heavey. He guided Phoenix to a play-off semi-final. With crowds averaging no more than 2,000 per match, Phoenix suspended operations. The arena was sold to the Anschutz Corporation in spring 2004.

MILTON KEYNES

Opened:	18 June 1990	Address:
Ice Size:	197ft x 98ft (60m x 30m)	Planet Ice
Total Spectator Capacity:	2,600 (2,500 in 1990)	Milton Keynes Arena
Seating Capacity:	2,300 (a proportion with a restrict-	1 South Row
	ed view)	Milton Keynes
Ice Hockey – First Match:		Bucks
27 June 1990: England Select 1 *v.* Dutch Select 6 (challenge).		MK9 1BL
		England

Teams:

Milton Keynes Kings	1990/91 English League Division 1; 1991/92 British League Division 1; 1994–96 British League Premier Division; 1998/99 English Premier League; 1999–2002 British National League
Milton Keynes Lightning	2002–05 English Premier League
Milton Keynes Monarchs	1995/96 English Conference
Milton Keynes Thunder	2001–05 English National League
Milton Keynes Kings	1994/95 & 1998–2004 English Under-19 League
Milton Keynes Storm	2004/05 English Under-19 League
Milton Keynes Junior Kings	1992–96 & 1998–2004 English Junior/Under-16 League/Conference
Milton Keynes Storm	2004/05 English Under-16 League
Milton Keynes Pee-Wee Kings	1991–96 English Pee-Wee League/Conference
Milton Keynes Kings	1998–2003 English Under-14 League
Milton Keynes Storm	2003–05 English Under-14 League
Milton Keynes Kings	1991–96 & 1998–2000 English Under-12 League/Conference
Milton Keynes Storm	2003–05 English Under-12 League

Honours:

Kings	1993/94 Winners British League Division 1 – South; 1992/93 Winners Autumn Trophy
Lightning	2002–05 Play-off Champions English Premier League; 2003–05 Champions English Premier League
Kings	1999/2000 Winners English Under-19 'B' League – South
Junior Kings	1998/99 Winners English Under-16 'B' League – South; 2000/01 Winners English Under-16 'A' League – South
Kings	1996/97 & 1999/2000 Winners English Under-12 'B' League – South

A demonstration of the spectator sightline restrictions. (Walter Bayliss/*IHNR*)

The rink – Milton Keynes Leisure Plaza – was produced by a combination of Milton Keynes Development Corporation and First Leisure. Inadequacies in the design process led to a severely restricted view from many seats. Eight columns are located in the middle of the tiered seating. Handrails and balustrades at landings to stairs project out a couple of feet, obscuring a clear view of the ice, as does the horizontal handrail at the front row of seats. The building and ice hockey have a chequered history.

It was abruptly closed on 19 April 1993 by the original operator – First Leisure. it reopened, under the name Bladerunner Ice Arena, on 2 August of the same year by MK Ice Limited who had taken over the lease. They went into liquidation in summer 1995. A group headed by Alan Teale took over the running of the rink and the ice hockey. They closed the rink from 14 June 1996, seeking additional funding. The building did not open again until 13 April 1998, with a consequent disruption to the youth development pro-gramme. For a year some teams played out of the Stevanage rink.

Mike Sirant, a coach from Manitoba University was engaged by First Leisure, with Tony Oliver, previously with Peterborough, as team manager. The imports of Dublin-born Patrick Scott and Troy Kennedy led the short-benched team to promotion to the British League (BL). In Kings' first match at home on 1 September Richmond Flyers were defeated 7–5 in the Autumn Trophy. Scott, the leading league points scorer at 101+87, become a favourite with crowds that averaged 1,171. Rich Strachan joined as the BL third permitted import. Seventh and missing out on the play-offs were offset by reaching the final of the Autumn Trophy. It took a penalty shoot-out to eliminate Kings. Twelve months later under Don Depoe, Kings lifted the Trophy on 12 December 1992 at Sheffield Arena. They came from 3–2 down as Solihull were beaten 11–4. Strachan replaced Depoe, and signed a trio from Peterborough – goalie Scott O'Conner, Andy Allen and import Trent Kasse.

A fifteen-match winning streak before Christmas shot Kings to the head of BL 1– North. A record twenty straight victories clinched the regional title. Back-to-back wins over Telford gained Kings promotion to the Premier Division.

Strachan was named Coach of the Year. He was also voted onto the All-Star squad, along with Scott and Doug McCarthy who were first–second in divisional scoring. Attendances had risen to an average of 1,705 – eighth highest in the land. Few changes were made in summer 1994 to meet the higher standard with inevitable consequences. Nine victories in the Premier's 44-game schedule resulted in eleventh place. Scott made the top ten with 69 goals plus 71 assists. They were saved from relegation by Edinburgh's withdrawal from the top flight. New coach Stan Maple built on a roster recruited for the lower division. Kings ended one step above the cellar floor. They did top their group in the play-offs. Doug

Note the columns amid tiered seats.

McCarthy made the Premier top ten, at eighth with 80 points. Crowd levels increased by 10.31 per cent. A couple of months later the rink closed down.

Planet Ice purchased the building, for a seven-figure sum from First Leisure, to reopen the facility at Easter 1998. Businessman Mike Darnell bid for the hockey franchise, to appoint Mark Mackie as player-coach and enter Kings into the English League. Scott returned, joined by Dan Pracher, Marc Twaite, Norman Pinnington and Bobby Brown among others, with Brad Kirkwood as netminder. Kings justified their comeback, winning the inaugural English Cup in front of a capacity crowd and ending as runners-up in the EL and finalists in the play-offs. This took Kings back to the BL the following autumn. History repeated as the team ended ninth, two points above last. Rob Coutts replaced Mackie. Crowd support dropped 17 per cent to 1,291. A one-place improvement in the BNL, over the previous season, saw Kings into the play-offs. Twelve months on came an exact repetition; the team finished eighth in the league and fourth in their play-off group. Strachan had returned, as player-coach, after a six-year absence. Promising British youngster Dave Clarke was the best scorer with 45 league points. Planet Ice (PI) showed Kings the door, stating that MK Kings Ice Hockey Ltd had gone into receivership.

On 12 May 2002 the PI-run Lightning joined the English Premier League. Eleven of the new team had previously played for Kings, including coach Nick Poole and Simon Howard, his assistant. A crowd of 1,190 turned out for Lightning's first game, a 7–7 tie with Romford. A 35-match winning spell from late October was good enough for second in the EPL. With Dumas making a comeback close rivals Peterborough were beaten for the play-off championship. Gary Clarke, a Brit from Telford, led the league in scoring.

Twelve months on Lightning were league and play-off champions. Clarke headed the club in scoring with Allen Sutton the EPL's best netminder. The year 2005 saw a repeat performance from Lightning with player-coach Nick Poole third in league scoring on 61 points. Sutton again topped the netminders with a 90.7 saves percentage. A crowd of 1,550 attended the play-off final held at Coventry on 17 April as Kings defeated Peterbough 7–2.

NEWCASTLE

Opened:	18 November 1995	Address:
Ice Size:	197ft x 98ft (60m x 30m)	Metro Radio Arena
Total Spectator Capacity:	5,500 (10 VIP boxes), 7,000	Arena Way
	for non-ice events	off Railway Street
Seating Capacity:	5,500	Newcastle Upon Tyne
Ice Hockey – First Match:		NE4 7NA

19 November 1995: Newcastle Warriors 4 *v.* Fife Flyers 6
(BL Premier)

England

Teams:
Newcastle Warriors	1995/96 British League Premier Division
Newcastle Cobras	1996–98 Superleague
Newcastle Riverkings	1998–2000 Superleague
Newcastle Jesters	2000/01 Superleague
Sunderland Chiefs	2000–05 English National League – North
Sunderland Tomahawks	2000–05 English Under-19 League
Sunderland Arrows	2000–05 English Under-16 League
Sunderland Commanchees	2000–05 English Under-14 League
Sunderland Cherokees	2000–05 English Under-12 League
Newcastle Vipers	2002–05 British National League

Honours:
Vipers	2002/03 Winners BNL Findus Cup

Taylor Woodrow's remarkable ten-month construction period of the Arena commenced in February 1995. It was conceived, and part financed, by Park Arena Ltd's partners, the late Chas Chandler and Nigel Stanger, formally of The Animals pop group, who wanted a venue to host concerts. The remainder of the £10 million cost was met by facilities managers Ogden Entertainment Services (£5 million), the Bank of Scotland (£2.5 million), plus a grant from the Tyne & Wear Development Corporation. Now owned and operated by SMG it was previously known as the Telewest Arena, being renamed in January 2004.

The building was incomplete when Warriors from Whitley Bay transferred to the Arena in November 1995, to compete in the British League as Newcastle. The opening match was seen by 4,089 people, a record crowd for the sport in the North-East, and not repeated since. Attendances for the season averaged out at 2,904. With the move Gary Douville took over as coach from Terry Matthews. He brought in imports Scott Morrison, Richard Laplante and Rick Fera, all familiar with the game in Britain. A further import, Scott Campbell, a Scottish-born Canadian, signed in January. With this talent an eighth place in the league and the quarter-finals of the B&H Cup and Play-offs was less than anticipated. Warriors returned whence they came.

Sir John Hall, chairman of Newcastle United football club, and honorary president of the rookie Superleague, moved his Durham Wasps from Sunderland to Newcastle to rename them Cobras in August 1996. Hall bought the Durham Wasps title from Tom and Paul Smith in May 1995, for his short-lived N.U. Sporting Club. Coach Rick Brebant and

The internal view at completion.

The finished exterior.

Finnish assistant Timo Turunen retained eight of the former Wasps. They added a mix of Canadian and Finnish imports, who failed to gel, finishing fifth in Superleague.

Come the autumn, with a couple of exceptions, the Finns were gone. In came Brett Stewart, Randy Smith, Frank LaScala and Jonathan Weaver, a Brit from the North-East, who enjoyed an outstanding year. After seven consecutive league defeats Brabant quit. Dale Lambert took over as coach, and the team finished eighth. Spectator support was down by 10 per cent. Frustrated by the local authority refusing permission to build his own arena, partly on publicly owned land, Hall put Cobras up for sale in December 1997. There were no takers, so the league took the franchise back the following June. Sir John and ice hockey went their separate ways.

Former Durham import Mike O'Conner was appointed GM, and he engaged Alex Dampier as coach of the Riverkings. The frugal budget ensured imports were mainly aging veterans. These included Kevin Conway (35), Hilton Ruggles (35) and Stephen Cooper (32), a Brit. Four other homegrown players joined. Riverkings, with 14 wins, finished one place higher than their immediate predecessor. Attendance fell 14 per cent.

A couple of days before the next campaign the wealthy Finnish owner of Jokerit Helsinki injected a rumoured £170,000 for a share of the club, with Jukka Jalonen taking over as coach. By season's end twelve Finnish players had donned Kings' colours. The attack line of Iiro Jarvi, Kim Ahlroos and Mikko Koivunoro were extremely effective, ending as Riverkings' top three scorers. Koivunoro set a new Superleague record for most assists at 39. Back-to-back victories over Nottingham and a tie in overtime, took Newcastle through to the British finals weekend. After holding London 2–2 at the end of twenty minutes in the final the energy had gone, Knights powered to a 7–3 victory.

In April 2000 Helsinki took control of the club from Superleague. By August the London based Eye Group and their parent company Fablon Investments held a 49 per cent stake. Eye's deputy chairman and MD was Paul Smith, previously involved with Durham, and he soon became club chairman. The name was changed to 'Jesters', seen by some fans as not inappropriate. Most of the Finns had gone, although newcomer goalie Tommi Satosaari kept Newcastle in many a match. Jesters defeated London 5–3 over two legs, to contest the B&H Cup final, losing 4–0 to Sheffield. Eye Group then bought out Helsinki's controlling stake. Poor recruiting, injuries and illness saw Jesters end in the cellar. In February Eye defaulted on wages. According to the players union around £148,000 was owed at the end of the season. Crowd levels had increased by 5 per cent, to average 1,965. Smith resigned as club chairman in early September and on 24 October 2001 Superleague again took the franchise back. Jesters were alleged to have debts of £250,000. Eye Group went into liquidation as a result of a court compulsory winding-up of 27 November 2002.

The ice was removed in November 2001, to be restored the following August with the birth of Newcastle Vipers in the British National League (BNL). Team owner, Newcastle speedway promoter Darryl Illingworth, engaged Alex Dampier and Clyde Tuyl as GM and coach. Mikko Koivunoro and Rob Wilson signed up. Homebred talent Ian Defty, Simon Leach, Stuart Potts, Richie Thornton and goalie Stephen Wallace all wore Vipers uniforms. Winning two and tying a third of their home qualifying games propelled Vipers into the BNL Cup finals weekend, held at Newcastle. Vipers overcame Guildford 4–3 in overtime to reach the final. Urged on by a 3,620 strong crowd on 24 November, goalminder Pasi Raitanen shut out Coventry 3–0, on goals from Mike Lankshear, Wilson and young Brit Michael Bowman. Satosaari returned to guard the Newcastle goal for 2003/04, along with Raitanen. Wilson became player-coach with Tuyl as general-manager. A training injury kept Longstaff off the ice and less than anticipated funding forced a wages cut. Third in the cup, with fifth in the league and play-offs was not unreasonable. The fans thought otherwise as attendance averages dropped from 1,403 for the cup to 1,092 in the play-offs.

On the ice 2004/05 was Vipers' best season to date, with a runners-up finish, although missing out on a final four play-off spot. Goalminder Doug Teskey and Longstaff were voted onto the All-Star second team. Off the ice Illingworth finally put the club into voluntary liquidation in mid-February due to a sizable debt to the Inland Revenue. A consortium headed by ex-Durham Wasps player Paddy O'Connor (29) took over.

The Sunderland club continue to play their 'home' fixtures at Newcastle as their own rink closed in the summer of 2000. A few were held at Whitley Bay in 2001/02 during the iceless months in the Arena.

NOTTINGHAM – ICE STADIUM

Opened:	10 April 1939 (Reopened post-Second World War on 31 August 1946)	Address: The Ice Stadium Lower Parliament Street
Closed:	27 March 2000	Nottingham
Ice Size:	185ft x 85ft (56m x 26m)	NG1 1LA
Total Spectator Capacity:	2,950 (originally 3,000)	England
Seating Capacity:	2,850	

Ice Hockey – First Match:
12 April 1939: Harringay Greyhounds 10 v. Harringay Racers 6 (challenge)

Teams:

Nottingham Panthers	1939/40 challenge games; 1946–54 English National League; 1954–60 British National League; 1980–82 Inter-City League; 1981/82 English National League; 1982/83 British League Division 1 – Section C; 1983–96 British League Premier Division; 1996–2000 Superleague
Nottingham Wolves	1949–59 'Home' tournaments; 1951–55 Midlands Intermediate League
Nottingham Wildcats	1959–60 'Home' tournaments (probably no home ice)
Nottingham Trojans	1981/82 Inter-City Intermediate League; 1982/83 British League Division 3; 1983–87 & 1986/87 British League Division 2; 1987/88 English League – North; 1988–91 English League Division 2; 1991–93 English Under-21 League
Nottingham Jaguars	1993/94 English League; 1994/95 English Conference
Nottingham Lions	1998–2000 English League Division 1
Nottingham Leopards	1994–2000 English Under-19 Conference/League

Nottingham Cougars   1982–2000 English Junior/Under-16 League/Conference
Nottingham Tigers   1982–90, 1991–2000 English Pee-Wee/Under-14
                        League/Conference
Nottingham Tiger Cubs   1989–2000 English Under-12 League/Conference

Honours:

Panthers   1950/51 Champions English National League; 1955/56
                        Champions British National League; 1955/56, 1986/87,
                        1991/92, 1994/95, 1996/97 & 1998/99 Winners British
                        Autumn Cup; 1989/90 Champions British Play-offs
Trojans   1985/86 Winners British League Division 2 – Midlands;
                        Winners 1988/89 English League Division 2 – North &
                        Play-off Champions; 1991/92 Winners English Under-21 'A'
                        League – North & Midlands and Play-off Champions
Leopards   1999/2000 Winners English Under-19 'B' League – North
Cougars   1987/88, 1989/90 & 1998/99 Play-off Champions English
                        Junior League & Winners English Northern 'A' Section;
                        1989/90 British Junior Under-16 Champions
Tigers   1987/88 Play-off Champions English Pee-Wee League and
                        Winners Northern Section
Tiger Cubs   1995/96 Winners English Under-12 Conference – Midlands

Publications:

Nottingham Panthers, 1982, Breedon Books
Nottingham Ice Hockey Club Official Year Book 1982/83 & 1983/84
Black & Gold, Litchfield, David, 1988, News Review Publications
Nottingham Panthers Statistical Guidebook 1946–2000, Chambers, Michael A., 2000
The Official Nottingham Panthers Yearbook 2000/01, ed. Moran, Gary

The Stadium, built by Messrs Sims, Sons and Cooke Ltd, was respected by opposition players and fans alike for its tradition and intense atmosphere. It was sold to Nottingham
Corporation in the summer of 1957. The ice pad was replaced in the spring of 1983. But

The Panthers *v.* Brighton Tigers 1956/57. Nottingham star Chick Zamick is number ten on the
extreme right.

The warm-up prior to the final match, 27 March 2000.

by the 1990s it was like a once-beautiful lady, who had seen better times in her youth, now a bit shabby and down at heel, but still much loved and valued by young and old.

The souvenir brochure issued for the opening of the stadium referred to Nottingham Panthers' entry for the English National League (ENL) the following autumn. A team was recruited, one or two even had a brief look at the new rink, but wartime travel and spectator restrictions caused them to head straight back to Canada. A 'Nottingham Panthers' did play a handful of challenge games in the winter of 1939/40; the core probably consisted of Canadians serving in the armed forces. The first recorded encounter took place on 15 November 1939 in front of a crowd of 1,500. Panthers lost 11–7 to RAF Canadians. Nottingham's listed line-up: Torgalson, Spencer, J. Block, H. Block, R. Brown, Rivett, Lee, Max Keeler, White, Jones, Raines. During the war the building served as a munitions store.

A couple of weeks prior to Nottingham's ENL debut Harringay Greyhounds defeated Harringay Racers 8–4 in front of a full house. The first post-war Panthers faced off in the Ice Stadium on 22 November 1946, to beat Wembley Monarchs 3–2 in the ENL. A minute into the second period George Stevens took a pass at centre-ice to net Panthers' first league goal. The line-up was: Jack Warwick, Bob Lyons, Ken Westman, Reg Howard, Jim Herriot, George Stevens, George 'Red' Burke, Mac McLachlan, Les Strongman, H. 'Mutch' Mollard, Ed Young, Art Coyston. London-born coach Alex 'Sandy' Archer, a 1936 Olympic gold medallist, recruited the team from around the Winnipeg area. They averaged just over twenty-one years of age and were reputed to be on a wage of £10 per week. Three members of the first post-war team spent many years in Nottingham – defender Jim Herriot, Ken Westman and Les Strongman. Les returned to live in Canada in January 2003, at the age of seventy-six.

Although playing to near-capacity crowds, success was far from instant. In the Festival year of 1951 Archie Stinchcombe, another Olympic gold medal winner, guided Panthers to the ENL title by a one-point margin. A 2–2 tie with Brighton on 4 May in Nottingham and Panthers' 9–4 victory over Rangers at Earls Court, in their final game eight days later, was sufficient. The league's top scorer, centre-ice Chick Zamick (67 points), was named to the All-Star 'A' team as was Strongman at left wing. Three years later, with Jack Siemon in goal, supported by the defender Gerry Watson (25) and Zamick and Strongman up front,

An aerial view c. 1948. The entrance hall is in the right-hand corner.

Panthers won the last ENL title of that era, also by a single point gained in their last game on 4 May – a 5–5 tie at Brighton. Zamick scored his 500th goal to level at 4–4, with Ernie Dougherty netting the fifth just before the final gong. Zamick topped the league scoring for a third time. Watson was voted onto the 'A' Sextet.

The English and Scottish Leagues amalgamated in the autumn of 1954. Panthers' opponents increased from four to ten. They met the challenge ending as runners-up to Harringay. Superstar Zamick's 65 goals and 47 assists led all comers. Chick and Strongman were selected to the 'A' All-Stars. A few months later, with Zamick as player-coach, Panthers won the Autumn Cup by seven points from Paisley. His charges held off a late surge by Wembley to lift the BNL title on goal average. Nottingham scored 15 more than the Londoners and conceded 5 fewer goals. Zamick collected two All-Star accolades, an 'A' as centre as he headed the points scorers, and a 'B' as coach. Siemon collected his third successive 'B' rating as goalie. In the last gasp of the first pro BNL, play-offs were instigated. Panthers defeated league champions Streatham to meet Brighton in the final. From 5–4 down from the first leg Panthers battled Tigers to a 3–3 deadlock on 6 May 1960 at the Ice Stadium in the last game. Fittingly Les Strongman cancelled out a Brighton goal. During these years Panthers also took on the national sides of Canada, Sweden, Czechoslovakia, USA and the USSR at the stadium.

The management gave little encouragement to developing local homegrown talent. Although Nottingham Wolves were in action by 1950 and competed in the Midland League, ice time for games and training was refused from 1956. Several Wolves helped out the Panthers on occasion. Scottish-born forward Dave Ritchie dressed on 131 occasions to contribute 2 goals and 9 assists. Sam Strachan had 44 outings.

It was twenty years before hockey was seen again at the Ice Stadium. The bulk of Sheffield Lancers, from the Inter-City League, under Nottingham-born manager Gary Keward formed the reborn Panthers. Keward persuaded the new stadium manager Malcolm Balchin and in particular director Charles Walker, to allow hockey back into the building. After two games behind closed doors, and with Strongman as coach, they defeated Solihull Barons 7–4 in a challenge on Nottingham ice on 20 September 1980, drawing a crowd of around 850. By mid-November full-house signs were out. Fourth in the Inter-City, Panthers moved to runners-up in their second campaign and occupied the same position in the new English National League. Founder members of the British League, results were mid-table or lower. This changed from autumn 1985 with the appointment of Alex Dampier as non-playing coach. Twelve months on Panthers topped their group of the Norwich Union-sponsored Autumn Cup, eliminating Whitley to reach the final. An over-time goal from Layton Eratt gave Nottingham a 5–4 victory over Fife and the first major piece of silverware in thirty-one years. A bronze-medal finish in the Premier Division followed with Dampier elected to All-Star coaching slot. The import trio of Fred Perlini, Jim Keyes and Terry Kurtenback provided firepower. Brian Cox and Ian Woodward, both British, shared netminding duties. Two years on Dampier brought in Darren 'Doc' Durdle to partner Kurtenback on the blue line, with Bruce Thompson as the lone import forward. This unusual move took Panthers to the British finals at Wembley for the first time. League champions Durham were beaten 8–6 in the semi-final. Next day in the final Ayr went down 6–3. Dampier was named 'Coach of the Year', with goalie David Graham and Durdle voted onto the All-Star team.

The youth programme, commencing almost as soon as hockey returned to Nottingham, was now producing not only championship teams, but also a steady talent stream for Panthers. During the 1990s, the league title continued to elude the Midlands club, although they almost made the Autumn Cup their own, with four wins in nine years. In 1991 Cardiff went down 6–4 in the semi-final. Local lad Simon Hunt (18) netted a hat-trick in the 7–5 triumph over Humberside. Youngsters Randall Weber, Simon Perkins and Stuart Parker shone in Panthers colours. The cup returned to Nottingham's trophy cabinet three years later with Mike Blaisdell as coach. Winning seven of their eight matches took Panthers to the semis where Edinburgh were defeated 25–11 on aggregate. In the final Cardiff lost 7–2. The coach netted a hat-trick. Third in the league, All-Star accolades went to Gareth Premack and Chuck Taylor on defence, forward Rick Brabant and Blaisdell. Sweet home and away victories in the semi-final over Sheffield, with a 5–3 defeat of Ayr in the final, provided the cup. In the Superleague era all scoring came from the imports with Greg Hadden potting a brace. Premack and Paul Adey made it to the All-Stars. After a tough preliminary round in autumn 1998, Panthers edged Manchester and Ayr by one-goal margins for their fourth cup of the decade. Third in the league and an agonising 2–1 loss in the British final followed. Adey and Hadden gained end-of-season recognition.

At the conclusion of Panthers' last game in the Ice Stadium on 27 March 2000 the emotional crowd mingled with the players on the ice. Happy spectators were permitted to dismantle and take away signs, seats and other removable items as souvenirs before the bulldozers moved in.

NOTTINGHAM – TEMPORARY RINK

In May 2000, due to demand for public skating and practice ice by Nottingham's ice hockey teams, prior to the completion of the second ice pad, and with numerous non ice bookings in the main stadium, a temporary rink opened on Handle Street NG3 1JE, near the Ice Centre. This was located in the disused Robinsons Fruit and Veg cold store. The 100ft x 80ft (30m x 24m) ice surface, was directly enclosed by walls with two small viewing areas, being accessed via the store's loading bay and corridor. This facility closed down in June 2001.

NOTTINGHAM – ICE CENTRE

Opened: 1 April 2000 (main stadium),   Address:
                           7 April 2001 (second ice pad)   National Ice Centre
Ice Size: Two pads both 197ft x 98ft (60m   Lower Parliament Street
                           x 30m)   Nottingham
Total Spectator Capacity: 6,500 (48 VIP boxes) main   NG1 1LU
                           stadium   England
Seating Capacity: 6,500 – main stadium, 300 –
                           second ice pad – training/
                           public skating rink

Ice Hockey – First Match:
9 April 2000: Nottingham Vipers 3 v. Slough Phantoms 4 (Women's League)

Teams:
Nottingham Panthers   2000–03 Superleague; 2003–05 Elite League
Nottingham Lions   2000–03 English Premier League; 2003–05 English National
                               League
Nottingham Leopards   2000–05 English Under-19 League
Nottingham Jaguars   2004/05 English Under-19 League
Nottingham Cougars   2000/05 English Under-16 League
Nottingham Jaguars   2002/03 English Under-16 League
Nottingham Lynx   2004/05 English Under-16 League
Nottingham Tigers   2000/05 English Under-14 League
Nottingham Ice Cats   2003–05 English Under-14 League
Nottingham Tiger Cubs   2000–05 English Under-12 League

Honours:
Panthers   2003/04 Winners Challenge Cup
Leopards   2000–02 Champions English Under-19 League
Tiger Cubs   2001/02 & 2004/05 Champions English Under-12 League
Tigers   2003/04 Winners English Under-14 'A' League – North;
                               2004/05 Champions English Under-14 League

Publications:
Nottingham Panthers Official Yearbook 2001/02, 2002/03, 2003/04 & 2004/05, all ed.
Moran, Gary, Nottingham Panthers IHC

Built on the inner-city site of the demolished Ice Stadium, the NIC has been designed by
Nottingham City Council department of Design & Property Services, in association with
Faulkner Browns and constructed by Laing. The cost was approximately £40 million, with
£22.5 million from Sports Council Lottery Fund. The NIC Charitable Trust contributed
£11.1 million with English Partnerships adding a further £1 million. It is owned by
Nottingham City Council, via a trust set up to manage and operate the Centre. The first
complex in Britain with twin Olympic size ice pads, it was officially opened on 17 May
2000 by Kate Hoey MP, then Minister for Sport.

   A crowd estimated at 4,800, the largest in the history of ice hockey in Nottingham,
watched Panthers' first game in their new home on 2 September 2000. Barry Nieckar and
ex-NHLer Jim Paek scored in Nottingham's 2–1 B&H Autumn Cup win over London.
The team progressed to the semi-final where they met Sheffield who won both legs. The
fans became convinced that the short-staffed Panthers, owned by Neil Black since August
1997, via his operating company Aladdin Management, were being deprived of funds. At

Interior view.

Christmas Peter Woods, a former GB coach, was engaged for his technical expertise. Four wins out of six in the Superleague over deadly rivals Sheffield, including a 5–0 blanking of Steelers at the NIC in the play-offs, helped ease concerns. P.C. Droin (26) from Quebec led the Panthers in scoring with 20+34, for fourth place overall among the nine league teams. Just two Brits iced for Panthers. Ashley Tait, who enjoyed regular shifts to contribute 26 points, and the young Paul Moran. He suited-up nineteen times. Paek was the sole Nottingham recipient of All-Star acknowledgement – with an 'A' rating.

Thirteen newcomers for 2001/02 and a coaching duo of Dampier and Paul Adey, a rookie behind the bench, moved Nottingham up four places in the league. Droin still headed the Panthers in scoring, with support from Vancouver-born stalwart Greg Hadden and new signing Lee Jinman (26). Consistency in the nets helped; Canadian Danny Lorenz faced more shots than any other netminder. Runners-up in the qualifying round of the Challenge Cup provided a two-legged semi-final with Ayr. Shut out 3–0 in Scotland, Panthers could only hold the eventual winners to a 4–4 tie at the Ice Centre. Average attendance for the season rose by 5.9 per cent to 4,374. For the third winter in the NIC, Panthers finished third in the league, with Superleague membership down to five. With Adey now in sole charge Tait and Moran were still the only homegrown on the roster. Panthers possessed three of the leading four league scorers in Jinman, Greg Hadden and Mark Cadottee. Nottingham ended the most penalised side, averaging just over thirty minutes a match. In the play-off semi-final Panthers conceded two late goals to London when 3–2 ahead. Winning their qualifying round of the Challenge Cup and a 3–2 victory over Belfast, took Panthers to their first final since moving into the NIC. At Manchester, Panthers slipped 3–0 behind to Sheffield by the fiftieth minute. Briane Thompson and Hadden provided respectability. At the end-of-season voting by the British Ice Hockey Writers' Association Jinman made the first team. Spectator levels again increased to average 4,654.

For season 2003/04 the bankrupt Superleague metamorphosed into the eight-member Elite League, with Panthers' owner Neil Black extending his lease of NIC ice. The Elite's reduced wage cap provided additional Brits: David Clarke, Mark Levers and back-up net-minder Geoff Woolhouse. Levers and Daniel Scott were products of Nottingham's youth development system. Thirty-two-year-old American Afro-haired right-winger Jim Craighead could score goals and indulge in the rough stuff. With 23 victories Panthers ended as runner-up to Sheffield. Revenge came in the Challenge Cup final. At the Ice Centre on 9 March Nottingham held Steelers 1–1 in front of nearly 5,000 fans, via a Clarke goal. Eight days later in Yorkshire Kim Ahlroos slotted in a sudden-death goal fifty-three seconds into overtime to clinch the silverware 3–2. In Panthers' second final of the

The external view.
(Mike Smith/*IHNR*)

campaign Sheffield regained the lead in the second period, to win the play-off final by the odd goal in three. Craighead was named to the first All-Star team. Strangely the crowds were down to average just under 4,000 per game. Much was expected from Panthers for 2004/05 but they struggled to clinch fourth for the last play-off slot. Following a dose of mumps Craighead moved to Cardiff. The acquisition of NHL holdovers Steve McKenna, Nick Boynton and Ian Moran helped Panthers to a superb closing display in the EL Final, a 2–1 loss to Coventry. Panthers' top scorer was David Clarke with a total of 62 points.

Foreign opposition had not been neglected as Panthers met two German and a Norwegian Elite team in successive seasons of the short lived Ahearne Trophy. Russian sides visited the NIC in 2001. AK Bars Kazan beat Panthers 6–1 in late August. Highlights of the Boxing Day 3–3 draw with Dynamo Moscow were shown later on Sky TV. Next year Panthers defeated the Americans of Princeton University 5–2.

From its opening the Ice Centre has provided a home to the traditional end-of-season play-off weekend for the British Championship, usually to sell-out crowds.

OXFORD – BOTLEY ROAD

Opened:	7 November 1930	Address:
Closed:	9 March 1934	100/120 Botley Road
Ice Size:	200ft x 100ft	Botley
Total Spectator Capacity:	Approximately 3,000	Oxford
Seating Capacity:	Estimated at 1,200	England

Ice Hockey – First Match:
19 November 1930: Oxford University 3 *v.* Berlin SC 1
(challenge)

Teams:
Oxford University 1930/31 Challenge games; 1931-34 English League Division 1
Oxfordshire 1931–33 English League Division 2

Honours:
Oxford University 1931–33 Champions English League

Designed by architect J.R. Wilkins, with the front façade in 'Guidstuc', which was floodlit at night. 'Daylight' lamps were installed internally for moonlight effects. There was also a club lounge with 'writing tables, books and comfortable chairs'. Like so many rinks at that time it was soon converted into a cinema – the Majestic. Wartime evacuees were housed

Above: An artist's impression. (*Skating Times*)

Right: England 2 Canada 3 – the programme.

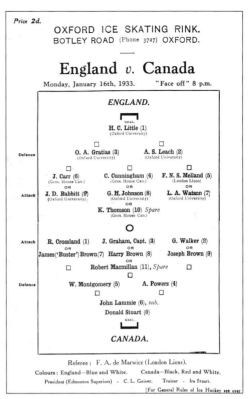

Price 2d.

OXFORD ICE SKATING RINK.
BOTLEY ROAD (Phone 3727) OXFORD.

England *v.* Canada

Monday, January 16th, 1933.　　"Face off" 8 p.m.

ENGLAND.

GOAL
H. C. Little (1)
(Oxford University)

Defence　　O. A. Gratias (3)　　　A. S. Leach (2)
(Oxford University)　　(Oxford University)

Attack

J. Carr (6)　　　C. Cunningham (4)　　F. N. S. Melland (5)
(Gros. House Can.)　　(Gros. House Can.)　　(London Lions)
OR　　　　　OR　　　　　　OR
J. D. Babbitt (9)　　G. H. Johnson (8)　　L. A. Watson (7)
(Oxford University)　　(Oxford University)　　(Oxford University)
OR
K. Thomson (10) *Spare*
(Gros. House Can.)

O

Attack　　R. Crossland (1)　　J. Graham, Capt. (3)　　G. Walker (2)
OR　　　　　OR　　　　　　OR
James ('Buster') Brown (7)　Harry Brown (8)　　Joseph Brown (9)
OR
Robert Macmillan (11), *Spare*

Defence　　W. Montgomery (5)　　A. Powers (4)

John Lammie (6), *sub.*
Donald Stuart (0)
GOAL.

CANADA.

Referee : F. A. de Marwicz (London Lions).

Colours : England—Blue and White.　　Canada—Black, Red and White.

President (Edmonton Superiors) - C. L. Gainer.　　Trainer - Ira Stuart.

[For General Rules of Ice Hockey see over

---

there in 1940, then until 1949 it served as a workers' hostel. The next year it became the home of Coopers' Oxford Marmalade until 1967. The building became an MFI furniture store and saleroom, until it was demolished in the early 1980s.

The opening of a rink in Oxford coincided with probably the strongest intake of Rhodes Scholars who also played ice hockey, since the university team was formed as Oxford Canadians in 1906. A large crowd turned out to watch the opening match. The Dark Blues then met and beat Princes and Manchester in front of an 'enthusiastic audience'. Upon returning from their annual Christmas continental trip they hosted touring teams including Davos and the University of Manitoba, who blanked Oxford 4–0 on 9 March. Eleven days later at Botley Road England defeated France 4–1. England returned on 26 March to tie Vienna 3–3. The university's outstanding netminder, Herbie Little from Toronto, played for Great Britain in the 1931 World Championships. During the Second World War he was director of Canadian Navy Intelligence. Oxford's captain that season, Ronald Martland, became Canadian Supreme Court Justice in 1958.

The sport took off at Oxford the following winter. With the students practicing four times a week, they only conceded a single goal in their five English League (EL) home league fixtures. Grosvenor House Canadians and Princes were shut out 3–0 and Sussex 4–0. Lee Watson (4), Larry Bonnycastle (3) and Searle Leach were the goal scorers in the 8–0 whitewash of Manchester, in front of 'a large crowd' on 29 January 1932. Earlier that season France beat the university 3–1. Returning from the continental tour, where they won the prestigious Spengler Cup, the Dark Blues held the powerful Boston All-Stars 0–0 on 18 February. The first forward line of Babbitt, Bonnycastle and Watson stayed on the ice throughout the match. One report states 'that there were four thousand spectators jamming the rink side and corridors and many hundreds were turned away'. Eight days later, in the 7–1 thrashing of Zurich SC, John Babbit, from New Brunswick, struck four times with Bonnycastle, Leach and Archie Humble also scoring. As champions of the English League, they beat the Rest of England 2–1 on 4 March as Bonnycastle netted both markers. The mayor of Oxford presented 'the individual members of the Oxford team with gold medals

Street elevation at night. (*Skating Times*)

in commemoration of their successes'. A team of mainly home-bred players competed in Division 2 as Oxfordshire, winning three games at Botley Road, to finish second. In other games staged at Oxford the English League held the Scottish League 1–1 on 7 January, and Gerry Davey hit a hat-trick on 15 April in England's 5–1 win over Vienna.

The university, with a virtually unchanged team, retained the EL title next winter, going undefeated. In November Grosvenor House and Manchester were again shut out at Botley Road, this time 4–0 and 16–0, with Babbitt and Watson hitting four apiece into the Lancashire net. In the Varsity match on 20 January, which doubled as an EL fixture, Gordon Johnson scored the only goal. Following the 0–0 tie with The Rest on 10 March the League Cup was presented to Oxford by 'Peter' Patton, president of the BIHA. In the internationals the university blanked Berlin SC in front of a 'record crowd' on 12 November, with Johnson scoring both goals. Edmonton Superiors won by a similar score on 1 December and beat England by the odd goal in five on 16 January. Five Varsity players represented England, including Orvald Gratias who scored in front of a full house. Four weeks later Toronto Nationals tied Oxford 1–1. In the BIHA International Trophy on 23 March Toronto and Boston Olympics, the new world champions, deadlocked at three apiece. The season closed with a flourish on 14 April as England shut out Scotland 4–0.

Gratias joined Streatham with Edward Hopkins taking over in goal and James Coyne as captain. He served as governor of the Bank of Canada 1955–61. With London clubs starting to use paid imports from autumn 1933, Oxford University lost at home in the EL for the first time in three seasons. Streatham triumphed 2–1 on 3 November, with G. Andrews scoring late on for the losers. Queens, with two third period goals, took both points on 19 January by 3–1. The students settled for third place with G. Johnson, on 12+3, one of the league's leading scorers by the time the rink closed. In their last game at Botley Road the university defeated the luckless Manchester 6–1 on 3 March.

The postgraduates beat France 4–2 on 24 November with Johnson and Babbit scoring a brace. They had lost 1–0 to Austria in late October in their first game of the season. Hopkins, in making a diving save in the first minute of the match with Ottawa on 30 November, suffered a deep cut near the left eye. He insisted in carrying on, heavily bandaged and only seeing out of one eye. Not surprisingly the university lost 10–0. In other matches at Botley Road England met Ottawa Shamrocks, billed as 'Canada', on 12 February. The visitors, who included Lou Bates, later to star with Wembley Lions, triumphed 5–2 in a brilliant game watched by a large crowd. The USA beat England 2–0 on 6 January. In the final game, a day before the rink closed for good, England had their revenge. In a match played at a tremendous pace the home country were victorious by the odd goal in three.

OXFORD – OXPENS ROAD

Opened: 1 December 1984
Ice Size: 184ft x 85ft (56m x 26m)
Total Spectator Capacity: 2,000
Seating Capacity: 1,025
Ice Hockey – First Match:
2 December 1984: Oxford City Stars 8 *v.* Oxford University 5 (British League Division 2)

Address:
Oxford Ice Rink
Oxpens Road
Oxford
OX1 1RX
England

Teams:

Oxford City Stars 1984/85 British League Division 2 – Midlands; 1985–87 British League Division 1; 1987/88 British League Division 2; 1988–92 English League Division 1; 1992/93 English Conference A; 1993/94 British League Division 1 – North; 1994–97 & 2000–02 English South Conference; 2003–05 English National League – South

Oxford University 1984–86 British League Division 2 – Midlands; 1986–2005 challenge games

Southampton Vikings 1984/85 British League Premier Division

Oxford City Satellites 1985–87 British League Division 2; 1987/88 English League; 1988–91 English League Division 2; 1994–2000 English Under-19 League

Oxford City Stars 2000–05 English Under-19 League

Oxford City Planets 1989–91 English League Division 3; 1991–94 English Conference

Oxford Blades 1998/99 English League Premier Division; 1999/2000 Cup games only

Oxford City Comets 1985–91 & 1992–2000 English Junior/Under-16 League/Conference

Oxford City Stars 2000–05 English Under-16 League

Oxford City Horizons 1985–2000 English Pee-Wee/Under-14 League/Conference

Oxford City Stars 2000–05 English Under-14 League

Oxford City Meteorites 1988–2000 English Under-12 League/Conference

Oxford City Stars 2000–05 English Under-12 League

Honours:

Stars 1984/85 Winners British League Division 2 – Midlands and Champions of Play-offs; 1990/91 Champions English League; 1995/96 Winners English South Conference

Planets 1990/91 Winners English League Division 3 – South; 1991/92 Winners English Conference – South

Horizons 1997/98 Winners English Under-14 'B' League – South

Meteorites 1997/98 Winners English Under-12 'B' League – South

Designed by architect Nick Grimshaw, to a controversial design, for Oxford City Council – the owners and operators – at a construction cost of £2.4 million. The architect, in a lecture at the Royal Institute of British Architects in March 1985, explained the reasoning behind his scheme, the twin slender steel masts supporting the roof being akin to a ship moored alongside the Thames.

The first rink manager, John Harris, told the press: 'We have time allotted to ice hockey from five to eight every Saturday and Sunday and for juniors and pee-wees for two hours every weekday evening.' Council finances enabled Stars to engage three experienced imports in Canadians Tom Smith and Jimmy Shand, both defencemen, plus Swedish junior international Urban Johansson. The latter pair headed the scoring chart on 87 and 77 points respectively. Stars' nearest rivals (literally) were Oxford University. The first 'Town v. Gown' match, won by Stars, drew an 800 crowd. In April 1985 the four divisional winners of Division 2 of the British League met over one weekend at Oxpens Road. Stars defeated Sheffield Sabres 10–2 to meet Aviemore Blackhawks in the final. Fittingly the newcomers won 6–1 on goals from Johansson with three, Shand, Paul Simpson and Mark Lewis, to gain promotion to Division 1.

Southampton Vikings, newly promoted to the Premier Division of the British League, were forced to play a few of their 'home' fixtures here during 1984/85 as Mecca, the new owners of the Southampton rink, refused to provide sufficient dates.

The imports were not up to the required standard at the higher level. Ill discipline and poor results led to a fall off at the gate. Five wins were good enough for ninth from twelve. The second and last winter in an expanded Division 1, with Stars now managed by American serviceman Ken Taggart, also yielded five victories, with relegation back to Division 2. Eight imports were tried, with Jari Virta, a Finn, contributing 99 points in a team whose penalty minutes had risen to 23.9 per game. Average attendance dropped to 474. A mid-table place for 1987/88 and the club's first major sponsor helped boost crowds. Over 1,000 were present on 21 February for the clash with Romford Raiders – the eventual divisional winners. Seven netminders had been tried. Discipline remained a problem, rising to 32.58 minutes, the highest of the three divisions.

For the next four years Stars competed in Division 1 of the English League. The third campaign under Canadian coach Don Jamieson, supported by Dan Pracher, an American with 141 points and Scotsman Scott Gough, was the most successful. Runners-up in the Autumn Trophy was followed by the league championship, with 23 victories in the 28 games. Stars won the Fair Play award with fewest penalties, averaging 9.4 minutes a game. Fifth out of six, in their section of the EL in spring 1993, the club could not resist the invitation to rejoin the Northern Section of an expanded and regionalised Division 1 of the British League, with consequent increased travel costs. Lacking a major sponsor and funding, imports came and went, as did coach James Cameron, with Stars losing 41 of their 44 matches. Oxford's senior team was back in the English League for the next three winters. At their second attempt they captured the Southern title, winning 21 out of their 22 fixtures. Gough and American-born player-coach Richard Boprey were second and third in Conference scoring with 116 and 109 points respectively.

A new team, Chill, intended to replace Stars, decamped to Swindon in early autumn 1997 as the ice plant at Oxpens Road developed a major fault. Senior hockey returned after twelve months. A group of local businessmen hockey fans formed the Blades, to compete

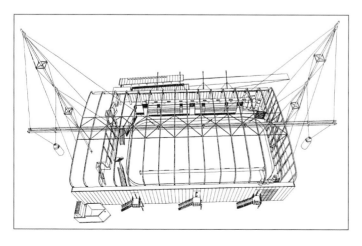

The roof of Oxford's ice rink is supported by masts and tension rods made of stainless steel for minimal maintenance, principally because only four clusters of four deep piles found the structure on its marshy site.

in the Premier Division of the English League. The core consisted of mainly locally trained youngsters with the addition of Canadian imports Brian McLaughlin, Jeff Sinnott and Sami Saarinen – a Finn. Coach succeeded coach without a single victory in the 32 matches. By January 2000 Blades had run out of money. Their results, other than eight games in the Millennium Cup, were expunged from the records. From autumn 2000 a virtually all amateur Stars contested the English Conference – South. They occupied a mid-table position, with Derek Flint one of the South's leading scorers. Missing for winter 2002/03, Stars returned the following season to the renamed English National League for a very creditable runners-up place. They repeated the feat the next winter.

The students of Oxford University tried league hockey for two seasons, before reverting to the occasional challenge match in preparation for the biannual Varsity match with deadly rivals Cambridge University. This fixture, which commenced in 1900, attracts a packed house of enthusiastic students. The 100th anniversary game, held at Oxpens Road, and fittingly won 4–2 by the 'Dark Blues', was attended by two alumni, Hugh Morrison and the late Herbie Little, from the squad which won the English League in 1932.

PAISLEY – EAST LANE

Opened:	9 April 1940	Address:
Closed:	May 1970	Paisley Ice Rink
Ice Size:	197ft x 97ft	9–11 East Lane
Total Spectator Capacity:	5,000 in 1940 (4,500 post- Second World War)	Renfrew Paisley
Seating Capacity:	5,000 in 1940 (4,500 post- Second World War)	Scotland

Ice Hockey – First match:
19 April 1940: North Scotland *v.* South Scotland

Teams:

Paisley Pirates	1946–54 Scottish National League; 1954–60 British National League
Glasgow Bruins	1947/48 Scottish National League
Paisley Wildcats	1946–50 Scottish 'Junior' Leagues and 'Home' tournaments; 1968/69 Northern Second League
Paisley Mohawks	1959–66 'Home' tournaments; 1966–70 Northern League

Honours:

Pirates	1947/48 Winners Western Section Scottish National League, Scottish Autumn & Scottish Cups; 1950/51 Champions Scottish National League and Play-offs & Winners Scottish Cup; 1953/54 Champions Scottish National League & Winners Scottish Autumn & Canada Cups; 1954/55 Winners Scottish Cup; 1958/59 Champions British National League
Mohawks	1966–69 Champions Northern League; 1967/68 Champions Northern League Play-offs; 1967/68 Winners 'Icy' Smith Cup and Autumn Cup

The concept of an ice rink at Paisley was launched with a share capital of £50,000 in 200,000 ordinary shares at five shillings (25p) each. Designed by architects F. Durret & Boston, with an ice plant installed by Lightfoot, the building occupied part of the site of the pre-1920 Abercorn Football Club. The rink functioned throughout the Second World War with many Canadian services hockey contests.

Above: The rear of the rink shortly before demolition.

East Lane entrance following closure.

Paisley Pirates joined the first post-war campaign of the professional seven-team Scottish National League (SNL), ending fourth. Canadian Jack Thaler (19) from Ontario, on the right-wing, was fifth best in league scoring with 26 goals and 23 assists. He was voted onto the first ever Scottish All-Star 'A' team, to be joined by teammate Art Hodgins (18), a defenceman, born in Canada of Scottish parents. For 1947/48 the rink ran two pro teams as Glasgow Bruins joined Paisley in the Western Section of the SNL, won by Pirates. Both Thaler and Hodgins again made the 'A' All-Stars. The experiment of two teams was not repeated. The signing of centre-ice Stu Robertson and Ken Head, a right-winger, in autumn 1949, provided fearsome shooting skills. Twelve months on the addition of Bob Kelly and defencemen Bernie Hill and Ed Shell, allied with the coaching of Aberdeenshire-born Red Thompson, an ex-referee and stern disciplinarian who took over from Perth native Tommy Lauder, brought the SNL crown to East Lane. Pirates demolished Dunfermline 17–5 in the two leg-leg semi final for the Anderson Play-off Trophy, and Falkirk 7–3 in the finals. Robertson and Head, one-two in league scoring, Shell and Thompson all made the end of season 'All-Star 'A' squad. Kelly (22) from Alberta, on the 'B's at left-wing, was named 'Rookie of the Year'. Not surprisingly the crowds returned.

Three seasons elapsed before Pirates collected further silverware under the shrewd recruiting and coaching of the bespectacled Keith Kewley. Backstopped by Ed Lockhead (22) from Ontario, with the defensive pairing of Tuck Syme (25), George Coulter (25) of Winnipeg and sharpshooting centre-ice Hal Schooley (25) from Hamilton, Ontario, Pirates took the SNL by a 14-point margin. All were named to the All-Star 'A' team. Paisley did not lose a home league encounter and only two in cup competitions. Coulter, with a total of 43 assists, was named 'Rookie of the Year' for 1953/54. Like most Scottish rinks Paisley encouraged home-grown talent from the start. In 1953/54 Bill Brennan, Bill Crawford and Dave Ferguson came of age, gaining regular berths with Glasgow-born Crawford (24) contributing 55 points. Brennan (21), a Paisley native, notched 9+26 in 54 games. The brothers 'Tuck' and 'Tiny' Syme and Joe Brown, all Scottish-born and trained and in their mid-twenties, had been regular defencemen in the SNL for some time.

The following autumn the Scottish and English Leagues combined into an eleven-member British League. Pirates claimed the bronze medal in both the Autumn Cup and BNL. Falkirk pipped them by one point in the cup with Paisley, three points behind Nottingham, heading the Scottish clubs in the league. Lockhead retained his place on the All-Star 'A's, with Kewley named to the coaching slot. George Samolenko (24) from Oshawa, at 65+57, made the 'B' squad. In the Scottish-only knockout competition Paisley defeated Falkirk in the final 6–5 on aggregate. Tommy Lemon (22) from Haileybury, Ontario, Pirates' centre-ice, became Scotland's 'Rookie of the Year'.

Paisley was the only Scottish rink to remain with pro hockey until the BNL folded in spring 1960. With the league down to four in 1958 (Edinburgh dropped out after the Autumn Cup campaign), Pirates beat Wembley by three points for the league crown. Lemon's playmaking, with 55 assists, aided the goalscoring of Ernie Domenico (30), from Timmins, Ontario, and Ike Scott. They occupied the top three places in BNL points scoring. The latter two gained All-Star 'A' accolades, as did defenceman and player-coach Bill Simpell at both positions. In the final fling of the first BNL, Pirates' fourth place finish provided a home and away semi-final with Brighton in the first play-offs of that era. Beating Tigers 5–3 in Paisley, they lost the tie 8–5 on the South Coast. Ted McAskill (23) from Ontario, who later spent four games in the NHL, headed Pirates' scorers with 27+17 for an All-Star 'B' place. Points runner-up Des Moroney went one better, collecting an 'A'.

With the collapse of pro hockey, home ice for training was only available to the all-amateur Mohawks on a spasmodic basis. Although home games were not permitted Paisley entered the reformed Scottish League in autumn 1962 and proceeded to win Section 'B' for three seasons. They triumphed over the Play-off 'A' winners Fife in spring 1965, defeating Flyers 6–4 at Kirkcaldy. Crawford, Robert Stevenson, Billy Miller, Brennan and younger brother Alistair were the top five Section 'B' scorers. Boxing promoter Peter Keenan negotiated with the rink directors for an experimental six-game series in early 1965. A near-capacity crowd attended the first game in nearly five years on 10 February. Mohawks beat Wembley Lions 6–3 on goals from Stevenson, Brown, Crawford, Miller, youngster Dorry Boyle and ex-pro Tom Lemon, making a return to the sport.

The formation of the Northern League in 1966 provided Mohawks with a genuine hat-trick of titles. Season 1967/68 saw a grand slam as Mohawks won all four competitions, losing just one game in each of the NL, 'Icy' Smith Cup and Play-offs for the Spring Cup. In the All-Star vote Billy Brennan made the 'A' team for defenceman and the 'B' as coach. Brother Ally joined him in the right-wing selection. Next year they made the 'A's. The Brennans, McBride, Miller, Ferguson and emerging youngster Al McRae were consistently in the top-ten scorers' lists. The netminding duo of Tommy Newall and Billy Laird kept the pucks out. By 1969 Mohawks were decimated by retirements and emigration. Younger players from the Wildcats replaced them, the drop in standard being reflected in lower crowds.

After closure as a rink the building became a venue for professional wrestling until 1973. It was demolished, with a supermarket built on the site for Fine Fare in 1975 designed by the Glasgow office of London-based architects Newman Levinson. Somerfield are the current occupiers of the unit.

PAISLEY – LAGOON

Opened:	August 1992	Address:
Closed:	3 September 2006	Lagoon Leisure Complex
Ice Size:	184ft x 85ft (56m x 26m)	off Mill Street
Total Spectator Capacity:	1,258	Paisley
Seating Capacity:	850	Renfrew
Ice Hockey – First Match:		PA1 1LZ
12 September 1992: Ayr Raiders 3 v. Fife Flyers 2 (B&H		Scotland

Autumn Cup).

Teams:

Ayr Raiders	1992 B&H Autumn Cup only
Paisley Pirates	1992/93 Scottish League Division 1; 1993/94 British League Division 1 – North; 1994–96 British League Division 1; 1996–98 Northern Premier League; 1997–2002 British National League; 2002–05 Scottish National League
Paisley Mohawks	1994–96 Scottish Under-19 League; 1996–98 Scottish Under-21 League; 1998/99 & 2000/01 Scottish League Division 1
Paisley Cherokees	1999–2005 Scottish Under-18/19 League
Paisley Chiefs	1994–2005 Scottish Under-16/17 League/Conference
Paisley Tomahawks	2002/03 Scottish Under-16 League
Paisley Warriors	1994–2005 Scottish Under-14/15 League/Conference
Paisley Tomahawks	2000/01 Scottish Under-14 League
Paisley Braves	1995–2005 Scottish Under-12/13 League/Conference

Honours:

Pirates	1992/93 Champions Scottish League Division 1; 2004/05 Winners Scottish Cup
Cherokees	2001/02 Winners Scottish Under-18 League Cup; 2004/05 Champions Scottish Under-19 League
Chiefs	2000/01 Champions Scottish Under-16 League; 2003/04 Winners Scottish Under-16 Cup; 2004/05 Champions Scottish Under-16 League
Warriors	1997/98 Winners Scottish Under-15 'B' Conference; 2000/01 & 2003/04 Champions Scottish Under-14 League; 2003/04 Winners Scottish Under-14 Cup
Braves	1997/98 Winners Scottish Under-13 'B' Conference; 1998/99 Champions Scottish Under-13 League; 1999–2001 & 2002/03 Champions Scottish Under-12 League

Publications:

Paisley Pirates Official Yearbook 2001, ed. McFadyen, Lisa

Developed under the auspices of Renfrewshire District Council, the building combines an ice rink and swimming pool. Participation rather than spectator sport must have been uppermost in the design brief, as viewing is restricted from the upper rows of the high level seating seats, with only about eighty per cent of the ice visible.

The homeless professional Ayr Raiders, who were coached by Jack Dryburgh provided the first hockey, played in front of near capacity crowds. Three class imports in Len Hachborn (109 NHL games), Kevin Lavallee (398 NHL games) and Chris Norton, combined with experienced home-bred Scots to qualify for the quarter-final of the Benson & Hedges Cup. Then the operating consortium, headed by Spanish-based self-proclaimed millionaire David Gardner-Brown, ran out of money. Three games into the British League Raiders were expelled by the British IH Association.

The Sports & Leisure Department of the council injected £25,000, enabling Colin Shields to set up Pirates and enter the Scottish League. Three imports were engaged, a rarity for the near amateur competition. Canadians Graham Garden and Mike Bettens joined from Telford, with Robert Koutney, a Czech previously with Aviemore, completing the trio. Five home-bred Scots signed from the Edinburgh club. In Pirates' first home, on 20 December 1992 they defeated a Scottish Select 8–2, in a challenge encounter in front of 350 fans. With two games a weekend required due to the late start, Pirates swept to the league title, winning 22 of their 23 matches. The imports occupied the first three places in the SL scoring table. Despite losing all four encounters in the three-team play-off group for

The interior. (Graham Knowles/*IHNR*)

promotion to the British League, Paisley joined the expanded Division 1 next autumn.

Six home games were lost in their Northern section for a fifth-place finish. Shields recruited an experienced defensive core in netminder Gerry Anderson and ex-Ayr player John Kidd (31). Canadian Peter Buckridge, from Ontario, led the attack with 119 goals. Doug Marsden (27), a defender, joined Bettens as the third regular import. With BL1 now back to one region reduced to fourteen teams, Pirates pushed for promotion to the Premier. At one point they topped their division, falling back to third. Bettens, now captain, was retained, to be joined by Ukrainen Alex Koulekov and Danuse Bauba, a Latvian. Dave Rook, a home-bred goalie from Irvine, played the majority of the games. Their play-offs group proved too tough. Shields won the 1995 All-Star coaching vote. With high-scoring Ukrainian Vasily Vasilenko added the following autumn went well, including a tie with the Premier's Newcastle Warriors in the B&H Cup. Inconsistency set in, players were discarded. Cash flow problems led to the release of Koulekov as Pirates settled for seventh.

Following talks with the council a consortium of businessmen, headed by Edinburgh-based Alan Maxwell as GM, took over from the departed Shields. Marsden came in as player-coach, as Bettens quit days before Pirates' opening 1996/97 fixture, in the new Northern Premier League of seven members. With the recruitment in late October of the much-travelled import Rick Fera and ex-Whitley Bay native Simon Leach, Pirates chased Fife all the way, to end as runners-up. In 1997/98 Paisley competed in the NP, plus the inaugural British National League, ending second and fifth respectively. With the dismissal of Marsden for an off-ice offence, Paul Hand took over as coach. The next three seasons Pirates ended at the foot of the table, with lower gates and little sponsorship. Some players shone through the ever-changing rosters, including the high scoring Jason Heywood, Chris Jamieson, Dominic Parlatore, born at Niagara Falls, Canadian goalies Craig Lindsay and Dave Trofimenkoff, and the home-grown Steven Lynch. In spring of 2000 Maxwell, losing money, was forced to step down, with terminal cancer. A new board, saddled with a huge debt struggled on for a couple of years, which saw Jim Lynch briefly behind the bench until Marsden came back for a third stint of coaching. In spring 2002, owing the Inland Revenue £20,000, professional hockey ended at the Lagoon.

In April 1999 Paisley announced a three to five-year plan to develop local talent. This move paid off, with all four youth teams winning their leagues since then, and providing sufficient talent for senior hockey to continue in Paisley, with Pirates playing in the Scottish National League. The runners-up spot in April 2004 followed a first-season fifth placing and the Scottish Cup a year later.

PERTH – DUNKELD ROAD

Opened:	1 October 1936	Address:
Closed:	1989	Central Scotland Ice Rink
Ice Size:	175ft x 97ft	Dunkeld Road
Total Spectator Capacity:	3,200 (when opened)	Muirton
Seating Capacity:	3,065	Perth
Ice Hockey – First Match:		Scotland

1 October 1936: Glasgow Mohawks 1 *v.* Kelvingrove 2
(challenge)

Teams:

Perth Panthers   1936–40 Scottish National League; 1946–54 Scottish National League; 1954/55 British National League; 1955/56 Scottish Amateur League; 1956–58 and 1961/62 'Home' tournaments

Perth Black Hawks   1937/38 Scottish National League; 1962–64 Scottish League; 1959–66 'Home' tournaments (most games played away)

Perth Blackhawks   1946–54 Scottish 'Junior' League(s) and 'Home' tournaments

Perth Panthers Cubs   1948–52 Under-17 tournaments

Honours:

Panthers   1937/38 & 1946/47 Champions Scottish National League; 1939/40 Champions Scottish Points Tournament; 1939/40 & 1948/49 Winners Simpson Trophy; 1948–50 Winners Bairns Trophy

Panther Cubs   1949/50 Winners McDonagh Trophy; 1950/51 Winners Scottish Juvenile Cup

Built by D. Beveridge & Co. to ensure that curling could be maintained regardless of the weather outside. L. Sterne & Co. of Glasgow installed the ice making plant. Perth was the second rink to be opened in Scotland after the First World War, enabling hockey to move from the Glasgow-based (Crossmyloof) Scottish 'house' league towards a National League. The Duke of Atoll performed the opening ceremony.

Canadians were recruited to staff Panthers with Les Tapp (23) from Ottawa as player-coach. Fellow countrymen the Forsythe brothers, Bert and Jimmy, and ex-Birmingham Maple Leafs defender Biff Smith joined him. They finished third in the five-team league behind Glasgow Mohawks and Mustangs. Next autumn the rink added Black Hawks, with Montreal-born Les Lovell as coach to a small squad. He spent the rest of his life in Scotland where his sons and grandsons also played ice hockey. Glasgow-born 'Scotty' Milne guarded the goal with Tommy McInroy, who played for GB in 1939, up front, along with Art Schumann from Saskatchewan. Finishing three points behind Panthers the experiment was not repeated. For the second year Panthers strengthened, with Scottish-born 'Red' Thompson (23) a 6ft defender who learnt his hockey in Canada, Earl Morley, left-wingers Jimmy Lightfoot (22), Ernie Pratt (21) and Len McCartney (20) coming in. This talent clinched the league title with 19 victories. Games were sold out, sometimes weeks in advance. Brighton Tigers visited Dunkeld Road on New Year's Day 1938, to crush Perth All-Stars 10–2. Next season Panthers, with Milne in goal and Bunt Roberts on defence, were pushed into second place by Dundee. For the first and last Second World War campaign Perth topped the league format-based Scottish Point Tournament, winning 12 of their 20 fixtures. 'Breezy' Thompson, with 26 points, and Schumann with 24 were sixth and eighth in the overall scoring table. The knockout

Panthers' Bob Purdie eludes a Fife defender at Perth on 16 December 1938. (*Perth Star*)

Simpson Trophy concluded on 17 May as Pirates defeated Dundee 5–1 in Perth, to collect the silverware 12–5 on aggregate.

Requisitioned in 1941 for use as a Fleet Air Arm store during the war, the building reopened as an ice rink in 1946. None of the pre-war Panthers signed for the 1946/47 version, although Laurie Marchant had turned out for Dundee, Kelvingrove and Glasgow pre-1940. Perth swept to the SNL crown, winning 15 of their 24 games. Johnny Sergenese at left-wing, tenth overall in league scoring, notched up 43 points. Danny MacNamara was voted onto the first time ever Scottish All-Stars. He made the 'A' team, with a 'Bs' for goalie George Laird, Jim Ross in defence and centre-ice Sam McNabney. Ross, born in Edinburgh in 1926, turned out 62 times for New York Rangers from 1951 to 1953. Two years later McNabney was awarded £2,500 damages in the Scottish Courts for the loss of an eye and his hockey livelihood, in an accident with Panthers.

Left-wing Bruce Hamilton (21), from Kinistino, Sakatchewan, signed for Perth in the autumn of 1948 to remain until pro hockey ended at Dunkeld Road. Alternating as the club's top or second-highest scorer he was eighth in the Scottish League in his rookie campaign with 31 goals and 20 assists, gaining an All-Star 'B' accolade. His team, finishing sixth, won the Bairns Trophy consolation tournament. In December Panthers defeated Sudbury Wolves, Canada's representatives in the forthcoming world championships. The 1940 Simpson Trophy triumph was repeated over the same opponents. Dundee Tigers lost 17–14 in the two-legged final. Next year Panthers slipped into the cellar, retaining the Bairns by beating Dundee and Ayr. Most games played to a full house. The acquisition of netminder Jack Siemon (22) from Kitchener, Ontario for 1950/51 improved Panthers' fortunes as they moved to the SNL runners-up slot. Siemon and Hamilton were named to the 'A' All-Stars. Leading Dunfermline 6–2 on 10 March Panthers were awarded a penalty shot. The captain signalled Siemon to take it – he missed. Perth's coach, Glasgow-born Tommy Forgie gained an All-Star 'A' award for his achievement in getting Panthers to third place in the 1951/52 Autumn Cup and into the play-offs final. They went down 6–2 at Falkirk and could only manage a 2–2 in the return on 19 April. Ken Doig, on right-wing, and Hamilton, second and third in SNL scoring, were named to the 'B' All-Stars. Panthers were third for the next two years, with Hamilton among the top ten SNL scorers to retain his All-Star rating, as did Forgie. Edinburgh-born, Perth-trained Jimmy Spence was tenth with 22 goals and 17 assists. With Siemon moving on, Panthers elected to go for Scottish-bred natives as Rolly Miller (19) from Perth and Ayr-born Stan Christie (29) split the netminding role. Perth, third again the following winter, had Gar Baker (22) from Seaforth, Ontario, taking over in the nets from the Scots tandem. He was second best in the Autumn Cup, where his team were runners-up, with a shots-per-goal average of 10.39 and two shutouts. Eighth in Perth's one and only season in the British League was a disappointment. Hamilton left for Switzerland a few games into the Autumn Cup to return for the close of the BL campaign. In his 405 games with Panthers he had totalled 447 goals and 375 assists.

The frontage in 1986.
(David Gordon)

Early Saturday morning coaching of local lads had started almost as soon as the rink first opened; although interrupted by the Second World War much talent was honed on Perth ice. In that last season of pro hockey Panthers' top scorer was J. Spence with 43 goals and 81 points. Ian Forbes was fourth with 62 points. George Watt and Sammy McDonald were among other Perth products who contributed to the scoring in the 1950s. All played for Great Britain in the World Championships.

Although crowd levels had remained high at Perth the directors, along with other Scottish rinks, pulled out of the BNL to set up an amateur league. This collapsed with an uncompleted schedule. Panthers did enough to make the play-offs, losing in the semi-final to Edinburgh. Durham Wasps made a rare trip to Perth in March 1957 for an 11–6 loss enjoyed by a 1,600 crowd. The player-run amateur Panthers, later Black Hawks, staffed by veterans and a handful of juniors, struggled on with little or no practice ice. Winning one of their twelve Scottish League games 1962–64, they still hoped to persuade their rink to stage home games. Ice hockey faded completely after the late 1960s, as curling interests took over. The width of the ice was increased to around 100ft, two corners were squared off and the seating capacity was reduced to 1,200 as a glass-fronted lounge was built across one end.

The building was located next to the St Johnstone football ground, with both being acquired in 1988 by a property developer and demolished shortly afterwards, to make way for a supermarket.

PERTH – DEWAR'S

Opened: September 1990
Ice Size: 151ft x 118ft (44m x 36.8m)
Total Spectator Capacity: 500 via viewing galleries
Seating Capacity: Minimal
Ice Hockey – First Match:
Scheduled for 14 January 1996 but cancelled: Perth
Panthers *v.* Kirkcaldy Kestrels (Scottish League)

Address:
Dewar's Ice Rink
Dewar's Centre
Glover Street
Perth PH2 OTH
Scotland

Teams:

Perth Panthers   1995/96 Scottish League (all games away, mainly at Aviemore); 1996–98 challenge games (all away); 1998-99 Scottish League (all 'home' fixtures at Aviemore – until December); 2000–02 Scottish National League (all 'home' fixtures at Dundee)
Perth Hawks   1999/2000 Scottish Under-18 League
Perth Lightning   2000–02 Scottish Under-18 League
Perth Lightning   1997–99 Scottish Under-17 Conference/League

Perth Blackhawks   1999–2002 Scottish Under-16 League
Perth Blackhawks   1995–00 Scottish Under-14/15 League/Conference
Perth Panther Cubs   2000–03 Scottish Under-14 League
Perth Panther Cubs   1995–2000 Scottish Under-12/13 League/Conference
Perth Piranhas   2000–05 Scottish Under-12 League

Built on the site of Dewar's Drinks warehouse, the centre, combining the rink and an indoor bowling hall, is owned by Perth and Kinross District Council. The boards surrounding the ice are too insubstantial for a robust form of ice hockey; the 'corners' are also square. The rink is mainly the dominance of curlers with 'senior' hockey not permitted, in spite of several representations, even up to MP level.

Youth ice hockey commenced at Under-12 level in late 1991. Veteran Canadian player the late Mike Muzur and others ran fortnightly training sessions from the next spring. Richard Harding, the newly appointed rink manager in the summer of 1993, encouraged the sport with a bi-weekly youth contest.

Perth Panthers' senior team was Perth in name only. Their first game was held on 17 December at Irvine – a 16–5 loss to Flyers in the Scottish League Division 1. The home game scheduled for 14 January 1996 was cancelled due to the unsuitable rink surrounds. Panthers had previously been the Glenrothes Jets before their rink closed in 1994, with the core of the players first coming together in 1984 as the Glenrothes Under-11 team.

PETERBOROUGH

Opened: 20 November 1981   Address:
Ice Size: 184ft x 85ft (56m x 26m)   Planet Ice Arena
Total Spectator Capacity: 1,700 (1,250 prior to 1994)   1 Mallard Road
Seating Capacity: 1,400   Bretton
Ice Hockey – First Match: Peterborough
23 May 1982: Peterborough Pirates 1 v. Streatham Bruins 6   PE3 8YN
(challenge)   Cambridgeshire
                                                               England

Teams:

Peterborough Pirates   1982/83 British League Division 2 – South; 1983–85, 1986/87 & 1995/96 British League Division 1; 1985/86 & 1987–95 British League Premier Division; 1996/97 Premier League; 1997/98 Southern Premier League; 1997–2002 British National League

Peterborough Phantoms 2002–05 English Premier League

Peterborough Pumas   1983/84 British League Division 2

Peterborough Titans   1984–88 British League Division 2; 1988/89 English League Division 1; 1989–91 English League Division 2; 1991–94 English Under-21 League

Peterborough Patriots   1993–95 English Conference

Peterborough Islanders   1996–98 English Conference; 1998/99 English League Division 1; 2000/01 English Conference; 2001–05 English National League

Peterborough Fen Tigers   1997–2003 English Under-19 League

Peterborough Phantoms   2003–05 English Under-19 League

Peterborough Jets   1982–2001 English Junior/Under-16 League/Conference

Peterborough Pythons   2001–03 English Under-16 League

Peterborough Phantoms   2003–05 English Under-16 League

Peterborough Caribous   1984–2003 English Pee-Wee/Under-14 League/Conference
Peterborough Phantoms   2003–05 English Under-14 League
Peterborough Beavers   1989–2003 English Under-12 League/Conference
Peterborough Phantoms   2003–05 English Under-12 League

Honours:

Pirates	1982/83 Champions British League Division 2; 1984/85 & 1986/87 Winners British League – Division 1
Phantoms	2002/03 Champions English Premier League; 2002–04 Winners Premier Cup
Titans	1989/90 Winners English League Division 2 – Midlands
Fen Tigers	1997/98 Winners English Under-19 'B' League – South
Jets	1987/88 Winners English Under-16 'B' League – North; 1992/93 Winners English Under-16 Conference – Midlands; 1996/97 Winners English Under-16 'B' League – South
Caribous	1995/96 Winners English Under-14 Conference – Midlands; 1996/97 Winners English Under-14 'B' League – South
Beavers	1993/94 Winners English Under-12 Conference – Midlands; 1999/2000 Winners English Under-12 'A' League – South

Publications:
Champions 1984/85 (pamphlet), author unknown, 1985
Ten Years of The Pirates, Potter, Simon and Caroline, 1992

Built by East Anglia Leisure as a private venture in ten months, and originally known as the East of England Ice Rink. The landlords were the Commission for New Towns with the venue opened by the Minister for Sport – Neil MacFarlane MP. Constructed as a basic industrial unit, suitable for conversation if the rink failed commercially. This it did on more than one occasion. It was abruptly closed on 4 October 1993 when the original operator, Dennis Adams, ripped out and burnt about 17 miles of the under-ice plastic refrigeration piping, claiming the rink had failed as a business. The hockey club's board of directors, headed by David Thorpe, negotiated a three-year interest-free loan from the council to purchase the rink plant and equipment. Around 200 volunteers, including players and Pirates' coach, the late 'Heavy' Eveson, worked shifts around the clock to repair the damage for the reopening on 18 December. The ice was decreased from its previous dimensions of 190ft x 92ft (58m x 28m), with the notorious mid-ice hump removed and seating accommodation increased.

An ice hockey club was formed in November 1981 when twenty-three enthusiasts met at the rink. Sunday lunchtime practices run by John Burke drew the three Hunter brothers, who learnt the rudiments of the sport in Canada, a group from Bradford headed by Granville Raper, two roller skaters – the Cade brothers – plus a couple of British and American servicemen. Three names were suggested – Pirates, Petes or Penguins, with the former being favourite. The first venture into league hockey drew 250 spectators. Winning nine of their ten home games pushed the crowds to average over 1,000. Sponsorship from two local businesses enabled two quality imports – John Lawless and Rob Carnegie – to be engaged. They piled up 171 and 85 points respectively. With national sponsorship from Heineken the British League formed a Division One, with Pirates a founding member.

Canadian Ron Katernyuk backstopped the team for a year of consolidation. Twelve months on, with Katernyuk behind the bench and third import Shannon Hope, who hailed from Peterborough, Ontario, Pirates swept to the divisional title and promotion to the Premier for autumn 1985. Although Hope had left, a moderate start was assisted by a £10,000 grant from the city council. Team manager David Thorpe departed after a dispute with the rink management, to be followed by Katernyuk in a clash with the club's directors. Seven players signed a letter demanding their reinstatement. They were shown the

The entrance, looking towards the cafe, when newly opened. (Fred Dean)

The arena in 1994 with a relaid ice pad. (Mike Smith/*IHNR*)

door. Between mid-November and the end of March Pirates lost 26 consecutive matches. Lawless finished ninth in the division's scoring with 72 goals and 67 assists, before leaving to form Cardiff Devils. His number 9 sweater was retired. It was only the second time in Britain that a player had been so honoured.

Back in Division 1 ex-Pirates player Steve Rattle took over the coaching. The class imports of Doug McEwen (23), new to Britain, and ex-Fife Flyer Todd Bidner (25) were joined by thirty-nine-year-old Gary Unger, the ex-NHL 'iron-man', with 914 consecutive games. Peterborough lost two matches, with the divisional title clinched by a nine-point margin. Unger scored at the rate of almost eight points a game. Crowd levels averaged 1,388. McEwen was released at season's end, much to the fans' surprise.

The second stay in the Premier was almost as shortlived as the first. With Bidner and Unger on the second year of their contracts Jim McTaggart, with 71 games in the NHL, finally joined them. In March Unger replaced Rattle as coach. Bottom of the ten-club heap, with 4 wins and 28 losses Peterborough were saved by the introduction of relegation play-offs and an Unger goal. In the 10 April 1988 second leg at Mallard Road with Telford, winners of Division 1, Pirates trailed 18–15 overall going into the third period.

Unger, in his last game, banged home a rebound off the goalie for the winning goal 82 seconds from time. The 2,400 crowd who jammed the building went wild. Pirates managed to remain in the Premier Division for the next seven years. Unger was relieved of his duties the following January. The team finished seventh and then eighth. By now the youth programme was producing senior players of the calibre of Jason Porter, Carl Stripling, Jonathon Cotton and Grant Budd. The decade of the 1990s dawned as the charismatic Rocky Saganiuk came in as coach. A disciplinarian and motivator with 265 NHL games to his credit, he rebuilt the team, replacing all the imports and bringing in Kirkcaldy-born netminder Scott O'Connor (21). A run of eight victories closed out the league, with Pirates third and into the play-offs. Three wins and a tie took Peterborough to their first British Championship weekend at Wembley. Disposing of Cardiff they lost out 7–4 in the final to league champions Durham. It was still Pirates' finest hour. Next season the club struggled financially. Against all the odds, including suspensions and injuries, Saganiuk inspired Pirates to seventh and a play-off position. Six points from twelve saw Pirates at Wembley again, to go down to Nottingham in the first semi-final.

Ninth for the next three years, the last saw Pirates lose their relegation play-off battle, with local youngsters including Cassie Dawkins and Darren Cotton as regulars. Back in Division 1 for 1995/96, Pirates finished eleventh. On 14 January an own goal by Chris Brant of Bracknell allowed Tony Melia (30) to become the fourth goalminder to be credited with scoring a goal with his opposite number in place. Eighth in the one-year Premier League was followed by five years in the British National League. Directors-cum-club owners, struggling with the rising costs, came and went. 'Mad Dog' Troy Walkington coached Pirates to consecutive fourth-place finishes, and the Christmas Cup of 1998, before departing the next October amid yet another cash crisis. Fifth twice, Pirates sank to tenth in the final winter of their existence, as director Paul Macmillan fell out with Planet Ice owner Mike Petrouis. Amid all the troubles for pro hockey the Peterborough youth teams won their leagues at every age level during the 1990s.

Phil Wing, a previous Pirates director, formed a new set up in summer 2002, entering Peterborough Phantoms into the lower-budget English Premier League. With the core of Pirates' home-bred talent, backed by the forty-year-old Doug McEwan, returning import Jesse Hammill and Duncan Cook from Solihull, the rookie outfit swept to the EPL title. Cook notched 120 points, with Scotsman Kevin King replacing Luc Chabot as coach in mid-season. Phantoms defeated near neighbours and closest rivals Milton Keynes Lightning in the Premier Cup. For 2003/04 Phantoms had to settle as runners-up, in both the league and play-offs, to MK. They did retain the cup. Average attendances rose from 513 of the previous season to 563.

Canadian-born Marc Long (25), a British passport holder, headed Phantoms' scoring with 20+29 by spring 2005 but again his team trailed Peterborough in the EPL and post-season play. Allen Sutton topped the goalies' averages.

RYDE IoW

Opened:	May 1991	Address:
Ice Size:	165ft x 80ft (50m x 24m – some	Planet Ice Arena
	sources state 44m x 22m)	Quay Road
Total Spectator Capacity:	1,000	Esplanade
Seating Capacity:	800	Ryde
Ice Hockey – First Match:		Isle of Wight
31 August 1991: Solent Vikings 3 v. Streatham Redskins 10		PO33 2HH
(challenge)		England

Teams:

Solent Vikings	1991/92 English League
Wightlink Raiders	1992–93 English Conference South; 1993/94 English League; 1994–97 English Conference South; 1997/98 English National League; 1998/99 & 2003–05 English Premier League
Isle of Wight Raiders	1999–2003 English Premier League
Wight Wildcats	1995–97 English Under-19 Conference; 2001–05 English Under-19 League
Wight Wolverines	1994/95 English Under-16 Conference
Wight Thunder	1997–2005 English Under-16 League
Isle of Wight Lightning	1996–2003 English Under-14 League
Isle of Wight Tornadoes	1995–2000 & 2002–05 English Under-12 Conference/League

Honours:
Raiders   1993/94 Champions English League and Cup; 1994–96
                                 Winners English Cup; 1994/95 Champions English Southern
                                 Conference & Play-offs; 1995–97 Champions English
                                 Conference Play-offs; 2000/01 Winners Premier Cup

Publications:
Isle of Wight Raiders – 10th Anniversary Book comp. Wall, Deborah, Price, Steve & Hart,
Steve, 2000

The original development and management company, Peterborough-based Gaul & Co., went
into receivership shortly after the rink opened. Their management functions were taken over
by Medina Borough Council. From 1993 to 1998 the rink operator was Civic Leisure. Wight
Leisure, a department of the Isle of Wight Council, ran things for 1998/99 until Planet Ice
took over a year later. The building is a brick-clad structure, with a friendly compact atmosphere on game night, situated a five-minute walk from the pier, with its electric train con-
necting to the fifteen-minute catamaran journey from the mainland at Portsmouth.

On 25 June 1996 the local authority pledged, at a council meeting, that the island would
either have a new rink or the existing one would be extended for season 1998/99. A year
later their application for lottery funding was turned down. Several groups have explored
the possibility of extending the building, to provide at least the minimum regulation ice size
of 56m x 26m, necessary for the higher levels of ice hockey in Britain. All found, as for similar ideas at other small rinks, that this is not a cost-effective proposition.

The hiring of two Canadians both to play hockey and work in the rink was about the
last act of Gaul & Co. Dave McGahan and centre-ice Sean Murphy from Ottawa compiled
199 and 193 points from their 32 games. Sussex-based physical education teacher and ice
hockey super enthusiast Mick Green took over team management to add homegrown players, mainly from the Southampton area. The inexperienced Solent team struggled on the
ice and financially, ending eighth, six points from the cellar. From around 200, spectator levels picked up to about 800.

A new regime ran the hockey from the following autumn, with sponsorship for the next
six years from a ferry company. Dan Sweeney (25) from Montreal, previously with Sheffield
and Solihull, came in as Director of Hockey/player-manager. McGahan was replaced by
Dave Cannon and a third import in defenceman Don Breau. Nick Rothwell also returned.
Fourth place gave way to the revamped English League and cup triumphs of 1993/94, with
one loss on the road to Sheffield Lancers. Sweeney at 214 points, Rothwell on 171 and
British youngster Ivor Ambridge with 157 were one, two and three in EL scoring, with
another Brit, Mel Brassett-Grundy, heading the netminders' averages. Extensive public relations led to crowds of 1,300 – 300 over the published capacity.

The EL reverted to a two-region 'Conference', with the south expanded to twelve
members. Raiders went undefeated in all three competitions, with the netminding tandem of Gareth Phillips and Keith Martin leading the way. Almost every game on the
island sold out. Losing the 1995/96 Southern Conference title by three points, Wightlink
won all six games in their play-off group. In the two-leg semi-final Altrincham were
crushed 40–2! Raiders 8–0 blanking of Durham City Wasps the next Saturday at Ryde
was sufficient to clinch the play-offs for the EL Championship 15–8 on aggregate.
Ambridge became the club's leading sniper. Earlier in the season Sweeney and Breau
returned to the island after playing on the mainland. For the fourth consecutive spring
Raiders peaked to collect the English League Championship. Canadian Dave Standing,
later joined by his younger brother Anthony, helped Wightlink to triumph in their play-
off group. Altrincham were dismissed 25–9 in the semi-final. Next weekend Raiders beat
Chelmsford 5–2 on Quay Road ice. The following day at the Essex rink Raiders clinched
the title by the odd goal in nine. Sweeney's 94 points in the Conference and 37 in the
play-offs topped both competitions. The team was the second most penalised, assisted by

Fans queuing in the sun.

Waiting for the Raiders.

the combined 361 penalty minutes of the Standing brothers plus, the 213 accumulated by Mark Wallace.

With the formation of the English National League defenceman Drew Chapman became coach as the squad finished fourth. Club leading scorers Canadians Pete Cooper and Jamie Nagle had paid their way across the Atlantic. The 'English Premier' replaced 'National' from autumn 1998 as Raiders turned to Scandinavia for its imports, as many as six. Luc Chabot (34) took over from Swedish Peter Nyman as player-coach a year later, as Wightlink gave way to Isle of Wight. He led them to a runners-up place. His first silverware came in March 2001 as Raiders beat Swindon 3–2 in Wiltshire. Twenty-four hours later a packed arena watched their team clinch the cup with a 2–0 shutout. Next year, third in the EPL, they went down to Invicta 6–3 on aggregate in the play-off final.

From 2002/03 Bournemouth-born Andy Pickles (29), who joined Raiders in 1999, and import Jason Coles, who signed on twelve months later, took over as the managing/coaching duo. With a sixth place the crowds had dropped to around 500. The following winter Wightlink returned as main sponsor. Raiders improved, progressing to the play-off semi-final. Rob Lamey, a Brit, led the five imports in club scoring. By spring 2005 Raiders just missed out on silver in the EPL, tying Peterborough on 40 points, although failing to collect a point in the play-offs. Coles pipped Lamey in club scoring.

SHEFFIELD – QUEENS ROAD

Opened:	30 November 1965	Address:
Closed:	25 May 2005	Sheffield Ice Sports Centre
Ice Size:	180ft x 80ft (55m x 24m)	Queens Road
Total Spectator Capacity:	1,500	Sheffield S2 4DF
Seating Capacity:	400	South Yorkshire
Ice Hockey – First Match:		England

4 October 1975: Sheffield Lancers 2 v. Blackpool Seagulls 29 (Southern League)

Teams:

Sheffield Lancers	1975–78 Southern 'A' League – Midland; 1978/79 Midland League and Northern Reserve League – England; 1979/80 Inter City League; 1992/93 English Conference – Wharry Division; 1993/94 English League
Sheffield Knights	1975–78 Southern 'B' League; 1978/79 Midland League Division 2
Sheffield Knights	1979/80 Midland League
Sheffield Saracens	1979/80 Midland League Division 2
Sheffield Sabres	1980–82 Midland League & 1980/81 Northern Reserve League – England; 1982–85 British League Division 2 – North; 1985/86 British League Division 1; 1986/87 British League Division 2 – North; 1987/88 English League – North; 1988/89 English League Division 2 – North; 1989–91 English League Division 1
West Yorkshire Raiders	1980/81 Midland League Division 2 (withdrew)
Sheffield Scimitars	1990/91 English League Division 2; 1991–94 English Under-21 League
Sheffield Scimitars	1994–98 & 2000–03 English Conference – North; 1998–2000 English League Division 1 – North
Sheffield Steelhawks	1994–2003 English Under-19 Conference
Hallum Rink Rats	2004/05 English Under-19 League
Sheffield Rapiers	1989/90 & 1993–2003 English Under-16 League/Conference
Sheffield Greyhounds	1997–2003 English Under-16 League
Hallum Rink Rats	2004/05 English Under-16 League
Sheffield Stormers	1993–2003 English Under-14 Conference/League
Sheffield Sabres	1998–2003 English Under-14 League
Hallum Rink Rats	2004/05 English Under-14 League
Sheffield Lasers	1994–2003 English Under-12 Conference/League
Hallum Rink Rats	2004/05 English Under-12 League

Honours:

Lancers	1978/79 Champions Midlands League
Sabres	1983–85 Winners British League Division 2 – North
Scimitars	2002/03 Winners English Conference – North
Rapiers	2000/01 & 2002/03 Champions English Under-16 League
Greyhounds	2002/03 Winners English Under-16 'B' League – North
Stormers	1996/97 Winners English Under-14 'B' League – North; 2000–03 Champions English Under-14 League
Lasers	1999/00 Champions and Play-off Winner English Under-12 League; 2000/01 & 2002/03 Champions English Under-12 League
Rink Rats	2004/05 Winners English Under-19 League Division 2 – North

One of the breed of new rinks created in the 1960s by the then Mecca Company – later a subsidiary of Grand Metropolitan – similar in concept and style to Bradford and Bristol. The original seating was removed later to combat vandalism.

   An ice hockey club was formed in spring 1975 by Tom Shipstone, Jim McGarrigle and Colin Maitland – the first netminder and coach. With nearly all novice players they entered teams in the amateur Southern 'A' and 'B' Leagues later that year. It was not long before Nottingham-based businessman Garry Keward took over as coach. He had lived in Canada for some years. In their inaugural campaign Lancers won two of their 16 matches, with fourteen-year-old Dwayne Keward, on left-wing, the leading scorer with 10+2. Keward Snr was named SL Coach of the Year. An attendance figure of 600 is recorded for the opening match.

In 1978 the Southern and Midland Leagues separated. Sheffield edged the long-established Blackpool Seagulls by a single point for the steel city's first league championship. Keward topped the league in goals at 26, with Canadian Scott Jones third with 15. Lancers made it to the semi-finals of the 'Icy' Smith Cup, emblematic of the British Championship. Next season the ambitious Lancers moved to the higher-standard Inter-City League, ending seventh, and in the autumn of 1980 the core of the team formed the resurrected Nottingham Panthers.

Knights, the younger second team, took over the mantle of the seniors for one winter, to become the Sabres for the next twelve. It took time to recover from the loss of players to Nottingham. By 1983 Sheffield were back in contention. Sabres won all 12 games in their section of Division 2 of the British League. Tony Griffith, Tony Newman (18) and Paul Legdon occupied second to fifth spot in points scoring. Andrew Havenhand, with two shutouts, was runner-up in the goalie averages. Next year Sabres repeated the triumph, again unbeaten, although not commencing at home until January due to rink refurbishment. The young squad was backstopped by some fine netminding from Havenhand. They lost their national semi-final to hosts Oxford, who won the championship. Sheffield's one and only season in the semi-pro British League, albeit Division 1, was a disaster; there was just one victory. Of the two Canadian imports, Larry McNeil was forty-one years old, and through lack of sponsorship Kevin Harrington returned home at Christmas. Practice ice was in short supply as the rink closed for a couple of midwinter months. Most points came from club stalwart Bernie Serafinski with 13 goals and 23 assists, followed by McNeil with 20. At least Sabres were the cleanest team, averaging 8.67 penalty minutes per match. A return to semi-pro hockey, 1989–91, produced modest returns, sixth and then fifth in the English League. Leading scorer in the first year Mark Stokes (23), on 117 points, was succeeded by Quebec-born Dan Sweeney, another twenty-three-year-old, with 66. Financial support from a local company and the city council was not available for the second season.

Three years elapsed before senior hockey reappeared at Queens Road with the all-amateur Scimitars, which soon drew crowds of around 350. They were run in conjunction with an active and increasingly successful youth development programme. Scimitars, with veterans of the calibre of Dean Smith (28), Les Millie (29) and Neil Abel (41), combined with young talent such as Keith Leyland, won their league in spring 2003, dropping three points in 18 games. The Under-16, Under-14 and Under-12 squads also all won titles.

With the opening of iceSheffield later in 2003 all the Queens Road-based league teams moved their operations to the new facility. A full youth league hockey programme. the Hallum Rink Rats, at four age levels, returned in autumn 2004 with immediate success for the Under-19s. This revival ended when the building was converted to a roller rink in late-spring 2005.

SHEFFIELD – ARENA

Opened:	31 May 1991	Address:
Ice Size:	197ft x 98ft (60m x 30m)	Sheffield Arena
Total Spectator Capacity:	8, 500 (can be increased to 10,200)	Broughton Lane
Seating Capacity:	8,500 (can be increased to 10,200 by use of 'stage' end)	Sheffield S9 2DF South Yorkshire
Ice Hockey – First Match:		England

26 September 1991: Sheffield Steelers Select 1 v. Durham Wasps 7 (challenge)

Teams:

Sheffield Steelers 1991/92 English League; 1992/93 British League – Division 1; 1993–96 British League – Premier Division; 1996–2003 Superleague; 2003–05 Elite League

Honours:

Steelers   1994–96 Champions British League and Play-offs; 1995/96 & 2000/01 Winners B&H Cup; 1996/97 Champions Superleague Play-offs; 1998–01 & 2002/03 Winners Challenge Cup; 2000/01 Champions Superleague and Play-offs; 2001/02 Champions Superleague Play-offs; 2002/03 Champions Superleague; 2003/04 Champions Elite League and Play-offs

Constructed for Sheffield City Council, at a cost of £35 million, as a multi-sports venue for the 1991 World Student Games. The first of Britain's post-Second World War breed of ice arenas, as opposed to rinks, setting new standards for spectator comfort and back of house facilities. There are thirty-two high-level corporate entertainment suites, each capable of holding twelve people. Two high-level press benches were an innovation, albeit providing a distant view of the ice.

Steelers joined at the third level, to reach the Premier Division in two campaigns. Owned by David Gardner-Brown and George Dodds, the team exceeded their expectations. The first league game on 6 October 1991, a 3–3 tie with Chelmsford, drew 300 people. By the time they qualified, early the next spring, for the promotion play-offs, the demand for tickets was such that extra seating had to be installed, setting a post-war British attendance record at 9,750. A family ticket for two adults and two children cost £10, while car parking was free. Pop music at ear-shattering volume, accompanied by hand jive and Mexican waves were not to everyone's taste. But it created a unique atmosphere at the 'House of Steel'.

Steelers were built with imports Rob Shudra (24), with 10 games in the NHL, and Mark Mackie, a couple of experienced Brits in Ronnie Wood and Phil Lee and the best of the home-grown talent from the established Sabres at the Queens Road rink. Shudra, Lee, Wood and Paul Thompson came from the cash-strapped Solihull club. Steve Nemeth (34), who had enjoyed twelve games with New York Rangers, joined in late autumn. Former Sabres goalie Andy Havenhand, Robert Saunders, Gary Cox and team captain Bernard Serafinski contributed to Steeler mania. Led by Nemeth with 39 points and newcomer Andy Donald in goal, three home wins from three ensured promotion to the British League. The claim that Lee played while suspended was the first of many controversies that would envelop the Yorkshire club in succeeding years.

Alec Dampier was drafted in in December 1992 to mastermind the push for promotion to Premier status. This was accomplished, aided by Tommy Plommer (24) from Ayr and Murrayfield native Scott Neil. As for year one, Steelers ended as runners-up, then won five of their six play-off contests. The BIHA imposed a £2,000 fine for the submission of a forged letter endeavouring to prove American Steve MacSwain was eligible for a British passport.

Player-manager Ronnie Wood resigned in February and publication of the first-year accounts showed a £50,000 trading loss. Dampier signed imports Chris Kelland (36) and Selmer Odelein from Nottingham, to kickstart a rivalry with Panthers' fans. Runners-up in the Premier, an 8–0 defeat of Nottingham in the British Championships at Wembley added intensity. The BIHA docked five points, dropping Steelers to third and levied a £5,000 fine, claiming Sheffield had broken the wage cap. In January majority owner Dodds parted company with Gardner-Brown. With a thirty per cent increase in attendance, the top-drawing club in Britain lost £174,000 in its second year.

The signing in December of twice Stanley Cup winner Ken Priestlay (27) provided the impetus for a late surge. Sheffield went nine games undefeated in February, to clinch the title on 25 March, coming from 5–2 behind at Nottingham. Winning all three group play-off games at Sheffield provided a second successive Wembley appearance. Steelers lifted the British Championship with a 7–2 victory over Edinburgh. Topping the goalies averages in the BL and play-offs, Edinburgh-born Martin McKay (26) was voted an All-Star. Twelve months later the club won all three trophies on offer. The coaching tandem of Dampier and

The B&H Cup final, December 1992.

Clyde Tuyl signed the homegrown talent of Nicky Chinn, Tony Hand and David Longstaff. Anglo-Canadian Wayne Cowley (31) took over in goal. A record 10,136 crowd at Sheffield on 2 December watched a Hand hat-trick clinch the Benson & Hedges Cup by 5–2 over Nottingham. With Hand leading the Premier with 123 points (46+77) Steelers won 27 of their 36 games, retaining the title. Attendances increased to marginally over 8,000. Three straight play-off victories at the House of Steel sent the club to the Wembley weekend. They cruised past Humberside to meet Nottingham in the final. It took nine penalty shots to settle the issue 2–1 in Steelers' favour. All-Star accolades went to Cowley, Hand and Priestlay.

In October 1996 Dodds placed Steelers on the market. Eighteen months on, with no takers, he confirmed a rental agreement with Apollo Leisure, recently appointed to run the arena. In April 1999 Sheffield Steelers Ltd was forced into liquidation owing £592,528. Darren Brown (28), the previous MD, formed a new organisation, holding a sixty-five per cent stake with the supporters group owning the remainder. Gates had fallen to around 5,500. In the newly launched Superleague final, at Manchester in March 1997, Nottingham were despatched 5–1. Despite signing ex-NHL forward Ed Courtney (30) that October, it took a further eighteen months to win another trophy – the newly instigated Challenge Cup. Nottingham were beaten 4–0 in the final and again in Millennium year by 2–1. Nottingham's ex-coach Mike Blaisdell masterminded Steelers' second grand slam to be named 'Coach of the Year'. Tynesider Longstaff (27), on 69 points, led all Steelers in scoring, to be named to the All-Star team along with Shayne McCosh. The players threatened to strike as wages faltered. Chesterfield-based Brown stood down as chairman in March. Superleague later revealed that the club had exceeded the wage cap by up to thirty-seven per cent.

A summer of prolonged turmoil followed before seventy-five-year-old Norton Lea, despite opposition from fan groups, concluded a deal with the arena in late August 2001. Three months on he acquired the rights to Steelers' name and logo. Crowds dropped to just over 4,000. Sheffield regained the play-off crown, led by the goalscoring of Rick Brabant (37) on 56 points and the puck-stopping abilities of Ryan Bach (28). Blaisdell, with a reduced budget for 2002/03, replaced Bach as Joel Laing (27) topped the averages, for Steelers' last Superleague title. Laing, together with defenceman Marc Laniel and Blaisdell gained All-Star status. At Manchester on 23 January Steelers saw off Nottingham to lift the Challenge Cup for a fourth time, by a 3–2 margin. The reduced wage cap of the new Elite League did not hinder another Blaisdell-inspired title and play-off double. Netminder Rob Dopson and his replacement Christian Bronsard ended first and second in the averages. Blaisdell collected the 'Coach of the Year' award to be elected to the Hall of Fame before leaving Sheffield for a job back home.

The late appointment of replacement Rob Stewart and the uncertainty surrounding Lea's future ownership plans affected Steelers' on-ice performance. Paul Heavy took over coaching in late winter. He led Steelers to second in their play-off group although they were blanked 3–0 by Coventry, the eventual champions, in the first match of the finals weekend.

Sheffield staged the qualifying tournament between 28 August and 4 September 1993 for the following year's winter Olympic Games. Britain ended last behind Slovakia, Latvia, Poland and Japan. A tournament for Group A of the World Championships took place in November 1999. GB drew all three of their matches, including a heartbreaking 1–1 tie on the last day. A win would have sent Britain through. Kazakhstan scored with two seconds remaining.

SHEFFIELD – iceSHEFFIELD

Opened:	21 May 2003	Address:
Ice Size:	Two pads – both 197ft x 98ft	iceSheffield
	(60m x 30m)	Coleridge Road
Total Spectator Capacity:	1,550 – Pad 1 (Performance), 200	Attercliffe
	– Pad 2 (Recreational)	Sheffield S9 5DA
Seating Capacity:	1,500 – Pad 1, 130 – Pad 2	West Yorkshire
Ice Hockey – First Match:		England

16 August 2003: Midland Summer Cup Play-offs

Teams:

Sheffield Scimitars	2003–05 English National League – North
Sheffield Steelhawks	2003–05 English Under-19 League
Sheffield Scorpions	2003–05 English Under-19 League
Sheffield Rapiers	2003–05 English Under-16 League
Sheffield Greyhounds	2003–05 English Under-16 League
Sheffield Stormers	2003–05 English Under-14 League
Sheffield Sabres	2003–05 English Under-14 League
Sheffield Lasers	2003–05 English Under-12 League
Sheffield Swampfrogs	2003–05 English Under-12 League

Honours:

Scimitars	2003–05 Champions English National League; 2004/05 Winners English Cup
Greyhounds	2003/04 Winners of English Under-16 'B' League – North
Lasers	2003/04 Champions English Under-12 League
Steelhawks	2004/05 Winners English Under-19 League Division 1 – North
Rapiers	2004/05 Champions English Under-16 League

Located between the Don Valley Stadium and the Sheffield Arena. Construction commenced in March 2002, with the bulk of the £15.6 million cost being met by £12.9 million from the Sports England Lottery fund and a £2 million bank loan underwritten by Sheffield City Council. Designed by the Sheffield office of Building Design Partnership, from a concept by local architect Chris Marriott, and built by HBG Construction North East Ltd. The facility is part of Sheffield City Trust, whose operating arm – Sheffield International Venues Limited – manage the Sheffield Arena.

All youth ice hockey league teams, including the senior Scimitars, previously based at Queens Road, moved their operations to iceSheffield. League matches commenced in September 2003, with Scimitars attracting an average crowd of 400. Headed by veteran Brits Les Millie and Neil Abel, Scimitars retained their ENL play-off supremacy in spring 2005. The iceSheffield venue was used for Manchester Phoenix's 'home' play-off match with Sheffield Steelers in March 2004, which attracted 1,376 spectators. Group A of Division 1 of the World Under-20 Championships was also held here in December 2004. Six nations competed in front of disappointingly low crowds, with Norway winning all five encounters and Britain being relegated despite spirited opening performances against France and Austria.

SLOUGH

Opened:	13 October 1986	Address:
Ice Size:	184ft x 85ft (56m x 26m)	The Ice Arena
Total Spectator Capacity:	1,500	Montem Lane
Seating Capacity:	1,000	Slough
Ice Hockey – First Match:		Berkshire
4 October 1986: (behind closed door – no public safety cer-		SL1 2QG
tificate) Slough Jets 15 v. Richmond Flyers 3 (BL – Division 1)		England

Teams:

Slough Jets   1986–95 British League Division 1; 1995/96 British League Premier Division; 1996/97 Premier League; 1997/98 Southern Premier League; 1997–2002 British National League; 2002–05 English Premier League

Slough Harrier Hawks   1989–91 English League Division 2; 1991–94 English Under-21 League; 1994–98 English Conference; 1998–2000 English League Division 1; 2000–05 English National League

Slough Comets   1994–2005 English Under-19 Conference/League
Slough Spitfires   1987–2005 English Junior/Under-16 League/Conference
Slough 'B'   1999–2000 English Under-16 League
Slough Bombers   1987–2005 English Pee-Wee/Under-14 League/Conference
Slough Mini Bombers   1990–94 English Under-12 League/Conference
Slough Hurricanes   1994–2005 English Under-12 League

Honours:

Jets   1988/89 Winners London Cup; 1989/90 Winners British League Division 1 & Southern Cup; 1993/94 Winners British League Division 1 – South; 1997/98 Winners Benson & Hedges Plate; 1994/95 Winners British League Division 1; 1998/99 Champions British National League

Comets   1997/98 Winners English Under-19 'A' League – South
Spitfires   1989/90 Winners English Junior 'A' League – South; 1993/94 & 1995/96 Winners English Under-16 Conference – South-East; 2004/05 Winners English Under-16 League Division 1 – South
Bombers   1987/88 Winners English Pee-Wee 'B' League – South; 1989/90 Champions English Pee Wee League; 1994–96 Winners English Under-14 Conference – South-East
Mini Bombers   1991/92 Winners English Under-12 'B' League – South
Hurricanes   1995/96 Winners English Under-12 Conference – South-East; 2000/01 Winners English Under-12 'A' League – South

Publications:
Slough Jets – The First Five Years, Potter, Simon, 1991

This was the second of three similar rinks to be designed by architects Building Design Partnership (BDP), the others being Lee Valley and Chelmsford. The rink is owned and was originally operated by Slough Borough Council, and is now managed by Slough Community Leisure.

In the early years Slough Jets were in possession of local authority funding and lucrative business sponsors. From summer 1999, Jets became an independent operation, with finances being difficult to obtain. Gary Stefan, from Brantford, Ontario, previously with Streatham, was hired as a player and to run the hockey programme. He recruited a netminder, two defenders and three forwards from his old club. Six more came from Richmond, with American-born netminder Charlie Colon (23) joining from Billingham, all coached by Paul Ferguson. The first match to take place in front of the public, subsequent to the granting of a safety certificate by the local authority, was on 18 October 1986 when Jets defeated Kirkcaldy Kestrels 7–5 in a British League (BL) fixture. Richard Boprey (27), from New York State, via Holland and Bournemouth, joined soon afterwards. In his 26 games he contributed 79 goals and 67 assists as Jets finished sixth, winning all their home games, in the sixteen-member division. Captain Mark Howell and Dave Rapley, both twenty-four-year-olds and homegrown products from Streatham, were Slough's best scorers, after the three imports. Jets attracted an average attendance of 777, with a high of 1,250.

Silverware arrived in spring 1989 with the London Cup, not competed for since 1953. In the two-leg final Streatham Redskins were beaten 25–11. Twelve months on it was retained, re-branded the Southern Cup. It was joined by the British League's First Division trophy, won by a six-point margin, with one loss at home. Boprey with 139 points and Brett Keller, with one fewer, were sixth and seventh in the division. Ferguson picked up the 'Coach of the Year' award, then retired, as did Boprey. For the next two campaigns, Jets ended as divisional runners-up, their ambition for promotion being frustrated, firstly by a recurrence of Colon's knee injury, then a controversial dismissal of All-Star offensive defenceman Brian Mason in the 1991/92 play-off contests. Two years on, with the council-backed Sport and Leisure Management taking over, Boprey returned to Slough as coach. Jets, unbeaten at home, won Division 1 South by a 14-point margin. Colon headed the goalies' averages in both the league and play-offs, where Jets failed to oust Peterborough for the Premier place. In their ninth season, with ex-player Scott Rex behind the bench, the divisional title was theirs. It was secured at Motem Lane by Darren Zinger's goal at 59.45. Slough had needed a nine-goal winning margin over Paisley to beat Peterborough to the Premier.

Zinger left and Howell retired and, although the replacements were three British-Canadians, including goalie Jamie Organ (24), Slough ended in the cellar. With the demise of the fourteen-year BL Gary Stefan became a prime mover in the formation of the Premier League, in which Jets finished third. This evolved next year into the British National

The fans call it 'The Hanger'. (Mike Smith/*IHNR*)

League. In December 1997 at Sheffield Arena Jets defeated Telford 4–3 to win the B&H Plate final. The next, and to date last, trophy arrived the following season. Colon replaced Scott as coach to do a superb recruiting job. Stefan's younger brother Joe returned. In came wingman Perry Pappas (24) and Adam Lamarre, a defenceman, both from Canada, together with Ulrik Larsen (28), a Dane. Winning all but two games at the 'Hanger', near-neighbours Basingstoke were pipped to the title by two points. Goalie Richard Gallace (25) was the league's best. With 49 points, Pappas was fourth. Both made the first All-Star team. Colon collected the coaching award to go alongside his All-Star 'A' goalie citations for 1992 and 1994. Crowds averaged 1,000, down 245 from the high of 1995/96. Gary Stefan retired, having accumulated 1,050 points in his 453 competitive games for Jets. During the next two campaigns Slough reached the finals in the B&H Plate and BNL Semi-final Play-offs, before the directors revealed a debt of £27,000 to the Inland Revenue.

A reconstituted club, coached by Warren Rost, of mainly local players from Slough's prolific youth programme, has competed in the English Premier League since autumn 2002, in front of about 400 fans. A third-place finish was followed twelve months on with a play-off final loss to Milton Keynes. The same two squads met in April 2005 as Jets lost 2–1 in a semi-final nail-biting cliffhanger at Coventry.

SOLIHULL

Opened:	18 February 1965	Address:
Ice Size:	185ft x 90ft (56m x 27m)	Solihull Ice Rink
Total Spectator Capacity:	2,200 (2,000 prior to 1975; 1,500 in 1995)	Hobs Moat Road Solihull
Seating Capacity:	1,200 (1,500 prior to 1975)	West Midlands
Ice Hockey – First Match:		B92 8JN

16 May 1965: Solihull Barons 4 v. Brighton Ambassadors 3 — England
(challenge)

Teams:

Solihull Barons	1965–68 'Home' tournaments; 1972–74 Southern League; 1974/75 Southern 'A' League; 1975/78 Southern 'A' League – South; 1978–82 Inter-City League; 1982/83 British League Division 2 – South; 1983–86 British League Division 1; 1986–91 British League Premier Division; 1991/92 English League Division 1; 1992/93 English League Conference 'A'; 1993/94 British League Division 1 – South; 1994–96 British League Division 1; 2000–02 English Premier League
Solihull Vikings	1964–70 'Home' tournaments; 1970–74 Southern League
Solihull Buffaloes	1979–82 Inter-City Intermediate League; 1982–84 British League Division 3
Solihull Knights	1984–88 & 1989–91 British League Division 2; 1988/89 English League Division 1; 1991–94 English Under-21 League; 1997–2005 English Under-19 League
Solihull Crusaders	1994/95 English Under-19 English Conference (all games away)
Solihull Blaze	1996/97 Premier League; 1997/98 English National League & Conference; 1998/99 English Premier League; 1999/2000 British National League
Solihull MK Kings	2002/03 British National League
Solihull Kings	2003–05 English Premier League
Solihull Squires	1985–91 English Junior League
Solihull Sabres	1991–2005 English Under-16 League/Conference

Solihull Baron-Mites	1984–91 English Pee-Wee League
Solihull Flames	1991–2005 English Pee-Wee/Under-14 League/Conference
Solihull Blues	2004/05 English Under-14 League
Solihull Kings	1989–2005 English Under-12 Conference/League

Honours:

Barons	1977/78 Champions Southern 'A' League; 1994/95 Winners Autumn Trophy; 1982/83 Winners British League Division 2 – South and Promotion Play-offs; 1985/86 Winners British League Division 1; 1992/93 Winners English League Division 1 – South
Buffaloes	1979/80 Champions Inter-city Intermediate League
Knights	1997/98 Winners English Under-21 'B' League – North
Kings	1992/93 Winners English Under-12 Conference – Midlands; 1999/2000 Winners English 'B' League – North
Blaze	1997/98 Champions English National League & Play-offs and Winners English Conference – North; 1998/99 Champions English Premier League and Play-offs

Publications:

Team Solihull Barons – Souvenir Brochure 1985/86, Ross, Tom, 1985
Red & White Hockey – The Year Book of Solihull Ice Hockey Club, Huxley, David, 1990
Red & White Review – Solihull Ice Hockey Club Yearbook, Buxton, Andy, 1995

The original owner – Cresta Ice Rinks – sold the building to Solihull Borough Council in autumn 1973. At that time, a car showroom occupied the street frontage adjacent to the rink entrance. Closed in April 1975 for major repairs including a new ice pad, plant and lighting, the rink reopened 1 December 1975. The current owners are St Modwen Properties Plc, who spent £1.8 million on a refurbishment programme completed in October 2000. Seating, which had been missing for some time, was reinstated along with new barriers, PA system and an upgrade to lighting, changing rooms and refreshment areas.

For years teams consisted of enthusiastic amateurs, grabbing a handful of games where and when ice was available. Some had played previously at Birmingham. Among the pioneers of the 1960s and 1970s was Reg Williams who said: 'Everything you did you did yourselves. We even had to clean the ice, after practice as well as matches.' Others of that era included Brian Lidsey, Art Hambidge, Terry Troman, Len Bettney, netminder Dave Randall, John Morris and Bob Chesterman. With the formation of the Southern League, an internal dispute led to the revival of the Barons and the demise of the Vikings. Emerging players included Paul O'Higgins, Clive Healey and Tony Cross. Attendances hovered around seventy-five.

Jack Dryburgh, the new rink manager in 1977 doubled the training sessions and home games, and appointed veteran ex-Scots pro Jimmy Mitchell as player-coach. Midlands-based foreign students such as Canadians Gilles L'Esperance, Vic Conte and Rusty Moore helped Barons to a Southern 'A' League championship in 1977/78. Crowds increased, topping 1,000 that January. Ontario-born, English-based Glen Skidmore was voted an All-Star 'A' in 1982. TV commentator Gary Newbon, soon to be club chairman, arranged for sponsorship from a truck manufacturer. Canadian imports Chuck Taylor and Barry Skrudland, joined, crowds increased as Barons moved up to Division 1 of the British League. Suspensions, changing imports, increased sponsorship and attendances, with an abandoned game culminating in the resignation of Newbon early in 1985. Next year, under the chairmanship of Tony Norcott, with imports Brad Schnurr born in Kitchener, Ontario, Jay Forslund and Doug McDonald, Solihull gained promotion to the Premier. Tynesider Ian Finlayson was named 'Coach of the Year' and Schnurr to the All-Stars. With average attendances at 1,641, the country's fourth highest, Barons, in financial turmoil plunged to the foot of the table.

They hung on at the top level for a further four seasons as John Parkinson headed a new board. Fourth in 1989/90 was the best, with Barons top of the Fair Play standings. David Simms, who had been on the club committee since 1987, took over as manager three years later. The next autumn, to relieve the debt burden, Sheffield Steelers attempted to buy the club and thereby their place in the Premier. Thwarted by the BIHA, Barons lost players to Steelers, to survive and drop to the affordable English League. Of the many imports of the Premier period, among the best were Jamie Crapper (1986/87), Rick Fera (1987/88), Brian Mason (1987–89) with 405 games in the NHL American Jere Gillis (1988–90) and Steve Chartrand (1990/91).

In spring 1993 Solihull, managed by John Butler, and spearheaded by Luc Chabot and Chartrand defeated Guildford in the play-offs to move back to the BL. With the addition of Dan Pracher, originally from New Jersey, and import Ian Pound, Marc Chambers coached the team to Autumn Trophy silverware before resigning. David Graham, from Newcastle, a previous Barons netminder took over. Early in the next campaign he left as Barons acquired a new owner. Neil Ratcliff of Cheshire-based Anderson Baillie Marketing planned to relocate the club to the nearby NEC. Financial disaster ensued. He relaunched the team as Solihull Blaze, but on 5 March 1997 the company went into voluntary liquidation with alleged debts of £280,000. Although the players' wages remained unpaid most continued, with Blaze as runners-up in the newly formed Premier League.

Andy Buxton, a director of Barons from 1994, together with a group of dedicated supporters, resurrected the team. He was joined by Grant Charman, team manager John Doyle and coach Paul Thompson. Sheffield-based businessman Mike Cowley came in later. With three regular imports the new Blaze lost one game in sweeping to a trio of titles. French-Canadian Chartrand totalled 302 points. Solihull-born Stephen Doyle (22), with his wacky style, led the play-off netminders. With the English National League now relabelled 'Premier' Blaze repeated the double. Jukka Vaisanen and Seppo Rajpar from Finland joined the established foreign players. Chartrand and Anthony Kelham (24) ended first and second in EPL scoring. Blaze moved up, to finish seventh out of ten in the recently revived British National League. Chartrand and Kelman ended fourth and fifth overall, with forty per cent of Solihull's goals. Having complained long and hard regarding delays to rink improvements Blaze decamped a few miles, to set-up in the new Coventry Skydome.

A new Barons, under the chairmanship of Jeff Porter, with Paul Walker as GM, joined the Premier Division of the ENL. Veteran import Don Beau, Jake Armstrong and locals S. Boyle and Neil Adams remained at Hobs Moat Road. Dan Pracher returned, along with veteran Brit Phil Lee and homegrown Jason Price. Another aging import, Kevin Conway, also joined, to end runner-up in EPL scoring with 81 points. The opening match attracted around 1,000 spectators. With a restricted budget sixth was reasonable, as attendances dropped alarmingly. Despite signing two good import scorers in Canadian Duncan Cook and Antii Makikyro from Finland, to finish runners-up in the league, spectators stayed away. From 730 in September they dropped to around 225 by February. Porter and Walker had had enough.

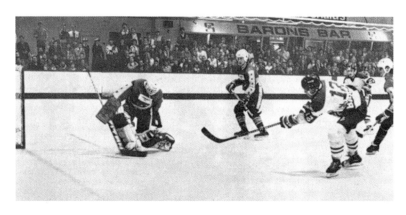

Jere Gillis scores in his second match for the Barons (v. Durham Wasps, 8 January 1989).

The frontage in April 1974. The entrance to the rink is on the left.

Husband and wife Mike and Sue Pack, previously backers of Milton Keynes, set up at Solihull as MK Kings with Rich Strachan as coach. Only Jeff Daniels, netminder Domenic DeGiogio, from Niagara Falls, of the imports previously with the Packs, and Brits Paul Moran and Danny Meyers moved north. The team ended in the cellar, winning just three times at Solihull. Kings were the cleanest in the BNL, at 13 penalty minutes per game. Attendance averaged out at 349, insufficient to sustain semi-pro hockey in the BNL. For 2003/04 Kings, minus the 'MK' prefix and the Packs, operated in the English Premier League. The long-suffering Solihull fans, reduced to a rump of less than 200, watched a repeat wooden-spoon performance. At least they were able to witness the sole win, as the importless Telford were beaten 7–5 at Hobs Moat Road. Season 2004/05 saw the total number of victories doubled.

Buffaloes were formed in 1979 to provide opportunities for youngsters and by 1985 the junior Squires included names still playing into the twenty-first century, such as Jon Rodway and Trevor Pickering. Youth hockey continues to flourish at all age levels at Solihull, producing home-grown Barons of the future.

SOUTHAMPTON – BANISTER COURT ROAD

Opened:	18 July 1931	Address:
Closed:	16 November 1940	Southampton Ice Rink
Ice Size:	180ft x 80ft	Banister Court Road
Total Spectator Capacity:	3,000	off Archers Road
Seating Capacity:	Estimated at approximately 1,500	Southampton
Ice Hockey – First Match:		Hampshire
13 October 1931: England 0 *v.* Germany 7 (challenge)		England

Teams:

Southampton 1931–33 English League – Division 2; 1933/34 challenge games
Southampton Vikings 1936/37 English National League
Southampton Amateurs 1937/38 challenge games
Southampton Imperials 1938/39 challenge games

Constructed at a cost of £80,000, with all spectator accommodation at ice level, the light steel-framed structure was located on the site of a pond previously used by the Southampton Skating Club. Changing rooms with showers were added in summer 1932. In November of that year tenders were invited by the receivers for the sale of the rink, which continued to

The result of a parachute
mine on 15 November
1940. (Jack Knott)

function. The name was changed to Sportsdrome in 1939 when local businessman Charlie
Knott Sr (1889–1973) purchased the building. It was operated as a roller rink, to revert to
ice on Good Friday 1940. French troops, evacuated from Dunkirk that spring, were billeted
at the rink, which later that year was destroyed by a parachute land mine during a massive
air raid.

A four-team (Bassett, New Forest, Shirley and United Insurance) house league briefly
operated in the autumn of 1931. The better local players formed a representative team. After
three away defeats, two in the second division of the English League, they met and shut out
Streatham 4–0 in their first home game on Saturday 5 December. Frank Goulden (21), who
scored, later made a name for himself in speedway. The other goals came from Derek Lister,
son of the rink manager, with two, and H. Bromley. By the end of March the six-team
uncompleted league standing shows Southampton with 4 losses and a tie. Three internationals were staged, with England losing 5–0 to Zurich SC on 25 February. The Scottish
League lost 5–2 to their English equivalent on 5 January. Among England's players were
goalie Vic Gardner, Carl Erhard, Gerry Davey, Neville Melland and the Canadian-born
Blaine Sexton, William McKenzie, the first manager of Harringay, John Magwood, Ernie
Ramus and Frank de Marwicz. Next season Southampton again had no success in the
league, with six recorded losses. G.W. Clode joined as player-coach. A switch to Sunday
mornings at 11.45 a.m. and the inclusion of guest players in a programme of challenge
matches worked. Investment in publicity saw attendances rise by February, averaging over
1,000, with two tiers of raised seats 'built around the entire rink'.

From late autumn A. Cooke and Ivor Nesbitt, from the nearby Bournemouth club, were
regularly seen in Southampton colours. Only seven of the previous year's squad of sixteen
had been retained. Later in the winter Southampton iced McKenzie, Magwood, Erhardt
and others, and on occasions the Bournemouth goalie G.K. Harper. Opposition included
Warwickshire, Cambridge University, Essex, Surrey and the Royal Canadian Navy. The
highlight was the unexpected win, 4–3 on 7 April, of Southern England over the USA, the
newly crowned world champions. Southampton's L. Clarke scored with D. Lister assisting
Nesbitt on another. Erhardt and Davey also netted.

Only three games are recorded at in late autumn 1933, then apart from a women's international game next March, ice hockey vanished for three years. The explanation can be
found in the minutes of a BIHA meeting of November 1936 where A.W. Lister, the rink
manager, states: 'when Southampton commenced to play Hockey about four years ago they
lost a lot of goodwill… in throwing together different scratch teams which did a lot of
harm'. During November and December 1933 Frank le Blanc, W. Kerr, Archie Creighton
(21), all Canadians from Queens and fellow countryman Jack De Denus of Warwickshire
joined some of last season's guests. Bournemouth and Grosvenor House were beaten with
Streatham winning 2–0 on 3 December. Centre ice seats cost 2s (10p).

For season 1936/37 the professional English National League (ENL) expanded to eleven
teams, including Rapides and Francais Volants based in Paris. They were soon in financial

difficulties and ceased operations. On 11 November Lister attended a meeting of the BIHA where he said: '…he wanted to make sure that they had a good team, and could now keep faith with their public'. The same day the local press reported: 'Players, trainers, masseurs and manager have been to Southampton to start their careers anew as the Southampton Vikings.' The ex-Volants, at the players' request, was domiciled in London. They practised at Wembley and travelled to Southampton for the Friday evening games, where admission for the public ranged up to five shillings (25p).

Hugh Farquharson, who went to Montreal's McGill University at the age of fifteen, became Vikings' player-coach and captain. A centre-ice, he had been his nation's leading goalscorer in the 1936 Olympics. He fulfilled the same role for Southampton with 34 goals and 20 assists. Tony Demers went on to play right-wing to Maurice Richard in the 'Rocket's' NHL rookie season for Montreal. Goalie Francois 'Kick' McCann was replaced in early March by F.A. 'Buster' Amantea. The two BIHA-required British-born players were George Horne and Irishman Frankie Green, both Canadian-trained. Also, briefly, Tommy Grace, a Londoner and Art Child – back-up GB Olympic netminder – played. The first home game was a 10–5 challenge win over London All-Stars on 20 November. A crowd, variously reported as 2,000 or 3,000 watched 'Doc' Ethier level in the first period for Vikings' first goal. Farquarson scored four with Theo Hamel (2), Gerry Philbin, Green and Wib Landymore also on target. In the four months on Southampton ice Vikings were victorious twice in the ENL. The first, a 10–4 win over Earls Court Royals, came on 4 December. Richmond were the losers, 5–2, six weeks later. A further six ended in deadlock, including the final three, for eighth place. Vikings also defeated Wembley Combined 4–3 on 19 February. In summer 1937 the league dropped four clubs including Southampton.

Locally based lads had practised during Vikings' season. Next winter the 'Amateurs', average age twenty-one, staged games at Southampton between January and April. Five of the opposing teams would today be classified as 'recreational'. In the sixth, on 27 March 1938 Amateurs, with goals from Jack Sproule and B. Currie, both Canadians in the RAF, lost 4–2 to Richmond Redwings of the London Provincial League (LPL). Twelve months on an expanded programme commenced in January, with the team relabelled Imperials and an 11 a.m. Sunday face-off. Among the eight victories was a 6–0 shutout of Cambridge Grads. Imperials also tied the two LPL Earls Court teams and Wembley Terriers. Harringay Hornets drew 3–3 and then returned on 23 April to win 7–5. A week later the season closed with a 7–2 victory for the all-Canadian Bristol Bombers. Of the 'Amateurs' only goalie Bill Selby, a Canadian from Ontario, Norman 'Lofty' Daniels, also a Canadian, E. 'Podge' Fuller and Isard, a 1931 veteran, turned out for Imperials. Other than Selby they all learned their hockey at Southampton, as did George Lane, who won a DFC in the Second World War along with Canadian utilityman Grant Fleming.

SOUTHAMPTON – ARCHERS ROAD/BANISTER PARK

Opened:	27 March 1952	Address:
Closed:	12 August 1988	Mecca Ice Rink (known as
Ice Size:	170ft x 72ft (52m x 22m)	the Sportsdrome pre 1964)
Total Spectator Capacity:	1,500 (2,000 prior to 1964)	Banister Park (pre 1964 –
Seating Capacity:	800 (approximately 1,500	Archers Road)
	prior to 1964; 300	Southampton
	between 1976–78)	Hampshire SO1 2JS
Ice Hockey – First Match:		England
18 June 1952: 'Canada' 13 v. 'London' 12 (challenge)		

Teams:

Southampton Vikings	1952/55 Southern Intermediate League; 1955–63 'Home' tournaments; 1976–78 Southern 'A' League – South; 1978–82 Inter-City League; 1982/83 British League Division 1 – Section C; 1983/84 British League Division 1; 1984/85 British League Premier Division; 1985–87 British League Division 1; 1987/88 British League Division 1 – South
Southampton Juniors	1955–63 and Southampton Redwings 1962/63 challenge games
Southampton Redwings	1971 challenge games
Southampton Danes	1977/78 Southern 'B' League; 1978–80 Inter-City Intermediate League
Southampton Knights	1982–84 British League Division 3; 1984/85 & 1987/88 British League Division 2
Southampton Vikings 2	1985–87 British League Division 2
Southampton Junior Vikings	1978–82 Inter-City Junior League; 1982–87 English Junior League
Southampton Kings	1987/88 English Junior League
Southampton Redwings	1987–89 English Pee-Wee League (all 1988/89 games away)

Honours:

Vikings	1952/53 Champions Southern Intermediate League; 1953/54 Winners Liverpool Tournament; 1953–56, 1957/58 & 1959/60 Winners BIHA Cup – Southampton Tournament; 1956/57 & 1959–61 Winners Southern Cup; 1983/84 Winners British League Division 1

Publications:

Southampton City Vikings Ice Hockey Club – Golden Jubilee 1937–87, Kemp, Paul, 1987
Southampton Ice Hockey Club – The 1987/88 Review, Harper, Peter, 1988
The Stadium Southampton, Bayley, C.R., 1992 (includes both Southampton ice rinks)

Work on the replacement rink, on the same site as that destroyed in the 1940 Blitz, commenced during the winter of 1950/51. The ice plant came from the recently closed Purley rink. Tiered seated balconies along one side and at both ends were added a year after opening.

With no local players available, a chance meeting between the Charlie Knott Jr (1914–2003) Southampton's MD and Benny Lee, his opposite number in Brighton, came up with the solution. The Sussex home-grown team in the Southern Intermediate League played behind closed doors. A quick meeting followed between Knott and the players and

The entrance in 1952.
(E.G. Patience/Jim Knott)

GREETINGS FROM THE TOP RANK ICE RINK SOUTHAMPTON

A postcard of the late 1970s.

the second Vikings were born. They travelled from their homes around Brighton each weekend, although their opening match was on the Monday evening of 27 October 1952. Skating out to 'Anchors Aweigh', a capacity crowd watched Des Palmer with three goals and singletons from Jimmy Knight and Roy Yates (20), tie 'London' (Wembley Terriers) 5–5 in a challenge. After four Sunday afternoon matches, the action switched to Saturday evenings. Undefeated in the league at home Vikings set a new SIL record by scoring 128 goals in the 20-match schedule, as did Dublin-born centre-ice Mike O'Brien,with 27+17, followed by Knight, Al Antram (26), Palmer and Gordie Crossley in the points table. Player-coach Ray Hammond (24) steadied the blue line with his sweep-checks. England, Nottingham Wolves and Swiss club Herisau also visited Southampton. The season concluded on 18 April as Vikings defeated The Rest.

Vikings were runners-up to Wembley Terriers for the next two seasons. 'Home' tournaments were introduced, commencing in 1953 with the Southampton Tournament for the BIHA Cup. The Southern Tournament followed three years later, which, after an interval of two seasons became the Southern Cup. Roy Harnett (25), with pro and international experience, joined for Vikings' second season with Colin Buckoke taking over in goal from 'Fish' Robertson. The outstanding London-born centre, Ken Gardner, displayed his scoring prowess at Southampton in October 1954. Support tailed off with weak opposition and one-sided scores; consequently Vikings did not appear for autumn 1957. Four National League sides were due to meet on Tuesday evenings for the Southampton Cup. Only the opening match on 29 October took place. Nottingham Panthers defeated Brighton Tigers 7–4; and that was the last seen of the competition. By January Vikings were back by public demand.

The first home-grown player to ice for Vikings was Dave Thomas in October 1956. The revived Vikings consisted of six of the by-now not-so Juniors. Winger Mike Madine (17) went on to play for Great Britain in the 1963 World Championships. They were mixed with six 'veterans' from the previous season. Defenceman Al Smith (27), signed from Streatham in September 1955, took over the captaincy. The new Kings won seven and lost four. On the afternoon of 22 November 1958 BBC TV *Grandstand* showed live action during Vikings' 11–2 win over Streatham Royals. Two cup triumphs sandwiched an 11–6 loss to Glasgow before the BNL folded in spring 1960. This released experienced Brits and Canadians. Several, including ex-Wembley Lions Roy Shepherd (30), John Murray (36) and Canadian centre George Beach (34) wore Southampton colours during the next three campaigns, although the only silverware of significance won was the Southern Cup in 1961. Edinburgh, then Altrincham, followed by Vikings' nemesis Brighton Tigers were too strong. For 1962/63 class Canadian defender Vic Fildes (32) and Andy Anderson (28), a centre from Toronto, proved popular with the fans, who still packed the rink on Saturday evenings. During these eleven years the national teams of Czechoslovakia, Sweden and the

USA plus Swiss and German club sides, All-Stars and England *v.* Scotland clashes all graced Southampton ice. Kings played a total of 262 matches.

The Sportsdrome was sold by Southern Sporting Promotions Ltd to Top Rank in the late summer of 1963. The new owners closed the rink on 21 October, took out the barriers surrounding the ice, walled off the upstairs balcony seating and removed all the seats at ice level. Rank banned ice hockey and the use of ice hockey skates by the public. Nine of the Vikings formed the bulk of the revived Wembley Lions.

In spring 1971 Redwing gained permission to stage three games by installing temporary scaffold board barriers. They beat Solihull and Wembley Vets, losing 4–3 to Sussex. The sport was then barred again. With closure on 5 April 1976 for a £330,000 reconstruction including a new ice pad, freezing plant and barriers, plus 300 rinkside seats, came a reversal of policy by Rank. Following a reopening gala on 5 September 1976 ice hockey returned twenty days later. The third incarnation of Vikings beat Streatham Taverners 7–6 in a challenge encounter. Terry Gilmour (29) scored Southampton's first goal, with Allan Hindmarch (29), the captain and veteran NL star Rupe Fresher (44) netting a pair, watched by a 1,200-strong crowd.

The core of the 1960s Redwings returned from five years of exile at Bristol. Coach Pete Murray (37), along with Tony Highmore (36), Rod Noble (29), Colin Bennett (30), Bob Turnbull (29) and Kenny Flood (38) had all played at least once for the pre-1963 Vikings. Canadian-born Walter Dirks (27) joined from Bristol along with the bespectacled Anglo-Canadian Steve Parrish (23). At the age of 45 burly Roy Shepherd returned to the team, taking over as coach the following season. Six foot five Pete Lane, a newcomer to hockey, kept goal. Playing a total of 36 matches Vikings won 28, finishing as runners-up to Streatham in the Southern 'A' League and to Kirkcaldy in the national knock-out 'Icy' Smith Trophy. Attendances averaged 1,000. Youth coaching commenced in early October and by the following spring Jim Maidment (23) was backing up Lane, with Gordon Baird at right-wing getting limited ice time.

With additional rinkside seating added, recorded attendances totalled 16,432 for 1977/78. The team was co-managed that season by the previous rink boss Charles Knott Jr. He signed Ron D'Amour, a Canadian from Streatham, fiery Liverpool Leopards' youngster Bernie Snagg and pre-1963 Viking Tony Whitehead as coach. Southampton were again placed second in the league and 'Icy' Smith Cup. Parrish was named to the All-Star 'A' sextet. Vikings had to look beyond their junior programme, and for 1979/80, with Czech native Bob Mitura in the nets, Vikings finished runners-up in the Inter-City League and play-offs. A new stream of youngsters joined by 1981 including Jamie Adams (GB Under-20 in 1984) and Mark Lewis (GB Under-20 1980). Next autumn Vikings competed in the interlocking Section B of Division 1 of the newly formed three-division British League. Foreign-trained players now required payments. American Greg Vasicek joined Mitura as a goalie tandem. With sufficient cash in 1983/84 Vikings acquired the Sims twins, Bruce and Brian, as co-player-coaches. Canadian defenceman Jim Shand and Streatham's English netminder Brian Cox (18) also signed. With nine wins from nine on Southampton ice, the tenth clash with contenders Solihull drew the largest crowd in eight years. Coming from 5–3 behind Bruce scored four goals, Brian the tying goal and game winner, with Shand assisting five times for a 7–6 victory. A week later the 5–5 tie with visiting Glasgow gave Vikings the title by one point and automatic promotion.

New rink owners Mecca refused to provide sufficient weekend dates, forcing Vikings to arrange some 'home' fixtures at Oxford. Keith Eccott, the club chairman, resigned in November, saying the sport now required a limited company structure. Ten Canadian imports, three coaches and a trio of managers later saw Southampton finish the campaign in the cellar. Kevin Murphy arrived from Canada in November 1986 as full-time non-playing coach. His disciplined approach provided stability. From 23 victories Vikings secured third place, from 16. Attendances averaged 724 with a crowd high of 1,056. Murphy gained the BL Division 1 'Coach of the Year' accolade. Next autumn he clashed with club chairman Jesse Fielder and was sacked. The revolving-door import policy restarted, with rumours of financial problems. The arrival of Brett Kelleher (27) as player-coach settled the floundering side. He netted 83 goals, a third of Vikings' total.

Four years after buying the facility Mecca closed the rink without prior warning, claiming that defects in the foundations were uneconomic to repair. Following numerous attempts by Rank from the early 1970s, then Mecca, to gain planning permission for luxury housing on the site of the rink, the local authority finally caved in, with the building being demolished by December 1988.

In spite of an initial campaign by the *Southern Daily Echo* and promises by the city council, seventeen years on Southampton still remains without a replacement ice rink.

STEVENAGE

Opened:	15 April 1988	Address:
Closed:	April 1997	The Ice Bowl
Ice Size:	184ft x 85ft (56m x 26m)	Roaring Meg
Total Spectator Capacity:	1,200	London Road
Seating Capacity:	1,000	Stevenage
Ice Hockey – First Match:		Herts SG1 1XH

30 October 1988: Brighton Royals 5 v. Chelmsford Renegades 4   England
(EL 2 – behind closed doors as rink not licensed for spectators)

Teams:

Stevenage Strikers   1989/90 English League Division 3 – Central; 1990/91 English
                         League Division 3 – South; 1991/92 English Conference
                         National Division; 1992/93 English Conference – South
Stevenage Sharks   1992/93 English League – Conference B
Stevenage Oilers   1996/97 English League – Southern Conference
Stevenage Cobras   1996/97 English Under-16 League
Stevenage Rattlesnakes   1996/97 English Under-14 League

The development of the Ice Bowl was a combination of private enterprise and the local authority. Eighteen months after opening a squad of twenty-two youngsters, many Under-21, had gained sufficient skill to enter the all-amateur, non-import Third Division of the English League. Strikers' first coaches were experienced players resident in the area, who had both represented GB at World Championship level, Pete Ravenscroft in 1950 and 1951 and the late John Baxter in 1966. Roy Cooke, who started in roller hockey, was leading scorer in the early days. Crowds of around 400 were not uncommon. In the four years of their existence Strikers struggled, winning 17 out of 63 games. The best performance was third in 1990/91 with 11 victories. Veteran Bristol-based goalie Chris Lowden guarded their nets in the final season, finishing with the Conference's second-best averages. That same winter Stevenage iced the Sharks, a semi-pro outfit, in the English League. The first game attracted over 1,200 spectators. Coached by Steve Rattle, with Tom Sheard as chairman, they ran out of money by Christmas. A small group of supporters took control, for Sharks to finish fifth from six, with five wins at the Ice Bowl.

Of the total of nine imports, Trent Andison and 6ft 2in Dave Hyrsky from Laurentian University stuck with the team, as did netminder Chris Newton (30). Hyrsky contributed 109 goals, nearly half the team's total output. The rink closed down on 26 April 1993, to be bought by local sports promoter Chris Roberts seven months later, reopening in December. Three seasons passed before senior hockey returned. For a first-year operation Oilers' third place, with 16 victories, was commendable. Canadian Mark Mackie was fourth best in the South with 34+40. Ironically, as the rink finally ceased operations in April 1997, Stevenage youth teams entered league competition for the first time.

Graham Trianer, managing director of Laax Investments, then running the rink, claimed that Stevenage Council had refused to grant an entertainment licences for non-ice musical events. He told the press: 'the ice arena is not financially viable and, as such, has to close down.'

STIRLING

Opened:	October 1980	Address:
Ice Size:	150ft x 90ft (45m x 27m)	Stirling Ice Rink
Total Spectator Capacity:	Minimal	Williamfield
Seating Capacity:	Nil	Torbrex Farm Road
Ice Hockey – First Match:		Stirling FK7 9HQ
Unknown		Scotland

Teams:
Stirling Wolves   1983–2004 (recreational only)
Stirling Cubs   (non league junior development)

Built primarily for curling, with limited public skating permitted at weekends. Wolves formed in 1983 mainly by 'ice boys' Craig Turnbull, Steph Martin and Gavin McMillan. The name was chosen because the last wolf in Scotland is reputed to have been killed near Stirling.

SUTTON-IN-ASHFIELD

Opened:	1975	Address:
Ice Size:	95ft x 80ft (27m x 24m)	Sutton Leisure Centre
Total Spectator Capacity:	Approximately 50	High Pavement
Seating Capacity:	Nil	Sutton-in-Ashfield
Ice Hockey – First Match:		Nottinghamshire
Not applicable – too small to host home fixtures		NG17 1EE
		England

Teams:
Ashfield Islanders   1984–87 British League Division 2 – Midland; 1987–89 English
                     League – South; 1989–91 English League Division 3 –
                     North; 1991–93 English Conference – South

Honours:
Islanders   1987/88 Winners English League – Southern Division

Part of a leisure complex. Access to one side and an end only, the opposite end of the ice is adjacent to a wall, with the other side formed of a glass wall separating the rink from a bowls area. Alcoves within the two adjacent walls provide off-ice bench accommodation for skaters and ice hockey players. An ice hockey club was formed in 1984, with some 'home' ice for games pre-1992 mainly at Hull. For 1992/93 season it was at Sheffield (Queens Road). Islanders' best season was 1987/88 with Johnny Pusztai, the late Chris Dirks and Shaun Leak, all previously with Nottingham, second, fourth and fifth in divisional scoring at 77, 44 and 40 points respectively. Islanders played a few challenge games in the 1990s as interest in the sport faded at the leisure centre.

SUNDERLAND

Opened: December 1977
Closed: June 2000
Ice Size: 184ft x 85ft (56m x 25m)
Total Spectator Capacity: 1,050
Seating Capacity: 950 (as at 1995 – originally nil.
200 seats added in August 1978)

Address:
Crowtree Leisure Centre
Crowtree Road
Sunderland
Tyne & Wear
SR1 3EL
England

Ice Hockey – First Match:
21 October 1978 : Crowtree Chiefs 4 v. Murrayfield
Racers 11 (challenge)

Teams:

Crowtree Chiefs 1978/79 Autumn Cup – Group 2; 1979/80 Northern League; 1980–82 Midland League; 1981/82 English National League; 1982/83 British League Division 1 – Section C; 1983–86 British League Division 1

Sunderland Chiefs 1986/87 & 1988/89 British League Division 1; 1987/88 British League Division 1 – North; 1989/90 English League Division 1; 1991/92 English League; 1992/93 English Conference A; 1993/94 English League; 1994–98 English Northern Conference; 1998–2000 English League Division 1 – North

Sunderland Indians 1990/91 English League
Durham Wasps 1995–96 British League Premier Division
Crowtree Tomahawks 1978–81 Northern Reserve League; 1980–82 Midland League Division 2; 1982/83 British League Division 3; 1983–86 British League Division 2

Sunderland Tomahawks 1987/88 English League; 1988/89 English League Division 2; 1992–94 English Under-21 League; 1994–2000 English Under-19 Conference/League

Crowtree Apaches 1979/80 Northern Junior League
Crowtree Arrows 1980/81 & 1982–86 Northern Junior League
Sunderland Arrows 1986–2000 English Junior/Under-16 League/Conference
Crowtree Commanches 1982–84 & 1985/86 English Pee-Wee League
Sunderland Commanches 1986–2000 English Pee-Wee/Under-14 League/Conference
Sunderland Cherokees 1994–2000 English Under-12 Conference/League

Honours:

Chiefs 1994/95 Winners English Northern Conference
Tomahawks 1982/83 Winners British League Division 3 – North; 1994/95 Winners English Under-19 Conference – North; 1997–99 Winners English Under-19 'A' League – North
Arrows 1990/91 Winners English Junior 'A' League – North; 1996/97 Champions British Under-16 League
Commanches 1988/89 Champions English Pee-Wee League; 1989/90 Winners English PW League – North; 1995/96 Winners English Under-14 Conference – North; 1997–99 Winners English Under-14 'A' League – North
Cherokees 1995/96 Winners English Under-12 Conference – North

The rink, at first-floor level, built as 'a low-cost windowless box', was part of a £7 million sports complex with a swimming pool, climbing wall, squash courts and indoor bowling. The

View of part of the interior c. 1979

original design proposals by architects Gillinson, Barnett & Partners indicated an S-shaped ice surface, with a 'removable peninsula projecting into the ice for informal seating'. Intervention by officials of the Northern Ice Hockey Association resulted in the adoption of a conventional configuration. Prince Charles formally opened the complex on 31 May 1978.

The first Chiefs recruited four established players from Durham – Hep Tindale (41), Gordon Manuel, Rod Binns (33) and Ernie Pinkey plus Jim Pearson (29) and Keith Havery (31) from Whitley Bay. Both clubs and rinks were owned by the Smith family, a powerful force in the Northern Association. Initially Chiefs were barred from official competitions; the NIHA then relented, permitting Crowtree to enter the 1978 Autumn Cup. Next winter in a full league schedule, with Canadian centre-ice Doug Wilks earning an All-Star 'A' rating and 'Overseas Rookie of the Year', Chiefs won four games. The expense of travel dictated a move to the less competitive Midland League for the next two years. In the first winter 12 points were deducted for use of unregistered players. Crowtree joined the revived one-campaign English National League for autumn 1981. Cal Land (27) arrived from Canada to join local players including goalie Joe Dunn (26), Kevin Musther (21) and Richard Howe (18). Finishing fourth in Section C of the inaugural BL, Land was fifth in scoring with 62 points. His team averaged 29.04 penalty minutes per match.

Crowtree were a founder member of the revamped second tier in autumn 1983, and initially a serious contender for promotion. Chiefs, led by the import trio of Paul Skjodt, Dwayne Rosenberg and late signing Glen Bertello, battled Southampton and Solihull all season. On 11 February Bertello struck the game winner at Crowtree in the 10–9 defeat of Solihull, with an attendance of 575. Seven weeks on Southampton went down 16–11 in a shoot-out on Sunderland ice. Chiefs missed the Premier by one point. Skojodt headed the division scoring by 19 points on 83+64. Next winter with a change of imports Crowtree slid to fourth. Although Mitch Duncan and Darrell Levine were good enough for fifth and seventh in points on 150 and 133 respectively. Duncan stayed on in Sunderland for a further winter, moving up to runner-up in scoring 59+93. The division's top British scorer was eighteen-year-old homegrown Stephen Nell with 40 goals and 37 assists.

The renamed Sunderland Chiefs came fourth in the Northern section in 1988. They picked up just one point the following winter to be relegated to the English League. 'Finn Hockey' ran the club, followed by a name change to Indians in a tie up with Durham. Neither lasted beyond one season. Crowds were down to 300. A reorganised near-amateur English League for 1993/94 suited Chiefs. They came second with 14 wins from 24 starts as Troy Butler finished with 115 points, fourth overall. Next winter Sunderland triumphed from further tweaking of the league, with seventeen victories in the eleven-member Northern Conference. Milan Dvoracek ended sixth in the points race on 59+20.

Full-blown pro import hockey was seen the next winter at the leisure centre. The homeless Newcastle United Sporting Club-owned Durham Wasps came third in the BL Premier Division, with 13 wins at Sunderland. Crowds were often over 1,000. Local lad Jonathan Weaver, a Chiefs mascot at six years old, contributed 17 points for Wasps.

Chiefs reached the play-offs in 1997 and 1998 and in the following campaign progressed to the final. For their last year on Crowtree ice, the team won the Northern 'Fair Play' award. Home-bred Stuart Potts came fifth overall in scoring with 48 points. This was indicative of the club's successful youth programme in the 1990s, particularly at Under-14 level.

Water leaks from the ice pad into the shops below resulted in closure of the rink in summer 2000. The club found a home at the newly opened Newcastle Arena. From early 2004 the iceless Crowtree rink was adapted, on a two-year lease, at a cost of £200,000, for use as an indoor football pitch for Sunderland AFC.

SWINDON

Opened:	26 April 1985	Address:
Ice Size:	184ft x 85ft (56m x 26m)	The Link Centre
Total Spectator Capacity:	1,650 (1,500 when opened)	Whitehill Way
Seating Capacity:	1,000 (750 on first floor balcony)	Westlea
Ice Hockey – First Match:		Swindon
20 July 1985: Bournemouth Stags 1 *v.* 'Southampton' All		SH5 8NU
Stars 5 (challenge)		England

Teams:

Bournemouth Stags   1986 British League Division 1; 1985/86 Brighton Royals British League Division 2 – South

Swindon Wildcats   1986/87 & 1988–93 & 1994–96 British League Division 1; 1987/88 & 1993/94 British League Division 1 – South; 2004/05 English Premier League

Swindon IceLords   1996/97 Premier League

Swindon Chill   1997/98 English National League; 1998–00 English Premier League

Swindon Phoenix   2000/01 English Premier League

Swindon Lynx   2001–04 English Premier League

Swindon Cougars   1987–89 English League; 1989/90 English League Division 2; 1990/91 English League Division 2 'A'; 1991–94 English Under-21 League; 1994–2005 English Under-19 Conference/League

Swindon Leopards   1988–2005 English Junior/under League/Conference

Swindon 'B'   2004/05 English Under-16 League

Swindon Pumas   1987–2005 English Pee-Wee/Under-14 League/Conference

Swindon Lions   2004/05 English Under-14 League

Swindon Jaguars   1988–2005 English Under-12 League/Conference

Swindon Lions   2004/05 English Under-12 League

Honours:

Wildcats   1991/92 Winners Autumn Trophy

IceLords   1996/97 Champions Premier League and play-offs

Phoenix   2000/01 Champions English Premier League

Cougars   1988/89 Winners English League – South & West; 1994–97 & 1999–2001 Winners English Under-19 Conference – South; 1998/99 & 2002/03 Champions English Under-19 League

Leopards   1991/92, 1998–2000 & 2001–03 Winners English Junior 'A' League – South; 1993/94 Champions English Junior Conference; 1994/95 Winners English Junior/Under-16 Conference – South-West

Pumas   1989/90 Winners English Pee-Wee 'B' League – South; 1991/92 Champions English Pee Wee League; 2000/01 &

	2004/05 Winners English Under-14 'A' League
Jaguars	1989/90 Champions English Under-12 League; 1997/98
	Winners English Under-12 'A' League – South

Publications:
Swindon Wildcats 1986–92 – The Story So Far, Chapman, Richard, 1992

The rink is an integral part of a complex that includes a swimming pool, sports hall, library, health centre etc under one roof. Thamesdown Borough Council designed and financed the Link Centre at a total construction cost of approximately £10 million. York supplied and installed the refrigeration system. The rink opened later than intended.

During January 1986 Bournemouth Stags staged two of their British League matches at the Link Centre. Brighton Royals also used the centre as a base. In late summer advertisements appeared for an ice hockey development officer, at a salary of circa £7,000 via a Sports Council grant. Dan Walker, an American previously at Deeside, was appointed with a budget of around £45,000. Injury curtailed his on ice appearances. He scored Wildcats' first goal at Swindon, seen by 370 spectators, in the 15–11 loss to Altrincham on 13 September 1986, assisted by Daryl Lipsey (23) and Richie Howe. The latter was one of several from the North-East of England, including netminder Joe Dunn (31), Stephen Nell (19), the team's top British scorer that winter, and Micky Stafford. Swindon piled up Division 1's most penalty minutes at 808, leaving Wildcats one point clear of relegation. The rink assumed financial control while the team for many years enjoyed generous sponsorship from local business. Lipsey co-ordinated hockey and set up an extremely successful youth development programme.

Wildcats gained moderate success, sustaining the support of the fans that saw dazzling scoring exploits from the imports. Kenny Kipp netted 151 times between 1987 and 1989. His second year was Wildcats' best to date as average attendances swelled to 1,252. Drew Chapman became the first homegrown Wildcat to gain an international cap, being selected for the England Under-16s. Defender Scott Koberinski, followed later in the 1989/90 season by Louis Haman (28), became an instant hero. Haman notched up 68 points in 14 matches. Koberinski, from North Battleford in Saskatchewan, stayed with Swindon through four campaigns, assuming the captaincy in his second. He played 128 times in official competitions, scoring 130 goals with 219 assists. He was joined in autumn 1990 by French-Canadian Luc Beausoleil who left next spring as Swindon's leading scorer on 192 points.

Under chairman Bill Roche the club became a limited company with Lipsey as general-manager. Imports Ryan Stewart and Bryan Larkin (24), from Montreal's McGill University, made an impact as Wildcats won their group of the Autumn Trophy. They faced Milton Keynes at Sheffield Arena on 23 November. From 4–0 down Larkin drew Swindon level at 5–5 early in the third period. Lipsey, Larkin and Stewart scored in the penalty shot finale, for Wildcats' first silverware. Leopards and Pumas won their groups in the youth leagues. Fifteen-year-olds Alan Amour and Allan Bishop graduated to the 'Cats. Next winter Swindon archived their best finish in Division 1 at fourth, a position they maintained for the next four winters.

Link Centre employee John Fisher, as hockey co-ordinator, was prominent within the sport as chairman of the Division 1 management committee. Dunn retired. Import Gary Dickie (25) notched up 200 points. The Under-16 Leopards tied Fife at Wembley in the 1994 British final. Lee Braithwaite, assisted by defenceman Neil Liddiard, scored in the final period. The following autumn ex-Cardiff import Steve Moria (33) signed. Next spring he was named 'Player of the Year' and voted onto the All-Star team with the divisional scoring title and 221 points. Local lad Jamie Thompson (19) and Jeff Smith (33) provided goalie rotation.

Locally based businessman Bob Dewar, Wildcats' ambitious sponsor, clashed with both the BIHA and the Link Centre. By April 1996 he replaced Roche as chairman. Lipsey moved to the new Manchester Storm, holding Wildcats' record for most league points at 874. Veteran Wayne Crawford (34), originally from Toronto, joined from Telford as

The rink combines with other facilities under one roof.

The interior.

player-coach. New to Britain, Calgary-born Brad Rubachuk (21) broke Moria's single season club points record in the BL by one. He was also the divisional 'bad-man' with 323 penalty minutes. Swindon's fourth place propelled them into the play-offs to finish second behind Superleague-bound Manchester.

The demise of the fourteen-year-old British League coincided with that of Wildcats. Dewar brought in a new name, along with substantial finances, reported to be around £250,000, plus a flood of foreign-trained players. Thirteen wore the short-lived IceLords uniform, including Barcley Pearce (26), Karry Biette (23) and Todd Dutiaume (23). All three were in the top-eight scorers list next spring. Coach Stan Marple, from defunct Milton Keynes, retained four of the 'Cats imports – Larkin, Dickie and the Finnish pair of Jari Virtanen and Petri Murtovaara. Twenty-six home wins ensured the new Premier League trophy. A second-leg 3–1 play-off semi-final victory over Slough secured a place in the final at Manchester. Ex-Team Canada netminder Mark Cavallin (25) shut out Fife Flyers 5–0. 'My eighteen-month dream ends here,' said Dewar.

Ex-netminder Mike Kellond formed the Chill to play out of Oxford in the English National League. He swiftly relocated westwards. The last of their three-year existence at the Link Centre was the best. Darcy Cahill (28), Swindon's highest-scoring import in 1998/99, became Chill's fourth coach the following autumn. Ron Bertrand (27) in the nets topped the league and play-off averages. At the other end the scoring of Canadians Lamonte Polet, Ken Forsee (24) and rugged defensive play of Ryan Mair (23), took Chill to third in the league and to the finals of the play-offs and the Millennium Cup. Kellond lost interest as plans for a nearby super arena evaporated.

Swindon resident Phil Jeffries formed the Swindon Phoenix, built around the retained imports Bertand, Forsee and Sean Tarr (25). Larkin returned as coach. Combined with a core of experienced and rising Brits they only lost one game at the Link, to take the English Premier title by three points. Bertand led the goalies with a save percentage of 91.8 per cent.

A legal challenge forced another change of name, this time to Lynx. it also led to a mid-table performance, the best being fourth in the 2002/03 EPL and Cup, despite money problems post-Christmas. Veteran home-grown Gareth Endicott, Fiddes, Armour and Braithwaite, with Durham-born Robin Davison continue to remain loyal to Swindon. Crowds now average 270.

In 2004/05 a revived Wildcats, with Lipsey back at the helm and three young Canadian College imports, finished fifth. In March 1989 Swindon hosted three games in Pool C of the World Junior Championships. Great Britain, who drew 2–2 on the 22nd with Bulgaria, included Wildcats' defenceman Toby Chamberlain and Lee Elliot. Swindon's own youth programme opened the new millennium with league triumphs at Under-19, Under-16 and Under-14.

TAVISTOCK

Opened: Autumn 1989   Address:
Closed: *c.* 1991   Tavistock Ice Studio
Ice Size: 50ft x 20ft (18m x 6m)   Tavistock
Total Spectator Capacity: Minimal   Devon
Seating Capacity: Nil   England
Ice Hockey – First Match:
A group of local youngsters practised the sport

Teams:
Tavistock Tom Cats   No record of any games played.

The ice was installed in a disused bus garage, which became a supermarket after the rink ceased to operate.

TELFORD

Opened: 10 October 1984   Address:
Ice Size: 184ft x 85ft (56m x 26m)   Telford Ice Rink
Total Spectator Capacity: 2,500 (originally 2,125)   St Quentin Gate
Seating Capacity: 2,300 (750 on first floor balcony) Town Centre
Ice Hockey – First Match: Telford
23 October 1984: Solihull Barons 7 *v.* Altrincham Aces 3 (challenge)   Shropshire TF3 4JQ
                                                                England

Teams:
Telford Tigers   1985–87, 1988–93 & 1994–96 British League Division 1;
                            1987/88 British League Division 1 – South; 1993/94 British
                            League Division 1 – North; 1996/97 Premier League;
                            1997–99 British National League
Telford Timberwolves   1999/2000 Benson & Hedges Cup only
Telford Wild Foxes   2001/02 English National League – South: 2002–05 English
                            Premier League
Telford Tornadoes   1986–88 British League Division 2; 1988–91 English League
                            Division 2; 1991–94 English Under-21 League; 1994/95
                            English Conference
Telford Falcons   1995/96 English Conference (withdrew December 1996)
Telford Tigers Royal   1997–99 English Conference
Telford Royals   1999–2001 English Conference
Telford Trojans   1994–2005 English Under-19 Conference/League
Telford Hellcats   1986–89 English Junior League
Wrekin Rockets   1989–91 English Junior League
Telford Rockets   1991–2005 English Under-16 League/Conference
Telford Tiger Cubs   1988–2000 English Pee-Wee/Under-14 League/Conference
Telford Venom   2000–05 English Under-14 League

Telford Terrahawks   1989–03 English Under-12 League/Conference
Telford Venom   2003–05 English Under-12 League

Honours:

Tigers   1987/88 Winners British League Division 1 – South and
     Division Play-off; 1993/94 Winners Autumn Trophy

Tornadoes   1991/92 Champions English Under-21 'B' League
Rockets   1993–96 Winners English Under-16 Conference – Midlands
Tiger Cubs   1992–95 Champions English Under-14 Conference; 1996/97
     Winners English Under-14 'A' League – North
Terrahawks   1989/90 & 1991/92 Winners English Under-12 League – North;
     1994/95 Winners English Under-12 Conference – Midlands
     2002/03 Winners English Under-12 'B' League – North
Trojans   2002/03 Winners English Under-19 'B' League – North;
     2003/04 Champions English Under-19 League

Publications:
Telford Tigers – The Story, Facts And Figures, Smith, Mike, 1988, Peerless Press Ltd

A Borough of Telford & Wrekin Council-owned and operated rink in the central complex of a 'New Town'. Built at a cost of £2.5 million it was officially opened by Princess Anne. The barriers surrounding the ice were formed in concrete blocks. The next summer £18,000 had to be spent on facings to render them suitable for ice hockey.

Exhibition matches took place the first winter involving teams from Altrincham, Blackpool, Nottingham and Solihull. Encouraged by the rink manager, entertainer David Ismay (chairman) and Gary Newbon, a Central TV sports commentator, formed Telford Tigers IH Club Ltd. They engaged Canadian defenceman Chuck Taylor (25), originally from Saskatoon, as director-player-coach. Local businessman Peter Sinclair provided support as sponsor, soon taking over as chairman, with Canadian Peter Kane as team manager. Newbon and Taylor had previously been associated at Solihull Barons, as had initial sign-ings import Mark Budz (26), Gordie Patterson, Paul O'Higgin and Dave Welch. Netminder John Wolfe (19) and Andy Steel (22) joined from Grimsby.

Setting high standards for marketing and presentation Tigers never fulfilled their potential. Having pressed their case for inclusion and direct entry into Division 1 in their inaugural season, Telford missed out on the runners-up spot by a point. Near sell-out crowds saw Budz reach 134 points, for fourth overall in divisional scoring, with Taylor voted onto the All-Star side.

A crowd of 2,000 attended the first game for 1986/87. Tigers did not lose at home with Budz, named to the All-Stars, and new boy Dean Vogelgesang from Saskatoon, second and third in divisional points with 200 and 196 respectively. The use of an ineligible player led to the deduction of nine points, dropping Tigers to fourth.

In the third campaign, the division split into two regions, Telford headed the South by two points, winning 12 out of 14 home games. They faced Peterborough for the coveted Premier place. On 2 April in Shropshire the visitors broke the deadlock late in the third period to win the first leg 14–12. Eight days later at Peterborough, Tigers were 6–1 in front after forty min-utes, but Pirates retained their Premier position by a single goal aggregate margin. This was as close as Tigers would get. Coming bottom of the 'Fair Play' heap, with a total of 763 penal-ty minutes did not help. Imports Kevin Conway (24), a centre, and right-winger Tim Salmon (23) gained All-Star – South accolades. Taylor was named 'Coach of the Year'. Gates averaged 2,006 with several at capacity. It would be six seasons before Tigers climbed as high again.

Kane returned to Canada to be replaced by Bob Koral. From a poor 1989/90 campaign centre-ice Gerald Waslen (27) was named 'Player of the Year' and an All-Star, as the division's top scorer with 201 points. In the summer Telford Ice Hockey Ltd went into liquidation. Former directors Jerry O'Reilly and Korol, with Chuck Taylor carrying on as MD, formed Telford Tigers Ice Hockey Club (1990) Ltd, with Ish Patel as chairman. Crowd levels returned to average 1,332 a year later, under new coach Jere Gillis. He had 405 NHL games to his credit. Kirkcaldy-born David Smith (19) was the club's second-best scorer with 51 goals.

Tornadoes, a development team, and, under the guidance of Tom Sheard, the junior (Under-16) Hellcats were formed in 1986. Soon home-grown talent, first Geoff Lane (20) and then sixteen-year-olds Norman Pinnington and Mark Hazlehurst, was suiting up for Tigers. By the late 1980s the Under-12 Terrahawks, the Under-21 Tornadoes and the Tiger Cubs were league winners.

Kevin Murphy replaced Gillis in autumn 1993 to introduce a three-line system of forwards. Telford faced Medway in the final of the Autumn Trophy. The 8–3 victory at home on 22 March clinched the silverware 11–7 on aggregate. The same month the club was presented with a winding-up order for £30,000 of unpaid VAT. Tony Emms, as chairman and GM Julie Harte formed a new board. Taylor moved to Nottingham. A second successive league runners-up place was secured. Long-serving goalie Wolfe gained All-Star recognition, as the home-grown Plant brothers Russ (19) and Ricky (17) blossomed.

The signing of Claude Dumas (28) who hailed from Thetford Mines, Ontario, provided the club's top scorer during Tigers' last years and beyond. He was named an All-Star 1996–99 for a total of 443 goals plus 316 assists, and was twice named 'Player of the Year'. Money troubles reoccurred with a winding-up order issued in December 1996. Ken Crickmore took over, with a share floatation on the unregulated OFEX market. Twelve months on John Lawless flew in from Canada as coach. Tigers won the Christmas Cup and finished second in the rookie BNL. By December 1998 Tigers had reached the B&H Plate final, helped by the netminding duo of Joe Watkins and Belfast-born Gavin Armstrong (30). Director Roy Williams resigned before Telford Tigers Ice Hockey plc slid into oblivion, to be wound up in the High Court in March 1999, leaving players and Lawless unpaid.

During the Tiger years they hosted Vandaalit from Finland, Moscow Dynamo, SKA Leningrad and a Ukrainian Select.

In the summer Gabe Gray launched Telford Timberwolves, minus an agreement with the council as to practice times and ice rental. They folded after losing all six B&H Cup matches. Attendances had been around 500.

Senior hockey returned to Telford eighteen months later, in the amateur English National League. Wild Foxes ended third from ten, in the Southern section, with Daniel Heslop top netminder. The ghost of Tigers' poor discipline persisted as Foxes averaged 51 penalty minutes per match. From autumn 2003 they moved up to the English Premier League, with a clutch of youthful talent, including Danny Mackriel (22), Adam Brittle (16) and Jared Owen. They more than halved the penalty minutes. A one-place improvement to eighth occurred in 2003/04 as Dumas returned, primarily to coach. The games attracted an average audience of 359.

Although eighth again by spring 2005, Foxes won 11 times and were only one point behind seventh-placed Chelmsford. Dumas played in all 32 games for runner-spot in the EPL points at 36+30. The team just missed out on the cup final, tied on points with Swindon in the preliminary group.

In winning their all-England play-off final at iceSheffield in May 2004, the Under-19 Trojans demonstrated the depth of home-bred talent available to ensure the future of ice hockey in Telford.

WHITLEY BAY

Opened:	30 May 1955	Address:
Ice Size:	186ft x 81ft (56m x 24m)	The Ice Rink
Total Spectator Capacity:	3,200 (3,500 when first opened)	Hillsheads Road
Seating Capacity:	3,200 (3,500 when first opened)	Whitley Bay
Ice Hockey – First Match:		Tyne & Wear
1 December 1956: Whitley Bay Wasps 6 v. Streatham		NE25 8HP
Royals 2 (Northern Tournament)		England

Teams:

Whitley Bay Wasps	1956/57 Northern Tournament
Whitley Bay Bees	1957/58 North British League and Northern Tournament
Whitley Bees	1958–61 Northern Tournament
The Wasps	1963–64 Northern Tournament; 1963–65 Scottish League – Section A
Whitley Warriors	1963–66 'Home' tournaments; 1966–82 Northern League; 1981/82 English National League; 1982/83 British League Division 1 Group B; 1983–95 British League Premier Division; 1996–97 Northern Premier League; 1997/98 English Conference – North; 1998–2000 English League Division 1 – North; 2000–05 English Conference/National League – North
Whitley Bay Bandits	1969/70 Northern League
Whitley Braves	1968/69 Northern Second League; 1971–77 Northern Second League; 1977–81 Northern Reserve League; 1983/84 & 1985–87 British League Division 2; 1987/88 English League; 1988–91 English League Division 2; 1991–94 English Under-21 League; 1994–2005 English Under-19 Conference/League
Whitley Renegades	1994–96 English Conference
Whitley Tomahawks	1975–77 & 1978–80 Northern Junior League; 1985–2005 English Junior/Under-16 League/Conference
Whitley Devils	1985–88 English Pee-Wee League
Whitley Mohawks	1988–2005 English Pee-Wee/Under-14 League/Conference
Whitley Arrows	1989–2005 English Under-12 League/Conference

Honours:

Wasps	1956/57 Winners Northern Tournament
Bees	1958–60 Winners Northern Tournament
Warriors	1971/72 Winners Autumn Cup; 1973–75 Champions Northern League; 1972–74 Winners 'Icy' Smith Cup; 1999–2001 Champions English Conference Play-offs; 2001/02 Winners English Conference – North and English Cup
Braves	1983/84 Winners British League Division 2 Play-off; 1990/91 Winners English League Division 2 Play-offs; 2001/02 Winners English Under-19 'B' League – North
Tomahawks	1998/99 Winners English Under-16 'B' League – North
Arrows	1993/94 Winners English Under-12 Conference – North; 1996/97 & 2000/01 Winners English Under-12 'B' League – North

The second of the Smith family-owned and operated rinks, with 'Icy' Smith's son Tom as manager and the second post-Second World War English rink to be built.

As Durham Wasps disbanded at the conclusion of the 1954/55 season, players were available. The Smiths decided to try ice hockey, from December 1956, at their new rink. In the first game, watched by 2,000 people, the Wasps' line-up consisted of: Jimmy Carlyle, Bill Booth, Mike Jordan, Stubby McManus, Hep Tindale, Robert Burns, Bobby Robinson, Ian Dobson, Johnny Weston, Norman Young, Derek Elliott, Cyril Metcalfe, Jim Thicke and Bob Exley. Only Thicke from Whitley Bay and Exley had not turned out for the previous Durham side. Young scored the first goal for the new Wasps at the sixteen-minute mark. He went on to complete his hat-trick. Winning 13 of their 17 matches in the Northern Tournament (NT) Wasps met and beat Glasgow, tied with Perth and lost to Wembley Terriers in the play-offs. Booth was non-playing coach and two Canadians had joined. Bob Bergeron, a veteran ex-pro, and Earl Carlson, previously with Durham. Wembley returned

Left: The entrance in 1957.

Below: The interior in 1990. (Whitley Bay Ice Rink/*IHNR*)

to contest the final on 27 April, won 8–2 by Wasps, who also defeated Scotland 9–3 at Whitley Bay on Easter Monday.

Next winter Durham Wasps were revived as Whitley Bay became the Bees. For four seasons the Northern Tournament was staged at both Whitley and Durham. The visiting teams appeared at Durham on Saturday and travelled to Hillsheads Road for a Sunday evening face-off. Bees lost their first game at Whitley on 6 October, 9–7 to Streatham. The line-up was: Carlyle, Joe Thicke, Bob Arnott, Derek Bryon, Phil Lumsden, Bryan Taylor, David Organ, Bergeron, Matt Docherty, Bill Smith (a nephew of Tom) and Terry Matthews (17). Other Bees were the returning McManus and Elliott plus Dave Lammin (22), John 'Scotty' Reid (37) and ex-Wasps and British international defender Butch Cartwright. By spring Durham topped the table, with Bees second; they met in the final at Whitley Bay. Wasps triumphed by the odd goal in seven on 13 April with Smith, Elliott and Lammin scoring for Bees, watched by a crowd of 3,000. Twelve months on Bees progressed to the NT final to defeat Edinburgh Royals 12–5 at Durham and 9–4 on Whitley ice. Topping the table in 1960, with 26 wins from 32 matches, Bees beat Paisley Mohawks 8–6 and 10–1 in the final to retain the tournament title. The Scottish defenders Bert Smith (34) and Jimmy Mitchell were snapped up by Bees. Dave Cassidy (18) and Bobby Green had also broke into the roster. Scotland defeated England 6–2 on 12 February 1961, with Bees' Jordan, Green and Lammin icing for the losers on their home ice. By spring, with the few visiting teams appearing eight times, crowd interest dwindled such that the tournament lapsed.

As the Durham players had fallen out with rink management the NT was revived at Whitley as Wasps played a mere six games in 1963. They shut-out Perth 7–0 in the final. With the demise of Bees, a 'house' league (North-East League) functioned between 1962 and 1964 consisting of Backworth Apaches, North Shields Red Wings, Wallsend Vikings and Whitley Bay Lions. Among home-bred players introduced to the sport Derek Adamson, George Emmonds (21), Walter Bell and Ronnie Stark were all icing with Wasps by early 1964. A further dispute with rink management caused Wasps to lose their ice at Whitley in March 1965. Warriors arose from the wreckage.

Whitley were a founder member of the amateur Northern Ice Hockey League (NL), which commenced in autumn 1966. They manged finish fifth after 28 matches. The team moved up one place in each of the next three campaigns. Warriors lost two league matches as they took the title for 1975 and 1976. They won the 'Icy' Smith Cup for 1973 and the following year, emblematic of the British Championship, together with the Autumn Cup for 1971. Initially the evergreen Terry Matthews carried the scoring threat, soon joined by centre-ice Alfie 'The Gent' Miller, Jim Pearson at left-wing and Paul Whitehouse, a right-winger. All won All-Star recognition and represented Britain in the World Championships. Miller was named NL 'Rookie of the Year' at the age of fifteen in 1970. Two years on the fiery defender Kenny Matthews was declared 'Player of the Year'. Brother Terry took to coaching to collect an All-Star 'B' rating in 1971 and an 'A' for seven years. Braves, a development team, joined the Second League in 1968. Tomahawks entered the Northern Junior League in 1975. Five years later they won the league format North–East Junior Shield.

The NL pioneered the post-1960 use of paid imports. Warriors were among the first with Jan Petterson. Warriors progressed from the Northern, via the English National, to the Heineken-sponsored British Leagues inaugural Premier Division in 1983/84. Prominent in the early 1980s were home-grown forwards Paul Towns, Peter Smith, defender Terry Ord and goalies Peter and David Graham, along with import Ron Butler with 134 points in 1983/84. In the autumn of 1987 Mike Babcock (24), who coached Anaheim to the Stanley Cup finals in 2002/03, with forwards Scott Morrison (23) and Luc Chabot (22) blended with the local talent to win all their home games, bar two, for second place. Crowds averaged 1,637. Morrison topped the league in scoring with 224 points as Whitley progressed to Wembley. Warriors failed to hold their semi-final lead. Babcock was elected to the All-Star team, as was Morrison, with Matthews named as 'Coach of the Year'. Miller retired after 550 matches with a total of 1,265 points. Next winter, Warriors bested Durham in their play-off group to return to Wembley, losing at the semi-final stage. Montreal-born Hilton Ruggles (25) was named to the left-wing All-Star position. Fifteen-year-old David Longstaff's 6 games and 3 goals was the high point the next year. Winning all three home play-off group games took Whitley to Wembley for the last time in April 1992. In the semi-final with Durham, Wasps won 11–4.

Warriors, now 'Newcastle', transferred to that city in November 1995. As Whitley Warriors once more, over 3,000 fans welcomed them back to Hillsheads Road and the new Northern Premier League the next September. They ended third. The following campaign saw Warriors as runners-up in both the English League National and Conference North under coach Mick Mishner. Imports Timo Loucasvuori and Kimo Saarinen, along with veteran homegrown John Iredale (31), were in the top-five scorers' list. With the return of native son Peter Winn to coach Warriors, they dropped out of the English Premier League to continue in the importless regional Conference.

Runners-up in spring 2000, Warriors defeated Billingham in the play-offs, with over 1,600 in attendance at Hillsheads Road. Top scorer Simon Leach helped Whitley to their first trophy in twenty-five years. Next season the league title and English Cup were added to the retained play-off silverware. Karl Culley (23) and Andrew Carter (24) with 67 and 58 points led the attack. Crowds averaged 1,000, but dropped back during 2003/04 as Winn departed to concentrate on the younger teams. Warriors slipped from third to sixth, moving up to third a year later.

Newcastle Vipers of the British National League staged four of their spring 2005 play-off matches at Hillshead Road.

PRINCIPAL SOURCES

Facts and figures gleaned over the years from a multiplicity of sources, newspapers and magazines too numerous to mention and journals that have from time to time covered ice skating and ice hockey have combined to build up the rink data in the files of the Harris Ice Hockey Archives upon which this book is based.

For the period 1930–40 *The Skating Times*, a monthly magazine, which also covered ice hockey, is an invaluable source, including numerous photographs of buildings long since demolished. Post-Second World War skating magazines – principally *Skating World* and *The Skater* – carried information on the few rinks built prior to the 1970s and those that ceased operations. The weekly *Ice Hockey World* (1935–40 and 1946–58) is another valuable source. From 1947 until 1955 the *Ice Hockey World Annual* carried a rink directory as does the contemporary *Ice Hockey Annual* from 1976 to date, plus a yearly page of useful 'rink news', and invaluable club information and player statistics, compiled and edited by Stewart Roberts – a close friend of over thirty years standing.

That excellent in-depth journal of record *Ice Hockey News Review* (1981–99) usually carried a detailed article on each newly opened rink, and from time to time carried accounts of some of the earlier venues. The magazine *Powerplay* (1991 to date) also provides useful data and background information on rinks.

The National Skating Association *Official Handbook*, from as early as 1914, listed artificially frozen rinks, with ice size, opening and closing dates, but with some inaccuracies. Issues 13 and 16 of *The South Westminster Local History Society Newsletter* contain details of London's Victorian rinks.

Powerplay is also virtually the sole printed source, from the early 1990s onwards, for the composition of youth ice hockey leagues, particularly the teams' nicknames, although some are occasionally assigned incorrectly.

BIBLIOGRAPHY

Publications devoted to specific rinks and or ice hockey clubs based in those rinks can be found listed under the heading of that particular rink. Where the publication names the publisher they have been included in the entry.

Ice Skating Rinks: J. & E. Hall Limited, Dartford, publication no. 889A (a pamphlet *c.* 1960s).
Ice Hockey: Patton, Major (B.M. 'Peter'). George Routledge & Son Ltd, London, 1936.
Ice Hockey: Erhardt, Carl. W. Foulsham & Co. Ltd, London, 1936.
Skating: Heathcote, J.M and Tebbutt, C.G. Longmans Green & Co., London, 1892.
The Skater's Cavalcade: Wade, A.C.A. Olympic Publications Ltd, London, 1939.

Virtually all other books about ice hockey in Britain lack detailed information on ice rinks.

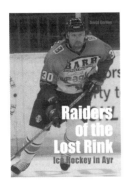

Also published by Stadia

Raiders of the Lost Rink Ice Hockey in Ayr
DAVID GORDON

Ayr has seen dramatic developments at every stage of the sport's history. Compiled by David Gordon, this absorbing and detailed account is rich in both anecdotes and statistics to chronicle the triumphs and tribulations of ice hockey in this Scottish west coast town over a period of 75 years. Containing many rare photographs, it is an essential read for anyone with an interest in the game.

978 0 7524 3073 7

If you are interested in purchasing other books published by Stadia, or in case you have difficulty finding any Stadia books in your local bookshop, you can also place orders directly through the Tempus Publishing website

www.tempus-publishing.com